Russian Literature

Cultural History of Literature

Ann Hallamore Caesar and Michael Caesar, *Modern Italian Literature*
Christopher Cannon, *Middle English Literature*
Sandra Clark, *Renaissance Drama*
Roger Luckhurst, *Science Fiction*
Lynne Pearce, *Romance Writing*
Charles J. Rzepka, *Detective Fiction*
Mary Trotter, *Modern Irish Theatre*
Jason Scott-Warren, *Early Modern English Literature*
Andrew J. Webber, *The European Avant-Garde*
Tim Whitmarsh, *Ancient Greek Literature*

Russian Literature

ANDREW BARUCH WACHTEL AND ILYA VINITSKY

polity

Copyright © Andrew Baruch Wachtel and Ilya Vinitsky 2009

The right of Andrew Baruch Wachtel and Ilya Vinitsky to be identified as Authors of this Work has been asserted in accordance with the UK Copyright, Designs and Patents Act 1988.

First published in 2009 by Polity Press

Polity Press
65 Bridge Street
Cambridge CB2 1UR, UK

Polity Press
350 Main Street
Malden, MA 02148, USA

All rights reserved. Except for the quotation of short passages for the purpose of criticism and review, no part of this publication may be reproduced, stored in a retrieval system, or transmitted, in any form or by any means, electronic, mechanical, photocopying, recording or otherwise, without the prior permission of the publisher.

ISBN-13: 978-0-7456-3685-6
ISBN-13: 978-0-7456-3686-3(pb)

A catalogue record for this book is available from the British Library.

Typeset in 11.25/13pt Monotype Dante
by Servis Filmsetting Ltd, Stockport, Cheshire
Printed and bound in Great Britain by MPG Books Ltd, Bodmin, Cornwall

The publisher has used its best endeavours to ensure that the URLs for external websites referred to in this book are correct and active at the time of going to press. However, the publisher has no responsibility for the websites and can make no guarantee that a site will remain live or that the content is or will remain appropriate.

The publishers would like to thank the following for permission to reproduce copyright material: Page 26, The Yorck Project, Zenedot Verlagsgesellschaft mbH; 30, Alex Bakharev, Wikimedia; 41, GerardM, Wikimedia; 43, © The National Library of Israel, Shapell Family Digitization Project, Eran Laor Cartographic Collection, and The Hebrew University of Jerusalem, Dept. of Geography, Historic Cities Project; 62, Library of Congress, Prints and Photographs Division, Photocrom Prints Collection; 74, S. Barichev, Wikimedia; 90, S. Barichev, Wikimedia; 106, © Rem Sapozhnikov; 206, A. V. Shchusev State Museum of Architecture, Moscow.

Every effort has been made to trace all copyright holders, but if any have been inadvertently overlooked the publishers will be pleased to include any necessary credits in any subsequent reprint or edition.

For further information on Polity, visit our website: www.polity.co.uk

Contents

List of Illustrations vi

Chronology vii

Introduction: Labyrinth of Links: Russian Literature and its Cultural Contexts 1

1 The Origins: Russian Medieval Culture 7
2 The Spirit of Peter: Russian Culture in the Eighteenth Century 31
3 The Spirit of Poetry: Russian Culture in the Age of Alexander I (1801–25) 57
4 The Russian Idea: The Quest for National Identity in Nineteenth-Century Russian Culture 89
5 Russian Psychology: The Quest for Personal Identity in Nineteenth-Century Russian Culture 125
6 Life as Theatre: Russian Modernism 157
7 The Art of the Future: The Russian Avant-Garde 182
8 The Future as Present: Soviet Culture 204
9 After the Future: Russian Thaw Culture 233
10 Instead of the Apocalypse: Russian Culture Today 261

Conclusion: Whither Russian Literature 285

Notes 294
Bibliography 302
Index 308

Illustrations

1	Andrei Rublev, *Old Testament Trinity*	*page* 26
2	Vasily Surikov, *Boyarina Morozova*, 1887	30
3	St. Peter and Paul Cathedral, St. Petersburg	41
4	Plan of St. Petersburg, 1737	43
5	St. Isaac's Cathedral, St. Petersburg	62
6	Pavlovsk: a view of the gardens	74
7	Alexander Column, St. Petersburg	90
8	A. M. Opekushin, Pushkin monument, Moscow, 1880 © Rem Sapozhnikov	106
9	Ilya Repin, *They Did not Expect Him*, 1884–8	140
10	Cover from *A Trap for Judges II*, 1913	187
11	Vladimir Tatlin's "Monument to the Third International" (model), 1919–20	206

Chronology

862	Varangian Prince Riurik is invited to rule in Kiev. The Riurikovich dynasty lasts until 1598.
988	Baptism of Kievan Rus (a loose medieval association of East-Slavic principalities under the leadership of Kievan princes). Grand Prince Vladimir I accepts the eastern (Byzantine) form of Christianity. The Church of Rus' becomes a subsidiary of the Patriarchate of Constantinople (until 1448).
1051	Hilarion becomes the first Russian-born metropolitan bishop of Kiev.
1054	The split of Universal Christian Church into Roman and Greek (Byzantine). Grand Prince Yaroslav the Wise dies and Rus' is divided between his sons.
1240	The destruction of Kiev by the Mongols. End of Kievan Rus and beginning of the so-called Mongol-Tatar Yoke (lasted until 1480).
1242	Prince Alexander Nevsky defeats the Teutonic (Livonian) Knights during the Battle on the Ice.
1326	Seat of the Metropolitan transferred from Vladimir to Moscow, which becomes the major political power aimed at the "reunification of Russian lands."
1453	Fall of Constantinople to the Ottomans. Moscow princes soon proclaim themselves heirs of Byzantine emperors and the Muscovite Tsardom as a new and the final reincarnation of the holy Christian empire (the Third Rome doctrine, 1510): "Pious Tsar! Listen and remember that all Christian kingdoms have now merged into one, your tsardom. Two Romes have fallen. The third stands firm. And there will not be a fourth. No one will replace your Christian tsardom."

1552 and 1556	Ivan the Terrible conquers Kazan and Astrakhan khanates. In 1582, Siberia is included in the Muscovite Tsardom.
1565	Ivan established the *Oprichnina*, a special institution and subdivision of his state, with the mission to punish evildoers and traitors (in his eyes). The reign of terror begins.
1589	The Metropolitan of Moscow Job becomes the first Patriarch of All Rus'.
1598-1613	Time of Troubles; Russian civil war caused by a dynastic crisis.
1613	Mikhail Romanov is elected tsar by the Assembly of the Land. The new, Romanov, dynasty begins.
1653–7	Russia gains Left-Bank Ukraine (including Kiev).
1653–4	Beginning of the Russian Schism. Patriarch Nikon (head of the Russian Orthodox Church) forbids the old Russian ritual; the Old-Believers' opposition.
1682	Archpriest Avvakum, the leader of the Old-Believers, is burned at stake.
1699-1700	Tsar Peter Alexeevich (1672-1725; Emperor of all Russia – Peter I – beginning 1721) initiates a great age of reforms.
1700–1721	The Great Northern War between Russia and Sweden. In 1709 Charles XII of Sweden is defeated at Poltava. Russia gains the Baltic territories.
1703	Peter founds St. Petersburg, soon to become the new capital of a "westernized" Russian Empire.
1762	Peter III issues his manifesto freeing nobles from obligatory state service: "[N]o Russian nobleman will ever be forced to serve against his will; nor will any of Our administrative departments make use of them except in emergency cases and then only if We personally should summon them."
1762–96	Reign of Catherine II (Great): the "Golden Age" of the Russian nobility.
1767	Catherine II published her political declaration of intentions *Nakaz* (*The Instructions to the Commissioners for Composing a New Code of Laws*): "[E]very Individual Citizen in particular must wish to see himself protected by Laws, which should not distress him in his

	Circumstances, but, on the Contrary, should defend him from all Attempts of others that are repugnant to this fundamental Rule."
1773–75	The Peasant Rebellion ("War") led by Emelyan Pugachev.
1772, 1793, 1795	Partitions of Poland. Russian Empire expands westwards.
1783	And southwards . . . Crimean territories annexed after series of successful Russo-Turkish wars.
1801	Unpopular Paul I (1796-1801), Catherine's son, assassinated. His son Alexander I ascends the throne and vows to return to the pro-gentry policies of his grandmother.
1812	War with Napoleon; the fire of Moscow.
1814	Liberation of Paris by the allied armies and establishment of a new European order under control of the major Christian powers (Holy Alliance).
1825	The Decembrist revolt.
1830–1	Polish uprising and its defeat.
1849	Nicholas I (1826-55) sends the army to help the Austrian Emperor defeat the Hungarian revolution.
1853–6	The Eastern (or Crimean) war; Russia's defeat and national shame.
1861–3	The emancipation of the serfs, the major action in a new series of Great Reforms initiated by Alexander II (1855-1881): "[T]hey are granted the right to purchase their household plots, and, with the consent of the nobles, they may acquire in full ownership the arable lands and other properties whichare allotted them for permanent use. Following such acquisition of full ownership of land, the peasants will be freed from their obligations to the nobles for the land thus purchased and will become free peasant landowners. (. . .) At the end of two years from the day of the promulgation of this decree they shall receive full freedom and some temporary benefits" (Manifesto of February 19, 1861). In the text when we talk about the abolition of serfdom we mean the actual abolition (1863) rather than the announcement.
1863–4	Polish revolution (insurrection) defeated.

1881	Alexander II assassinated by a terrorist.
1905	The first Russian revolution follows Russia's defeat in the Russo-Japanese War.
1914 – 1918	World War I (or the "German War").
1917	The liberal (February) and Bolshevik (November) Revolutions. End of the Russian Empire and beginning of the Soviet state (from 1922 – The Union of Soviet Socialist Republics) with Moscow as the capital.
1918–21 (or 23)	Civil War between "Reds" (Bolsheviks) and "Whites" (monarchists).
1921	Relatively liberal New Economic Policy (NEP) introduced. Ends in 1928 with the adoption of the First Five-Year Plan, the proclamation of new policies of accelerated industrialization and, beginning in 1929, collectivization.
1924	Death of Vladimir Lenin, the leader of the Bolshevik Revolution. In the 1920s, Joseph Stalin gradually consolidates absolute power.
1937	Peak of Stalin's "purges": many members of the literary and artistic intelligentsia are arrested and executed or imprisoned.
1941–5	Great Patriotic War with Nazi Germany. In 1945 the Soviet army captures Berlin. Formation of the socialist camp in Europe, with Warsaw Treaty signed in 1955.
1953	Stalin dies.
1956	XX Congress of the Communist Party: denunciation of Stalin's cult of personality by Khrushchev. Millions of inmates return from labor camps. The "Thaw" period begins.
1961	Yuri Gagarin becomes the first human in space.
1962	Cuban Missile Crisis.
1968	Soviet army invades Czechoslovakia to prevent it from leaving the socialist camp.
Mid-1960s	The end of the "Thaw." The Soviet dissident movement emerges.
Late-1960s–mid-80s	"Period of stagnation" of the Soviet regime. "Afghan" War of 1979-89.

1971–2	The start of the "third wave" emigration (with the first wave following the Revolution and the Civil War and the second after the World War II). In 1972, 35,000 people left the Soviet Union (mostly representatives of the intelligentsia).
1985	Gorbachev's Perestroika (a futile attempt to reconstruct the centrally planned Soviet economy) begins.
1991	The USSR is dissolved. Russia, Ukraine, Belorussia, Kazakhstan, and other former Soviet republics announce independence.
1994–6, 1999–2006	Russo-Chechen wars. Vladimir Putin becomes President of the Russian Federation in 2000.

Introduction

Labyrinth of Links: Russian Literature and its Cultural Contexts

Russian literature (like any other literature) is not an island, but part of a complex cultural process. A journey through its "labyrinth of links" (to use a phrase of Lev Tolstoy) is a fascinating and, we hope, helpful adventure: we learn not only about curious facts, names, and works, but also acquaint ourselves with the experience of a particular Other. Let us begin with a case that illustrates the complexity of this process. Our choice may seem strange: the hero is not a well-known writer, the event is not significant, and the work under discussion does not belong to the canon of famous literary texts (it was never completed, in fact). However, this case serves as a fitting introduction to our narrative, since it presents as if in a miniature the ways in which a literary process originates and develops.

On August 8, 1801 the twenty-year-old poet Andrei Turgenev, son of the director of Moscow University, leader of a literary group of enthusiastic young men that included the future founder of Russian Romanticism Vasily Zhukovsky, recorded in his diary:

> I bought *Werther* from Horn today and decided, without any particular goal, to have it translated.... Without knowing what I would need it for. Just now a quick thought came suddenly to mind.
>
> *So eine wahre, warme Freude ist nicht in der Welt, als eine große Seele zu sehen, die sich gegen einen öffnet,* Werther says in one passage. Earlier, I read this indifferently and dispassionately; now, a trivial word in a conversation between Ivan Vladimirovich [Lopukhin] and [Archbishop] Platon showed me the noble firmness of his soul and made me feel pleasure, although he wasn't speaking to me. Another thought came to me instantly after that. I remembered that passage in Werther, and in my new Werther I will check my feelings against his, and note for myself the things that I felt the same as he did.
>
> So I began *within* myself. I jumped up and ran to my room to write these lines.
>
> Morning – its arrival chased away the peaceful sleep which had embraced me softly; I woke, and with a fresh soul went up the hill from my humble

hut; at every step I was delighted by a new flower, heavy with dew and bending towards the earth; the young day was rising with joy, everything about me was coming to life and bringing me to life.

As I ascended, the mist slowly spread [. . .] Soon it was as if I was surrounded by clouds and I was in twilight.

Suddenly the sun seemed to break through and light appeared in the darkness. It fell now below, now rose again, splitting itself over the groves and hills. With what great impatience I waited to welcome the bright sun; I awaited its doubled charm after the gloom. The airy fight had not finished yet; brilliance surrounded me, and I stood blinded.

Soon a feeling within my heart roused me to gaze about. I had to do it quickly, as everything was blazing and burning all around.

The Divine Woman slowly descended onto the clouds before me; I had seen nothing in my life more beautiful; she looked at me and slowly came to rest.

"You do not recognize me?" she said in a voice overflowing with love and grace – "You do not recognize the one who so often poured the purest balm over the wounds of your heart? No! You do know me; your passionate heart has formed the closest, eternal bond with me. Even as an infant, you reached your hands out to me, weeping bitter tears."

"It is so!" I cried, blissful, bowing toward the earth; "I have sensed you for a long time; you brought me peace when passion raged furiously through my limbs, you sent me the best of life's gifts; and any blessing I receive, I want to receive only from you.

"I do not name you. Many give you names, and consider you their own; every eye seeks you, and for almost every gaze your radiance is happiness.

Oh! When I was misled, I had many friends; when I came to know you, I lost almost everyone; no one but myself have I to share in my joy."[1]

This diary entry requires a brief commentary. It dates from August 1801, the fifth month of the reign of the young Emperor Alexander I, who had ascended the throne after the death (assassination) of his tyrannical father Paul I. It was a period of great aspirations and enthusiasm, "the clear morning of the century," as contemporaries called it. *The Sorrows of Young Werther* (Die Leiden des jungen Werthers, 1774) is an epistolary novel by Johann Wolfgang von Goethe, one of the most important works of German *Sturm und Drang* movement. The German citation from *Werther* says that the greatest joy in the world is to see how a great soul opens itself to the other. Horn owned a bookshop in Moscow (there were very few bookshops at the time, with no more than a couple of hundred Russian readers). Ivan Lopukhin was a Russian statesman, influential freemason, religious writer, and philanthropist. He was one of the leaders of the

Russian spiritual Awakening movement (which derived from its German counterpart) and a good friend of Andrei Turgenev's father. At the center of his mystical doctrine was an idea of universal Love-Wisdom presented in the feminine symbol of Divine Sophia. Bishop Platon was the Metropolitan (Archbishop) of Moscow and also an amateur poet. The situation described in the diary may be reconstructed as follows: A young man bought Goethe's volume in the German book store; then he witnessed a conversation; between two religious men; he was deeply moved by the beauty of their souls, as this was revealed in this conversation, recalled Werther's opinion concerning the soul which opens itself to the other; decided to test himself to see whether he was also able to feel and express such lofty emotions; rushed home and started to write a piece about the dawn, ascension of a mountain, and the vision of a beautiful woman.

However, here is a paradox. The young man's work is actually a verbatim translation of Goethe's poetic "Zueignung" (Dedication), which opens the edition of *Werther* Turgenev used ("Der Morgen kam; es scheuchten seine Tritte. . ."). In this magnificent poetic introduction, the Poet ascends a mountain, sees a beautiful divine woman who welcomes him, gives him the veil of Poetry and demands that he return to the world of men to share their hardships and show them the way to the truth. It is as if the young Russian poet composed someone else's poem. In fact, a diary translation for him was a means of self-comprehension and self-establishment: if I can feel like Goethe, then I also belong to the "chosen natures." This translation exemplifies the formative period of Russian Romantic poetry when "someone else's" might mean (or help to discover) "one's own." Such a translation does not merely introduce a great foreign work to the reader (in fact, Turgenev wrote it for himself and never completed it). It is rather a poetic initiation, a young man's attempt to discover the poet's self. Here German words become Russian, ideal poetic emotions and Western poetic mythology are filtered through the Russian poet's heart and find their new form in the Russian text.

Turgenev died a year later, having published just one serious poem. His friends created a peculiar myth of him as an unrealized genius (later on, the premature death of Russian poets would become a key Russian poetic myth). Eighteen years later his friend Zhukovsky would translate a part of Goethe's "Zueignung" and create a cycle of poems about the beautiful Spirit of Poetry descending from the heavens. The vision of a divine woman preoccupied the Russian socialist writer Nikolai Chernyshevsky in the 1860s and was central to the mystical philosophy of the religious thinker Vladimir Solovev at the end of the nineteenth century. The latter's ideal of eternal womanhood, in its turn, affected many Russian symbolist writers of the early twentieth century. In the late 1910s, the Russian avant-gardist poet Boris Pasternak would translate Goethe's poem and the symbolist Alexander Blok, known for his lyrics dedicated to the "Beautiful Lady," would severely criticize Pasternak's idiosyncratic translation and suggest his own.

Turgenev's diary entry was written at the dawn of the period known as the Golden Age of Russian poetry. It provides a glimpse inside the process of the formation of Russian poetic consciousness and reveals important tendencies and themes of the modern Russian literary tradition: the cult of poetry as a transforming force and the idea of the poet's sublime mission in the world; "echoes" between poets of different nations and times; the search for Russian identity inside or against the Western literary background; close links between literature and religious and mystical traditions; literature's confessional character, its attempt to transform everyday life into poetry, as well as to render "the spirit of the time."

To be sure, for most Anglophone readers Russian literature consists not of a series of topics such as those enumerated above, nor of a historical sequence of works and literary movements, but rather of a small number of individual writers. These include, first and foremost, the great nineteenth-century novelists Fedor Dostoevsky, Lev Tolstoy, and Ivan Turgenev, as well as Anton Chekhov, known primarily for his plays. From the twentieth century, these same readers know some works of Alexander Solzhenitsyn, perhaps Pasternak's *Doctor Zhivago*, Mikhail Bulgakov's *Master and Margarita*, and Vladimir Nabokov's *Lolita*. The brilliant tradition of Russian lyric poetry stretching from the eighteenth century to the present is almost completely terra incognita, as are the complex prose experiments of Nikolai Gogol, Nikolai Leskov, Andrei Bely, and Andrei Platonov. It is our job in this book to connect the known and the unknown, and to place both in a context that will allow the reader to appreciate works with which she is familiar and to stimulate her to explore new territory. We do so by considering these works in the context of a cultural history of Russian literature.

So what is a cultural history of Russian literature and how does it differ from a traditional history of Russian literature? A traditional literary history assumes, either explicitly or implicitly, that the most appropriate way to understand the development of a nation's literature is by focusing on the internal evolution of that tradition itself. Hence, the foreground tends to be occupied by the relationship of one group of canonized authors and texts to another. In its turn, if we are talking about the history of a Western nation's literature, those developments are set in the context of a broader European literary tradition with which the given national tradition interacts. As a result, if we are dealing with Russia for example, we can appreciate how Dostoevsky grew out of Gogol, how Russian realism grew out of Russian Romanticism, and how Russian Romanticism and realism both borrowed from and rejected features of European Romanticism and realism. In recent years, literary historians have begun to make this schema more complex by paying greater attention to writers and traditions that had earlier been excluded from the canon, such as women's writing, émigré writing, and so forth. While this broadens the list of authors and works under consideration, it does not change the basic concept.

Two things fall out of such histories. First, traditional literary histories behave as if writers produce their work in an environment in which literature is the only relevant art form. They therefore neglect the fact that writers are always part of a larger cultural milieu that includes composers, painters, architects, actors, dancers, choreographers, directors, photographers, and filmmakers, and that literary work frequently borrows from and interacts with other cultural forms. One of the major sea changes that has occurred in the study of the humanities over the past few decades has been instigated precisely by the concern to recognize the implications of these sorts of interactions, and much of the best recent work by cultural historians concerns this topic. Literary histories, even non-traditional ones, have been slow to recognize their importance. Although it is clearly impossible to elucidate all such interactions, the reader here will find a greater focus on Russian visual art, music, and theatre, than is generally the case in a literary history.

While interactions between literature and other spheres of art could be a focus of literary historians focusing on any national tradition, there is also one particularity of Russian literary development (at least in comparison to the better-known literary histories of West European countries) that a cultural history of Russian literature needs to take into account. It is a rare literary history that fails to mention the broader social and political context in which authors produce their work, but, for understandable reasons, such material generally remains in the background. After all, the basic periodization of English and Russian literature is deemed identical in the nineteenth century, passing from sentimentalism through Romanticism to realism, and then to modernism. Given that this line of development occurs despite enormous political and social differences between the two countries during the same period, it is hard to avoid the conclusion that the internal arc of literary development is more significant than the non-literary background.

When we speak about Russian literature, however, such an approach has significant problems. It may be true that from the Enlightenment forward in Western Europe literature lived a somewhat autonomous existence from the state, but in Russia the relationship between literature in general and its most significant producers in particular with the state remained close and highly salient. At almost every period, Russian literature attempted to play, and usually did play, a significant extra-literary role. Literature was frequently the primary medium for political discussion in Russia, as well as the locus for much of the country's significant philosophical thought. It worked either for or against the political power of the state, but almost never could it be said to have existed in an autonomous sphere. Literature did not merely reflect social and political reality, it frequently created social and political reality. As a result, if we are to provide a satisfactory cultural history of Russian literature, then the political and social context in which that literature was produced and the interrelationship between that context and the literary sphere must get at least equal billing with the internal development of the literary system.

We have chosen an unusual way to present the narrative of Russian literature in its broad cultural context, one that tries to retain a basic chronological framework without falling into an encyclopedic presentation. Our book is divided into ten chapters, each of which deals with a bounded time period from medieval Rus' to the present. In a number of cases, chapters overlap chronologically, thereby allowing a given period to be seen in more than one context. To tell the story of each period, we provide a longish essay touching on the highpoints of its development and then we provide a discussion of one biography of a significant individual, one literary / cultural event, and one literary work which serve as prisms through which the main outlines of development of a given period can be discerned. This makes our history primarily conceptual in nature, and it will encourage readers, from the casually interested to the professional scholar, to see Russian literature in surprising contexts and from unexpected perspectives. Certainly, there are many other events, works and authors on whom we could have focused, and we hope to create a sufficiently polemical atmosphere through our choices to invite colleagues and the public to propose different ones. Nevertheless, we are confident that the thirty nodal points selected are sufficiently representative to allow us to present the central mytho-poetic conceptions that have driven the development of Russian literature and simultaneously to provide a conceptually challenging history.

1

The Origins: Russian Medieval Culture

I

According to one influential view of Russian cultural history, a book devoted primarily to modern developments could well begin with a consideration of eighteenth-century Russian literature. Anything before that belongs to a completely different cultural formation, one no more closely related to modern Russia than classical Roman culture is to modern Italy. This attitude grows from a broadly accepted understanding of the import of the reign of Emperor Peter I (the Great). Peter, it is said, created Russia anew from the ground up, annihilating earlier Russian cultural practices and refashioning a new culture oriented to Western Europe rather than to the autarkic and/or "Asiatic" cultural tradition that had developed in the Russian lands over the previous 750 years. The historian and philosopher Mikhail Pogodin (1800–75) expressed this sentiment baldly in the first issue of his journal *The Muscovite* (Moskvitianin) in 1841:

> We cannot open our eyes; we cannot make a move; we cannot turn in any direction without encountering him: at home, in the street, church, school, court, regiment, at leisure. He is everywhere, every day, every minute, at every step. We wake up. What day is it? 1 January 1841. Peter the Great ordered us to number years from the birth of Christ. Peter the Great ordered us to take January as the first month. Time to get dressed – our clothing is sewn in the manner Peter the Great prescribed, our uniforms according to his design. The fabric is woven at a factory that he founded; the wool is shorn from sheep that he bred. Our gaze falls upon a book – Peter the Great introduced this alphabet and carved this type himself. You begin to read – Under Peter the First this language became a written, literary one, supplanting the earlier church language. The newspapers are brought in – Peter the Great founded them.

Although no one would dispute that much in Russia did change in the wake of Peter's reforms, we do not accept the claim that modern Russian literature can be understood without reference to medieval Russian culture, which in fact remained remarkably vibrant and influential in many spheres despite all attempts to suppress it and which played an important role in creating the distinctive outlines of modern Russian culture in general and literature in particular. That having been said, it is important to recognize that the cultural mentality of Russians, even well-educated Russians in the period before the eighteenth century was, from a modern Western perspective, peculiar, and needs to be understood on its own terms rather than as a direct precursor of modern Russian thought. Furthermore, although there are significant continuities in the culture of Russia from the tenth to the seventeenth centuries, it is dangerous to lump all of the dynamic development of this long time frame into a single "period" whose defining characteristic is that it is *not* identical to modern Russian culture. Recognizing and appreciating these difficulties, we nevertheless sketch a history of Old Russian culture, focusing primarily on those elements that remained salient into the modern period.

II

Before beginning, the ambiguity of the term "Old Russian" must be considered. The Rus', according to the best evidence that can be mustered, were a relatively small group of Norse (Viking) war lords, who came to rule over a group of speakers of East Slavic dialects in the area of today's northwestern Russia (around Novgorod), beginning sometime in the ninth century. In a relatively short time this ruling caste became Slavicized and extended its reach to other territories in the immediate vicinity and farther south along the trade route that connected the Baltic to the Black Sea. Though they shifted their base of operations depending on the vicissitudes of war, dynastic politics, and the personal preference of various warlord leaders, Kiev, in today's Ukraine became their most important stronghold by the tenth century. It remained the center of what has come to be called Kievan Rus' through the beginning of the thirteenth century when the city was sacked by the armies of Batu Khan.

As was the case with analogous political formations all over medieval Europe, the Rus' state was unified, insofar as it was unified at all, by a dynastic rather than a national conception, held together by the horizontal relationships of the rulers of its various territories rather than by a vertical conception of the cultural or ethnic solidarity of its inhabitants. Thus, while the ruling class had a fairly strong notion of the Rus' territories, which comes through clearly in various literary works, they had no interest in the creation of a homogeneous Rus' nation. After the destruction of Kiev, Rus' fragmented and a number of formerly peripheral cities attempted to take up the mantle of Rus' in the forest regions that the Mongols could not control (or did not find worth controlling). Among these were Vladimir-Suzdal in the northeast, Novgorod in the northwest, and Volhynia in the southwest. In the course of the fourteenth and fifteenth centuries, however, Moscow, which had been unimportant during the heyday of Kievan Rus', became the most powerful East Slav city, eliminating rival Slavic centers of power as a vassal state to the Tatars, and eventually leading a coalition against the Tatars by the late fourteenth century. As Moscow gained political hegemony, it also claimed religious and cultural centrality and its leaders came to view their state as the natural heir, not only to the cultural patrimony of Kievan Rus' but to that of all Orthodox Christianity. The Byzantines had seen themselves as Romans and Constantinople was dubbed the Second Rome. After its fall to the Ottomans in 1453, Moscow was the only remaining Orthodox Christian power, and Muscovite ideologues developed the theory of Moscow as the Third (and final) Rome.

When modern European notions of the nation appeared in the mid to late eighteenth century, Russian nationalists created a narrative of political and cultural development that outlined a natural arc from Kievan Rus' through Muscovy to modern Russia. This narrative remained more or less unchallenged as long as Russia was the only East Slavic national state. More recently, however, nationalist-oriented scholars in Ukraine, and to a lesser extent Belarus, have claimed the culture of Kievan Rus' as their ancestor, dubbing it not Old Russian culture, as had been the standard usage, but Old Ukrainian or Old Belarusian culture. Recent, post-nationalist scholarship has emphasized the problematic nature of any such assertion, focusing on the wide variety of proto-national cultural formations among the East Slavs and noting the artificiality of any narrative that seeks to assert a single, teleological line of national cultural development. From our perspective this controversy misses the point. Certainly other modern cultures can plausibly claim to be the heirs of what has traditionally been called Old Russian culture. Rather than engaging in polemics regarding who owns the legacy of this culture, however, we prefer to explicate some of its specificities and to point out ways in which it affected the formation of modern Russian culture. We will, however, use the term Old Rusian to describe the culture of Kievan Rus' and reserve Old Russian for the culture that developed in the Eastern portions of the Rus' lands after the Mongol invasions of the early thirteenth century.

Event – The Christianization of Rus'

According to the *Primary Chronicle* (Povest' vremennykh let) the crucial historical source for our knowledge of Kievan Rus' as well as a key early literary work (see below), the Rus' prince Vladimir agreed to be baptized and to convert his people to Byzantine-rite Christianity in the late 890s. This choice was undoubtedly the single most important cultural event of the entire pre-modern period, as Christianization laid the foundations for practically every cultural development that would occur on the Russian lands over the next seven hundred years.

According to the Chronicle account, Vladimir chose Byzantine-rite Christianity having carefully considered alternative monotheistic religions – Judaism, Latin-rite Christianity, and Islam. Islam was rejected because of its prohibition against alcohol – "Drink is Rus's love," Vladimir is quoted as saying, "we cannot do without it." Judaism was rejected because its contemporary Diasporic reality suggested that it lacked the ability to be the basis for a strong political state, and there is no doubt that Vladimir was interested in conversion at least as much for political as for spiritual reasons. While Roman Christianity impressed Vladimir's envoys, they were awed by the pomp and circumstance of Christianity as practiced in Constantinople, then the greatest city in the Western world. "The Greeks led us to the edifices where they worship their God, and we knew not whether we were in heaven or on earth. For on earth there is no such splendor or such beauty, and we are at a loss how to describe it. We know only that God dwells there among men, and their service is fairer than the ceremonies of other nations."[1]

To be sure, the Chronicle account must be taken with a grain of salt, or at least it must be recognized that the choice of Byzantine-rite Christianity was over-determined. The Byzantine Empire had been the main civilization with which the Rus' had been trading for more than one hundred years, and a religious alliance with the Greeks made more sense than one with religions professed by groups whose center was more distant. Constantinople was, after all, the capital of the most powerful empire of its day, and could likely provide the Rus' lands with some added protection. As had been the case with South Slav rulers who had converted earlier, Vladimir also probably recognized that Christianity could be a unifying force in his kingdom. Furthermore, individual members of the Rus' elite had been converting to Byzantine Christianity for many years (including Vladimir's grandmother Olga who had been baptized some fifty years earlier by the Byzantine Emperor himself) so the religion was not completely unfamiliar. Finally, according to the Chronicle, Vladimir reaped significant personal benefits from his willingness to convert, including the ultimate trophy wife: the sister of the Byzantine Emperor. A marital union with the most powerful empire in the Western world was an obvious sign that Vladimir and his realm were important.

Nevertheless, just because a ruler agreed to convert did not necessarily mean that his subjects thought the same way. For the rank and file, the benefits of conversion were unclear. The pagan gods had provided a sense of security for many, and it is difficult to believe they were eager to give up familiar idols for the abstract, text-based Christian faith. As the Chronicle account states when recounting that Vladimir forced the sons of the "best people" to study Christian books: "The mothers of these children cried over them; for they were not yet firm in their faith and they cried over them as if they had died" (132). Given that we can find exhortations against various pagan practices in texts by Christian clerics for hundreds of years, we can guess that despite Christianity's ability to fold pagan customs into its practices, Christianity and paganism continued to exist side by side for a long time. Indeed, ethnographers could still find echoes of pre-Christian practices in the life and folkways of nineteenth-century Russian peasants, though they had lost any connection to an organized pagan Slavic belief system.

Regardless of how quickly or thoroughly the masses embraced the new religion, the adoption of Christianity in Rus' was of critical importance for further cultural and social developments. In accepting the Orthodox religion, Rus' became part of the Byzantine Orthodox world and unavoidably assimilated many Byzantine political customs and assumptions. The Byzantine Empire was first and foremost a Christian state, whose basic doctrines were defined by the church fathers, the church councils, and the decisions of the various Byzantine emperors. Although during earlier centuries the church had been racked by heresies and doctrinal disagreements, after the final victory of those in favor of icon veneration in 843, the doctrine of the Eastern Orthodox Church was essentially fixed. By comparison with Catholicism (not to mention later Protestantism), Orthodoxy was a traditionalist religion, which placed great stock in liturgy and ritual and tended to be less concerned with individual achievements. To be sure, at the time of the conversion, Christianity had not yet split definitively between Orthodoxy and Catholicism (this would occur only in 1054). Nevertheless, for both political and ecclesiastical reasons the two wings of the church had been drifting apart for hundreds of years, and by the late tenth century, they were clearly distinct. As the Chronicle account indicates, the Rus' were particularly impressed by the liturgical and sensory aspects of Orthodoxy, rather than by its theological principles, and they would remain attached to the somewhat more mystical and less rational practices of Orthodoxy.

In the Byzantine scheme of things, the emperor, chosen by God, was more powerful than any Western ruler. It was the emperor, not the patriarch (the title given to the spiritual leader of the Orthodox church), who presided over church councils and expounded dogmatic pronouncements. While Catholic popes could make even the most powerful Catholic kings bend to their will at times, the Byzantine patriarch was appointed by the emperor and could be dismissed by him. When one eleventh-century patriarch tried to challenge this arrangement he was arrested, beaten, and thrown into prison where he died before a trial could occur. In the Orthodox world, therefore, the linkage between church and state was tighter than in the West, and state interference with church affairs was more pervasive.

Because the Byzantine church permitted the liturgy to be celebrated and the central religious texts translated into local languages and because some southern Slavic groups had converted earlier (the Bulgarians, for example, had done so by the early 860s) translations of many basic theological texts already existed in a comprehensible Slavic idiom. The rapid influx of "pre-packaged" religious texts was of cardinal importance to future literary developments. There is no evidence that the Rus' possessed any writing system before their conversion to Christianity. The provenance of the religious texts translated by Saints Kiril and Methodius for missionary work among the Eastern and Southern Slavs ensured that their language (which would later come to be called Old Church Slavonic) and the language of everyday conversation in Rus' would not be identical. Linguists use the word diglossia to describe a cultural system in which two languages or linguistic registers exist side-by-side in a given cultural milieu and can be called upon to serve different functions. This is a useful term and applies well to the situation in Rus', though it would be better to imagine the two spheres as more like poles on a continuum than separate and impermeable systems. Thus, the religious texts brought to Rus' and copied by local scribes quickly took on features of the local spoken dialect, and the local dialect rapidly began to absorb words and grammatical constructions borrowed from the bookish language of the church.

Throughout the history of Russian literature writers have exploited the diglossia between Church Slavonic and spoken Russian for stylistic effect, and this rich linguistic potential is one of the most significant long-term influences of Old Rusian culture on modern Russian literature. In the 1750s

Mikhail Lomonosov (1711–65) developed a theory of "three styles" for modern Russian literature distinguished by the relationship of Slavonicisms to colloquial Russian. The high style, suitable for epic and tragedy, was to contain a preponderance of Slavonic forms, a middle style, suitable for lyric poetry, verse comedy, and prose, would exhibit a mixture of Slavonicisms and Russian forms, while a low style suitable for fables and other popular genres would primarily employ colloquial Russian. Battles between proponents of Slavonicisms and those who favored a more colloquial idiom would continue from the mid-eighteenth century into the 1820s, after which time Russian forms generally gained the upper hand. Nevertheless, Slavonicisms continue to exist in parallel to more standard Russian forms to this day. To an extent, the modern usage is analogous to the option writers of English have to choose between more colloquial Germanic words and rarified Latinate synonyms (to find someone innocent or to exculpate him, for example) except that in modern Russian the relationship is more consistent and more frequently exploited.

In addition to literary culture, the Rus' borrowed heavily from the architectural and visual lexicon of Constantinople. The first Russian stone churches were built by the late tenth century in Kiev and in Novgorod in the eleventh century, and a number of these edifices remained in a remarkably good state of preservation into the modern period. The domed church building (though not onion-domed – this characteristic Russian style did not appear until later, probably in the thirteenth century) became a ubiquitous feature of the Russian landscape. And the icon, again imported originally from Constantinople but quickly nativized by Russian painters, became a feature not only of church interiors but also of homes, both peasant and noble. Even after the Petrine reforms, the icon did not lose its central place in the traditional Russian home, and iconic images retained a significant place in the cultural memory of modern Russians.

Initially, the Rus' were satisfied to attach themselves to the great Christian narrative but did not claim to play a crucial role in it. This attitude shifted in the fourteenth and fifteenth centuries as Moscow gained influence and the power of other centers of Orthodox Christianity diminished (beginning with the Ottoman subjugation of the Balkans in the late fourteenth century and concluding with their capture of Constantinople itself). The Russians began to develop a more muscular attitude to their role in the Christian narrative. Thus, whereas earlier versions of the *Primary Chronicle* noted that no apostle had set foot in Russian territory, later versions present an apocryphal story claiming that the apostle Andrew visited not only the coasts of the Black Sea (as Byzantine legends had it) but also the Dnepr river basin and the site of the future city of Novgorod where he became acquainted with the Slavs. In particular it was asserted that he had marveled at the peculiar bathing customs of the Slavs near Novogorod: "I saw the land of the Slavs, and while I was among them I noticed their wooden bathhouses. They warm them to extreme heat, then undress, and after anointing themselves with tallow, they take young reeds and lash their bodies" (47). Such stories permitted the Muscovites to claim a direct connection, however, tenuous, with the earliest Christians. The marriage in 1472 of Prince Ivan III to Sophia Paleologus, the surviving niece of the last Byzantine emperor, allowed the Muscovite state to claim important symbolic trappings of the fallen Byzantine Empire.

At about this time the curious *Tale of the White Cowl* (Povest' o belom klobuke) was composed in Novgorod, which was in an increasingly desperate struggle with Moscow for its political autonomy. According to this narrative, in gratitude for a healing vision in which the pope had appeared, Emperor Constantine had given a white cowl to Pope Sylvester as a sign of the primacy of clerical over imperial power. This holy object remained in Rome until the popes fell into heresy (by this time the Orthodox considered Catholicism as heretical). It had been transferred to Constantinople where the Orthodox patriarchs had shown it due respect until such time as the Byzantine Empire itself began to collapse under the weight of its sins. At this point, sometime in the early fifteenth century, the cowl was claimed to have been transferred to Novgorod, making this Russian city the symbolic heir of the mix of political power and Christian ideology once characteristic of Rome and then Constantinople. This story was loosely associated with a broadly accepted theological theory that posited three Christian kingdoms – that of the Father, of the Son, and of the Holy Spirit. Russia, in the local interpretation, was the last of these.

Novgorod would eventually lose the struggle for primacy among the Russian pretenders. Its final political destruction would come at the hands of Ivan IV (the Terrible) in 1570. But the idea of Russia as the third and final Christian kingdom had been further developed in Muscovy by the monk Filofei in the 1520s. Filofei famously wrote that "two Romes had fallen, Moscow was the third, and there would be no fourth," thus putting Russia at the very center of Christian eschatological history. The belief, derived at least in part from this theory and its subsequent interpretations, that Russia had a special, messianic destiny would play a crucial role in Russian literary and cultural history in the nineteenth and into the twentieth centuries. It underpinned Emperor Alexander I's "holy alliance of Christian states" after the defeat of Napoleon, and was held by Nikolai Gogol (1809–52), who tried unsuccessfully to instantiate it in his epic "poem" *Dead Souls* (Mertvye dushi, 1842). This notion was held even more strongly by Fedor Dostoevsky (1820–81), who wrote about Russia's messianic destiny at length in his *Diary of a Writer* (Dnevnik pisatelia, 1873–9, 1880–1) and, in less obvious ways, in *The Brothers Karamazov* (Brat'ia Karamazovy, 1880). It remained central to the eschatology of Russia's most influential philosopher Vladimir Solov'ev (1853–1900) and would color the apocalyptic thinking of the symbolist generation, many of whom initially saw the 1917 revolution as the fulfillment of Russia's messianic destiny. Although Christianity was consigned to oblivion by the Bolsheviks, they never abandoned the idea that Russia had a messianic role to play in world history as their attempts to spread world communism attest. In the post-Soviet period Orthodoxy has begun to play an ever more prominent role in Russian society, and it is clear that Christianity, officially brought to Russia by Vladimir in the late tenth century, will remain a key component of Russian culture, literary and otherwise, into the future.

III

Before beginning a short survey of the cultural history of Old Rusian and Old Russian literature a few more broad questions should be considered. One has to do with the definition of literature. If by literature we have in mind written texts produced primarily for aesthetic enjoyment, it is safe to say that practically no literature was produced in Kievan Rus' and rather little in pre-modern Russia. If, on the other hand, we have in mind texts that have an aesthetic component regardless of their primary function, then it is possible to speak of literature in this period, for many writers were clearly aware of the expressive component of their texts. That is the sense in which we will use the term literature here, focusing, we repeat, on those elements of the literary / cultural system that would remain relevant for modern Russian literary culture.

Another important question relates to those who engaged in writing and reading in this long period. A few decades ago, the answer would have seemed fairly unambiguous, at least for the Kievan period: the vast majority of writing was believed to have been commissioned either by the church or the various Rus' princes. In the Muscovite period, especially in the seventeenth century, although clerics still dominated text production, some texts were created by and for members of the merchant caste. In the past few decades, however, archeological excavations, particularly in Novgorod, have turned up large quantities of written material incised on birch bark and these finds have forced a reconsideration of who wrote in the Kievan period and why. It now seems that writing, particularly in Old Rusian rather than Church Slavonic, was quite prevalent in the merchant milieu. Such communications, however, had an exclusively functional character, so the belief that what can be called literary writing in this period was produced exclusively by and for a small group of educated clerics and their patrons in the princely courts remains unchanged. The prevalence of literacy among merchants from the earliest period does, however, provide a convincing explanation for the rise of literary works in that sphere in later periods.

A final broad question regarding Old Russian literature relates to oral literary production. In the mid-nineteenth century, inspired by the German theoretical insistence on the importance and beauty of folk literature, as well as by the powerful works collected among their South Slavic "cousins," Russian ethnographers recorded a wide range of folk material including short epic poems (the so-called *byliny*), folk stories, and lyric poetry relating to various stages of life such as birth, death, and especially marriage. Both because of references in these works to ancient historical figures and events as well as to certain pre-Christian practices, it was assumed that this oral literature dated back to the Kievan period. In the twentieth century scholars became aware of the likely oral origin of some of the greatest epics of the Western tradition, Homer's *Iliad* and *Odyssey*. In this context it became apparent that the most aesthetically accomplished work of Old Russian literature, *The Lay of Prince Igor* (Slovo o polku Igoreve), which likely dates from the twelfth century and which had an enormous influence on a number of modern Russian literary works, had oral origins as well. Thus, in considering Old Rusian and Old Russian literary production, we need to keep in mind that not everything written was literature (far from it) and not all of what can be called literature was written.

IV

As noted earlier, the first written texts to appear in Rus' had been translated into Church Slavonic by speakers of South Slav dialects – primarily religious in character, they included most importantly such standbys as The New Testament and the Psalms, as well as some works by the Eastern Church fathers. Very quickly, however, East Slavs assimilated the Slavonic idiom and began to compose original works, based to be sure on translated models. The first substantial piece that can be definitively attributed to a native Rus' is the "Sermon on Law and Grace" by the Metropolitan Hilarion, written sometime in the late 1040s. Although the sermon's concern with demonstrating the superiority of the New Testament (Grace) to the Old Testament (Law) is a standard Byzantine topic, Hilarion, who after all belonged to a generation for whom even the concept of literacy was an innovation, demonstrates an exceptional ability to deploy complex rhetorical tropes and a deep knowledge of scripture and church history. Most remarkable is Ilarion's extended panegyrical apostrophe to Vladimir, the Christianizer of Rus', who is compared to Constantine the Great and exhorted to rise from his grave to observe how the seeds he planted have germinated in Rus': "Arise from your grave, venerated prince, arise and shake off your sleep . . . Behold your child Georgy [the Christian name of Iaroslav, the Wise], look upon your beloved one whom God has brought forth from your loins. Behold him embellishing the throne of your land . . . Behold Christianity flourishing, your city gleaming, adorned with holy icons and fragrant with thyme, praising God and filling the air with sacred songs."[2] Hilarion was not the only Rus'-born prelate to produce literary work in this period – Cyril, Bishop of Turov in the mid-twelfth century, left a substantial corpus, including prayers and sermons.

By far the most influential literary form in this period, however, was the *zhitie* (vita, Saint's life). Again, this genre was imported from Byzantium, where it was widespread. The saint was a person who had imitated Christ in a particularly exemplary fashion and who could, after death, intercede for the living. A life story was generally composed fairly soon after the death of a holy person and used as evidence in support of canonization. After a saint was canonized, a brief version of the life would be read in church on the day commemorating the saint. For a fledgling church like that of Rus', it was important to create a pantheon of local saints, both to indicate to local believers that the church had become fully integrated with the local culture and perhaps to convince outsiders that the new church had reached at least some level of parity with its parent. The kinds of saints selected for canonization provide a good indication of local church politics.

Prince Vladimir appears to have been elevated to sainthood for his role in evangelizing the Rus', despite the fact that his early life had been less than savory, including incidents of murder, rape, and polygamy. Vladimir's grandmother Olga, who had personally converted to Christianity in the mid-tenth century, was also considered a saint. More interesting than the canonization of successful rulers, however, is that of Rus's first officially recognized saints, Vladimir's sons Boris and Gleb. After Vladimir's death a fratricidal struggle ensued between his sons. According to the accounts in both the *Primary Chronicle* and in the saints' lives devoted to Boris and Gleb, Sviatopolk seized the throne after his father's death and killed the two before another brother, Iaroslav, managed to stop his murderous spree, drive him out of Kiev, and take power himself.

As history (and saint's lives) are written by the winners, there is no certainty that the events took place as described. What is important, however, is not "what really happened" but what the texts present as having happened. And here we find a consistent story – though both Boris and Gleb are said to have been aware of their brother's fratricidal urges, they made no attempt to defend themselves or to flee. Rather, in imitation of Christ, they chose the path of non-resistance to evil, interpreted by the hagiographers as martyrdom for their faith rather than political murder. Later Russian theologians and religious thinkers, including for example Lev Tolstoy (1828–1910), would claim that the idea of passive non-resistance to evil or *kenosis* (emptying out) exemplified by Boris and Gleb is a distinctive trait of Russian orthodoxy. Not all sainted princes were canonized for passivity, however. The vita of Alexander Nevsky, for example, celebrates primarily his military victories over the Teutonic knights and Lithuanians, which are understood to be in defense of Orthodoxy as the Teutonic knights were a Catholic order and the Lithuanians still pagan at this time. This work would later be used as a jumping-off point for the famous 1938 film directed by Sergei Eisenstein (1898–1948) with stirring music by Sergei Prokofiev (1891–1953).

Political leaders were not the only (nor even the majority) of Slavs chosen for canonization. Theodosius, founder of the influential Monastery of Caves in Kiev, is the subject of one of the earliest extended saint's lives. Written by the monk Nestor relatively soon after Theodosius's death, the work reveals practically all of the literary topoi associated with the genre. It begins with a short invocation, justifying the writer's task and confessing to his inadequacy to complete it properly. The life proper mixes commonplaces of the hagiographical tradition with some details particular to Theodosius. As is typical, he was born to god-fearing parents, and preferred scholarly pursuits to amusements as a young man. Not typical, though by no means unheard of in this context, is his extended effort to break free of his mother, who opposes his choice of a holy vocation. Nestor spends the bulk of the narrative describing Theodosius's efforts to build a monastic community and to stand up to contemporary political leaders in its defense, as well as to resist the blandishments of the devil through humility, prayer, and feats of ascetic self-abnegation. The requisite miracles are described as well, although Theodosius's are fairly prosaic.

The so-called holy fool is a saintly type that, while not unique to Russian culture, seems to have had a particularly strong appeal there. The earliest of these is Isaac, who, having awakened after lying immobile for two years without eating and drinking as a result of demonic possession, engaged in such peculiar actions as standing barefoot in the Russian winter until his feet froze to the ground, and playing such (unspecified) tricks on the abbot and brothers of the cave monastery that these holy men beat him – all in the name of conquering devils who continued to pester him while he was praying. Holy fools would remain prominent in Russian culture through the seventeenth century, and would play important roles in such modern works as Alexander Pushkin's (1799–1837) play *Boris Godunov* (1825; later Modest Musorgsky's [1839–81] opera [1874] of the same name) and Dostoevsky's *The Idiot* (Idiot, 1869).

Stylistically, the saints' lives written during the Old Rusian period are relatively unadorned and lack the elaborate rhetorical fireworks of, say, Ilarion's sermon. Lives from the late fourteenth and early fifteenth centuries, however, become far more elaborate, even as they retain many of the basic thematic topoi of the earlier works. Particularly notable are two lives written by Epiphanius the Wise. Employing a complex stylistic system that has been called word weaving by scholars, Epiphany fashions exceptionally compelling texts whose rhetorical flourishes create a literary analogy to the mystical and practical feats of his heroes: St. Sergii of Radonezh and St. Stefan of Perm. The former was, like Theodosius, the founder of an influential monastic community. His support of Moscow's pretensions to leadership of the surviving Russian princedoms in the late fourteenth century was instrumental in making that city and its rulers first among equals in the struggle against the Tatars. The latter is remembered as a proselytizer who risked martyrdom in his attempts to convert the pagan Permians to Christianity.

Saints' lives were read in churches and collected in various incunabula and later published collections. The basic outlines of the saint's life were, therefore, well known to the majority of modern Russian writers (at least those born before 1917), and the zhitie was undoubtedly the single most influential Old Rusian / Old Russian genre for nineteenth and twentieth-century Russian literature. Dostoevsky, for example, made extensive use of this tradition, most specifically in *The Brothers Karamazov*, where the lives of both Father Zosima and Alesha Karamazov bear obvious relations to those of Russian saints. The short story "Father Sergii" (published 1912) by Lev Tolstoy is another classic Russian work based on the saint's life paradigm. Even more interesting is the use of the saint's life by Nikolai Chernyshevsky

(1828–89) in his novel *What is to be Done?* (Chto delat'?, 1863). This work, ostensibly anti-religious but riddled with topoi taken from the Christian traditions, was Lenin's favorite and has been called the most influential Russian novel of the nineteenth century because of its canonized status among the revolutionary youth. A central character is the revolutionary "man of iron" Rakhmetov, whose feats of asceticism include sleeping on a bed of nails.

Literary Work – *The Primary Chronicle* (Povest' vremennykh let)

In a short essay devoted to *War and Peace*, Tolstoy says that his book is "not a novel, even less is it a poem, and still less an historical chronicle." This, he goes on to claim, is not an anomaly: "from Gogol's *Dead Souls* to Dostoevsky's *House of the Dead*, in the recent period of Russian literature there is not a single artistic prose work rising at all above mediocrity, which quite fits into the form of a novel, epic, or story."[3] Had he chosen to, Tolstoy could have removed the word "modern" from his account of Russian literature, and noted that one of the key texts from the Old Rusian tradition is equally multi-generic and difficult to pigeonhole. The *Primary Chronicle* is Russia's original loose and baggy monster, containing legends, historical narrative, hagiography, original documents (treaties, wills, and testaments), and practical advice for ruling and living.

A chronicle is, in its simplest form, a piece of historical writing in which entries are made according to a chronological principle. Thus, in principle at least, the chronicler tells about all relevant happenings in a given year, regardless of their internal heterogeneity, before turning to events of the following year. Chronicles are additive: each new chronicler copies the entries from before his time and adds new material to bring the chronicle forward. Chronicle writing was widely practiced in the Byzantine empire, and Byzantine chronicles were among the earliest secular works with which literate Rus' became acquainted soon after Christianization (probably through earlier translations done in Bulgaria).

No original manuscript of what has come to be called the *Primary Chronicle* survives, but its text was incorporated, with various excisions and amendments, into multiple later Chronicles. This allows scholars to recreate with a reasonable degree of certainty the likely "original text" which was, it appears, composed in the second decade of the twelfth century in Kiev, almost certainly by a monk associated with the Monastery of the Caves. It is possible, though unprovable, that this text itself was based on even older versions, and it is certain that the chronicler had available many oral sources as well as documents that have not survived. Stylistically, the *Primary Chronicle* is written in an accessible and straightforward version of Old Rusian, for the most part lacking Slavonicisms and less rhetorically complex than contemporary ecclesiastical works. Not only is it the first extensive text in Old Rusian, it is also, despite obvious flaws and factual errors, the most important source text for historical knowledge of Rus'. Thus, it can be seen as the progenitor text for Russian literary and historical writing, and this may well have contributed to the fact that these types of writing never entirely diverged in Russia.

The basic concerns of the text are signaled by its title "This is the tale of bygone years, where the Rus' land came from, who first began to rule in Kiev, and how the Rus' land came to be." Thus, the focus is on the history of a group of people, their rulers and their political life. Nevertheless, as is the case with some of its Byzantine sources, the *Primary Chronicle* begins with prehistory – the creation of the world derived from the Old Testament. Moving quickly through the flood, the chronicler provides an origin for the Slavs in one of the seventy-two tongues that spread over the world after the destruction of the Tower of Babel. While the ethnographic details are not convincing in the light of modern scholarship, the claim that the Slavs originate from one of the original world tribes is significant, for it implies they had a position in the original divine plan. The Chronicle moves quickly forward to recount the legendary founding of Kiev by three brothers Kii, Shchek, and Khoriv and their sister Lybed'. It continues with an ethnographic survey of the various Slav tribes who lived in the Dnepr and Danube basins. A number of the customs described in the text have been corroborated by archeological evidence.

The first dated events in the Chronicle begin with the middle of the ninth century and focus on the position of the Slavs between the Byzantine Empire on the south and the Varangians (Norsemen, Vikings) in the north. As the territories inhabited by the East Slavs lay precisely on the trade route connecting the Baltic to the Black Sea, such a concern is by no means surprising. By far the most controversial of the early chronicle stories is the "Calling of the Varangians," dated by the Chronicler to 862 (6370 by the chronology of the Chronicle, which numbers years from the "creation of the world"). According to this legend, a group of the Slavs had been paying tribute to some Norsemen but rose up in revolt against them. Having successfully ridden themselves of these foreigners, however, the Slavs realized that they could not prevent their lands from descending into anarchy and invited back some of the Norse, called Rus', to rule over them. "Our land is great and abundant, but there is no order here. Come and rule over us," the Slavs are reported to have said to three brothers (the magic three is almost certainly not accidental): Riurik, Sineus, and Truvor. Regardless of whether Norse overlords were actually invited or invited themselves over local opposition (a later version of the Chronicle asserts that in 864 "Riurik executed the courageous Vadim and killed many of his [Vadim's] advisors"), it does appear certain that the ninth-century rulers of the East Slavs around Novgorod and a bit later Kiev were indeed Vikings and that the Rus' (and later the Russians) adopted their name from these warriors. However, within a few generations the ruling class of Vikings became fully Slavicized and were absorbed by the more numerous Slavs.

Whether the ancestors of the Russians had originally been ruled by Slavs or by Norsemen and what the relations were between the two groups became exceptionally controversial in both literature and history when nationalism in its modern form arrived in Russia in the late eighteenth century. From the end of the eighteenth century to around the 1830s the terse chronicle account of Vadim was used as a jumping-off point for plays, poetry, prose fiction, history, and even an opera libretto by writers as diverse as Empress Catherine the Great (1729–96), Iakov Kniazhnin (1740–91), Vasily Zhukovsky (1783–1852), Nikolai Karamzin (1766–1826), Kondraty Ryleev (1795–1826), Alexei Khomiakov (1804–60), Stepan Shevyrev (1806–64) and Alexander Pushkin. Vasily Tatishchev (1686–1750), Russia's first modern historian, was probably the first to provide a "nationalist spin" to the Chronicle account: "In these times the Slavs fled from Novgorod to Kiev, away from Riurik who killed the courageous Vadim, a Slavic prince, for not wanting to be a slave to the Varangians."[4] Although Empress Catherine is best known for her political and military achievements, she was an accomplished and prolific writer as well. In both a history and a "Shakespearian" drama, she chose to slant Vadim's revolt quite differently, emphasizing that it was caused by the Novgorodian's envy of the Varangians.

In supporting Riurik while emphasizing his non-Russian background, Catherine was aligning herself with the so-called Norman theory, which "came to regard the Varangians (Normans) as true founders of the Russian state. The founding of this Norman school dates back to the first half of the eighteenth century, traced largely to group of German scholars."[5] Historians of Russian descent generally rejected this theory, primarily because of "its tendency to consider the Slavs not only a backward people, but as incapable of governing themselves."[6]

As the *Primary Chronicle* moves closer to the historical time of its composition, the text becomes denser and more detailed. The compiler clearly had access to some original documents, as indicated, for example, by his inclusion of what seems to be the entire text of a trade treaty between the Byzantine Empire and Prince Igor of Kiev in 945. The multi-generic quality of the *Primary Chronicle* really becomes apparent at this point, for the exceptionally dry provisions of the treaty are followed almost immediately by the colorful stories of the revenge that Igor's widow Olga takes on the neighboring Drevlian people after they murder her rapacious husband. To be sure, this juxtaposition may have been a mere accident, a function of the paucity of materials available to the chronicler from the period before there were many written records or eyewitnesses.

Whatever the reasons, generic heterogeneity remains a significant feature of the *Primary Chronicle* even as it begins to cover material that would have been more readily available to the first chronicler. Thus, for example, the year 1015 begins with a dry and factual account of Vladimir's death (stylistically typical for the *Primary Chronicle*), which occurred just as he was simultaneously attempting to control his son Iaroslav and defend his kingdom against the marauding Pechenegs. "Vladimir sent Boris to oppose them [the Pechenegs], but he himself fell seriously ill. He died at Berestovo but his death was hidden because Sviatopolk [another of his sons and the one who would later attempt to usurp the kingdom] was in Kiev" (144). Almost immediately, however, the chronicler launches into an encomium to Vladimir in a completely different style: that of the hagiographer. "He is the new Constantine of great Rome; just as the latter agreed to be baptized and baptized his people, so did the former. If earlier he had given in to vile passions, later he was zealous in penitence, as the apostle says: 'Where sin is plentiful, there grace abounds.' The amount of good he did Rus' by converting it is amazing. We, having become Christians, cannot possibly honor him sufficiently for this gift."

The story of the murder of Boris and Gleb that follows introduces to the narrative an important line of moralizing political admonition: the lands of Rus' can be powerful and flourish only when their rulers live in harmony. When fratricidal rivalries come to the fore, unfortunate consequences result, not merely for the ruling class but for all Rus'. The dangers of such feuding will be referenced time and again in the chronicler's account, and are his preferred explanation for various calamities that befall the land. This interpretation of Rusian history, along with the concomitant claim that Russia requires a powerful and autocratic ruler in order to flourish, would be central to Nikolai Karamzin's interpretation of Russian history (see chapter 3), and is referenced to the present day as an explanation (and sometimes a justification) for the political behavior of Russia's rulers.

This message also lies at the heart of the single greatest literary work of Old Rus', *The Lay of Prince Igor* (Slovo o polku Igoreve). This brief, brilliant epic, describes the failed campaign of 1185 led by Igor, prince of Novgorod-Seversk, against the Kumans, a nomadic tribe that roamed the south-eastern borders of Rus'. Without proper consultation with or support from his fellow princes, Igor sets out to win glory for himself but is ultimately defeated. This disaster leads the poet to consider other episodes in which lack of unity led to defeat, and he admonishes the princes to harmony: "You've lowered your banners, / You've sheathed your sundered swords, / For you have leaped out of your grandfather's glory. / For with your feuding / You brought the pagans / Onto the Russian land.'" The *Lay* was not discovered until the late eighteenth century, but after its publication its exquisite rhetoric, tight composition, and brilliant imagery became a source of inspiration for many works of modern Russian literature and culture including Alexander Borodin's (1833–87) opera *Prince Igor* (first performed 1890) and Alexander Blok's (1880–1921) exquisite poetic cycle "On the Field of Kulikovo, 1908" (Na pole Kulikovom).

Alongside admonitions to brotherly love, the chronicler does not fail to emphasize the importance of the church as the other central institution of the state. Thus, Iaroslav is lauded not merely for banishing his usurping and fratricidal brother Sviatopolk and for restoring central order, but also for his support of the church: "And it was under his rule that Christianity became fruitful and spread, and monks began to multiply and monasteries to appear. And Iaroslav loved ecclesiastical rules, and he also loved the priests, especially the monks." Given that the chronicler himself was almost certainly a monk, one could chalk up this statement to self-interest, but, whatever the reasons, religion becomes the second pillar on which the chronicle's narrative rests. In the world-view of the chronicler, the history of Rus' becomes a mighty battle between the forces of God and the devil. "And, seeing the multitude of churches and Christians, Iaroslav was overjoyed, while the devil was dismayed and vanquished by the new Christians" (167).

Iaroslav's testament to his sons (the will is another genre that fits seamlessly into the Chronicle's narrative) displays a political version of the same binary philosophy wherein a life lived morally leads directly to good consequences, while misfortunes inevitably follow moral transgressions. "If there be love among you [Iaroslav's sons], then God will be with you and you will vanquish your enemies. And you will live in peace. But if there be hatred among you, quarrels and fights then you will be destroyed and you will destroy the land that your fathers and grandfathers created through hard work" (175).

The *Primary Chronicle* comes to an end sometime in the second decade of the twelfth century, but by no means does this mark the end of chronicle writing in Rus'. The period around 1116 appears to have seen the *Primary Chronicle* copied and slightly altered three separate times in or around Kiev. From these three redactions a branching tree of chronicles spread as chronicle writing began to be practiced in a variety of locales. Recognizing, at least implicitly, that history is not what happened but what can be convincingly said to have happened, local princes commissioned chronicles to play up their role and that of their towns at the expense of their political rivals. They also used the chronicles to assert their connection with the legacy of Kievan Rus', particularly in the wake of the political fragmentation that occurred in the thirteenth century after the Mongols destroyed Kiev. In time, certain types of writing that had originally been developed in the chronicle tradition, such as battle tales, became self-standing genres of writing even as chroniclers continued to employ them. The tradition of narrating history using the chronicle format remained vital until well into the seventeenth century. In the eighteenth century the manuscript chronicles came to be seen as invaluable historical sources and were among the earliest books of Old Rusian literature to be published. And although new methods of historical narrative came to supersede the chronicle approach, the chronicle texts have continued to echo in modern Russian cultural memory. Such echoes can be heard not only in their use by historians, but even in works of late twentieth-century Russian literature such as Alexander Solzhenitsyn's (1918–2008) sprawling *Red Wheel* (Krasnoe koleso) tetralogy, each volume of which is titled by month and year.

Biography – The Archpriest Avvakum (1621–1682)

One frustrating aspect of Old Russian culture for the contemporary reader is the seeming absence of individuality among both its producers and its subjects. Accustomed as we are to an essentially romantic ideal of the individual artist, the struggling, striving hero, and the equally romantic ideal of the overarching value of innovation, it can be difficult to appreciate a cultural system that does not put individuality and novelty on a pedestal. The comparative absence of the individual is particularly striking when we examine the question of biography. The saint's life, the only genre specifically devoted to biography is, in its essence, precisely opposed to the concept of individuality, for the saint becomes a saint insofar as his or her life is successfully imitates models provided by earlier saints and, ultimately, by Jesus or the Virgin Mary. This, according to the important Russian religious

1 Andrei Rublev, *Old Testament Trinity*. Rublev's icon, painted circa 1410, is considered the greatest achievement of Russian medieval painting. The soft colors and harmonious lines of the icon radiate a sense of tranquility.

scholar G. P. Fedotov, is the "general law of hagiographical style, similar to the law of icon painting: it demands the subordination of the particular to the general, the absorption of the human face into the heavenly glorified image."[8] Thus, even an icon of enormous power and beauty such as Andrei Rublev's celebrated "Trinity" (circa 1410) is not an original composition but rather one of many depicting this scene using similar imagery.

The same general principle can be said to apply to the biographies of rulers that appear within the chronicle texts. Rulers are described in terms of how their lives and deeds comport with certain models of behavior and tend to be described as either good or evil. Psychological motivation is generally absent as well, with good acts ascribed to a willingness to follow God's commands and evil deeds to the interference of the devil. One should not, of course, use the absence of individuality and nuanced psychological motivation in Old Russian literature to assume that these men and women were in fact one-dimensional and lacking an inner life any more than the absence of color in nineteenth-century photographs should cause us to think that our predecessors lived in a sepia-toned world. Individuality and psychology certainly did exist (and sometimes they can be sensed glimmering through the formulae of literary texts and icons) but they were not what the Russian formalists would later call "literary facts." They were outside the phenomena to be included in literary texts in much the same way as, for example, sex was not a literary fact in Victorian literature though it was a fact of Victorian life.

The most significant exception to the general impersonality of Old Russian literature is *The Life of the Archpriest Avvakum Written by Himself*, which was written in the period between 1669 and 1676. For hundreds of years a source of inspiration to his fellow Old Believers, Avvakum's autobiography was recognized as a seminal and powerful text by Russian readers and writers from the time of its first publication in 1862. In addition to its literary power, the *Life* is also recognized as a key source for understanding the great schism the occurred in the Russian church in the 1660s.

Avvakum was an exceptional figure in a turbulent time. The origins of his activity can be traced to a movement within the Russian church that began in the 1630s and was led by a group of radical conservative parish priests who came to be known as the Zealots of Ancient Piety (or, alternatively, the Lovers of God). They pushed for a series of reforms whose aim was to reinvigorate the Russian church, especially the liturgy. These efforts were at first supported by the pious Tsar Alexei Mikhailovich (reigned 1645–76) and clergymen from this sphere were appointed to positions of authority and influence. But in 1652 a man named Nikon (1605–81) was appointed patriarch of Russia – although Nikon had been affiliated with the reformers and as patriarch continued the process, he soon took the reforms in a different direction, revising the Russian liturgy to bring it into conformity with contemporary Greek practice. There is still disagreement as to why he did this, but in any case beginning in 1653 he introduced a series of symbolic changes in the liturgy which were soon followed up by new Slavonic editions of basic texts that, in the view of Nikon and those around him, were more in keeping with the Greek originals. These alterations provoked a violent and bitter reaction from most of the Lovers of God as well as many members of their flocks. In the course of the next decade and leading up to the "apocalyptic year" of 1666, the Russian church began increasingly to be rent by a split between those who accepted the "new books" and "new practices" pushed by Nikon and supported by the Tsar (even after 1658 when he sidelined Nikon himself) and those who refused to accept these texts and practices – the so-called Old Believers.

Avvakum, as can be seen both from his self-presentation in the *Life* and from other surviving documents, was a charismatic preacher and a fanatically devoted believer willing to survive torments and ultimately a martyr's death. For the student of Russian literature, however, the *Life* rather than the life is most significant. Written in a spectacularly expressive jumble of colloquial Russian and biblicly inflected Church Slavonic from Avvakum's place of confinement north of the Arctic Circle and poised uncomfortably between a medieval saint's life and a modern autobiography, it is the first in what would become a long line of Russian prison narratives. To be sure, it would be easy to exaggerate the extent to which Avvakum's autobiography anticipates modern autobiographical literature and breaks with the past. Avvakum is no Rousseau. The overall framework in which he understands his life and the lives surrounding him remains that of medieval Rus'. He views the world in black-and-white terms, and sees his life as evidence for the working out of God's plan on earth. Nevertheless, at a number of places and for all his conservatism, Avvakum recognizes that the traditional categories of thought by which he lived are simply not capable of expressing everything he thinks and feels.

Perhaps the most trenchant example is in Avvakum's attempts to understand his relationship with Afanasy Pashkov, to whose expedition in Siberia the exiled priest was assigned for some nine years. He begins this section of the narrative as follows: "As a reward for my sins he was a harsh man; he burned and tortured and flogged people all the time . . . And from Moscow he had orders from Nikon to afflict me."[9] Indeed, Avvakum describes a litany of suffering that he and his family endured at Pashkov's hands: beatings, starvation, forced labor. At one point in the narrative, Pashkov's son Eremei (who had secretly been sympathetic to Avvakum) is sent off with a detachment of Cossacks and asks a local Siberian shaman to prophesy the outcome of the expedition. Avvakum is convinced that the shaman is an instrument of the devil and, when the omens are said to predict victory for Eremei, he prays loudly and publicly for God to destroy Eremei and his men.

And then, a strange thing happens – Avvakum, who is normally absolutely sure as to the correct course of action, says: "And I started feeling sorry for him. Here he'd been a secret friend to me, and he'd suffered on my account" (72). For a moment God's will appears to be at odds with human feeling. Avvakum continues: "I started pestering the Lord that he should have mercy on him" (73). Nevertheless, when after some period of time Eremei does not return Pashkov prepares to have Avvakum executed, presumably convinced that his prayers had led to Eremei's disappearance: "We waited for them to return from war but they didn't turn up at the appointed time. And during this time Pashkov wouldn't let me see him. One day he set up a torture chamber and built a fire; he wanted to torture me. And I recited the prayers for the dying. I knew all about his hash-slinging, how few came out of his oven alive . . . And lo, two executioners came running for me. But marvelous are the works of the Lord and inexpressible are the designs of the Most High! Eremei, wounded, and another man rode along the little road past my hut and yard" (73). The juxtaposition of the elevated tone of the Church Slavonic Mass with the colloquial metaphor of the torturer Pashkov as a hash-slinger who cooks people in his ovens is typical of Avvakum's style as is the mixture of implied psychological explanation (for the bereaved Pashkov's actions) and overt recourse to a discourse of miraculous intervention.

The final ambivalent exclamation point on the relationship between jailor and jailed, however, comes just before Avvakum tells the reader of receipt of orders to return to Moscow. "Ten years he tormented me, or I him – I don't know. God will sort it out on Judgment Day." On the one hand, we still see an explicit belief that everything that happens in the world occurs because of the will of God and that his will can be known. But apparently it cannot be known in this world where the archpriest openly and simply admits that he does not know who was the victim and who the victimizer in this long-term forced relationship.

Though he was burned at the stake in 1682, the Old Belief and Avvakum's text lived on. Persecuted by the state, at times violently, the Old Believers nevertheless remained a significant presence in post-Petrine life, particularly among the merchant class, where they were disproportionately represented. Old Believers and other sects descended from the Old Belief were frequent subjects in nineteenth and early twentieth-century Russian literature, art and music: in the plays of Alexander Ostrovsky (1823–86), the short stories of Nikolai Leskov (1831–95), Modest Musorgsky's opera *Khovanshchina* (written 1872–80, first performed 1886), the painting "Boyarina Morozova" (1887) by Vasily Surikov (1848–1916), and Dmitry Merezhkovsky's (1865–1941) novel *Peter and Alexsei* (Petr i Aleksei, 1902). As for Avvakum's *Life* it was copied out by hand and passed from one Old Believer community to the other, becoming the first significant Russian samizdat text.

30   The Origins

2 Vasily Surikov, *Boyarina Morozova*, 1887. Surikov is best known for his large-scale dramatic historical canvases. Here, the noblewoman Morozova, who has refused to recant the old belief, is being arrested. She holds up two fingers to make the sign of the cross, rather than the three which were required as part of the liturgical changes that led to the great schism in the Russian church. The Holy Fool in the lower right responds with the same gesture.

2

The Spirit of Peter: Russian Culture in the Eighteenth Century

I

On March 8, 1725 Peter the Great (ruled 1682–1725) was buried in the new Russian capital of Saint-Petersburg. For the funeral a wooden church was erected inside the still-unfinished Peter and Paul Cathedral, which was destined to become the new resting place for Russian monarchs. After the liturgy, Archbishop Feofan Prokopovich (1681–1736), one of the main ideologues and propagandists of Peter's reforms as well as one of the first Russian eighteenth-century writers, came to the rostrum. His short emotional speech was frequently interrupted by "cries and moans from his listeners." "It seemed," said Ivan Golikov, a late eighteenth-century historian of Peter's reign, "that the very walls of the church and the battlements of the fortress were howling."[1]

In his eulogy, Feofan provided a canonical formula for the cult of Peter, which lay at the foundation of the official mythology of the Russian Empire (developed in its turn from an ancient Roman prototype). In keeping with the tradition of Christian rhetoric, Feofan found analogies for the Russian monarch's deeds in the Holy Writ, but these deeds were emphatically secular. Peter was a heroic conqueror, a latter-day *Samson*, who transformed Russia from a weak country to a powerful, stone (in keeping with his name) state through his creation of a mighty army. He was the new *Japheth*, who built the world's newest navy, thereby opening up paths "to the ends of the earth," and bringing Russia's "power and might to the farthest oceans." He was a Russian *Moses*, who had promulgated clear, firm, intelligent and beneficial laws and had developed a proper system of state administration. He was a Russian *Solomon*, who brought to Russia a "variety of philosophical arts," as well as "various previously unknown teachings, clever ideas and arts." He created a new system of positions and ranks (The Table of Ranks, 1722), civil attitudes and "honest models for daily life and useful habits and mores of behavior". Finally, Peter was the *Constantine* of Russia: like him, he pushed through reforms of the church, bringing it under state control (the "Spiritual-Religious Rules," 1721), and defeated the opposition of superstitious fanatics. A great transformer, the father of his country, Peter had made Russia powerful and terrifying to her enemies and good to her friends, glorious throughout the world, well-organized, happy and civilized. Peter's death, concluded Feofan, nevertheless did not mean the end of his Work, "for in leaving us his shattered body, he left us his spirit."[2]

II

The Spirit of Peter, "incarnated" in the new Russia, became the mythical source of a peculiar state religion characteristic of Russian culture through most of the eighteenth century. Writers, artists, architects, and scholars understood their work as service to an ideal state, the realization of the "commandments" of Peter and his successors, the imitation in their own particular field of the Tsar-Founder in the grandiose project of building new (albeit borrowed from the West), rational, and beneficial forms of social and cultural life for Russia's citizens, at least for that small percentage who belonged to the upper echelons of the gentry class. Despite the fact that most of the literary works of the eighteenth century were imitative and weak, the role of this period in modern Russian culture cannot be overstated: it prepared the way for the future development of literature and laid down the foundations of Russian cultural mythology.

The most significant cultural acts of this period were the translation and adaptation of the patterns of Western secular art, the creation of a new system of Russian versification, the borrowing and naturalization of the neo-classical aesthetic and the ideology of Enlightenment, the formation, from "nothing," of a local audience able to appreciate new works of art, the creation of national models of "pleasant and useful" forms and genres, and the "cleansing" and development of the literary language. In the second half of the century Russian theatre and ballet appear and develop rapidly, as do secular painting and sculpture, lyric poetry and instrumental music. Characteristically, the main cultural actors of this period perceive themselves and are perceived by their contemporaries not so much as imitators, but as demiurges, "Peter the Greats" of Russian art: Fedor Volkov (1729–63) is the founder of Russian theatre; Lomonosov is the father of Russian odic poetry; Alexander Sumarokov (1717–77) the creator of tragedy; Denis Fonvizin (1745–92) the inventor of comedy.

A characteristic desire for the eighteenth century is to "catch up to the Age of Enlightenment" as Pushkin would put it later. Beginning in the days of Peter, famous Western artists and writers were invited to Russia; schools, workshops, libraries, museums, academies and universities were founded; model texts of Western culture were translated into Russian; gardens were laid out – first regular "French" gardens and later "natural" English parks served to propagate new aesthetic ideas; the preferred language of conversation for the Russian elites became French in the course of the century, and a trip to Paris became de rigueur. At the same time, Russians quickly began to ask the questions that would, over the next few hundred years, plague every "developing country": what Western customs should be imitated and what should not? what is useful for us and what is dangerous? in which cases are our old ways of life superior to Western ways? how can we adapt foreign ideas for our own use? and, finally, what, if anything, is particular to us in the context of European culture? Often, we can perceive attempts to find the elusive Golden Mean: on the one hand, fanatical partisans of the old religious traditions (the "superstitious" in the language of the Russian Enlightenment) were mocked unceremoniously. But so were "brainless" imitators of the West ("petits maîtres" as they were called in Russian eighteenth-century comedies and satires). One scholar has called the Russian eighteenth century a careful listener, student, and critic of the European Age of Enlightenment, noting that it attempted "to incorporate the entire culture of humankind, encompass all spheres of culture and master all types of crafts."[3] This "eulogy to the eighteenth century" may sound like an exaggeration; however it formulates a peculiar cultural utopia of the age.

One of the most powerful cultural stimuli in the eighteenth century was the idea of Russia as the inheritor of Western civilization, called upon to complete the project of universal civilization. This latter-day transformation of Russia was understood by the ideologues of the new culture as a sign of her chosen status and was expressed in a variety of ways in the course of the century. Peter had learned from the Swedes in order to defeat them and create a powerful empire. Petersburg, which had been designed and built according to the latest architectural ideas, was to eclipse all European capitals in beauty and organization. The poet and scholar Lomonosov saw Russia's messianic importance in the progress of Russian science and expected Russian mariners to repeat the feat of Columbus (i.e. opening up a sea route through the North to India). The odic poet Vasily Petrov (1736–99) thought that the crowning achievement of Russian civilization would be the liberation of Constantinople from the Turks and the creation of a universal empire. The goal of the Russian Academy of Arts was to "glorify the Russian word" and its main achievement was the creation of the first explanatory dictionary of the Russian language (1789–94).

Toward the end of the century, the writer Nikolai Karamzin predicted that "soon all the nations of the world will come to light the wick of their candles in Russia" (*Poesie*, 1789).

III

Russian literature of the first two-thirds of the eighteenth century was tightly connected with the state and the court: it explicated, depicted, and propagandized the state's actions and simultaneously served to entertain and glorify the Imperial court, describing it as the fulcrum from which the new culture would spread to the periphery. Writers, together with ballet masters, visual artists and specialists in pyrotechnics, took part in the creation of large and small spectacles that depicted, in allegorical form, the greatness of the Russian state and the wealth and elegance of its ruling dynasty. This cultural *syncretism* of music, words, dance and pyrotechnics in the capacious envelope of the court spectacle lasted until the beginning of the nineteenth century, though diminishing in influence toward the end of the period.

Although literature was only one part of the state-court ritual, the position of the poet was, from the beginning, considered more prestigious than that of artist or composer. Gradually, literature, written and read almost exclusively by the gentry, began to escape from its position of dependence on the state, and to be seen as a key social institution, generally standing in opposition to the state apparatus. Literature began to be conceived as the incarnation of national honor, a salvific force balancing between the omnipotent monarch and the "wild" common people. In accord with this new vision, the author was to serve as the conscience of the nation, bravely speaking about Russia's flaws and appealing to the monarch to fix them. This ideology and ethics was expressed in different ways in Russian drama of the second half of the century (the tragedies of Sumarokov and Iakov Kniazhnin, and the comedies of Fonvizin), as well as in Gavriil Derzhavin's (1743–1816) odic poetry, the satirical journals of Nikolai Novikov (1744–1818) and – in the most radical form – in Alexander Radishchev's (1749–1802) passionate political poetry and prose, in which the first Russian "Jacobinian" lauded the high ideal of Divine Liberty, condemned the tyranny and moral and social vices of Catherine's Empire, and poured sentimental tears over the tragic lot of the Russian peasantry.

The idea of the Russian writer's superiority and national mission was powerfully expressed by the greatest Russian poet of the century,

Derzhavin, in his 1795 variation on the theme of Horace's ode "Exegi monumentum..." (Book III, xxx):

> I built myself a monument, eternal and miraculous,
> It's higher than the Pyramids, than metal it is harder;
> Swift winds and thunder cannot knock it down
> The flight of time cannot demolish it.
>
> Thus I won't really die! The part of me that's largest
> Will baffle death, and will escape decay,
> My fame will grow, and never wither,
> As long as Slavs are honored in this world.
>
> And word of me shall spread from the White Sea to the Black,
> Where Volga, Don, Neva and Ural rivers flow,
> Each member of the countless tribes will know
> How from obscurity I found my way to fame,
>
> By daring first in lively Russian speech
> To celebrate the virtues of Felitsa,[4]
> To talk of God with intimate simplicity,
> And with a smile announce the truth to kings.
>
> O Muse! take pride in your well-earned rewards,
> Disdain all those who show disdain for you,
> And with an easy and unhurried hand,
> With dawn eternal crown your brow. (trans. Andrew Wachtel, Gwenan Wilbur, Tanya Tulchinsky)

IV

It is difficult to understand the peculiarities of the new culture without a brief discussion of the social structure of the Russian Empire founded by Peter. It was characterized by the existence of four major estates (*sosloviia*) – nobility, clergy, merchants, and peasantry, with the leading role given to the first. As the nineteenth- century Russian historian-monarchist Mikhail Pogodin put it, "every estate has its own role in the state: the clergy pray, the nobles serve in war and peace, the peasants plough and feed the people, and the merchants are the means that provide each with what he needs."[5] This social structure was consolidated during the reign of Catherine the Great (ruled 1762–96). It responded to Peter's idea of a perfect, that is, rational and regular, military-bureaucratic absolutist state and, therefore, was a *new* creation, rather than a legacy of the feudal past.

The gentry's position was a bone of contention through much of the century, but was ultimately defined by Catherine's decree of 1785. The gentry had the exclusive right to own serfs, were not required to pay the individual poll tax, were not subject to corporal punishment, had the right to study at privileged educational institutions, and could choose where to live and in what capacity to serve the state. Although Peter I had required all gentry to serve, by Peter III's decree of 1762 gentry could choose not to serve at all if they so desired. A man's promotion in state service was regulated by Peter I's "Table of Ranks," as opposed to earlier practice whereby ranks and awards were dependent on the importance of one's family. Indeed, although gentry status was generally hereditary, a non-noble could become a member of the gentry class if he rose high enough in state service (depending on how high his gentry status could be exclusively his own or be passed on to his descendants).

The "Table of Ranks" divided service into military (considered more noble), civilian (which was generally less prestigious in the eyes of the gentry), and court. All positions occupied one of fourteen ranks, and emoluments and prestige were strictly regulated according to rank. Thus, the social standing of a person was defined by his place in the state hierarchy. This bureaucratic system had an enormous influence on human interactions in Russia in the eighteenth and nineteenth centuries. Russian officials (especially "little" ones, low down on the government ladder) became some of the most beloved figures of so-called humanist literature of the imperial period: they instantiated themes including protest against the total bureaucratization of society, and an interest in the internal moral world and psychology of human beings "ground down" by the state machinery and social prejudice.

A second privileged group was comprised of the clerics of the state Orthodox Church. Priests and monks were free from personal taxation, military service, and corporal punishment. They were not, however, allowed to own serfs nor to engage in trade. At the beginning of the eighteenth century, Peter eliminated the position of Patriarch and subordinated the church to the state. Church affairs were henceforward governed by a special bureaucratic organ called the Holy Synod, led by an Ober-Procurator appointed by the Tsar. Believers in other religions (Catholics, Lutherans and Muslims) had civil rights (which did not extend to Jews) but their presence in the Empire was strictly controlled, and Orthodox believers were forbidden to convert to other religions. Old Believers were also severely discriminated against in the eighteenth and first half of the nineteenth century (for a literary depiction of their position in this period see the wonderful story "The Sealed Angel" [Zapechatlennyi angel, 1872], by the underrated master of Russian prose Nikolai Leskov). The synod was even more zealous in its persecution of various mystic sects that spread among the populace in the course of the eighteenth century. Although the clergy was the smallest estate in Russia, its role in the life of every Orthodox Christian (from birth to death) was significant. Not a single holiday or significant social event took place in the absence of a clergyman (including such eminently secular events as the unveiling of statues devoted to writers). Nevertheless, in comparison to the pre-Petrine period, the influence of the church on the cultural life of the country was sharply diminished.

The third estate was that of the merchants. They were free from paying the poll tax, but were liable to pay a tax equivalent to one percent of their capital each year. They were liable for military service as well, but could pay to avoid it. As opposed to the gentry, the bulk of the Russian merchant class did not undergo a process of Westernization and preserved the mentality of pre-Petrine Russia. City dwellers who did not belong to one of the guilds and who were not members of the gentry or clergy were in a class by themselves. They were required to pay a yearly tax, serve in the military and were subject of corporal punishment. They did, however, have the right to engage in petty commerce and to work for wages. Unlike the situation in major European cultures of the eighteenth century, the role of "the third estate" in Russian culture was marginal. Merchants and artisans were portrayed in a number of "bourgeois comedies," which addressed and satisfied, in accordance with neo-classical aesthetic hierarchy, "low" tastes. The cultural discovery of the highly original world of Russian merchants occurred only in the mid-nineteenth century and is associated with the innovative plays of Alexander Ostrovsky and the social paintings of Russian realist artists.

The lowest estate, making up some 90 percent of the populace, was the peasantry. From the days of the Petrine reforms until the abolition of serfdom in 1863, peasants were either state serfs (required to live on state-owned land and work for the good of the state) or the property of individual gentry serf owners. Without special permission serfs were not allowed to move from their dwelling place or to leave their commune, were required to pay a personal tax each year (the poll tax), provide recruits to the army, and were subject to corporal punishment if their master so willed it (they could not be legally executed by their owner, however). The peasants were united into communes or assemblies of households, which met to make decisions regarding a variety of local affairs. The responsibilities of the serf commune included payments to the lord, distribution of land allotments among its members, and resolution of internecine conflicts. A senior male member of each household represented it in the governing body of the commune (women had no voice). The Russian word for the peasant community, "mir," means the world, universe. In the nineteenth century, Slavophile and some socialist thinkers would introduce an idealized vision of the peasant "mir" as an organic Russian form of economic, social, and religious life characterized by collective property, self-government, harmonious relationships between its members, and spiritual unity.[6] Other thinkers, however, saw the "mir" as an archaic feudal form which retarded Russia's economic and social development.

Peasant revolts were a frequent fact of Russian life in the eighteenth century. The most dangerous and widespread of these was the so-called Pugachev Rebellion of 1772–5, which came close to destroying the Empire. For many decades the Rebellion and its extraordinary leader haunted the historical imagination of Russian cultural elite – from the statesman Nikita Panin's "Political Testament," compiled by his associate Fonvizin, to Pushkin's *History of Pugachev* (Istoriia Pugacheva, 1834) and short novel *The Captain's Daughter* (Kapitanskaia dochka, 1836), to the "peasant poet" Sergei Esenin's lyrical drama of 1921.

The peasants' utter lack of human rights became one of the most important themes of Russian social thought from the end of the eighteenth century until the middle of the nineteenth century. Key literary works concerning this topic include Radishchev's *Journey from Petersburg to Moscow* [Puteshestvie iz Peterburga v Moskvu, 1790], for which the author was originally condemned to death but later, by the mercy of Catherine sentenced to a mere ten-year period of Siberian exile, Gogol's *Dead Souls*, and the story cycle *Notes of a Hunter* (Zapiski okhotnika, 1852) of Ivan Turgenev (1818–83). A deep sense of shame in the face of the undeveloped and unenlightened state of the peasantry was widespread among the Russian intelligentsia throughout the nineteenth century. One response to this feeling of collective and inherited guilt was the idealization of the Russian peasant as the vessel of national ideals and the preserver of organic values that had been lost by the Westernized gentry. Overcoming the yawning gap separating the most (i.e. the most Westernized) and the least privileged estates became an obsession in Russia and was perceived from the end of the eighteenth century as an exceptionally important task for society and culture.

We began this introduction to eighteenth-century Russian culture with Bishop Feofan's eulogy to Peter the Great. We conclude with a historical anecdote which illuminates some cultural consequences of the Reform.

Sometime in the early decades of the nineteenth century, the gifted satirical poet and aristocrat Petr Viazemsky (1792–1878) was visiting one of his remote estates. After a Sunday Mass, an educated (yet old-fashioned in his neo-classical literary tastes) local priest enthusiastically addressed the villagers: "You do not comprehend what kind of Master Our Lord gave you, my Orthodox brothers! He is the *Russian Horace*, the *Russian Catullus*, the *Russian Martialis!*" After each of these lofty attestations, as Viazemsky ironically (and sadly) comments, his pious peasants bowed to earth and vigorously crossed themselves.[7]

Cultural Event – The Founding of Petersburg

One of the most important and successful achievements of Peter's reformist reign was the establishment of its new capital city. The city gave its name to an entire period of Russian history and engendered a cultural myth of exceptional importance for Russian national thought from the eighteenth through at least the middle of the twentieth century.

August 1700 saw the outbreak of the Northern War between Sweden and a coalition of states which included Russia. Peter's goal was to reacquire direct access for Russia to the Baltic Sea, which had been lost by the Muscovite state during the sixteenth and seventeenth centuries. The young Tsar saw the "return" of these territories as an opportunity to break free of Russia's isolation and economic backwardness. The war began badly for the Russians, but Peter was able to reorganize his army quickly. On October 11, 1702 Russian forces were able to seize the Swedish fortress Nöteborg on the Neva River, and in the spring of 1703 the Swedes surrendered the nearby fortress of Nyenschanz (called Shlotburg by the Russians). At the military council following this victory, it was decided to build a fortress and pier on this newly acquired territory. The spot was of clear strategic importance and naturally protected. The cornerstone of a fortress was laid on May 16, 1703 and soon after, on the saints' day of Peter and Paul, was named Sankt-Piterburch in the Dutch manner. A bit later, the cathedral dedicated to Peter and Paul that was built inside the fortress was named the Petropavlovsk Church and the city that grew up around it began to be called Sankt-Peterburg. On October 4, 1703 the first Russian newspaper *Vedomosti* (News), which appeared at that time in Moscow, published the following announcement: "After the taking of Shlotburg, His Imperial Majesty decreed that a new and highly fortified fortress be constructed on an island about a mile from there. It has six bastions and twenty thousand people have worked to build them. And he has ordered that this fortress be given the name Petersburg in his name."⁸ Petersburg was not the only city founded by Peter, but it was his favorite child, his "New Holland," "Paradise," and the realization of his dreams of Russia's naval future.

The first Governor of Petersburg and Shlotburg was Peter's favorite, Alexander Menshikov (1672–1729). He oversaw the construction of the city and the fortress, which by the fall of 1703 was practically finished. Attempts by the Swedes to win back the lands at the mouth of the Neva were unsuccessful and after their crushing defeat at Poltava in 1709 (an event immortalized in Russian literature by Pushkin's narrative poem "Poltava" [1829]) there was no further danger to the new city from its northern neighbor.

The transfer of the capital to the new city took place gradually: the court moved in 1712, to be followed by the Senate, Russia's highest legislative and administrative organ, at the end of 1713. The diplomatic corps did not move until 1718. The cornerstone of the Peter and Paul Cathedral was laid in 1712 on Peter's birthday. This church (designed by the Italian architect Dominico Trezzini, 1670–1734) became the new sepulcher for the Russian ruling family (replacing the Archangel Cathedral in the Moscow Kremlin). All the Russian Emperors from Peter to Nicholas II are buried here (with the exception of Peter's grandson, Peter II, who died of smallpox in Moscow in 1730 after a short and insignificant reign, and the unfortunate Ivan VI who reigned in 1740–1 and then, having been deposed, spent twenty years in solitary confinement and was finally murdered in 1764). In 1710 Peter founded the Alexander Nevsky Monastery, which played an important role in cementing Petersburg's position as the Russian capital. In 1723 the relics of Alexander Nevsky, victor over the Swedes and the Teutonic Knights and one of Russia's most revered saints, were translated to the new monastery, and Nevsky became the city's patron. In 1721 the Holy Synod began its existence here.

Peter's transfer of the center of the state from Holy Moscow to Saint Petersburg did not by any means mark a turning away from traditional notions of the holiness of the Russian capital. The difference was that the object of veneration was understood differently – not the holiness of the religious tradition, but the holiness of the state itself, as incarnated in its monarch-founder. Feofan Prokopovich constantly compared the Tsar to the apostle Peter, playing on the Biblical notion of the latter as the stone on which the future building would be erected.⁹ The naming of the city was associated not just with the glorification of the Tsar's heavenly protector but also with "the idea of Petersburg as the New Rome."¹⁰ Even the choice of the city's coat of arms, which featured crossed anchors analogous

3 St. Peter and Paul Cathedral, St. Petersburg. The cathedral, the second to be erected within the walls of the Peter and Paul fortress, was built between 1712 and 1733. One of the enduring symbols of St. Petersburg, it is the burial place of almost all the Russian emperors and empresses from Peter the Great to Nicholas II.

to the crossed keys of the Vatican shield, was a conscious attempt to link Petersburg to Rome.

Despite the establishment of Petersburg as Russia's capital, Moscow continued to be considered the second capital, the religious center of the Empire, and the bastion of those gentry not in state service. The opposition of the Old and New capitals (the former more ancient and "national," the latter more "European" and modern) became one of the great antitheses of Russian culture from the eighteenth to the twentieth centuries. It is expressed frequently in literary works, most notably Tolstoy's *War and Peace* (Voina i mir, 1865–9), where Moscow, home to the old fashioned, warm and friendly Rostovs stands in stark contrast to the cold Petersburg of the Emperor and his court.

From the outset, the building of Petersburg was linked with a defined plan for the settlement of the city (albeit one that was frequently not fully realized): employees of the Admiralty were supposed to live on Admiralty Island, while those who worked for the court and on the wharves were to live on the Moscow side. Vasilievsky Island was for the key groups of urban citizens (the gentry, the merchants, and various petty officials), while artisans and soldiers were to live on the Petrograd side. Military personnel made up a large proportion of the population. Toward the end of the 1720s the first guards regiments – the Preobrazhensk and Semenovsk Guards – were transferred to the new capital from Moscow. They were soon joined by the newly constituted Izmailov and Horse Guards.

The city's population grew quickly. In 1725 it had somewhere between twenty-five and thirty thousand inhabitants. In the middle of the century there were perhaps seventy-five thousand Petersburgers. And by the end of the reign of Catherine, the period of the great flowering the "Palmyra of the North," the city could boast upwards of 200 thousand residents. A characteristic demographic feature of Petersburg was the disproportion between its male and female inhabitants, with the former outnumbering the latter by about two to one. Petersburg officials therefore tended to go to the old capital to find their brides. As Gogol would joke in the 1830s: "Moscow is feminine, Petersburg is masculine. All the brides are in Moscow, while the grooms are in Petersburg."[11]

Peter's idea was that the new city would become a powerful military port, "a window onto Europe," and the administrative, business, and cultural center of the Empire. From the beginning of its existence, Petersburg thus had two constituencies, internal and external, and two functions: it was to be a showpiece of the beauty and power of the new Russia as a

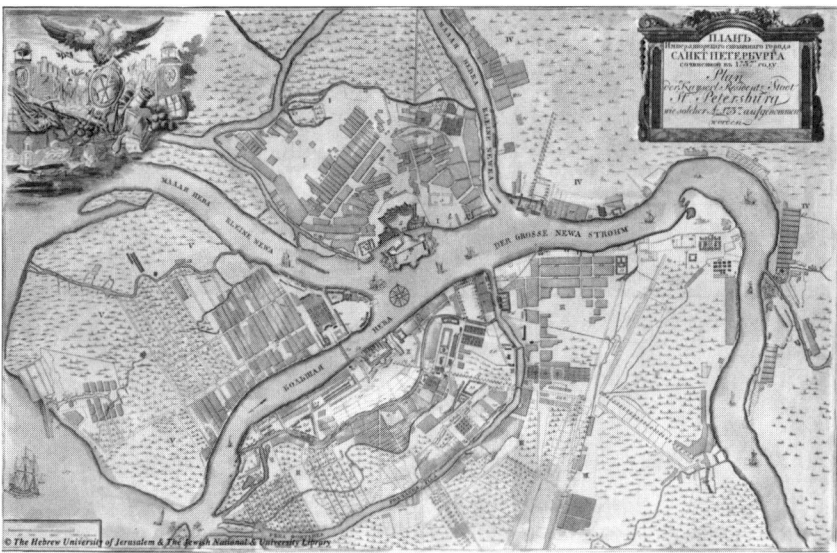

4 Plan of St. Petersburg, 1737. Built on the delta of the Neva River some 3 miles from the Gulf of Finland at around the 60th parallel north, St. Petersburg was designed by Peter the Great to be Russia's "window onto Europe." This plan shows the central sections of the city. To the south, encircled by the Fontanka River is the left bank of the Neva, the area that became the center of the city. Here are to be found such monuments as the Winter Palace (which now houses the Hermitage Museum), the Admiralty, St. Isaac's and the Kazan Cathedrals, and Nevsky Prospect. The oldest section of the city, however, is on the opposite side of the river in the center of the map, and is dominated by the Peter and Paul Fortress. In the center of the map and the west is Vasilievsky Island.

Western civilization and a propagandist of the benefits of Westernization for the Russian populace. On the banks of the Neva and her main tributaries, the Emperor ordered the construction of monumental stone buildings. In his desire to create a city equal to the great capitals of Europe, Peter commissioned architects, engineers and builders from all over Western Europe. The city plan, by the Frenchman J. B. Leblanc, envisioned the creation of an "ideal" city, the material incarnation of the concept of a well-ordered state. The plan called for a beautiful geometric schema of streets radiating out from the Admiralty building. Peter placed great emphasis on abundant street lighting by means of hempseed oil lamps and the construction of green spaces and city parks.

The most important stone buildings served symbolic functions and as sites for the development of the new state: The Peter and Paul Fortress stood for military might (later it would become a prison for offenders against the state); the Admiralty was the apotheosis of the navy; the building of the Twelve Colleges (Ministries) symbolized the orderly run state and the triumph of the rule of law; *Gostinyi dvor* [lit.: the Magnate Yard] stood for commercial development, the Kunstkamera and the Academy of Sciences for the growth of science and art, and the Winter Palace (modest at first but grandiose by the reign of Catherine the Great) was the residence of the monarch him or herself.

After the victory at Poltava an ambitious project of constructing palaces and houses for the nobility in the outskirts of town began: Peterhof, Ekaterinhof, and Oranienbaum were meant to demonstrate the greatness and beauty of the private lives of the Russian ruler and his immediate entourage. Petersburg's Summer Garden [*Letnii sad*] was designed to propagandize new European aesthetic sensibilities based on classical mythology through the strategic placement of large numbers of statues of scantily clad Greek gods and allegorical figures amidst wooded areas and fountains. Petersburg's "regular" squares were designed for military parades and outdoor spectacles that, in allegorical form, praised the political vision of Peter and his acolytes.

One such spectacle was the solemn "apotheosis" that began on September 15, 1721 in celebration of the successful conclusion of the Northern War. The festivities, including firework displays, cannon fire and a masquerade ball, ended with a Mass at the Holy Trinity Cathedral after which Chancellor Fedor Golovin, in the name of the Senate, asked the monarch to take the title "Peter the Great, Father of the Fatherland, Emperor of All the Russias." Peter agreed and Russia officially proclaimed herself an Empire, the only one in Europe besides the Holy Roman Empire with its capital in Vienna.

Petersburg gradually became the educational and cultural center of the Empire. New educational institutions of a secular character, capable of nurturing properly prepared personnel for the country were opened here (or transferred from Moscow). These included the Naval Academy, the Artillery and Engineering School, and the Medical School. Later, during the reign of Anna Ioannovna (ruled 1730–40; she was Peter's niece), a Marine Academy was opened. This would become the main finishing school for the Russian gentry in the eighteenth century, the breeding ground for many of the cultural ideologues: the poet and dramatist Alexander Sumarokov, the poet and enlightener Mikhail Kheraskov (1733–1807), and the dramatist Vladislav Ozerov (1769–1816) all studied here. In 1764 Catherine the Great founded the Smolny Institute for Noble Maidens in Voskresensk Convent. The ultimate goal of this first Russian girls' boarding school was the upbringing of an "ideal women," in accordance with the ideas of the eminent Russian enlightener Ivan Betskoy (1704–95). These ideal ladies of Catherine's reign are depicted in a series of portraits by one of the first and, perhaps, the greatest Russian portraitists Dmitry Levitsky (1735–1822).

Soon after Peter's death the Petersburg Academy of Sciences was founded. It served not only as the scholarly hub of the Empire ("a meeting place for educated and interesting men") but also as a site for teaching (both university and high school) and a cultural center. Beginning in 1728 the Academy began to publish its monthly "Notes," the first scholarly journal to appear in Russia. Petersburg also became the center for Russian book production. 1719 saw the beginning of construction of the first science museum in Russia, the Kunstkamera, which in addition to its baroque collection of oddities and freaks of nature (always a source of fascination for the curious Tsar), featured Russia's first anatomical theatre, observatory and public library (beginning in 1728). The first Russian military hospitals – the General Marine (1717) and the General Naval (1719) – were founded here.

Peter also planned to construct a psychiatric hospital, but this idea went unrealized until the 1780s when the mental ward of the Obukhovsky Hospital for the poor (the "Russian Bedlam") opened. It is remarkable that among the early patients of the ward were two young Russian scholars and freemasons (i.e. in Catherine's eyes, gloomy representatives of the spiritual opposition to her glorious and felicitous regime). Both young men had recently returned from abroad and both were diagnosed as hypochondriacs. From the time of the enlightened Empress psychiatric diagnosis has been used by the Russian authorities as a simple and effective way to discredit and/or isolate political and ideological opponents, including some of the Decembrists who revolted against the new Tsar Nicholas I in 1825, the first Russian religious philosopher Petr Chaadaev (1794–1856), and Lev Tolstoy. The insane asylum would also become one of the crucial locations in Russian literature of the "Petersburg period": it was the final stop for the hero of Pushkin's "Queen of Spades" (Pikovaia dama, 1833) and for Gogol's insane clerk Poprishchin ("Notes of a Madman" [Zapiski sumasshedshego, 1835]); this is where the deranged Goliadkin of Dostoevsky's *The Double* (Dvoinik, 1846) would be confined. One of the great paradoxes of Petersburg in the Russian cultural mind is that this city, designed as the incarnation of rationalism, became symbolically linked with the theme of madness.

As opposed to Moscow, which grew up over centuries without any plan, Petersburg from its founding was understood as a city built "in a day" by the will of a single person and as a symbol of a break with the national tradition. Opposition to Peter's project was already apparent by the 1710s. His opponents averred that the only holy city was Moscow, "the Third Rome," and insisted that "Petersburg did not exist at all, that it only seemed to exist and would vanish."[12] Prophecies about the inevitable disappearance of Petersburg were especially popular among the partisans of the restoration of Muscovite traditions, and also among the Old Believers, who saw the Tsar-Reformer as the Antichrist and his city as the New Babylon. In the nineteenth century the theme of the destruction of Petersburg entered literature: from Dostoevsky's descriptions of Petersburg as a mirage up through the "phantasmagoria" of the symbolists and their followers who saw with their own eyes the gradual decay of the city after the Revolution of 1917.

A constant theme in the Russian image of Petersburg is the clash of the city with the elements. If wooden Moscow was associated with fires, then Petersburg was linked with floods (though it had its share of fires). Symbolic fire (death and cleansing rebirth) and water (as a punishment for sins) are thus connected with these capital cities in Russian culture. As early as 1706 the city's inhabitants had to face the destructive power of the Neva in flood. Peter, by the way, laughed it off. "Three days ago," he wrote to Menshikov, "there was so much water that my palace had 21 inches inside it . . . On the other side of the street people were able to travel freely by boat . . . it was hilarious to see people on their roofs and in the trees." The letter is sent "from Paradise."[13] A rather different view was expressed by a contemporary witness to the flood of 1721, when the waters crested some seven feet above the river's banks: "It is impossible to describe the terrifying sight of the many loosed boats, some empty and some filled with people; whipped by the storm, they were swept along by the water toward practically inevitable destruction."[14]

The most famous and destructive flood occurred in 1824, the final year of the reign of Alexander I, and it served as one source for Alexander Pushkin's "Bronze Horseman, A Petersburg Tale" (Mednyi vsadnik, Peterburgskaia povest', 1833). The work begins with a solemn prologue describing Peter sitting "on the banks of the empty waters" of the Neva and ordering the construction of a new city in this wild place "to spite the haughty neighbor" (that is the Swedes) and in spite of the elements. The poet glorifies the "young city" of beautiful palaces, granite embankments, squares, and cast iron fences which has risen from "the muddy swamps." The glamorous and celebratory description of the city in the Prologue stands in stark contrast to the sad story told in the body of the poem. This is the tragic narrative of Evgeny, a poor member of the gentry class, who loses first his fiancée and then his mind as the result of the flood. The crazed hero makes a fist at the equestrian statue of Peter the Great (the so-called Bronze Horseman of the French sculptor Falconet, which was erected on the Senate Square at the behest of Catherine the Great in 1782), whom he sees as guilty for his personal tragedy. Evgeny's "rebellion" is immediately punished. It seems to the insane hero that the horseman turns to him in anger and he flees with the echo of the horse's hoofs behind him, only to die on the spot where his fiancée's home had stood before the flood washed it away.

Pushkin's poem is a central source for the Russian "Petersburg text" – a series of literary works in which the city is depicted not merely as the setting for the action but as a protagonist, problem and mystery of Russian history and fate. Other works generally considered to be part of this cycle are Gogol's "Petersburg Tales," many of Dostoevsky's stories and novels (including *Poor Folk* [Bednye liudi, 1845], *The Double, Crime and Punishment* [Prestuplenie i nakazanie, 1866], and *The Idiot*), Alexander Blok's poem cycle "The City" [Gorod, 1904–8], Dmitry Merezhkovsky's symbolist novel *Peter and Alexei*, Andrei Bely's masterpiece *Petersburg* [Peterburg, 1913–14, 1922], and Anna Akhmatova's *Poem Without a Hero* [Poema bez geroia, 1940–65].

Biography – Mikhail Vasilievich Lomonosov (1711–65)

Lomonosov was perhaps the most important Russian enlightener. The breadth of his interests is truly staggering: in the words of Pushkin, "historian, rhetorician, engineer, chemistry, geologist, artist, and poet, he experienced everything and examined everything."[15] As early as the end of the eighteenth century, Lomonosov's biography was seen as a model life for a Russian enlightener – a secular apostle of Peter's reforms who proved through his own life and work that "the Russian land is capable of birthing its own Platos and [. . .] Newtons." Some important motifs of the Lomonosov legend in Russian culture include the link between Enlightenment and the "free" traditions of the Russian north (Russia's supposed national roots), his peasant background, his love of science, his departure from home as a youth in search of education, his selfless service to Enlightenment and his constant battles with his enemies (religious fanatics, superstitious traditionalists, German academicians whom he saw as hindering the development of Russian culture, as well as Russian scholarly colleagues who were partisans, in Lomonosov's view, of incorrect views).

Lomonosov was born on November 8 (19th, new style)[16] 1711 in a small village in Arkhangelsk Province on the banks of the White Sea in Russia's far north. His father was a well-to-do peasant fisherman who engaged in long sea voyages, in which the young Lomonosov participated, across the White and Barents Seas. His childhood memories of the North had an important formative influence on the future scholar: among the topics that continually attracted his attention were "the aurora borealis, cold and heat, sea voyages, sea ice, the importance of sea life for life on dry land."[17] Lomonosov's pet scientific dream was the discovery of a northern sea route to America and India.

According to the apt formulation of one contemporary historian, Peter the Great inherited a country on the lam: serfs were running away from their masters, wandering the countryside looking for justice, plundering; Old Believers were fleeing to the forests, escaping from the Muscovite Kingdom that they saw as having lost God's grace. This eighteenth-century peasant nomadism found its reflection in Lomonosov's life but its outcome in this case was transformed by new opportunities that had appeared in the wake of Peter's reforms: Lomonosov does not run from injustice but rather in search of new, secular knowledge. Still, the key event in his life is his departure to Moscow in 1730 with a convoy carrying a load of fish. Concealing his peasant background, the young man enrolls in the Slavo-Greco-Latin Academy, Russia's most advanced seminary. It had been founded by Peter's father Tsar Alexei Mikhailovich, but by this time was already educating its students for careers in state service. Other important figures who studied at this institution in the early years of the eighteenth century included Antiokh Kantemir (1708–44), a diplomat and Russia's first poet satirist, the medical doctor and philosopher Petr Postnikov (1676–1710?), and the poet and academician Vasily Trediakovsky (1703–69), who was later to become one of Lomonosov's fiercest rivals.

Lomonosov was placed in the lowest grade, as he did not know any Latin, the language of instruction (the "pillars" of his early education, by his own admission, had been the *Grammar* of Melety Smotritsky and *Arithmetic* by Leonty Magnitsky – among the first books published in Russia in the Petrine era). In 1734, Lomonosov attempted, unsuccessfully, to attach himself to an expedition to the Aral Sea (in the Southeast of Russia) led by an eminent geographer. But in 1735, he was chosen as one of the school's twelve best students and as a reward sent to the Academy in St. Petersburg for further education. At that point the Academy consisted of the Academy of Sciences proper, an Academy-sponsored university and high school, the science museum (Kunstkamera), the anatomical theatre, the observatory, laboratories for physical and geological sciences, instrument shops, and a library. The lectures that made the greatest impression on the young man were those of the famous Swiss mathematician Leonard Euler (1707–83).

In 1736, along with two other promising students chosen by the Academy, Lomonosov was sent to Germany to study foreign languages, chemistry, and mining. At Marburg University his teacher was one of the most eminent philosophers of the Enlightenment, Christian Wolff (1679–1754), himself a student of Leibnitz. As early as 1738 Lomonosov submitted his first dissertation in Physics. Having finished his studies in Marburg he transferred to Freiburg to study chemistry and mining with Johann Friedrich Henckel (1678–1744).

Lomonosov's interests were not limited to the sciences, however. He was equally attracted by rhetoric and poetics. While in Europe he discovered the poetry of the late German Baroque, attempted to translate poetry from German and French, and thought about the reforms of Russian prosody that had recently been proposed by Vasily Trediakovsky, the secretary of the Russian Academy. In 1739 he wrote his innovative "Ode on the Capture of Khotin" (Oda na vziatie Khotina) in which he not only celebrates a Russian victory over the Ottomans, but attempts to show the results of his theoretical ruminations on the "nature" of Russian verse, which in his view should be based on the repetition of rhythmic patterns of stressed and unstressed syllables (so-called syllabotonic verse, as is typical for modern English and German poetry, rather than the syllabic verse, typical for Polish and French, that had been used heretofore in the rather meager Russian secular verse tradition). Lomonosov laid out his theoretical conclusions in his "Letter on the Properties of Russian Versification" which he sent to the Academy together with his "Ode." Written in iambic tetrameter (which would become the most commonly used verse form in Russia) the "Ode on the Capture of Khotin" would eventually come to be recognized as the first work of modern Russian literature. The Russian poet and critic Vladislav Khodasevich (1886–1939) would write "the first sound of the Khotin Ode became the first sound of our life."[18]

Lomonosov understood poetry as a kind of creative laboratory in which to test theoretical conclusions about the nature of the Russian language and create models for future writers. Russian critics have often compared Lomonosov with Horace and Malherbe, lawgivers to their respective national poetic traditions. In the eyes of his contemporaries, Lomonosov was seen as the inventor of the Russian celebratory ode, though his rival Trediakovsky had in fact preceded him, with its clear ideological program and complex rhetorical structure that can be seen in the topic and the overall construction as well as in the grammar and phonetics of the verse lines themselves. Nevertheless, it would be wrong to think that Lomonosov's literary experiments were all successful. He failed, for example, to realize his "most important" literary project – a model epic poem about Peter the Great (in the hierarchy of neo-classical genres the epic was considered the highest genre). At the same time, as a theorist he set to Russian literature the task of writing such a work.

In May of 1740, having quarreled with Henckel, Lomonosov left Freiburg, on foot, as was his wont. On June 6, 1740 he married the daughter of a Marburg brewer, but he departed almost immediately after the wedding on further wanderings. Along the way Lomonosov got into real trouble: he was waylaid and impressed into the Prussian army. Having escaped from his garrison, he made his way back to Marburg (on foot once again), where his former professor Wolff helped raise sufficient money to send him back to Petersburg.

In 1742 Lomonosov was appointed an adjunct member of the Academy of Sciences in Physics, and in 1745 was named professor of chemistry. Lomonosov and Trediakovsky were the first native-born Russians to be named academicians. At this time, the research of the Academy was divided into three sections: Mathematics (theoretical mathematics, astronomy, geography, navigation, mechanics), Physical Sciences (theoretical and experimental physics, anatomy, chemistry, and botany), and Humanities (rhetoric, ancient and modern history, and "law together with politics and ethics"). The Academy was charged not merely with research, but also asked to provide expertise regarding inventions, judging them on the basis of innovation and "usefulness." Furthermore, the Academy was supposed to provide literary propaganda for the state, and to design mass celebratory spectacles. As such, Lomonosov's literary work was a regular part of his Academy service; a considerable part of his literary oeuvre consists of odes and panegyrics written on commission from the Academy, texts for court spectacles, and other poetic works devoted to different aspects of court life.

The breadth of Lomonosov's scientific interests in the 1740s and 1750s is astounding: he writes papers and gives talks about physics, astronomy, chemistry, economics, history, and rhetoric. In 1748 he supervises the building of the first Russian chemical laboratory in which he carries out experiments and teaches students. In the 1750s he develops technology to make opaque glass of various colors which he needs to create a "color theory" and to make Russian mosaics. In his work in this latter area Lomonosov hopes to revive this ancient art using new technology: that is, he hopes to synthesize art, science, and technology in an aesthetic realization of the Enlightenment utopia. His first mosaic was an image of the Virgin Mary based on a drawing by the Italian artist Francesco Solimena. Lomonosov proudly announced that the picture was made from four thousand pieces of glass and that to produce them two thousand eight hundred and four experiments were required. In 1753 he received permission to open a factory for the production of colored glass for mosaics and later got an Imperial commission to build a monument to Peter the Great in the Peter and Paul Cathedral whose main feature was to be an enormous mosaic depicting the greatest events of Peter's reign.

The foundation of Lomonosov's varied activity was the belief in the unity of the world, which he saw as existing on the basis of God-given natural laws accessible to the human mind. Poetry plays an important role in this religion: the joy of scientific discovery turns out to be the foundation of poetic art, and poetry, in its turn, is a powerful means to propagandize scientific discovery, focusing the attention of private patrons and the government on the brilliant potentials opened by science. In the 1740s and 50s Lomonosov wrote his best poems. His "Evening Reflection upon God's Grandeur Prompted by the Great Northern Lights" (Vechernee razmyshlenie o Bozhiem velichestve pri sluchae velikogo severnogo siianiia, 1743) is perhaps his most characteristic shorter work. Suggested by a scientific phenomenon familiar to the poet from his childhood years in the Russian north, it provides an exceptionally satisfying description of and explanation for the aurora borealis in keeping with the deistic spirit of the Age of Enlightenment:

> The day conceals its brilliant face,
> And dark night covers up the fields,
> Black shadows creep upon the hills,
> Light's rays recede from us.
> Before us gapes a well of stars –
> Stars infinite, well fathomless.
>
> A grain of sand in ocean swells,
> A tiny glint in endless ice,
> Fine ash upswept in mighty gale,
> A feather in a raging fire,
> So I am lost in this abyss,
> Oppressed by thoughts profound.

The mouths of wise men call to us:
"A multitude of worlds dwell there,
Among them burning suns untold,
And peoples, and the wheel of time:
There, all of nature's strength
Exists God's glory to proclaim"

But where, O nature, is your law?
Dawn breaks from out of northern lands!
Is this the home of our sun's throne?
Or are the icy oceans burning?
Behold, cold fire envelops us!
Behold, now day has entered night.

O thou, whose lively gaze can see
Into the book of law eternal,
For whom the smallest part of things
Reveals the code in all of nature,
Thou comprehendeth planets' course,
Now tell us what disturbs our souls?

Why do these bright rays sparkle in the night?
Why does fine flame assault the land?
Without a thundercloud can lightning
Rise from the earth up toward the heavens?
How can it be that frozen steam
Gives birth to fire from winter's depths?

There, oily darkness battles water,
Or rays of sunlight sparkle bright,
Bend toward us through the thickened air;
Or do the peaks of stout hills glow,
Or have the sea winds ceased their song,
And smooth waves struck the space.

Regarding what lies right before us
Thine answer's full of doubts
O, tell us, how enormous is the world?
What lies beyond the smallest stars?
Are thou aware of all creation's end?
Tell us, how great is our Creator?
   (trans. Andrew Wachtel, Gwenan Wilbur, Tanya Tulchinsky)

In his poetic compositions, Lomonosov created a mythologized image of the poet as someone faithful to "Peter's tasks," willing to serve science viewed as the most important component of the state's civilizing work, unwavering in his opposition to the enemies of Enlightenment, completely selfless and straightforward, imbued with noble thoughts and the gift of prophecy.

Lomonosov died on April 4, 1765 and Moscow's university, which he had founded in 1755, is named after him to this day.

Literary Work – Gavriil Derzhavin's "Felitsa"

The ode "Felitsa" (1782) by Gavriil Derzhavin is one of the most original and significant works of Russian literature in the "Age of Catherine," the golden age of the Russian gentry state, a period marked by great military victories, successful legal reforms, and the rapid development of Russian national culture. Symbolic of the age was the fate of the poem's author, who in the wake of its appearance rose suddenly from being an "unknown" poet and modest bureaucrat in the Senate to one of the Tsarina's favorites and the leading poet of the Empire.

The impetus for the creation of the ode was the allegorical-didactic "Tale of the Tsarevich Khlor" written by Catherine in 1781 for her five-year-old grandson, the future Emperor Alexander I. The heroine of this fairy tale (one of the first works of Russian children's literature) is the merry and friendly Kirgiz Tsarina Felitsa (from the Latin felicitas – happiness), who helps her protégé, the young Tsarevich Khlor, to find a *thornless rose*, symbol of benevolent and rational government, on a rocky mountain. By orienting his work toward the Empress's light fairy tale, which was filled with characters based on concrete members of her entourage, Derzhavin was able to transform the solemn celebratory ode pioneered by Lomonosov into something more intimate. His "Felitsa" celebrates the personal image of the Empress rather than her public persona and consciously appeals to the personal tastes, experiences and light-hearted side of its addressee. The fairy-tale orientalism of the ode not only accorded with the recherché style of Catherine's court, distinguished by its theatricalized ceremonies in which the personal life of the Empress was depicted as something like an episode from the "Thousand and One Nights," but it also hinted allegorically at the Tsarina's expansionist policy, through which a number of "Eastern" peoples had become Russian subjects.

The poem is built around the appeal of the "sinner" noble Murza (a Tatar honorific), in whom it was easy to recognize various "weaknesses" of Catherine's favorites, to the god-like "Kirgiz-Kaisatsk Tsarina," in whose portrait the reader could easily see the Empress. Later, Derzhavin would emphasize that he chose the role of Murza for himself because of his own ancestry from a "Tatar tribe" and because he had his "own villages near the free Kirgiz nomads." The benevolent life of Felitsa is presented by the Murza as a model for imitation and is contrasted to the comic vanity of his own life: "Tell me, Felitsa, / How to live opulently yet justly, / How to subdue the storm of passions / And be happy in the world." At the same time, the key to the odic celebration of the Tsarina is not so much her innocence as it is her wise beneficence, which is based on a deep understanding of human nature and love for her subjects. These qualities are what raises the ode's heroine above previous "Kirgiz-Kaisatsk" (that is Russian) rulers and is the source of her rational and humane lawgiving which in its turn leads to the happiness and flowering of her state.

The ode expressed the Empress's favorite thoughts about enlightened absolutism, which she had laid out in her "Instruction" (Nakaz, 1767–8), and it successfully played on the "scenario of power" characteristic of her reign: the mythological representation of the Empress as the mother of her people and her rule as "by humane feelings, if not institutional guarantees."[19] Even so, by his own admission Derzhavin held back his poem for an entire year, fearing the anger of the nobles he had satirized (for his poetic rose definitely *had* thorns!). In the author's later retelling, inspired by his conscious attempt to construct his authorial biography as a story of divine calling, the appearance of "Felitsa" was the result of Providence. By accident the ode fell into the hands of one of his influential friends, who passed it on without the poet's permission to various people including Princess E. P. Dashkova (1743–1810), the director of the Russian Academy of Arts and Sciences. Dashkova, herself a talented author, decided to use "Felitsa" to open the first issue of the Academy's journal "Colloquy of Lovers of the Russian Word," meant to develop domestic literary production and to form public opinion in favor of Catherine's political positions. The poem was published anonymously under the jocular title "Ode to the Wise Kirgiz-Kaisatsk Tsarina Written by a Tatar Murza who Moved to Moscow Long Ago and is Living for Personal Reasons in Saint Petersburg. Translated from the Arab Tongue in 1782."

According to Derzhavin's account, Dashkova brought Catherine a copy of the journal and the next morning was called in to see the Empress who met her with tears in her eyes and asked her to reveal the name of the author "who was able to describe me so pleasantly that, as you see, I am crying like a little fool." A few days later Derzhavin received an envelope with the inscription "From Orenburg from the Kirgiz Tsarina to the Murza." The envelope contained a gold snuff box and 500 gold coins. Soon afterwards the poet was granted a royal audience. From that time forward

Derzhavin was seen as Catherine's *personal* poet, and the name Felitsa became the "cultural pseudonym" for the Tsarina who had turned down the titles "the Great," "the Wise," and "Mother of the Fatherland," all of which had been proposed by the Senate and the Petersburg gentry. In years to come the gallant masquerade of Catherine and Derzhavin as Felitsa and her Murza continued: on commission from the Empress (and in the absence of commissions) the poet produced a number of poems by Murza ("Gratitude to Felitsa," "The Murza's Vision," "Depiction of Felitsa," and others) which have come to be called his Catherinian cycle. In these poems Derzhavin not only extolled his benefactress, but even allowed himself to teach her and criticize her policies.

The success of "Felitsa" with Catherine can be ascribed to Derzhavin's ability to describe the Empress as she wished to see herself and as she presented herself in her correspondence and copious literary work: "naturally merry," the enemy of boredom and grumblers, and the foe of fanatical mystics and moralists who despise human nature.[20] The rational jollity that the Empress emphasized was not so much a character trait as it was a cultural mask, chosen by her in the ideological struggle for the political regime she personified and constantly defended. It was the mask of an enlightened philosopher on the throne, the incarnation of reason, goodness, empathy, optimism, and an ideal balance of emotions.

Though Derzhavin insisted that the triumph of his poem was the result of happy accident, the intervention of important state actors, partisans of Enlightenment and influential writer friends on his behalf speaks to a carefully thought out campaign at the height of Catherine's reign. Almost immediately after its appearance, a number of ecstatic reviews appeared in which Derzhavin's poem was said to inaugurate a new tradition of praise of the monarch ("without flattery") and to open "a new and untrodden path" for Russian literature. In fact, Derzhavin's candidacy as the star of the Russian poetic Olympus was pushed forward by Dashkova's party (with the shadow of Catherine standing behind it). The ode's grandiose success became, in turn, the basis for Derzhavin's brilliant political career, which continued even after Catherine's death: he was appointed at various times a provincial governor, the state secretary of the Empress, a member of the State Council, and the Minister of Justice. However, because of his difficult character Derzhavin did not last long in any of these posts and more than once he had to resort to poetry as a way to worm his way back into the Empress's good graces and to scourge his "enemies."

The importance of "Felitsa" in Russian literature is enormous. The poem is one of the most daring and most successful attempts to reform the central genre of Russian eighteenth-century poetry: the solemn celebratory ode. Derzhavin's turn away from the splendor and heavy-handed allegory typical of the older Lomonosov model of the genre, his unique mixing of solemnity with elements of anacreontic verse, satire, and "oriental" fairy tale while nevertheless avoiding any hint of the burlesque, his ability to turn the ode to more intimate themes which fit well with the pre-Romantic tendencies of the late eighteenth century, his use of colloquial speech and irony, his deflation of high themes while not giving up their importance, and his ability to imbue the narrator's voice with a strong individual personality – all serve to set this work apart from its predecessors. Perhaps even more important was that Derzhavin created a new model of a Russian poet: in place of an abstract odic singer, the linchpin of the Ideal State, he substituted a Russian gentry-poet, living his private life and choosing of his own free will to sing the praises of the Tsarina who is the source and guarantee for gentry liberty. "Felitsa" became the ur-text of a line of Russian poetic appeals to the ruler: it is the wellspring for such works as the "Aleksandriads" of Nikolai Karamzin, Pushkin's poems to Emperor Nicholas I, and Vladimir Mayakovsky's (1893–1930) poems to Lenin among others. Derzhavin's ode canonized the problematic status of the Russian poet as the Tsar's interlocutor and of poetry as an autonomous force that must be reckoned with by the powers that be.

3

The Spirit of Poetry: Russian Culture in the Age of Alexander I (1801–25)

I

In Russia the nineteenth century began on March 11, 1801; on that day (or more precisely sometime after midnight on the morning of the 12th) Emperor Paul I was deposed and killed by a group of conspirators in the Mikhailov Palace. In the course of his short (1796–1801) but extremely peculiar reign, Paul had managed to alienate the "leaders of society" who had been accustomed to the freedoms of the Catherinian era. Paul's son Alexander came to the throne. The young emperor announced that he proposed to rule "by the laws and in the spirit" of his most august grandmother, Catherine the Great. Gentry privileges were reinstated, some of Paul's more bizarre laws (including those forbidding foreign books and travel abroad) were rescinded, liberal regulations for universities (1802) and censorship (1804) were enacted, private publishing houses, which had been banned since 1796, were again allowed (1802), literary and social societies and Masonic lodges were permitted (1810) and new universities were opened (1802–4).

Under Alexander, literature was supposed to sing the power and harmonious beauty of the Empire, which was flourishing under the patriarchal care of the humane monarch – a "human being on the throne" as Nikolai Karamzin, one of chief ideologues and most visible writers of his reign, put it. In odes and panegyrics, the reign of Alexander (1801–25) was lauded as a Golden Age, the Russian analogy to the glorious era of the Roman Emperor Augustus. It was a period of heroic battles and hitherto unheard of artistic triumphs linked with a whole pleiad of important architects (Andrei Voronikhin [1751–1814], Toma de Tomon, Carlo Rossi), visual artists (Vladimir Borovikovsky [1757–1825], Orest Kiprensky [1782–1836], Fedor Tolstoy [1783–1873], Alexei Venetsianov [1780–1847]), dramatists (Vladislav Ozerov, Alexander Shakhovskoi [1777–1846], Alexander Griboedov [1795–1829]), and poets (Vasily Zhukovsky, Konstantin Batiushkov [1787–1855], Petr Viazemsky, Denis Davydov [1784–1839], Evgeny Baratynsky [1800–44],

Alexander Pushkin). In historical perspective, this was a period in which Russian culture enthusiastically assimilated a variety of Western ideas and schools: the Imperial neo-classicism of Napoleonic France, "democratic" English sentimentalism, German *Sturm und Drang* and the English "Gothic" school, and, a bit later, the Romanticism of Thomas Moore and Lord Byron. The rapid influx, coexistence, juxtaposition, and synthesis of these various styles lent the period a particularly dynamic character and prevented the appearance of a single dominant trend or style. In general terms, however, the arc of cultural development in the Alexandrine era can be seen as moving away from the normative thinking of neo-classicism to a Romantic mindset, from imitations of Western models to the formation of a national cultural model and the creation of the ur-texts of national culture.

In the Russian cultural mythology, this epoch, often called the "Golden Age," is a well-defined period with clear traits and cultural heroes. The latter are distinguished by paradoxical combinations of qualities: they are of aristocratic background but filled with "republican spirit"; their orientation is toward the West but they share a strong sense of national pride; they imitate classical models but are fascinated by folk culture and native traditions; they are heroic ascetics filled with sentimentality, they project both rationality and mystical exaltation; they combine theatricality with a cult of simplicity; they love solitude but serve the nation; they see Russian history as a subset of European history but believe in Russia's messianic potential.

II

The political history of the first fifteen years of the century was seen by contemporaries as a kind of heroic epic: military campaigns in the West (the anti-Napoleonic coalitions), the North (war with Sweden) and the South (against the Ottomans), the Napoleonic invasion of 1812, the Battle of Borodino, the burning of Moscow, which had been abandoned by her inhabitants, the flight of the French pursued by the armies of Field Marshal Mikhail Kutuzov [1745–1813], the "liberation of Europe" by Emperor Alexander, the triumphant entry of the Russian army into Paris in 1814, and, finally, the Holy Alliance of monarchs formed at Alexander's initiative which was supposed to guide the Christian nations until the Second Coming. Throughout this period there were nebulous, though constant promises from the Tsar regarding political reforms, the elimination of "slavery" (that is, serfdom), and even the possibility of a constitution.

These exceptional events struck contemporaries as proof of the predictions of some German and Russian mystics regarding the great historical mission of Russia and her Emperor as the destroyer of the Antichrist (Napoleon) and savior of mankind from the sins of the French Revolution. These messianic ideas were reflected in the manifestos and political activity of the Tsar, in the missionary and translation work of the members of the Russian Bible Society, in poetry (Zhukovsky's "Singer in the Kremlin" [Pevets v Kremle], "Vadim," 1815–16), in architectural design (the project for the Cathedral of Christ the Savior by A. L. Vitberg [1788–1855] in 1817), and later on in painting (the celebrated canvas *The Appearance of Christ Before the People* by A. A. Ivanov [1806–58]). They did not diminish in the period that stretched from the late teens until the middle of the 1820s, that is in the period of the formation of the "secret societies" that would produce the "Decembrists" – young officers, for the most part from aristocratic families, who imbibed French ideals of "citizenship, freedom, and constitutional rights" during their stay in Paris, enthusiastically adopted the Romantic nationalism of German patriots of the 1810s, were inspired by revolutions in Spain and Italy in the early 1820s, and dreamed of a radical transformation of Russia. The idea of a religious renaissance associated with the Tsar-Savior was transformed in the minds of these "Russian Jacobins" into a secular religion of freedom, lauded earlier by Radishchev in his ode "Liberty," and of national and political rebirth to which these chosen heroes would lead Russia and for which they would be willing to die.

The political goals of these enthusiasts of divine Liberty ranged from conservative constitutional monarchy to a strongly centralized republic. Alexander Pushkin, who was closely associated with the movement, although never a member of a secret society, described the agitated atmosphere of Decembrists circles in a coded poetic survey of Russian political history of the 1810s (only a fragment of this work has survived):

> The friend of Bacchus, Mars, and Venus,
> Here Lunin spoke impressively,
> From hesitancy strove to wean us,
> Then muttered on in ecstasy.
> Here Pushkin read his verse with swagger,
> And here the regidical dagger
> The sad Yakushkin, it would seem,
> Bared silently, as in a dream.
> The lame Turgenev for his nation,
> Alone had eyes, and every speech
> For him one moral had to teach;

> His object was emancipation,
> And in these nobles he would see
> The men who'd set the peasants free.
>
> (trans. Babett Deutsch).

The appearance of secret political societies in Russia toward the end of the 1810s was a result of the dissatisfaction of a significant portion of the intellectual elite with the Emperor's political orientation: his rejection of earlier liberal promises for Russia and support of a moralizing mysticism which was defended by the new state ideologues as necessary to save Russia's soul and protect the state from revolution; his reactionary foreign policy, particularly his "betrayal" of his "Orthodox brothers" (that is the Greeks) who were revolting against the Ottoman Empire, which Alexander and the Holy Alliance understood to be a legitimate monarchy. Most disquieting of all was the Emperor's growing detachment from affairs of state, which after 1816 were increasingly placed in the hands of the arch-conservative A. A. Arakcheev (1769–1834). Upon Alexander's death in December 1825, a group of rebellious army officers (the so-called Northern Society) refused to swear allegiance to the new Tsar Nicholas I. They led some 3,000 troops onto the Senate Square, but the revolt was quickly suppressed by soldiers loyal to Nicholas. A few weeks later, the leaders of the loosely connected rebel group (the Southern Society) led an equally ill-fated and short uprising. Nicholas I personally led the investigation into the rebellion, ordering execution for five of the ringleaders (including the poet Kondraty Ryleev), and long terms of imprisonment and exile for many participants. Thus ended the Alexandrine period, which had begun a quarter century before with high liberal hopes.

III

Russia's military and political successes in the first fifteen years of the nineteenth century got out in front of her cultural achievements, and the main task in the peacetime years that followed 1815 was cultural building: Russia felt the need to catch up to the West (or even surpass it) not merely in the military arena but in the cultural as well.

In this period Petersburg became an expression of the aesthetic tastes and messianic pretensions of the Emperor – the Northern Palmyra as a rival to Napoleonic Paris. Two generations of architects, from Andrei Voronikhin to Auguste de Montferrand, worked on creating a new image for the capital in imitation of Humanist Athens and mighty Rome: the monumental harmony of Voronikhin's Kazan Cathedral inspired by St.

Peter's, the straight arrow of Nevsky Prospect, the clear sightlines of Vasilievsky Island outlined by a triangle formed by the Stock Exchange building, rostral columns and the granite embankments along the Neva and Petersburg's Bolshoi Theatre designed by T. de Tomon, the main Admiralty building of A. Zakharov, and, a bit later, the immense St. Isaac's Cathedral of Montferrand (completed during the reign of Nicholas I). Art was meant to immortalize the men and events of this great age from the Emperor himself in the triumphant equestrian statue of R. Volkov, to the heroes of the war of 1812, to the battle canvases of V. I. Moshkov and the medallions of F. P. Tolstoy.

The Westernizing (Francophile) cultural program of Alexander was opposed by an unofficial alternate center of Russian cultural politics – the Russophile salon of the Emperor's mother Maria Fedorovna (a German by origin), which patronized home-grown musicians, artists and literati. The program of this salon (which became the prototype for a significant number of aristocratic literary salons of the period 1810–30) was oriented toward the "court Romanticism" of the Prussian queen Luisa, and called for simplicity, naturalness, fidelity to national traditions and religious practices, "correction" of artistic tastes and mores through imitation of classical models, as well as an adoration of nature, family values and an exalted sentimentality. The incarnation of this program was the summer residence of the Empress-mother, the elegant Pavlovsk (designed by the architects Giacomo Quarenghi and Pietro Gonzago) with its picturesque romantic park, "classical" pavilions and hospitable idyllic farm – a symbolic representation of the idea of an organic (natural) Russian monarchy filled with matriarchal concern for the well-being and morality of its subjects.

Monumental Alexandrine classicism and the elegant pre-Romanticism of the court at Pavlovsk matched the tastes of the big-city gentry. In the provinces, however, tastes ran more to sentimentalism, which had appeared by the end of the 1780s in patriarchal Moscow and spread to the periphery by the beginning of the new century. Imitating models derived from the Western and native sentimental tradition (Rousseau, Sterne, Goethe of the period of *Werther*; *The Works of Ossian*, and Karamzin's influential *Letters of a Russian Traveller* [Pis'ma russkogo puteshestvennika, 1797–1801] and his celebrated short story "Poor Liza" [Bednaia Liza, 1792]), the Russian sentimental landowner looked to the bosom of nature to escape the vanity of this world. He would visit cemeteries and ruminate about the fate of all mortal things, surround himself with symbols of sentiment (memorial stones, grottos, dark alleys in his garden, altars to Melancholy in his study), call his maid Celene rather than Akulka and his estate a Gothic

62   The Spirit of Poetry

5 St. Isaac's Cathedral, St. Petersburg. The neo-classical bulk of St. Isaac's Cathedral dominates the southwest corner of the Neva's left bank. It took a full forty years to build (1818–58) under the direction of the architect August de Montferrand. The interior is sumptuously decorated with multicolored granite and marble.

island rather than Nikolsk. He might sit for hours by a warm fire, thinking about the exploits of his countrymen under the command of Alexander ("the Phenomenon of Europe"), compose poems and prose for provincial and Moscow journals, and listen to the amateur musical performances of his lovely daughter.

Many contemporaries laughed at this kind of exalted sentimentality. In the acerbic words of the comic writer and classicist A. Shakhovskoi, "this style was born in England, ruined in France, became pretentious in Germany, and was brought to us in a truly laughable condition." Nevertheless, the sentimental tradition was of great significance for Russian culture. These islands of feeling, where the cultivation of love for the Russian landscape was melded with meditation, reading, modest versifying and musical performance, played an important role in the emotional emancipation of the Russian gentry, allowing them to feel and to express their inner life. This sentimental tradition would have a considerable influence on high culture in Russia in the first half of the nineteenth century: the elegiac tradition of Zhukovsky, Batiushkov, Baratynsky and Pushkin grows directly from it, as does Pushkin's ironic sentimental prose (*The Tales of Belkin* [Povesti Belkina, 1830] and *The Captain's Daughter*). In their turn these stories were of great importance for Turgenev's lyrical prose in the second half of the century. This tradition was also the point of departure for Gogol's sentimental humanism ("The Overcoat" [Shinel', 1842]) and the early novels of Dostoevsky, as well as the tradition of the Russian musical "romance" as practiced by Mikhail Glinka (1804–57) and Petr Tchaikovsky (1840–93).

IV

The liberalization of social life during the reign of Alexander I allowed for the appearance of literary and artistic circles and groups not directly dependent on the government and court. The most important of these set themselves the task of developing Russian culture from a wide variety of positions including the Moscow-based Westernizing group led by Karamzin and I. I. Dmitriev (1760–1837), the neo-classical salon of the director of the Imperial Public Library A. N. Olenin, the pre-Romantic "Friendly Literary Society" of Andrei Turgenev and Vasily Zhukovsky, the democratic "Free Society of Lovers of Belles Lettres, Sciences and Arts," the proto-Slavophile "Colloquy of Lovers of the Russian Word" of A. S. Shishkov (1754–1841) and G. R. Derzhavin, and the liberal-aristocratic "Arzamas." New journals (the modest precursors of the "thick journals" of the 1840s and beyond, which included articles on a variety of topics as well as original and translated literary work, became the mouthpieces of various ideological points of view in this period: the Western-oriented *Herald of Europe*, (Vestnik Evropy beginning in 1802), the patriotic, anti-French *Russian Herald* (Russkii vestnik, from 1808), the mystic *Herald of Zion* (Sionskii vestnik, from 1806).

In the 1810s and 1820s literature and art gradually became further emancipated from direct government control and began to reflect the interests and tastes of the educated gentry who had sufficient leisure time to devote to culture and who began to develop their own ideas about the world and history, frequently in opposition to the views of the state. This was a time of the consolidation and flowering of the gentry intelligentsia, and the diversification of Russian culture.

One characteristic phenomenon of the Alexandrine period was the cult of natural and beneficent classicism: it was apparent in a wide range of loci, from fashion and in the daily life of the gentry to court ceremonies and festivals, in art and in literature. The Emperor himself, who took command of the Russian armies in their European campaign of 1813–14, liked to play the role of the Russian Agamemnon. Young officers played the roles of Homeric heroes. Young men in the civil service thought of themselves as noble Roman republicans, and (later) as fighters against tyranny. The pantheon of the "Russian Jacobins" of the 1820s was augmented with contemporary heroes from the Spanish and Neapolitan Revolutions of 1819–21, and also with new "Brutuses" like the German student Karl Sand who assassinated the conservative playwright and "Russian agent" August Kotzebue in 1819. The behavior of this group was markedly theatrical and semiotically loaded: social life and history were understood as a kind of captivating performance played by a set of rules canonized in art and literature, a play in which everyone knew his role.

Naturally, theatre played an important part in the cultural life of the first decades of the century. It was not only a favorite source of amusement but was seen as an ideal school for developing the taste (the Imperial Ballet) and virtue (the dramatic theatre) of the gentry. The verse tragedies of Vladislav Ozerov were particularly popular at the beginning of the century. They sang the praises of duty and passion, the virtues of self-abnegation, and the role of heroism and individuality in creating a peaceful society. The monologues of the noble and sensitive heroes of Ozerov's plays, performed by the talented tragedians Alexei Iakovlev and Ekaterina Semenova (1780–1849), were taken by contemporaries, especially younger audiences, as moral imperatives, models for exalted imitation. The hero of the day was the orator, who drew on a loaded vocabulary that demanded from the listener an answering emotional echo. Words like "fatherland" and "freedom" were meant automatically to evoke pride and elation, while "tyranny" and "slave" functioned to call forth anger. The world was divided into noble heroes, filled with honor and national pride, and the unprincipled crowd, wallowing in selfishness.

The Romanticism of the 1820s brought this classical topos of the juxtaposition of the hero and the crowd to the level of tragic and irresolvable conflict. In *Woe from Wit* (Gore ot uma, 1824), the verse comedy of Alexander Griboedov the noble orator-patriot Chatsky clashes with a variety of characters representing the ignorant and unprincipled Moscow crowd. Having angrily dressed them down, he flees Moscow in despair. This comedy, which for political reasons had no chance of being staged at the time, read by its author at a number of Petersburg salons and circulated around the country in many handwritten copies, was taken by many members of gentry society as a kind of declaration of opposition.

An orientation toward the classical world did not exclude a simultaneous concern with "the national" in the Alexandrine period. In the pre-Romantic cultural mind, much affected by the ideas of the great German philosopher J. G. Herder, the fables of I. A. Krylov expressed the Russian spirit as organically as Homer had expressed the spirit of the Greeks. The poet Nikolai Gnedich believed he could transform Russian belles lettres in his translation of *The Iliad* by recreating Homer in all his primitive beauty and power. Vasily Zhukovsky hoped to nurture national feeling through his hexameter translations of J. H. Hebel's German idylls. Nikolai Karamzin tried to imitate the "narrative beauty" of Tacitus in his *History of the Russian State* (1803–26). Of particular importance to Russian cultural thought was the publication in 1800 of *The Lay of Prince Igor*. The heroes of this "Russian Iliad," including the reckless Prince Igor, his faithful wife Iaroslavna and the bardic singer Boyan became archetypical characters in Russian literature and art of the nineteenth century: from Zhukovsky's "Singer in the Russian Military Camp" to the historically inflected "Meditations" (Dumy) of the Decembrist poet Kondraty Ryleev, to the programmatic national opera *Prince Igor* (Kniaz' Igor', 1890) of A. P. Borodin.

V

The culture of the Alexandrine period was literocentric. As one contemporary put it: "Despite the terrible events sweeping Europe at the time, politics was not the main topic of conversation. It always took second place to literature." More to the point, the violent arguments about grammar, stylistics, and metrics so characteristic of this period were not merely about aesthetic issues. Rather, they were equally of a political and ideological character. They centered around the national essence of Russian culture, particularly its relationship to Western (primarily French) culture. Literature played the role of a parliament in which various points of view about important contemporary issues collided. Although the world of "real" Russian politics was the exclusive province of the Emperor and his court, here one could find liberals and conservatives, "Gallomaniacs" and "Slavophiles," monarchists, and republicans.

One of the hottest debates of the first half of the century began as a conflict between the partisans of the "old" and "new" styles (Alexander Shishkov vs. Karamzin and a group of his young admirers, including poets Konstantin Batiushkov and Petr Viazemsky). In the 1820s it transformed into a debate about national forms of art, which prepared the ground for the historiosophical arguments of the 1830s and 40s between the Slavophiles and Westernizers. Passionate arguments about literature (the "War on Parnassus") led to a previously unheard of flowering of literary parody, which revealed the conventionality of whatever artistic school or principle it mocked (*The New Sterne* [Novyi Stern, 1805] and *The Lipetsk Waters* [Lipetskie vody, 1815] of Shakhovskoi, Batiushkov's "Vision on the Shores of Lethe" [1809], Vasily Pushkin's "A Dangerous Neighbor" [Opasnyi sosed, 1811], Alexander Voeikov's "Insane Asylum" [1814], and finally Alexander Pushkin's *Ruslan and Liudmila*). By the beginning of the nineteenth century the writer had already become a figure of authority in the eyes of the educated public. By the end of the 1810s, he was a "shaper of minds" for the reading public.

Lyric poetry was by far the most important type of literature in the Alexandrine age. It became a kind of "sacred rite" in the words of a contemporary. The exceptional prestige of poetry in Russian culture throughout the nineteenth and twentieth centuries has its roots in this period, particularly in the "Friendly Literature Society" (1801) imbued with the pre-Romantic ides of Goethe and Schiller. Its young members espoused a cult of friendship of the beautiful soul and the religion of poetry. Poetry, according to the society's leader Andrei Turgenev, derives from God, awakens dreams and hopes in the human soul, explains the "mysteries of the divine," serves to console the unhappy and inspire people to activity (patriotic service). Poets are heaven-sent heralds, who form a holy fraternity. A rather different, carnivalized version of such a fraternity was the literary society "Arzamas"

(1815–18) – a literary order of like-minded aesthetes (the "Karamzinists" D. N. Bludov, Batiushkov, Viazemsky, and others) who banded together to eat, drink and make merry while defending proper poetic taste (the poetic system of Zhukovsky) from attacks by literary "retrogrades" (Shishkov's "Slavophilic heresy"). In this time the Romantic myth of the "immortal family" of chosen poets, the inhabitants of the eternal land of the imagination, arose. The idea of a literary fraternity, a "union of poets," runs like a crimson thread through this entire age. It is expressed in one of the most popular literary genres of the period, the friendly verse epistle, characterized by broad stylistic and emotional range, and its aesthetic of "poetic chatter" which is nevertheless able, under a veneer of light verse, to express deep thoughts and emotions.

VI

By the middle of the 1820s, Russia had formed its first true canon of poetic work. It included a wide variety of texts: Zhukovsky's ballads "Liudmila" (1808) and "Svetlana" (1811), Batiushkov's epistles "My Penates" (Moi penaty, 1811) and his elegy "The Dying Tasso" (Umiraiushchii Tass, 1817), Gnedich's (1784–1833) idyll "The Anglers" (Rybaki, 1811), the political lyrics of Viazemsky ("Indignation" ["Negodovanie," 1818]), and Alexander Pushkin ("Freedom: An Ode" [Volnost': Oda,1817]), as well as longer narrative poems by Zhukovsky (*The Prisoner of Chillon [Shil'oinskii uznik*, 1822]) and Pushkin (*Prisoner of the Caucasus* [Kavkazskii plennik, 1822], *The Fountain of Bakchisarai* [Bakchisaraiskii fontan, 1822], and *Gypsies* [Tsygany, 1823]). Russian aesthetic criticism also began in this period. Articles by such figures as Viazemsky, Orest Somov (1793–1833), Nikolai Polevoi (1796–1846), and Vilgelm Kiukhelbeker (1797–1846) allowed the public to access debates about trends in literature that had previously been confined to the oral culture of salons and discussion groups.

Poetry of this period is highly theatrical. In keeping with Western traditions, Russian authors took on specific roles for themselves, which continued to be attached to their life and works. From this period we have the myths of the Russian sybarite and dreamer Batiushkov, Ivan Krylov (1769–1844) the "Russian Aesop," Ozerov the exalted singer brought down by society, the "abject" melancholic poet Zhukovsky, the "Hussar poet" Denis Davydov, the "citizen poet" Ryleev, and the "poet exile" (Baratynsky and the young Pushkin). Naturally, the actual biographies of these men were richer than these masks and their poetry was more varied than such epithets might suggest. Nevertheless, this Renaissance-style play with classical roles was necessary for the formation of the young Russian poetic tradition: Western models needed to be naturalized and personalized, Russian poets had to feel themselves not as imitators but rather as the heirs or even the rivals of Western poets.

To sum up, by the middle of the 1820s, poetry had been transformed from a more or less mechanical collection of verse texts, genres, and names to a kind of republic of letters linked by shared themes, problems, and myths and populated by concrete authorial figures well known to readers. By the mid-1820s, Alexander Pushkin, the author of love elegies, frivolous poems, inflammatory political lyrics, and innovative Romantic narrative poems, was acknowledged by his fellow writers and the readers' public as the unquestioned head of the Russian literary Olympus.

Yet it should be mentioned that there were barely a few thousand readers in Russia at this time. Works of literature appeared in editions of between 200 and 600 copies, and they rarely sold out (this showed significant growth from the eighteenth century, when an edition of between fifty and eighty copies was considered good sized). Pushkin's "Fountain of Bakchisarai" came out in an enormous edition of 1200 copies as did, apparently, the collected fables of Ivan Krylov in 1809. The best-selling books of the entire age were the first volumes of Karamzin's *History of the Russian State*, which sold an unheard of 3000 copies in a month. We can get some idea of the number and composition of the Russian reading public from the subscriber list of the journal *Herald of Europe*, which started with 580 subscribers and quickly reached over 1200. The majority of readers were the nobles (most of whom resided in St. Petersburg and Moscow). There were a very few public libraries at the time in Russia. All in all, the most realistic number of readers was about one percent of the Empire's population (we are speaking, of course, about readers of literature; the literate population was undoubtedly greater).[1] This was a far smaller reading public than in enlightened Western countries.

Most Russian authors were from the gentry class and perceived their literary work as entertainment or Romantic calling rather than a source of financial reward. According to a contemporary historian, "in the first half of the nineteenth century, there had been no more than twenty to thirty individuals making a living from literature at any one time; and for the gentry, who had at their disposal a broad spectrum of opportunities for social advancement, the role of professional writer had held no attraction."[2] An exceptional role in the professionalization of the literary trade was played by Pushkin in 1820s-1830s. However, it was only in the 1850s-

1860s, with Alexander II's Great Reforms, substantial structural changes in Russian society and the development of the publishing industry, that "social strata such as the classless [*raznochintsy*] intelligentsia, minor and middle-ranking officials, and the gentry began to view literary work as both honorable and prestigious."³

VII

Alexander I, the symbolic initiator of the Russian cultural awakening of the first quarter of the nineteenth century, died on December 1 (new style) 1825 in the southern town of Taganrog, far from Petersburg. The later years of his reign had been marked by his mystic explorations and constant wandering around the Empire – something between an on-going fact-finding mission and a flight from reality. The liberal promises and grandiose projects of the early years remained unrealized. Reforms were supplanted by counter-reforms intended to guard Russia from "destructive" influences from the West (most importantly Romantic nationalism and political radicalism). Despite the generally negative view of the Emperor in Russian society of the time, his death was perceived as a tragic loss, the end of a great epoch. In place of the Golden Age, which is tied in the Russian cultural memory to the image of the "meek" Alexander, came the "Iron Age" associated with the new Tsar, the "severe and powerful" (in Pushkin's words) Nicholas I. This is the origin of the nostalgia for the "wonderful epoch" of young heroes and poets that became such an important component of the Russian national cultural myth. Aesthetic yearning for this particular paradise lost has tended to be expressed particularly forcefully during various crisis periods of Russian history: after the reforms of the 1860s (Tolstoy's *War and Peace* and Tchaikovsky's *Eugene Onegin*), the modernist epoch (Vladimir Solovev, Alexander Blok, Alexandre Benois [1870–1960], Osip Mandelstam [1891–1938], Anna Akhmatova [1889–1966], Marina Tsvetaeva [1892–1941], Iuri Tynianov [1894–1943]), and during the "years of stagnation" of the 1970s and 80s (books and films about the Decembrists and their wives, the scholarly and semi-popular books and lectures of Natan Eidelman [1930–89] and Iuri Lotman [1922–93]).

Biography – Vasily Andreevich Zhukovsky (1783–1852)

The importance of V. A. Zhukovsky for Russian culture is enormous: the founder of Russian Romanticism; a major reformer of prosody and poetic semantics; a translator of genius who acquainted Russophone readers with the Western literary canon from *The Odyssey* through the works of Byron; the "teacher" of Pushkin and Gogol; the creator of the first Russian religious philosophy of art as well as of the central "poetic myths" of the ages of both Alexander I and Nicholas I; the author of the words of the Russian national anthem, and the tutor of the Tsar-reformer Alexander II.

Zhukovsky had a long life. His poetic and social activity covered more than half a century and was closely linked to the cultural history of three distinct reigns – Paul I, Alexander I, and Nicholas I. Zhukovsky's mindset, however, was firmly of the Alexandrine era. In the words of G. Florovsky, precisely Zhukovsky "with his brilliant range of poetic and creative incarnations, with his heightened sensitivity and responsiveness, with his free and direct language" was able to express the "spirit" of this time.[4] Thus, the life and work of Zhukovsky can serve as an illustration of the psychological history of Russian society during the Golden Age of gentry culture.

Zhukovsky was born on January 29, 1783 in the village of Mishenskoe near the provincial city of Tula (some one hundred miles south of Moscow). His father, Afanasy Bunin, was a wealthy landowner. His mother Salkha was a Turkish slave girl. According to family legend, Salkha had been given to Bunin as a present by one of his serfs, who had captured her during the Russo-Turkish war of 1770. Following his father's wishes, the boy was adopted by Andrei Zhukovsky, a poor nobleman living on Bunin's estate. The future poet spent his childhood and youth on his father's estate and in the home of his half sister and godmother in Tula. He was brought up in the spirit of provincial sentimentalism and in a circle of women with broad cultural interests: literature, music, theatre. But, most importantly, the Bunin family life was characterized by the kind of warmth and friendly fellowship that Zhukovsky would always prize highly. The theme of the cozy home, a protected little oasis of camaraderie and sympathy amidst the large and cold world, would become one of his favorite poetic topoi.

In 1797 Zhukovsky was enrolled in the University Pension for Gentlemen in Moscow, one of the most progressive and successful schools of its day, which played an important role in nurturing the talents of many Russian intellectuals of the first half of the nineteenth century (the writers Griboedov, Vladimir Odoevsky [1803–69], Stepan Shevyrev, and Dmitry Venevitinov [1805–27] studied here, as did future statesmen A. P. Ermolov and D. V. Dashkov and a number of the Decembrists). At the end of the eighteenth century, the school was led by a group of pedagogue-masons who strove to provide an "Athenian" education (in contrast to the "Spartan" program of contemporary military academies and the typical "Roman" pattern of home-based schooling). The curriculum was encyclopedic, but the Humanities were stressed: foreign languages, literature, history, music, visual art. The teachers encouraged students to experiment with their own composition, even allowing them to produce a literary journal.

During his high-school years Zhukovsky made the acquaintance of Andrei Turgenev, lover of Rousseau, Goethe, Schiller, and Shakespeare. After finishing school, Turgenev, Zhukovsky, and some other young enthusiasts founded the "Friendly Literary Society," the first pre-Romantic circle in Russia. They saw the activities of this group as preparation for their future moral, social, and literary work, and it seemed to them that the coincidence of their coming of age with the beginning of the new century was an omen of their future success. But Schillerian ebulliance, noble striving for greatness, and great expectations for themselves were soon supplanted (in proper Wertherian fashion) by feelings of disappointment and deep melancholy, which in one form or another would affect all the members of the group.

Zhukovsky first achieved poetic fame with his translation of Thomas Gray's "Elegy Written in a Country Churchyard," which appeared in Karamzin's *Herald of Europe* in 1802. Filled with the spirit of sentimental humanism, this elegy provided a whole complex of themes and motifs that would become the distinguishing features of Zhukovsky's poetry: a celebration of the quiet life in the bosom of nature far from cold civilization, radiant melancholy, death as a bridge to another world, memory as a hope for a meeting *over there*, and a patient faith in resurrection. Zhukovsky's poetic discovery here was the image of the "abject singer," a sensitive lover of nature, an unknown genius doomed to an early grave. In 1803 Zhukovsky's friend Andrei Turgenev to whom the poet had dedicated this translation died at the age of twenty-two. Thus, the borrowed theme of the dead young poet took on personal resonance for Zhukovsky, and his poetry became associated with a prophetic gift.

Having finished school, Zhukovsky took a job in the civil service, but soon resigned in order to devote himself full-time to literature. Beginning in 1804 he gave private lessons to his nieces, the "melancholy" Maria and the "sunny" Alexandra (their mother was Zhukovsky's half sister) and fell in love with the former. Between 1806 and 1811 he dedicated a cycle of lyric poems to her and in 1812 proposed marriage. But her mother refused (Zhukovsky was, after all, their close relative, though not on paper). Unrequited love would become the main theme of Zhukovsky's poetry for years to come. Many of the poems of this "Russian Petrarch" would be set to music as romances, making Zhukovsky's verse a prominent feature of gentry living rooms throughout Russia.

In 1808, Zhukovsky published his translation of "Lenore," by the German "Sturm und Drang" poet Gottfried Bürger. The poem's atmosphere is gothic: night, a skeleton, ghosts who accompany the girl and her dead fiancé, a cemetery, open graves. Zhukovsky transferred the setting of the ballad to Russia, changed the name of the heroine (to the very Russian Liudmila, a name which has the further advantage of rhyming with the word *mogila* [grave]), smoothed out the somewhat primitive language of the original, and removed some images that might offend sentimental taste. "And that was the beginning of Romanticism in Russia!" as the influential critic Vissarion Belinsky (1811–48) would say years later. In fact, the ballad's power derives from the way in which Zhukovsky manages to make the world of the past – exotic, terrifying, passionate – come alive for the reader (the narrative begins in medias res and remains in the present tense throughout). This ballad became the prototype for the genre in Russian literature and the image of the melancholy Liudmila became canonical for Russian Romantic heroines.

Between 1808 and 1833 Zhukovsky would write (or more often translate) some forty ballads, whose central theme was generally that of crime and terrible punishment. Nevertheless, the horrors of his ballads are imaginary, a nightmare that dissipates as soon as the dreamer awakes. This was the mechanism of one of his most famous poems, the "Russian" ballad "Svetlana" (1811): here the vision of a corpse turns out to be a nightmare brought on by a fortune-telling session. In the poem's finale the heroine marries her beloved who has returned safe and sound. Zhukovsky's goal here was the creation of an ideal female character, "a Russian soul." Her distinguishing features are purity, humility, submission to God, fidelity, tenderness, and a radiant sadness. Dark forces are unable to harm such a pure soul, and the implacable judgment day of the Western ballad gives way to the actions of wise Providence. A few years later, Alexander Pushkin would employ the ideal image of Svetlana as the basis for his Tatiana in *Eugene Onegin* (Evgenii Onegin, 1823–30).

When war with Napoleon began in 1812, Zhukovsky signed up with the Moscow Volunteer Regiment. In the fall of 1812, he wrote his verse cantata "A Singer in the Russian Military Camp," which after its publication in 1813 became the most important Russian patriotic poem of the period. On the eve of the battle, the Russian bard glorifies the war heroes by name, remembers the fallen, and calls on the living to avenge them through victory. Every word resonates in the hearts of the listening soldiers, who repeat his concluding words as a refrain. Patriotic feeling is presented here as an emotional outpouring, uniting all Russians. In this and other patriotic poems of the first half of the 1810s, Zhukovsky set himself the daunting task of becoming a national poet, presenting the collective voice of the entire Russian people. He achieved this in typical Romantic style, not by turning away from a subjective point of view but rather by maximizing it, taking his lyricism to a state of mystical ecstasy, which, paradoxically, is meant to open the path to objective truth.

In the second half of the 1810s Zhukovsky gradually turned away from elegiac and patriotic poetry to verse descriptions of Alexander's visionary policy and mystically inspired prophecy ("The Singer in the Kremlin"). At the very end of the decade hymns to the Christian empire were supplanted in his oeuvre by works focusing on court life and on nature. As early as 1815, Zhukovsky had begun to be a frequent guest at the "small court" of Queen Mother Maria Fedorovna and at this time he wrote his elegy "Slavianka," a poetic description and symbolic interpretation of the palace and park at Pavlovsk. Soon thereafter Zhukovsky became a kind of official poet for the Queen Mother and he began a career at court that would span some thirty years.

In his "Pavlovsk poems" Zhukovsky describes the happy life of the Queen Mother's "little court," with its pavilions, chalets, gazebos, park, and river, its amusements, festivals, and little disappointments. His poetic goal is to give voice to this world and his poems are a kind of aesthetic sacralization of life among the highest Russian aristocracy, a world completely hidden from the Russian public. At this time Zhukovsky began to formulate his idea of poetry as an autonomous world, a "parallel universe," and of himself as a dweller in "two worlds" capable of revealing their secret correspondences to a few chosen readers.

In 1821 Zhukovsky traveled with the entourage of the Grand Princess Alexandra Fedorovna (the wife of the future Tsar Nicholas I) on a European tour. In Berlin he saw a luxurious court spectacle on motifs from the poem "Lalla Rookh" by the English Romantic Thomas Moore. Alexandra Fedorovna played the lead role – the Bukharan Princess Lalla Rookh, while her husband Nicholas took the part of her fiancé. In his poems "Lalla Rookh" and "The Appearance of Poetry in the Image of Lalla Rookh," Zhukovsky transformed the charming Princess into a divine symbol of beauty, poetry, and love. In that same year, he wrote an article about Raphael's "Madonna" – one of the first and most influential esthetic manifestos of Russian Romanticism and, later, Symbolism, (echoes of the central ideas of this article can be found in the work of Pushkin, Afanasy Fet

74 The Spirit of Poetry

6 Pavlovsk, a view of the gardens. Pavlovsk was originally built as the country residence of Catherine's son Paul. Though the central neo-classical palace is an impressive building, Pavlovsk is best known for its large English park.

(1820–92), Vladimir Solovev, and Blok). The poet creates his mystical philosophy about the "genius of pure beauty" who appears on earth in order to breathe energy into it for a moment and leave a memory as a harbinger of a better world.

In March 1823, Zhukovsky's half-sister Maria died. Zhukovsky interpreted the death of the girl he had always loved as the apotheosis of his existence. And in fact Zhukovsky could be called the poet of death. It is highly unlikely that in the entire history of Russian literature we could find a poet who wrote more frequently about death, corpses, cemeteries, and meetings beyond the grave. Nor is it likely that we could find a poet who parted with so many loved ones in his poetry: his best childhood friend and that friend's noble father, his beloved and her dear sister, poet and writer friends, several tsars, and even one countess's pet bird.

In 1826, Zhukovsky was appointed tutor to the heir to the throne, the future Alexander II. He took his pedagogical work seriously, creating detailed plans for Alexander's education. This did not prevent him from writing poetry, but it does seem to have altered his creative path; his work becomes more serious and philosophical. He begins to understand contemporary history as an alternating series of catastrophes (the Decembrist uprising, the cholera epidemic and peasant rebellions of 1830–1, the Polish uprising, the death of Pushkin) and periods of tranquility on the road to some future ultimate period of stability based on an eternal pact between a powerful tsar and his loving people. The poet is no longer the emotional prophet or singer of historical victories but rather the wise and calm interpreter of contemporary events for his young pupil. The crowning glory of Zhukovsky's pedagogical program was the Tsarevich's grand tour around Russia: the future emperor needed to understand his country. This took place in the spring of 1837: the heir to the throne and his tutor (like a latter-day Telemachus and Mentor) set off on a long journey. They got all the way to Western Siberia, traveled through the Urals, visited Kazan' on the Volga, the Crimea, and Ukraine, returning to Petersburg only in December.

In 1841 Zhukovsky completed his teaching assignment and soon afterward left Russia. He married a young German girl and bought a comfortable home in Düsseldorf. But the Biedermeier happiness he had dreamed of for his old age proved short-lived. His wife fell ill, and his relationship with Emperor Nicholas, who demanded his return to Russia, became strained. The poet looked for peace and tranquility in religion and work. In the second half of the 1840s he wrote articles about faith, morality, and politics, but the book containing them was not permitted by the Russian censor. He also conceived a plan for the creation of a Russian religious philosophy and for the language necessary to express it. He did, however, succeed in publishing religious and mystical stories, epic poems, and he began his translation of *The Odyssey*, which he understood as an enormous idyll expressing a patriarchal and harmonious world-view. Towards the end of the 1840s Russian idealist Romantics created a new myth of Zhukovsky: he is the prophet, the spiritual father of Russian poetry, fated in his late years to save his child from the aggressive and materialist poetic rabble.

He never returned to live in Russia. First there was his wife's illness, and then the European revolutions of 1848. Zhukovsky interpreted the latter events in eschatological terms, as can be seen from the reappearance of the imagery that had characterized his work during the Napoleonic wars. History is again seen as an apocalyptic battle in which the poet warrior is the herald of truth and harbinger of the last judgment. At this period Zhukovsky translates the second half of *The Odyssey* as a story about the restoration of order at the hands of the ordained monarch (in the margins of the translation he compared the suitors to contemporary parliamentary deputies fomenting revolution). He creates a verse translation of the *Apocalypse* of John, and begins his final long poem *Ahasueros* – a symbolic epilogue to the dying epoch, his own poetry, and his spiritual biography. Zhukovsky had imagined the role of the poet in a variety of ways in the course of his career. In this final work the ideal poet appears in the image of a sufferer enlightened by faith (Ahasueros the eternal Jew is the incarnation of historical experience and the suffering of humanity), and the ideal poetry as a heartfelt hymn of thanks to the Creator.

Zhukovsky died on April 22, 1852 in Baden Baden, having outlived his "students" Pushkin and Gogol. His body was brought to Petersburg and buried in the cemetery of the Alexander Nevsky Monastery, close to Karamzin. In 1881, in accordance with his will, Dostoevsky was buried next to him. Zhukovsky's gravestone bears an inscription taken from his programmatic poem "Camoens" (1839): "Poetry is God in the holy dreams of the earth."

Event – The Appearance of Nikolai Karamzin's *History of the Russian State*

The first eight volumes of N. M. Karamzin's *History of the Russian State* were published in February 1818. Covering a period of some eight centuries, from the formation of Rus' through the triumphant early years of the reign of Ivan IV (The Terrible), the *History* was an enormous success. The work was read and discussed at court and in the aristocratic salons, in literary circles and among army officers, in the capital and the provinces, capturing the attention of "the educated and the ignorant" in the words of Karamzin's friend Ivan Dmitriev. "Everyone, even women of high society, rushed to read the history of their fatherland, heretofore completely unknown to them" (Pushkin). To be sure, there had been histories of Russia before Karamzin's, but only Karamzin's became a cultural and social phenomenon, the object of furious polemics that continued throughout the nineteenth century. There were many reasons for this:

1. Karamzin's *History* appeared at a high water moment of Russian patriotic feeling and national pride, following the victory in the war of 1812 and the liberation of Europe from Napoleon.
2. Even without the stimulus of the triumph over Napoleon, there had been a growing interest in history in Russia from the turn of the century onward: the Imperial Academy of Sciences, the Public library, the Society of Russian History and Antiquity at Moscow University, various private patrons such as Count Nikolai Rumiantsev all encouraged historical scholarship, the collecting of antiquities, the translation and publication of older written texts.
3. In the first decades of the century, Russia had absorbed generally accepted Romantic notions about history as the expression of the spiritual particularity of the nation and the historian as a kind of magician capable of resurrecting the past. These new notions mixed with and were augmented by traditional Enlightenment ideas about history as a book containing moral lessons for rulers and citizens.
4. Russia lacked an authoritative historical text that would provide a generally accepted narrative and propose a coherent conception of the development of the country. Russians were searching for their own Tacitus or Livius.
5. Several competing conceptions of the historical process existed in the 1810s: mystical (history is God's work and Russia's recent triumph should be seen as the realization of a Providential plan), monarchical (history is the actions of tsars and generals), "Russophile" (the triumph of Russia is due to a people who are truly worthy of their history), liberal (history is the story of Russia's progress toward Europeanization and the ultimate triumph of law and a constitution).
6. From the turn of the century, Karamzin had been considered one of Russia's most important writers: creator of "Poor Liza" and *Letters of a Russian Traveler*, editor of Russia's first thick journal (*The Herald of Europe*). Toward the end of the first decade of the century he was seen

as the ideologue of the conservatives, who saw the Tsar's liberal reforms (for the most part promised but never promulgated) as a mistake. That he was writing a general history of Russia had been known for a long time, and the appearance of his book was eagerly anticipated.

Karamzin began working on the *History* in 1803. In October of that year he received the title of Court Historiographer, a position that provided economic independence, official status, and access to the relevant archives. By all accounts Karamzin immersed himself completely in his topic, consulting Russian and foreign chronicles, ancient documents and folkloric texts ("a meager source but not completely worthless" in his words). His project was grandiose. He not only wanted to cover Russia's history from its origins to the present day (in the end he only was able to reach up to the "Time of Troubles" at the beginning of the seventeenth century), but he also wished to present and prove his conception of the development of the Russian state: he saw it as a difficult journey, filled with diversions and failures, but one leading inexorably to the creation of an ideal enlightened monarchy in which autocracy was united with perfect civil and moral law.

Quiet and tranquility were necessary for work, but Karamzin's "cells" (his offices in Moscow and on his country estate Ostaf'evo) could not protect him from an agitated world. In August of 1812 the historian was compelled to leave Moscow just days before Napoleon entered the city. His library burned in the fire of Moscow. As he worked on the *History* he also wrote a series of tracts and memoranda addressed to the Tsar. His critique of Alexander ("A Note on Ancient and Modern Russia," 1811) is directly linked with his thoughts about history. Thus, Karamzin's work was not an escape into the past. It was rather an attempt to understand the tragic and heroic events of the present through historical experience, to present the contemporary greatness of the Empire as the result of a long process of Russian historical and moral development. He understood his own role as analogous to that of Titus Livius, the historian who lived during the reign of Caesar Augustus, and he saw his work as a monument to Russia's past erected at precisely the moment of the heretofore unknown triumph of Russia, her people, and her Emperor.

By all accounts contemporaries read the *History* as a discovery of the past and a manifesto of national pride. The government minister Mikhail Speransky (who was roundly criticized by Karamzin) wrote: "His *History* is a monument erected in honor of our age, our literature."[5] Karamzin's friend and relative Petr Viazemsky compared the writer to Field Marshal

M. I. Kutuzov, the victor over Napoleon: Karamzin "saved Russia from an invasion of forgetting, called her to life, and showed us that our fatherland is truly the place many of us discovered in 1812."[6] At the same time, the *History* elicited spirited attacks both from the right (he was accused of insufficient patriotism for his willingness to criticize some rulers and events) and from the left (he was charged with monarchism, preaching the status quo, and defending serfdom). His methodology was also criticized (too much credulity toward the chronicles) as was his "style" (a mix of barbarisms with Slavonicisms). The intensity of the polemic was linked to the fact that Karamzin had provided his contemporaries with something Russia had never liked: a compromise, a balancing act (in the spirit of the Age of Enlightenment) in which on the one hand, an enlightened monarchy was opposed to selfish oligarchy and the blind madness of the crowd, and on the other, to tyranny. In this work patriotism mixes with historical skepticism, monarchism with the republican cult of civic virtue, Enlightenment didacticism with Romantic imagination, the role of a loyal subject with the position of an independent and honest free citizen, poetic history with a professional historian's pedanticism, modern Russian with archaisms, "sentimentality" with " sobriety." It is characteristic that the main focus of criticism was not the *History* itself but rather the Dedication and Introduction that preceded the first volume. Let us examine the main points Karamzin makes there and their cultural resonance:

1. *"History belongs to the Tsar."* These words taken from the Dedication unquestionably reflect the author's monarchist views. In 1818 they elicited the anger of young radicals who saw in them an expression of servility. "History belongs to the people" retorted one of the Russian Jacobins. At the same time, the meaning of the Dedication is clarified by the moment at which it was written: November 8, 1816. Three months before, the Holy Alliance of Christian monarchs, the crowning glory of Alexander's historical mission, had been concluded. The Emperor saw the Holy Alliance as the beginning of a new era of Christian brotherhood of tsars and their peoples. From this mystical monarchist point of view Russian history seemed parochial. At this period the Emperor avoided all expressions of national feeling (in August 1816, for example, he refused to visit the battlefield of Borodino, that "holy" site of the war of 1812). Thus, in the Dedication and Introduction Karamzin was reminding the Tsar-Victor to pay attention to his people and his nation's history. But by 1818, when the first volume was actually published, Alexander's reputation in Russian educated society had been severely

tarnished and Karamzin's words sounded like an expression of ultra-monarchism.
2. *"History is, in a certain sense, the holy book of a people."* This was Karamzin's favorite thought. Earlier he had formulated it even more drastically: "what the Bible is for Christians, history is for peoples." In the context of the second half of the 1810s these words sounded like an attempt to present national history as a sacred text which expresses the creative work of the past, contains "the legacy of our ancestors to contemporaries," "explains the present and provides examples for the future." As a result, the historian is not so much a dispassionate chronicler as an explicator of the past and, to an extent, a prophet of the future.
3. *History is useful.* In the first place, the historian insists, leaders and lawmakers need to learn from historical examples to understand their people and guide their passions in the name of tranquility and happiness insofar as these are achievable in this world. Second, history is necessary for average citizens because it inures them to "the imperfection of the visible order of things" which has ever been the case. History consoles the average citizen in difficult times, telling him that catastrophes occurred in the past but the state was not destroyed. History feeds the moral feeling of the citizen and "leads him to act fairly." This preaching of the status quo infuriated Russian Jacobins.
4. *History is pleasurable.* Karamzin, always a literary writer, saw history as a kind of voyage through the past, which should give the reader pleasure and aesthetic nourishment. History stimulates the imagination: "History, opening graves, raising the dead, giving life to their hearts and putting words in their mouths, recreating kingdoms from the dust and putting before the mind's eye a series of epochs with their distinguishing passions, mores, and actions, expands the bounds of our own existence...through its creative power we live with people of past ages, see and hear them, love and hate them." This manifesto of historical illusionism was picked up by Russian writers and artists. Pushkin, developing Karamzin's thought and answering his critics, wrote: "History belongs to the poet!"
5. In the family of European nations Russia has her own history, of which she can and should be proud. *"Either all of Modern History must remain silent or Russian history has the right to be heard."* Thus, according to Karamzin, reading history feeds patriotic feelings and leads to the moral development of citizens. This thesis was welcomed by young patriots, but Karamzin's insistence that Russia's historical development was driven by autocracy evoked their anger.

6. *"Love for the fatherland"* gives the historian's brush *"passion, power, and beauty. Where there is no love there is no soul."* According to Karamzin, the historian had to be a talented writer and a moral, sensitive person. In his *History* he creates a powerful image of the historian-narrator (the implied author): an honest citizen, a passionate observer of the past who is yet able to restrain that passion in the interests of creating an objective narration and interpretation. The image of the Historian became an important component of Russian literary mythology in the first third of the nineteenth century.
7. *"The human soul is the only immortal thing in this world!"* According to Karamzin, the ever-moving narrative of history is in fact a story about the eternal – the human soul and its moral quest. This moral-spiritual plane was at the center of a programmatic speech he gave in December 1818 at the Russian Academy of Sciences ("everything for the soul!"). This view of history appears in modified form in the work of both Zhukovsky and Pushkin and, later, in Tolstoy's *War and Peace*.

From the point of view of genre, *History of the Russian State* is a heterogeneous work: it is simultaneously a "scholarly" (in the understanding of the period) investigation based on a critical reading of sources, a philosophical work (in the spirit of the Enlightenment and early Romanticism), and a literary composition, written "in powerful and colorful" language and creating the illusion of resurrecting the past. Karamzin's work stands at the beginning of a peculiar Russian "obsession with history" (in the words of Andrew Baruch Wachtel),[7] which is a distinguishing feature of Russian culture of the nineteenth and twentieth centuries. The main lines of Russian historiosophy and, more generally, social thought – grew out of the polemic surrounding Karamzin's *History*: Does Russia have a creative role to play in history? What is the connection between the past and present? Where did the Russian state come from and what form of government did the original Russians have (the Novgorod Republic or the Muscovite autocracy)? Does Russia need serious reform or are major changes destructive? Should the historian strive for truth, even if it is unpleasant, or is his task to support national pride through a conscious mythologization of the past? What moves history – God, tsars, or the people? What should the relationship between scholarship and artistry be in a historical narrative? From Karamzin's *History* we can see a straight path to the Romantic historiosophy of Zhukovsky, the historical skepticism of Petr Chaadaev, the Westernizing notions of Vissarion Belinsky and Alexander Herzen (1812–70), the Slavophile approach of Ivan Aksakov (1823–86), the "state centered" methodology of Konstantin Kavelin (1818–85), the "democratic" historiography of Nikolai Kostomarov (1817–85), the anarchistic historicism of Tolstoy (*War and Peace*), and the mystic history of Vladimir Solovev and the Russian religious philosophers of the turn of the twentieth century.

The History of the Russian State also became a *national historical source book* for Russian literature and art. Russian nineteenth-century authors were attracted by the fact that Karamzin treated in great detail the pre-Petrine period – the culture that Peter and his successors had repressed, thereby creating, in their view, insoluble conflicts in the present. Though they read the entire work avidly, contemporaries were most influenced by the later volumes, the writer's greatest achievement: his narration of the evil deeds of Ivan the Terrible (the tsar-tyrant, "scourge of mankind"), the meek Tsar Fedor Ioanovich, the wise Boris Godunov who was punished by Providence for killing the young heir to the throne. The "Karamzinian legacy" in Russian literature includes historical lyrics (the "Meditations" of Ryleev, the historical-political ballads of Pushkin, Nikolai Iazykov [1803–47], Pavel Katenin [1792–1853]), Mikhail Lermontov's (1814–42) Romantic poem "The Song about Tsar Ivan Vasilievich and the Young Oprichnik and Brave Merchant Kalashnikov"), drama (Pushkin's *Boris Godunov*, Kiukhelbeker's *Prokopy Liapunov* (1834), Alexei Khomiakov's slavophile-inflected *Yermak* [1826], the historico-mystic trilogy about Tsar Boris [1867–70] by Alexei Konstantinovich Tolstoy [1817–75], among others), painting (the unfinished "Siege of Pskov" [1836–7] by the Romantic Karl Briullov, "Ivan the Terrible and his Son" [1885] by Ilya Repin), opera (*Boris Godunov* by Modest Musorgsky, *The Maid of Pskov* [1873] and *The Tsar's Bride* [1898] by Nikolai Rimsky-Korsakov, and *Prince Igor* of Borodin) and, eventually, film (Sergei Eisenstein's *Ivan the Terrible*, 1944–5).

Pushkin wrote that "Karamzin, it appears, discovered Old Rus' as Columbus had discovered America."[8] To extend the comparison, we could say that Karamzin's opening up of Russia's past led to its colonization by an exceptionally broad range of philosophers, writers, and artists.

Literary Work – Ruslan and Liudmila by Alexander Pushkin

One of the most important tasks facing the young Russian Europeanized literary tradition was the creation of a national epic poem capable of expressing the essence of the nation and its historical fate. According to neo-classical genre notions, the appearance of such a work was a sign that a national literary tradition had matured to the point of being considered a peer of the developed European traditions. At the beginning of the nineteenth century, most Russians expected that such a work would be created based either on an imitation of the classical or neo-classical heroic epic (Virgil's *Aeneid* or Voltaire's *Henriade*) or on a model derived from the chivalric fairy-tale poem in which historical figures and events mixed with fantasical elements (*Orlando Furioso* of Ariosto or Wieland's *Oberon*). Many attempts were made (from the heroic poem *Pozharsky, Minin, Hermogen, or the Salvation of Russia* [1807] of Prince S. A. Shirinsky-Shikhmatov to Karamzin's unfinished "Ilya Muromets"), but all were unsuccessful. In 1810, Vasily Zhukovsky tried to write "Vladimir" set at the time of the Christianization of Rus' and based on a combination of Russian folk epics, the *Primary Chronicle* and his own imagination, but he also failed to complete the work. Instead, he produced "The Twelve Sleeping Maidens, A Story in Two Ballads" (1811–16), in the second, mystical part of which a "pure" Russian knight awakens twelve enchanted (and enchanting) sleeping virgins and enters into a heavenly marriage with one of them. This Romantic work canonized the theme of Platonic love in Russian literature and was rather popular, but it did not answer the need for a Russian national poem.

In the second half of the 1810s, Zhukovsky's young admirer Alexander Pushkin, the rising star of Russian poetry, began to compete with his erstwhile mentor, and in the years between 1818 and 1820 he wrote his magic poem *Ruslan and Liudmila*, a work he had been contemplating since 1815. The poem was created in the bubbling literary and intellectual cauldron of Saint Petersburg, where the young poet was an active participant in many literary and cultural undertakings: the "war on Parnassus" between the opponents of Zhukovsky's Romanticism and its supporters (Arzamas), debates about national history stimulated by the appearance of the first volumes of Karamzin's *History*, political discussions in the "secret" Union of Prosperity. In this period Pushkin wrote numerous elegies, parodies, epigrams, and political invective, all of which circulated rapidly in the hot-house atmosphere of the capital. He became a celebrity, acquired the reputation of the enfant terrible of Petersburg society, and ended up exiled from the capital by order of the Emperor himself. *Ruslan and Liudmila* was published when its author was far away from the capital, but its appearance marks the beginning of his countrywide fame.

Ruslan and Liudmila was the capstone not merely of an important period in the life and literary reputation of Pushkin, but also in the history of Russian literature and its cultural mythology. This dynamic, playful long poem is a monument to the era of the Russian poetic renaissance of the first two decades of the nineteenth century, with its literary battles, political opposition, and Romantic strivings for national specificity. It is also one of the relatively few truly joyous and light-hearted works of Russian literature, which has tended more toward satiric sarcasm or moralizing disapproval than to insouciant laughter.

Ruslan and Liudmila is written in iambic tetrameter (Pushkin's favorite meter) and consists of six sections. The action of the work occurs during the reign of Prince Vladimir of Kiev. Nevertheless, the Russianness of the poem is thoroughly conventional: although a number of episodes are borrowed from Russian fairy tales, the basic story (the kidnapping of a beautiful woman and her subsequent rescue by the knightly hero) is traditional for Western chivalric romances and fairy-tale epics. In Pushkin's day this basic story line was used frequently in magic poems and operas (Mozart's *Magic Flute*, for example). The story line is as follows (unfortunately, our paraphrase destroys the capricious plot turns of the original, which give the narrative much of its character):

> Great Prince Vladimir's daughter is marrying the brave Prince Ruslan. Boyan (the bard of Kiev) is singing a wedding song. After the wedding feast as the newlyweds are heading for their bedchamber a sudden thunderclap is heard and an "unknown force" carries off the young bride. The inconsolable father blames Ruslan for his inability to protect his wife and calls on his knights to search for the young woman. He promises to marry her to whichever knight can find her and to give him half of his kingdom. Ruslan sets off to search, as do his rivals: the passionate Khazar Khan Ratmir, the grim warrior Rogdai, and the boastful Farlaf.
>
> In his travels Ruslan meets the old wizard Finn, who tells him that his wife was kidnapped by the great sorcerer Chernomor, who lives in the distant and inaccessible north and has a habit of stealing beautiful young ladies (though due to his age he is no danger to their honor). Finn predicts that Ruslan will defeat his foe and be united with his wife. He also tells Ruslan the story of his own unhappy love for the beautiful Naina. Many years ago she spurned his love and in his grief he turned to magic in order to change her mind. Having spent many years mastering the magic arts Finn managed to cause her to fall in love with him, but by then she was a seventy-year old witch and he fled from her and her love.
>
> In the meantime, Liudmila wakes on a luxurious canopy bed. She is waited upon by beautiful girls in diaphanous clothing, while merry songs from an unseen singer waft through the air. In the garden outside are exotic trees, "diamond fountains," beautiful statues which seem almost alive. It is all like something out of 1001 Nights. But nothing can console Liudmila. She looks outside and sees depressing northern landscapes which do not gladden the

eye (but do remind the reader of Petersburg). Chernomor, accompanied by his armed moors enters. He is a disgusting bald dwarf with a long beard (the source of his strength, it turns out) and a tall hat. Scared by Liudmila's screams, this Slavic sorcerer runs away only to get tangled in his beard. In the ensuing chaos she manages to steal his cap of invisibility and now the kidnapper can no longer find her.

The gloomy Rogdai, filled with "useless envy" attacks Ruslan but Ruslan defeats him and throws his body into the Dnepr River where it becomes a trophy for a lascivious necrophilic naiad. Ratmir, who had headed off toward the south, is imprisoned in a castle filled with beautiful girls. They seduce the Khan, who forgets all about Liudmila.

Ruslan must surmount many obstacles. He battles with a disembodied head guarded by a charmed sword, and defeats Chernomor after a two-day battle. But the traitorous Farlaf kills Ruslan and proclaims himself Liudmila's deliverer. Fortunately, Finn arrives with some magic water that brings Ruslan back to life. He rushes to Kiev but his reunion with his bride is again delayed, this time by a horde of nomadic warriors who are besieging the city. The hero puts them to flight, enters Kiev in glory and removes the spell with which Chernomor had enchanted his bride. The happy father forgives the guilty Farlaf, and allows the now powerless Chernomor to remain at his court. It all ends with a feast and the happy couple's marriage is finally consummated.

Pushkin's poem was incredibly popular with readers, but contemporary reviewers were of two minds. Critics of Pushkin's generation and circle welcomed the poem as a manifesto of new, Romantic art (which they understood in terms of irony, national specificity, and the rejection of neo-classical norms). Older critics as well as some young members of the liberal opposition, found many deficiencies: the poem lacked any higher purpose, was a cacophony of genres and styles, was vulgar, mocked authority, did not contain "higher feelings," was immoral, immature, and silly. These accusations were consistent with the image of the poem's author and resonated with Pushkin's negative reputation in some circles – he was a talented joker with an unbridled imagination and unhealthy inclinations. In the apt formulation of a recent critic, the poem's opponents "could not figure out the author's point of view, but they recognized that irony had supplanted moralizing" (Lotman). Indeed, "pointless" parody of contemporary literature is pervasive in *Ruslan and Liudmila*: Pushkin gores the oxen of "Slavophiles" and Westernizers, the Platonic Romanticism of Zhukovsky, the neo-classical theatre of Ozerov, and Karamzin's conservative historiography. "High" and "low" styles are juxtaposed throughout, various neo-classical genres mix and seemingly mock one another: ode and elegy, ballad and idyll, chivalric poetry and fairy-tale opera.

By itself this sort of technique is not Pushkin's invention. *Ruslan and Liudmila* derives from a well-known tradition: the libertine "poésie fugitive" of Parny, Western and Russian mock-epic poems (Pope, Voltaire, Vasily Maikov [1728–78]), jocular "magic" epics (Ariosto) and fairy tales (*Dushenka* [1783] of Ippolit Bogdanovich). However, the artistic ideology of Pushkin's poem differs in important ways from its precursors. They had served not to erase but rather to enforce immutable laws of genre and style. Pushkin's work, on the other hand, is characterized by a Romantic irony, which functions to destroy traditional, normative ideas of the artistic word, and to emphasize the conventionality of literature. This mockery of evil and powerless sorcerers (both fairy-tale necromancers and contemporary mystics) is magic not merely in genre (marked by abundant fantastic elements) but also in form: it is a kind of "incantation by laughter," a poetic spell, through which a new poetic language is created from various unrelated ingredients.

Pushkin's central hero (and his main invention), who links this heterogeneous material, is the Poet-Narrator. He observes the heroes from a distance, appeals to the reader's sentiments and experience (the frequent turn to "my readers" would become one of Pushkin's trademarks), deviates constantly from the main narrative line, jumps from "ancient legends" to contemporary topics, piques the reader's imagination with seductive images thereby inducing a feeling of being present in the work, frustrates the reader's expectations, draws him into a game of hints and jokes filled with double and triple entendres to create a kind of matreshka-doll text that still attracts scholars wishing to unpack it.

Although many contemporaries faulted *Ruslan and Liudmila* for its lack of a coherent "message," the poem is quite tendentious in a way. Its ideology is organically anti-patriarchal. The central opposition is between old age and youth, with the latter having a clear positive valence: it is associated with elan vital, action, courage, lightness, and earthly rather than Platonic love. The latter, on the other hand, is linked with treachery, tyranny, malevolence, and weakness. This cult of youth is quite typical for Russian literature of this period, and distinguishes it from works like *The Magic Flute* with its celebration of wise old masons. One modern-day critic sees the anti-patriarchal jokes as subtle political and oppositional jibes (Chernomor's northern kingdom as Petersburg): *Ruslan and Liudmila* is "in fact irreverently and hilariously anti-imperial."[9]

Even the poem's eroticism carries a marked literary-parodic valence. Thus, one of the most famous seduction scenes is a parody of Zhukovsky's ballad about the awakening of the twelve sleeping maidens. In Pushkin's poem, the locale where the tender Ratmir discovers the twelve princesses and forgets all about Liudmila turns out to be some sort of harem or even perhaps a brothel. Pushkin is not only making fun of Zhukovsky's Platonic lyrical philosophy, but also of his biographical image: the older poet was, after all, spending most of his time in the fairy-tale atmosphere of Pavlovsk, the residence of the small "female" court of the Queen Mother, in the company of her ladies-in-waiting to whom he addressed many tender poems. On Good Friday, March 26, 1820 Pushkin read his still unpublished poem to Zhukovsky. In response the latter gave him his portrait with a jocular, though loaded inscription: "to the conquering student from the vanquished teacher on that high and solemn day when he finished his poem *Ruslan and Liudmila.*"

In August 1820, Emperor Alexander sent Pushkin into exile. As if lockstep with this event Pushkin wrote a biographical epilogue to *Ruslan and Liudmila*, hinting at his misfortune. This epilogue revises the tone of the poem: in hindsight it allows for an interpretation of the work as a nostalgic elegy to a happy and insouciant period – an important part of Pushkin's biographical myth would be formed by his period of exile. Pushkin compares himself to Ovid, who had, coincidentally, been sent into exile to the same region by Emperor Augustus some 1800 years earlier. The opposition age-youth in Pushkin's poetry is supplanted by another, Ovidian opposition of a carefree "then" and an unhappy "now." In his enchanting novel in verse *Eugene Onegin*, which can be considered in many ways as a continuation of the line of *Ruslan and Liudmila*, the happy days of youth are described as a kind of paradise lost.

In 1828, Pushkin returned to his early poem. He wrote a Prologue, which is a charming variation on themes from Russian fairy tales. The Prologue reflects the poet's new-found Romantic interest in Russian folklore as an expression of the national spirit (in the beginning of the 1830s he would write a series of brilliant verse fairy tales as well). This new material lends the poem the character of a folk song: "By the shore's a green oak tree . . . There's a Russian soul there, it smells of Rus'." At the same time the careful reader of the late 1820s might guess at a cunning authorial mystification in these lines and find not so much the sort of "Russian soul" that the ideologues of Nicholas I wanted to inculcate as a free and jocular "soul of literature."

In 1837 Mikhail Glinka, the father of modern Russian classical music, finished an operatic version of *Ruslan and Liudmila*. The idea for this five-act magic opera had been discussed during Pushkin's lifetime, but the libretto was written after his death. Only the most basic situations of Pushkin's story were retained: the kidnapping, the quests, the liberation and awakening of Liudmila. The opera eliminates Rogdai, gives Ratmir a wife, replaces the "historical" Vladimir with the invented king Svetozar, and enlarges the role of Naina. The action is presented linearly, without the zigzags and digressions so characteristic of Pushkin's poem, the irony is almost completely eliminated, and an aria is added for the tenth-century bard Boyan in which he predicts the appearance of Petersburg, where, Boyan tells us, a young poet would some day sing of Ruslan and Liudmila on his golden lyre.

Glinka's opera is a late Romantic work, filled with elegiac nostalgia (for the deep past, the happy world of fairy tales, and also for Pushkin), Romantic nationalism (we hear musical expressions of national spirit not only of Russia but also of Persia [the "Persian Chorus" of Ratmir] and of Finland [Finn's aria]), and philosophical meditation characteristic for the metaphysical strivings of the 1830s. The opera's premiere took place at Petersburg's Bolshoi theatre on November 27, 1842. Juxtaposing the two *Ruslans* allows us to appreciate the enormous changes that had taken place in Russia's cultural life in the twenty or so years between the writing of the poem and the staging of the opera: the poem expresses the life-affirming atmosphere of the friendly circles. Glinka's opera conveys the dreamy and somewhat hermetic mood of the more inward looking intellectual circles of the late 1830s and early 1840s.

The fate of *Ruslan and Liudmila* was similar to that of many of Pushkin's works: it entered the national literary canon where it quickly dissolved into fodder for school readers (particularly the "folksy" fairy tale segments such as the Prologue or Ruslan's battle with the head). It also became standard children's reading, though with several excisions. In 1972 the Mosfilm studios released a bad film by the good director A. L. Ptushko, in which Pushkin's poem was turned into a patriotic epos about glorious Russian heroes battling foreign invaders. The popular reaction to this patriotic sovietization of Pushkin's poem was predictable: it was ridiculed in such genres as schoolboy folklore ("By the shore they've chopped the oak down") to literary parody, as in the song of the famous Soviet-era bard Vladimir Vysotsky (1938–80) entitled "The magic shore has disappeared":

> So, this is no longer a secret
> There's no more Fairy Land.
> Everything the poet wrote about
> is nonsense.

4

The Russian Idea: The Quest for National Identity in Nineteenth-Century Russian Culture

I

On August 30, 1834, ceremonies on St. Petersburg's Palace Square marked the unveiling of the Alexander Column, erected by Emperor Nicholas I in memory of his brother's triumph over Napoleon. The column was taller than its classical predecessors, the columns of Trajan and Pompei, and it surpassed the Vendome column in Paris, which had been erected to honor the Russian tsar's great opponent. This new obelisk, created according to the plan of the French architect Auguste de Montferrand, was crowned with a sculpture by the Russian artist Boris Orlovsky depicting an angel with features that recall those of the late emperor. In its right hand the angel holds a cross, while its left hand is raised to the heavens. The Alexander column was not only a monument to the emperor but also to the heroic age associated with his name, an age in which Russia reached unheard of heights of glory. The monument also marked the end of the Alexandrine period. The new reign, which had begun in 1825 with the suppression of the Decembrist Rebellion, engendered a new political and cultural scenario. Alexander's cosmopolitanism, which saw Russia as part of the family of Christian nations, had been replaced by a project devoted to the perfection of the national state, capable of standing alone to protect itself from the whirlwind of a Europe swept by new revolutions.

Vasily Zhukovsky, the court poet and tutor to the crown prince, expressed this idea clearly in his description of the celebrations surrounding the unveiling of the Alexander Column: "Russia, having taken all that is rightfully hers, not dangerous to the outside world though an implacable and indestructible enemy, not the scourge but the guardian of the Europe that gave birth to her, has entered today a new and great period of her existence, a period of internal development, of the firm rule of law, and of the calm attainment of all the treasures of social life." "Like a fertilized field," he continued, "she seethes with the life that has been thrown into her depths, and is ready to produce a rich harvest of civil goods for the autocracy that

7 Alexander Column, St. Petersburg. Built between 1830 and 1834 by the architect August de Montferrand and topped by a statue designed by Boris Orlovsky, the Alexander Column dominates the Palace Square in front of the Winter Palace. The tallest monument of its kind in the world, it is dedicated to Alexander I and his victory over Napoleon in the campaign of 1812.

created and fortified her." The era of bloody wars, unbridled uprisings (from the Decembrists' coup d'etat to the war with the Ottoman Empire of 1828–9 to the Polish revolt of 1830–1) and even natural cataclysms (the cholera epidemic of 1831) was over; strict political order, solid legislation, and stability had been established in Russia as exemplified in Russia's strong monarch, and the age of self-sufficient national development had begun.

The official concept of the new Russian ideology had been proposed by S. S. Uvarov [1786–1855] in 1832. It rested on three inseparable ideas: orthodoxy, autocracy, and nationality (the trio was apparently a version of the traditional Russian military creed: "For the Faith, the Tsar, and the Fatherland," modernized in the spirit of German idealistic philosophy). Uvarov understood orthodoxy as the people's religion, the basis for morality and patriotism. Autocracy was seen as the optimal system for political order in Russia, the central condition for her political existence. By the third component of the trinity, Uvarov had in mind the historical legends, mores, and habits that made up the character of the people. Uvarov's doctrine, which historians came to call "Official Nationality," was conservative and defensive at base. It was an attempt to halt, or at least neutralize the ever-strengthening ideological influence of Western Europe, as well as put under official control potentially dangerous alternative nationalist models. This ideology was enforced through strict ideological control by the Ministry of Education over schools, textbooks (especially history textbooks), and a redoubled censorship of books and periodicals. It also led to government support for those historians who described Russia's past from a monarchist point of view (N. G. Ustrialov, M. P. Pogodin) and for patriotic art. The literary model of the latter became Nestor Kukolnik's (1809–68) historical drama *The Hand of the Almighty Saved the Fatherland, 1834* (Ruka Vsevyshnego otechestvo spasla), which celebrated autocracy as the perfect embodiment of the hopes of the Russian people.

But the idea of a new, self-sufficient period of Russian history appealed to a wider circle than the Tsar and his acolytes. The search for a national idea was a central concern for Russian Romantic thought of the mid-1820s (German culture had lived through a similar period in the preceding decade). From that time forward, and continuing until the present day, attempts to formulate a "national idea" have been a favorite parlor game of Russian intellectuals. To be sure, endeavors of this sort had been made even before the reign of Nicholas: one could point to the doctrine of Moscow as the Third Rome, and ideas about the resurrection of Constantinople that animated Catherine the Great's regime. But if previous definitions of the national idea had been the prerogative of state institutions or individuals who had the Tsar's ear, what changed in the 1830s was that Russian "educated society" in general got involved in the project of nation building. Debates about Russia, her particularity, the direction and goals of her development, began to be discussed in aristocratic salons and gentlemen's clubs, among university students, and in the editorial offices of journals. To a great extent the passion that animated these arguments can be explained by the particularities of Russia's historico-cultural situation: the enormous cultural divide between the educated, Westernized (to one extent or another) class and the majority of the nation; the dissatisfaction of a significant portion of the intelligentsia with the secular and state-oriented Russian culture that had been created during the reigns of Peter and Catherine; a sense of cultural isolation (neither West nor East) and a concomitant desire to reconnect with a lost organic whole; the fact of modern Russian culture's indebtedness to Western European culture coupled with the belief in Russia's uniqueness and special mission.

Rancorous arguments about national specificity and the particular paths of Russia's development formed the substrate on which most major developments in Russian nineteenth-century culture took place: national prose (from Pushkin to Tolstoy and Dostoevsky), theatre (from Gogol to Ostrovsky), music (from Glinka and Dargomyzhsky to Musorgsky and Rimsky-Korsakov), and visual art (from Briullov and Ivanov to Perov and Repin). In the sections that follow we highlight the most characteristic and influential of the national ideas formulated between the 1830s and 1870s.

II

In 1836 the journal *Telescope* published a *Philosophical Letter* (Filosoficheskoe pis'mo) by Petr Chaadaev. Written in 1829, it was part of a cycle of tracts devoted to Russia and her anomalous position in human history. The letter was addressed to an educated Russian woman who had complained that she was tormented by doubts and inexplicable anxiety. In the author's response, this seemingly personal psychological state is described as natural for Russian society, which finds itself stuck in the "emptiness of social experience." The reasons for this national apathy lie in the depths of Russia's past. The history of humankind, in Chaadaev's view, is controlled by the law of Providence, which is invisibly leading the world to its goal – the creation of God's kingdom on earth. Russia's tragedy is that, having accepted Christianity from Byzantium, she cut herself off from

Western civilization, Catholic at base, which is secretly doing the work of Providence. As a result, Russia finds herself outside the historical process.

"Our history," says Chaadaev, "is not connected to anything, explains nothing, proves nothing." Peter's Westernizing program did not lead Russia to true Enlightenment. From their triumphal march through the enlightened countries in Europe in 1813–14, the Russians brought back "only bad ideas and disastrous errors" which led to the calamitous events of December 1825. It appears that in the Russian makeup there "is something that resists all true progress." The only salvation, according to Chaadaev, is for Russia to return to the "universal work" of "developing the human race" which is being carried out by the Western nations. The contemporary state of the nation is emphasized by the symbolism of the place from which the letter was said to be written – not Moscow but Necropolis, the land of the dead.[1]

Nevertheless, at the same time, the future greatness of Russia, which is called to "unite in our civilization the history of the entire globe," is already implicitly present in the exaggeratedly pessimistic tone of the letter. As the law of Providence has a universal character, this means, for Chaadaev, if Russia has not done anything for the world there is a hint that she has not *yet* fulfilled her destiny. In other words, Chaadaev's historiosophical conception contains a sort of negative messianism quite typical for Russian religious thought; the proof of future greatness is the nullity of the present (another example of this sort of theology is the first, satiric, volume of Gogol's *Dead Souls*, on which the writer was working in the second half of the 1830s). In the philosophical letters that followed this one, Chaadaev developed his idea about Russia's future in great detail. But he only managed to publish the first letter.

The appearance of Chaadaev's work had the effect of a bomb blast. The journal was immediately shut down, the censor who had allowed its publication was fired, the journal's editor was exiled to the north, and Chaadaev was declared mad by the Emperor himself. This "insane" criticism of Russian history drew a terse response from A. Kh. Benkendorff, chief of the secret police: "Russia's past was amazing, her present is more than spectacular. As for her future, it is greater than can be drawn by the most powerful imagination."[2] Patriotically inclined readers accused Chaadaev of crazy enmity and slander toward Russia, of apostasy and Catholic proselytizing. Alexander Pushkin, who to a great extent agreed with the critical pathos of his friend, nevertheless could not agree with his thesis regarding the poverty and meaninglessness of Russian history: "Russia's awakening, the development of her power, her movement toward unity (toward Russian unity, of course) . . . can this really be called a pale and half forgotten dream. And Peter the Great, who himself embodies universal history! And Catherine, who brought Russia to Europe's threshold? And Alexander who brought us to Paris?"³

The polemic around Chaadaev brought to the fore two opposing positions that would for many years determine the character of Russian national thought: the Slavophile and the Westernizer. Both groups agreed with the Moscow philosopher that contemporary Russia, celebrated in official ideology and art, was not what it should be. But they disagreed on the topic whither Russia.

III

According to the views of the Slavophiles (A. S. Khomiakov, the brothers P. V. and I. V. Kireevsky, the brothers K. S and I. S. Aksakov, Iu. F. Samarin), Russian culture was different from Western culture because it had grown up on its own religious and social foundation. The attempt by Peter the Great to inculcate Western values and political forms (individualism, rationality, legality, and empire) had been a huge error. Russia's salvation, in their view, was not in a return to European culture (which the Slavophiles considered spent) but in a restoration of pre-Petrine patriarchal values. The Slavophiles viewed the peasant commune as the ideal social form for Russia. "A commune, – wrote K. S. Aksakov [1817–60], – is a union of the people who have renounced their egoism, their individuality, and who express their common accord; this is an act of love, a noble Christian act . . . in the commune the individual is not lost, but renounces his exclusiveness in favor of the general accord – and there arises the noble phenomenon of a harmonious, joint existence of rational beings (consciousness); there arises a brotherhood, a commune – a triumph of the human spirit."⁴

The following chart, based on an 1852 article "On the Nature of European Culture and Its Relation to the Culture of Russia" by Ivan Kireevsky (1806–56), one of the intellectual leaders of the Slavophile movement, provides an indication of how the Slavophiles viewed the dichotomy Russia – The West.

The West	**Ancient Russian culture (since 988)**
Roman Catholic Church	Orthodox Church
Theology became a matter of abstract logic	Theology retained the integrity of the Orthodox world's spirit
Fragmentation of the forces of the mind	Every effort to maintain them as a living whole

A search for the truth by establishing a logical sequence of concepts	. . . by concentration of spirit
A search for an external, dead unity	A striving toward an inner, living essence
The Church mingled with the state, uniting spiritual with temporal power and merging the ecclesiastical and the secular in a system of a mixed character	The Church remained aloof from worldly institutions and purposes
Scholasticism and law in the universities	Higher learning cultivated in the monasteries, in the midst of prayers
A scholastic and logical approach to the higher verities	An endeavor to grasp them spontaneously and completely
Pagan [Roman] and Christian civilization grow into one another	A constant effort is made to keep the [Christian] truth pure
Statehood is the result of violent conquest	State arose through the natural development of popular customs based on the unity of fundamental belief
A hostile separation of estates	Estates united in purpose of maintaining their natural differences
Land ownership is the basis of civil relationships	Society based not on private property to which persons were attached, but on persons to whom property was attached [the commune decides]
Law is built on formal logic, i.e. artificial	Law grows out of local custom, i.e. natural
The appearance of justice	The essence of justice
Codification of laws along logical lines	The link between legal doctrine and the precepts of faith and custom
Improvements are always effected by means of violent change	They occur through natural harmonious growth
The turbulence of the party spirit	The steadfastness of basic conviction
The whim of fashion	The stability of a way of life
The precariousness of individual willfulness	The solidity of family and social ties
Luxury and artificiality	Simplicity of needs and moral fortitude. The ideal of "holy fool" – an ascetic wanderer venerated by the common people.
The ideal of beauty is founded on the lies of the imagination. A tendency toward effeminacy, fancifulness, theatricality	An inner wholeness of being is essential not only for cognition of the truth but also for full esthetic enjoyment.

An inner anxiety coupled with an intellectual conviction of virtue	A profound tranquility of the inner self, coupled with constant self-mistrust and the incessant striving for moral improvement.[5]

In a word, Western culture, according to Kireevsky, represents ratiocination and dichotomy in all of its aspects, while ancient Russian culture demonstrates intelligence and integrity. Why, then, did the latter not develop more richly than the former? The answer is the will of Providence and the fatal mistake of Westernization made by Peter and the Russian ruling class. What is to be done? Educated Russians should throw off the yoke of Western logical systems, study Russia's past and, following "the special, living, integral philosophy of the Holy Fathers of the Church," develop Russian life on native principles. Characteristically, the future Russia in Kireevsky's vision is associated, first and foremost, with the flourishing of the arts, "growing from native roots" (207). Whether Kireevsky's philosophical dichotomies are correct is questionable. What is certain, however, is that they helped nineteenth-century Russian art to define its mission. One may easily find Kireevsky's analytical "roots" in Tolstoy's *War and Peace,* with its militant anti-rationalism and peaceful organicism, and in his philosophy of Christian (i.e. unifying and moral) art ("What is Art?" [Chto takoe iskusstvo], 1890); in Musorgsky's *Boris Godunov,* with its musical elevation of the voice of common Russian people; or in Dostoevsky's novels with their debates on ecclesiastical vs. secular justice, their accent on spiritual values, and passionate search for the essence of Russianness.

The government of Nicholas I viewed the Slavophile ideology with deep distrust, seeing it as a dangerous competitor to "official nationality." As a result, the Slavophiles had difficulty spreading their ideas in the print media. It was only in the late 1840s and early 1850s that they managed to publish some programmatic articles in the journal *The Muscovite* (Moskvitianin) and to bring out three self-standing collections of essays.

The late 1840s and early 1850s saw the rise of a movement related to Slavophilism: Pan-Slavism. If the Slavophiles looked for salvation in a return to the nation's roots, then the Pan-Slavists saw Russia's destiny in the realization of her "historic mission," the union in a single Orthodox empire of all the Slavic peoples under the rule of the Ottoman Empire. The result of this spiritual and political expansion would be a Slavic or even universal Empire envisioned in Fedor Tiutchev's (1803–73) exalted poem "A Russian Geography":

> Moscow and Peter's town, the city of Constantine,
> these are the cherished capitals of the Russian monarchy.
> But where is their limit? And where are their frontiers
> to the north, the east, the south and the setting sun?
> The Fates will reveal them to the future generations.
>
> Seven internal seas and seven great rivers
> from the Nile to the Neva, from the Elbe to China,
> from the Volga to the Euphrates, the Ganges to the Danube,
> This is the Russian empire and it will never pass away,
> just as the Spirit foretold and Daniel prophesied
>
> (1848 or 1849; trans. F. Jude)

The propagator of Pan-Slavism, Tiutchev, a diplomat who also happened to be one of Russia's greatest lyric poets, saw the Crimean War (1853–56) between Russia and a coalition of European nations supporting the Ottomans as an apocalyptic battle of Slavdom against the forces of the West. Russia's defeat in this war was a great shock for the Pan-Slav ideologues. A second wave of Pan-Slavic enthusiasm would come in the late 1870s in answer to the national union of the "Germanic world" and the Russo-Turkish War of 1877–8. Echoes of this second wave can be found in the final scenes of Tolstoy's *Anna Karenina* (1877), when the grieving Vronsky signs up to join the Russian volunteers heading off to fight in the Balkans.

The historian and naturalist Nikolai Danilevsky (1822–85) in his controversial tract "Russia and Europe: A Look at the Cultural and Political Relations of the Slavic World to the Romano-German World" (1869) formulated his theory of irreconcilable antagonism between the civilizations. This theory is based on the denial of any progress in history, which is seen as circular. Danilevesky distinguished several formative historical and cultural types. He also suggested that any nation as a cultural entity has its own stages: youth, adulthood, and senility. Danilevsky proclaimed that contemporary Western culture was reaching the end of its lifespan, whereas its Slavic counterpart had just reached its youth. The mission of Russia lies in the unification of the Slavic world with its capital in Constantinople. The Slavic nation, in his vision, is a collective Messiah.

Danilevsky's ideas had a deep impact on Dostoevsky, who gradually moved from his earlier nationalist ideas to his idea of the "Russian God," a vision of Russians as the chosen Christian nation. In his *The Devils* (Besy 1871–2), one of the most sympathetic characters, Shatov, takes the religious nationalism of the Slavophiles to an extreme:

> The purpose of every popular movement or motion, in every people and at every moment of its being, is, exclusively, the search for God; its own God, only its own . . . God is the synthetic personality of the whole people taken from its beginning until its end. There never had been one common God for all or many peoples, but each people had its own particular one. . . . When Gods are shared in common, then they die and the faith in them, together with the peoples themselves, also dies. The stronger the people, the more exclusive its God. There has never been a people without religion, that is, without the conception of good and evil and its own, unique, good and evil.

His renegade inspirer Stavrogin comments: "You have reduced God to a simple attribute of nationality." Shatov replies:

> Reduce God to an attribute of nationality? [. . .] on the contrary, I raise the people up to God. And could it be otherwise? The people is the body of God. Every people only remains such while it has its own God and while it rejects all other Gods in the world uncompromisingly; while it believes that with its God it will conquer and drive from the world all the other gods . . . A truly great people can never be reconciled to a secondary role amongst humanity, or even to a primary role, but only and exclusively to the first role . . . But truth is only one, and therefore, only one of the peoples can have the true God, even though the other peoples have their own great gods. The only "God-bearing" people is the Russian one . . .[6]

IV

The Slavophiles' opponents were the Westernizers, a term that united a group of intellectuals of the late 1830s and 1840s who shared the belief that Russia, whatever her particularities, was not a unique country developing according to some sort of special laws. It was a backward country but, thanks to Peter's reforms, it was now following the same path as civilized Europe. The Westernizers saw Russia's salvation not in a return to pre-Petrine social structures and not in a strict observance of Christian principles of social life, as the most influential writer of the day, Nikolai Gogol, proposed in his 1847 book of edifying essays (see the section on Gogol below), but rather in the creation of responsible and independent individuals, the formation of civil society, and in the social and economic modernization of the country. The forefather of this trend, the literary critic Vissarion Belinsky, formulated his vision of Russia's goals in his passionate letter to Gogol (1847):

> Russia sees her salvation not in mysticism or asceticism or pietism, but in the successes of civilization, enlightenment, and humanity. What she needs is not sermons (she has heard enough of them!) or prayers (she has repeated them too often!), but the awakening in the people of a sense of their human dignity lost for so many centuries amid dirt and refuse; she needs rights and laws conforming not to the preaching of the church but to common sense and justice, and their strictest possible observance. Instead of which she presents the dire spectacle of a country where men traffic in men, without even having the excuse so insidiously exploited by the American plantation owners who claim that the Negro is not a man; a country where people call themselves not by names but by nicknames such as Vanka, Vaska, Steshka, Palashka; a country where there are not only no guarantees for individuality, honor and property, but even no police order, and where there is nothing but vast corporations of official thieves and robbers of various descriptions. The most vital national problems in Russia today are the abolition of serfdom and corporal punishment and the strictest possible observance of at least those laws that already exist.[7]

Another prominent Westernizer, the writer and philosopher Alexander Herzen criticized the Slavophiles' negation of post-Petrine Russia:

> The whole Catherinian epoch, which our grandfathers remembered with a shake of their heads, and the entire Alexandrian period, which our fathers remembered with a shake of their heads, belong to what the Slavophiles call the "foreign period," for they consider everything educated as alien. They do not understand that the new Rus' was still Rus', they do not understand that with the Petrine break into two Russias our real history begins. For all that is grievous about this division, it is responsible for all we have – a bold state development, the emergence of Rus' on the scene as a political individuality, and the emergence of Russian individuals among the people. Russian thought becomes accustomed to express itself, literature appears, heterodoxy appears, questions trouble us, national poetry develops, from the songs of Kirsha Danilov to Pushkin.[8]

Like the Slavophiles, the Westernizers were never a group with a unified ideology or program. First and foremost, they were divided on the question of the tempo the process of modernization (Westernization) should take, from those favoring gradual reform (V. P. Botkin [1812–69], T. N. Granovsky [1813–55], Ivan Turgenev) to those believing in the complete destruction of the existing order (M. A. Bakunin [1814–76]). Nor did they agree on the question of religion. The idealist Westernizers (Granovsky, Botkin) argued passionately with the Westernizer materialists (Herzen, Bakunin), who saw the words "God and religion" as synonyms for "darkness, chains, and the whip" (as Belinsky put it). This difference of opinion ultimately led the

Westernizer movement to break into two streams, one liberal and the other radical (including socialist and later Marxist groupings). The central organs for Westernizer thinking in the 1840s were the thick journals *Notes of the Fatherland* (Otechestvennye zapiski) and *The Contemporary* (Sovremennik).

Alexander Herzen's influence on Russian political thought was tremendous. He was a writer, a philosopher, and the founder of the free Russian press in London which ended the Russian government's monopoly on the printed word. He also "created" his own biography as the story of an individual's search for freedom as described in his masterwork *My Past and Thoughts* (Byloe i dumy, 1854–66, 1919). Herzen was more than a Westernizer. He was, rather, a man of the West: a political refugee, he spent more than twenty years in Western Europe, where he became one of the most eminent political figures of the socialist movement.

Unlike the liberal Westernizers, Herzen severely criticized Western bourgeois democracy. Unlike the radical socialists, however, he believed that personal freedom did not contradict the interests of Communist society. Towards the end of his life he engaged in fierce polemics with "the militant, boorish anti-humanism of the younger generation of Russian revolutionaries – fearless, but brutal, full of savage indignation, but hostile to civilization and liberty."[9] Herzen's political periodicals, *The Polar Star* (Poliarnaia zvezda) and *The Bell* (Kolokol), were strictly forbidden by the Russian authorities, but they were smuggled to Russia, illegally copied and circulated throughout the country, thereby beginning the Russian tradition of political samizdat (literally self-publishing) that would flourish during the late Soviet period (to be sure, works had circulated in manuscript during the "Golden Age," but generally within closely circumscribed circles). In the 1850s, Herzen introduced the theory of "Russian socialism." Its basic tenet is that "the man of the future in Russia is the muzhik [the peasant], just as in France he is the proletarian."[10] In Russia's peasant commune (here Herzen echoed the Slavophiles, but with completely different conclusions), he found the seed for future socialist society and a hope that it would be possible to avoid the path of Western bourgeois society.

V

Russia's defeat in the Crimean War was seen by educated Russian society as proof of a deep malaise that threatened the very existence of the state. The politics of Nicholas suffered a total defeat and the colossus of the Russian Empire, which had been puffed up by the official ideology, appeared to stand on legs of clay. The new Emperor Alexander II (who was crowned in 1855 after the death of his father) would push through a series of fundamental reforms in the 1860s, of which the most important was the liberation of the serfs. These reforms changed Russian society in major ways, and led to a new state ideology that concentrated on the gratitude of Russia's citizens toward their Tsar-Liberator.[11] But the official doctrine proposed by the state and those cultural institutions that depended on it, still failed to take hold of educated society.

In this period debates about the national essence and mission migrated from salons and discussion circles to thick journals which embodied particular "directions": the democratic *Notes of the Fatherland* (edited by the leading poet Nikolai Nekrasov (1821–78) and the satirist M. E. Saltykov-Shchedrin [1826–89]) and *The Russian Word* (Russkoe slovo) edited by D. I. Pisarev [1840–68]; the liberal *Library for Reading* (Biblioteka dlia chteniia) under the direction of P. V. Annenkov [1814–77] and *Herald of Europe* (Vestnik Evropy) under M. M. Stasiulevich [1826–1911]; the conservative *Russian Herald* (Russkii vestnik) of M. N. Katkov [1817–87]; Slavophile and neo-Slavophile ideas were presented in *The Russian Colloquy* (Russkaia beseda), *The Muscovite* (Moskvitianin) as well as *Time* (Vremia) and *Epoch* (Epokha) of Dostoevsky; Katkov's *Moscow News (*Moskovskie vedomosti) took the lead in presenting the pro-government position.

The intelligentsia's populism, with its sense of guilt before the uneducated and politically suppressed masses, was a powerful cultural movement, which found its expression in literature (Nekrasov's social poetry), painting (the so-called Peredvizhniki [Wanderers], a group of Realist artists, among them Ivan Kramskoy [1837–87], Vasily Perov [1834–82], and Ilya Repin [1844–1930], who formed the Society for Traveling Art Exhibitions to propagate democratic values in art), and music (the composers of the Russian national school Mily Balakirev [1836–1910], Alexander Borodin, César Cui [1835–1918], Modest Musorgsky, and Nikolai Rimsky-Korsakov [1844–1908]). A new ethics of art was proclaimed – an artist was seen to have a social calling, a responsibility to address important social issues, portray real life objectively and instruct the nation as to how to make things better.

The major themes of Russian art of this period were the tragic lot of the Russian peasants, the sufferings of women and children; harsh criticism of the upper classes; the search for a solution to the riddle of Russia's unhappiness in her troubled history. It was also a search for national forms of art (which had been proclaimed, as we recall, by the Slavophiles), i.e. rooted in Russian popular culture and effective enough to infect the educated public with ideas of social activism. Musorgsky, the leader of the Russian national school of music, wrote in a letter to the painter Repin:

> It is the people I want to depict; sleeping or walking, eating, or drinking, I have them constantly in my mind's eye – again and again they rise before me, in all their reality, huge, unvarnished, with no tinsel trappings! How rich a treasure awaits the composer in the speech of the people – so long that is, as any corner of the land remains to which the railway has not penetrated.[12]

The most powerful expression of his aesthetic beliefs was his historical opera *Boris Godunov* (the plot was derived from Pushkin's tragedy, which had been based, in turn, on Karamzin's account of the sinful Tsar Boris's reign and the Time of Troubles). A multi-voiced "chorus of people" presented the collective image of the Russian masses, which judges, suffers, and weeps over their poor lot. Russia's tragic destiny, concealed from both common people and their rulers, is revealed by the Simpleton (Holy Fool) who serves as embodiment of the national conscience in Musorgsky's opera:

> Flow, flow
> bitter tears!
> Weep, weep,
> A soul of the Orthodox faithful.
> The enemy will soon be here,
> Darkness approaches,
> With the impenetrable
> Blackness of the night.
> Woe, woe to Russia, weep,
> Weep, ye Russian people,
> Ye starving people!

VI

Literature played the leading role in Russia's nineteenth-century nation building. As early as 1847, the godfather of Russian Realism, Belinsky, had introduced the idea of a supreme national mission for Russian literature and formulated a characteristic moral code of the Russian writer in his letter to Gogol. According to Belinsky, the Orthodox Church, in which Gogol saw the key to the spiritual awakening of Russia, cannot claim moral leadership:

> Only literature, despite the Tartar censorship, shows signs of life and progressive movement. That is why the title of writer is held in such esteem among us; that is why literary success is easy among us even for a writer of little talent. The title of poet and writer has long since eclipsed the tinsel

of epaulets and gaudy uniforms. And that especially explains why every so-called liberal tendency, however poor in talent, is rewarded by universal notice, and why the popularity of great talents that sincerely or insincerely give themselves to the service of orthodoxy, autocracy, and nationality declines so quickly. [. . .] And here the public is right, for it looks upon Russian writers as its only leaders, defenders, and saviors against Russian autocracy, orthodoxy, and nationality, and therefore, while always prepared to forgive a writer a bad book, will never forgive him a pernicious book. This shows how much fresh and healthy intuition, albeit still in embryo, is latent in our society, and this likewise proves that it has a future.[13]

In Belinsky's messianic vision (rooted in Hegel's philosophy of the Absolute Spirit), literature "would be the means by which the Spirit would come to self-expression in Russia, the form wherein the Russian people would make their original contribution to world culture and the evolution of world history." This social mission of literature, it has been claimed, forced writers to "move outside their profession and take on themselves roles to which they were by nature less well-suited: those of political commentator, public tribune, even religious prophet."[14]

In the course of the nineteenth century the writers' profession gradually became more popular and prestigious. In the first half of the century there had been no more than twenty to thirty professional writers. In 1855 their number was close to 300, and by 1880 had increased to 700. According to a contemporary observer, "never, neither before nor since, has the writer occupied here in Russia such a position of honor"; he "has become society's teacher, educator, and prophet, opening up vistas of the future and indicating the ideals and goals to which to aspire." The 1870s saw a real publication boom: "[N]ow anyone who possesses even a modicum of the ability to communicate in print is striving to be published" and "the demand for writers has outstripped the supply, bringing into print everyone who is even slightly literate and can write with fluency and animation."[15]

In the age of Alexander II, literature became the arena for sharp ideological struggle and each major author had partisans and bitter enemies. The Russian novel of "the golden age of prose" (1860s-1870s) became a unique stage on which the nation's fate and direction was discussed. In this sense it was the center of Russian political life: *Fathers and Children* (Otsy i deti [1862]) of Turgenev; *What is to be Done?* (Chto delat'? [1863]) by N. G. Chernyshevsky with its socialist utopia of the New Russia (located between the Euphrates and the Tigris, a latter-day Garden of Eden); *War and Peace* by Tolstoy; the novels of Dostoevsky; Leskov's stories about seekers of truth.

One of the most characteristic features of Russian literature of this period was an attempt to define the peculiarities of the *Russian* national character in terms of *Western* culture: Russian authors claimed that the nation possessed its own Hamlets, Lady Macbeths, and Don Quixotes who were depicted as even more complex and intriguing than their Western counterparts. The adjective "Russian" became a moral, ideological, and even existential category, rather than an ethnic name. Note the rhetorical questions raised by Russian writers of this period: How do Russians die (presumably, Westerners die in different ways)? What is Russian boredom (toska)? What is "a Russian man at the rendez-vous"? What are "Russian women"? What are "Russian boys" (i.e. the young generation)? What is the Russian way (the symbol of Gogol's troika)? In this period Russian literature became world-famous and contributed to the creation of the Western vision of the "enigmatic Russian soul," – a myth which is still alive.

VII

The cult of literature led to a peculiar cult of its "material" – the national language. To be sure, the diverse and rich Russian tongue had been praised as early as the eighteenth century, the formative age of Russian literature and Russian lexicography. In the early nineteenth century Admiral Shishkov proclaimed that the future of Russian literature lay not in the imitation of "the French elegance," but in following the tradition of Church Slavonic. However, the vision of Russian language (its grammatical structure, phonetics, syntax, and vocabulary) as the material vessel of the Russian national spirit originates in the Slavophile milieu. Thus, according to Kireevsky, Western languages inherited from the Latin their rigid and artificial grammatical constructions which "stifle all natural freedom and spontaneity of emotion." By contrast, Russian "has overthrown the dry, formal category of tense and has developed within itself forms which express its lively property – namely energy or . . . duration of a manifestation."[16] It is not accidental that the 1850s-1860s (the heyday of Russian nationalist culture) are marked by a tremendous interest in linguistics and lexicography – from K. S. Aksakov's "On Russian Verbs" (1855) to Vladimir Dahl's (1801–72) *Explanatory Dictionary of the Living Russian Language* (Tolkovyi slovar' zhivogo velikorusskogo iazyka, 1863–6), a grand monument to the speech of Russian people. In his *Dictionary* Dahl grouped words in "nets" or "families" according to their mutual attraction, i.e. around shared roots. An eminent writer, ethnographer, and spiritualist (he was a follower of a

Swedish mystic Swedenborg), he saw the word as a spiritual entity, a bridge between "material man" and "the Spirit," and a window onto the national soul.[17] In a sense, Dahl was not a linguist, or a collector of words, or a writer, but rather a "language seer" who, by traveling through lexical worlds, tried to reveal how a national language functions ("lives" and "breaths") in its countless verbal "families" which express the spirit of the nation, that, in turn, mirrors the Divine Word/World.

The veneration of the beautiful and redemptive Russian language was also characteristic for Westernizers. Thus, toward the end of his life Ivan Turgenev wrote a prose poem called "The Russian Language," a manifesto of Russian linguistic patriotism:

> In days filled with doubt, in days of heavy thoughts about my motherland, you are my one support, oh great, mighty, truth-telling and free Russian language! Were it not for you, how could I avoid despairing at the situation my land? But it is impossible to imagine that such a language could have been vouchsafed any but a great people![18]

But in a single language, even a great one, it is possible to express the most varied thoughts. And toward the end of the 1870s a crisis caused by a surplus of competing national ideas arose. "Educated society" began to feel the need for a truce. The excuse for this truce became the ceremonies surrounding the unveiling in Moscow of a monument, the work of A. M. Opekushin, to Alexander Pushkin on the 81st anniversary of his birth – June 6, 1880 – one of the most important cultural events of the entire nineteenth century in Russia. Pushkin had been canonized by Russian culture in the 1850s and 1860s as the first Russian poet, the creator of the Russian literary language, and the ideal incarnation of a Russian person in his historical development (Gogol's definition). After a Mass conducted by the Metropolitan of Moscow, a requiem was pronounced in the name of "the Boyar Alexander." At noon, a solemn procession moved from the church to a stage covered in a red carpet. Among the honored guests were the poet's children, famous writers, and graduates of the Lycee that Pushkin attended. State-Secretary F. P. Kornilov read an official document turning the monument over to the mayor of Moscow S. M. Tretiakov. To the sound of music and the ringing of Moscow's church bells the attendees bared their heads, and the General Governor of Moscow, Prince B. A.Dolgoruky pulled away the monument's covering to loud hurrahs.

The sculptor chose to show Pushkin wearing a long jacket covered by a wide cloak. His head is slightly bowed to one side and the poet seems to be in deep thought. Inscribed around the sides of the pedestal are lines from

8 A. M. Opekushin, Pushkin monument, Moscow, 1880. Dedicated on the 81st anniversary of Pushkin's birth (June 6, 1880) and built with funds raised by public subscription, this monument, which stands in almost the exact center of Moscow, has become a legendary meeting site for Muscovites. The statue was the excuse for an extravagant three-day Pushkin celebration that codified the poet as the Russian national writer.

the poem "The Monument," a free translation of Horace's *Exegi monumentum*, which had earlier been translated into Russian by both Lomonosov and Derzhavin:

> I shall be noised abroad through all great Russia,
> Her innumerable tongues shall speak my name:
> The tongue of the Slavs' proud grandson, the Finn, and now
> The wild Tungus and Kalmyk, the steppes' friend.
>
> In centuries to come I shall be loved by the people
> For having awakened noble thoughts with my lyre
> For having glorified freedom in my harsh age
> And called for mercy toward the fallen.

In this poem, Pushkin stated that his monument "not made by human hands" would rise "above the Alexander column" on the Palace Square in Petersburg. Its unveiling, as we noted earlier, had been greeted by a military parade. Now in 1880, the new monument was surrounded by the self-appointed representatives of the Russian people, the intelligentsia, led by the most influential writers and critics. Then, what was celebrated was the power of the Russian state, symbolized by the dead Emperor-Victor. Now, Russia's culture had become pre-eminent, symbolized by her greatest poet. Many of the most famous Russian writers gave public speeches at these festivities, and each presented his own view of the essence and tasks of Russia. The problem, however, was that each one, be it the Slavophile Aksakov, the Pan-Slavist Dostoevsky, the Conservative Katkov, or the Westernizer Turgenev, saw in Pushkin the expression of his ideology and his ideology alone.

Biography – Nikolai Vasilievich Gogol (1809–1852)

Perhaps the most outstanding Russian literary historian of the twentieth century began his article on Gogol with the words "Gogol was a liar."[19] And indeed, Gogol, who was born on April 1, loved to mislead relatives, friends, and admirers, invented or presented in a completely fantastic way the facts of his biography, surrounded his life and works with an atmosphere of mystery, and in answer to the question "why?" responded simply "for some reason." The mystery in which the author enveloped himself was not so much a Romantic mask, as a hint at his belief in his own unique and inscrutable role in Russian history. In his later years he would admit that he felt the presence of the hand of Providence as he wrote, and he demanded that his friends and admirers follow his advice and teachings quite literally. Gogol saw the goal of his central literary work, *Dead Souls,* as nothing less than the spiritual salvation (and resurrection) of the nation. With Gogol begins the history of Russian literary messianism, a distinguishing characteristic of Russian culture.

Gogol hailed from a relatively poor Ukrainian gentry family. His father was an amateur writer, the author of comedies in the Ukrainian language and popular style. From his father, Gogol inherited a deft comic touch, a taste for a motley and earthy linguistic register, and an actor's timing. His mother's influence was religious. The writer would later recall that one of the deepest impressions of his childhood was his mother's narration of the Last Judgment. Horror in the face of the world beyond the grave, often hidden beneath a mask of comic narration, is a constant theme in the works of the mature Gogol. Gogol spent his childhood on his parents' estate not far from Poltava. Nearby was the village of Dikan'ka, the place to which the writer would later attach the cycle of fantastic "Ukrainian" tales that would bring him fame throughout Russia. Also nearby was the estate of Troshchinsky, an influential figure from the Catherinian age, a distant relative and patron of the Gogols. This estate was a kind of provincial cultural center, a Ukrainian Athens with a rich library and a theatre where among others the plays of Gogol's father were performed.

From 1821 to 1828 Gogol studied in the town of Nezhin at the local Gymnasium, which, at that time, was an excellent school. The teachers tried to stimulate the students' literary talents, and encouraged the production of hand-written journals, one of which was edited by Gogol. The students' literary idols were Zhukovsky and Pushkin; they also read Schiller and Byron. Gogol's first literary efforts were in verse. Toward the end of his period in Nezhin he would write the long poem "Hans Kiuchelgarten." Its dreamy hero, having tired of bucolic life, leaves his village and his beloved maiden to wander the world. But, having become disillusioned in his efforts to find his romantic ideal in romantic climes, he returns home where he discovers that his Luisa still loves him. The heroes marry and everything ends well. Gogol placed high hopes on this simple poem, which at times shows flashes of talent but is in the main comically clumsy.

At the end of 1828, Gogol arrived in St. Petersburg, which astounded the young provincial with its brilliance, its cultural variety (especially musical), while at the same horrifying him with its bureaucratic and physical "coldness" (the symbolic theme of coldness would become central to the writer's Petersburg stories). Gogol had come to the capital with the goal of becoming famous – quickly and throughout Russia. Precisely how this would be accomplished, the young man did not know. His attempts to make a career in the bureaucracy ended in failure, as did his plans to become an actor. His literary debut was no more successful: the publication of "Hans Kiukhelgarten" in 1829 elicited nothing more than a few ironic commentaries. In response, the author bought up all the unsold copies, burned them, and unexpectedly left Petersburg to go abroad. Then, equally unexpectedly, he returned. He told his mother he had run away to escape an unhappy love affair.

In 1830, Gogol took a minor clerical job. His short stint in the bureaucracy would give him all the material he needed for his brilliant Petersburg stories (including "Notes of a Madman," "The Nose," "The Overcoat"), which depict the tragicomic sufferings of lower-level clerks squashed by the bureaucratic machine. This type of the "little man" was, in the opinion of Russian critics of the 1840s and 1850s, Gogol's great contribution to Russian literature. It was, in point of fact, a Russian echo of the social Christianity and its accompanying sentimental philanthropism that had swept Europe in the 1830s. Also in 1830, Gogol published his first "Ukrainian" story in *Notes of the Fatherland*, the best literary journal of the day. Its subject matter was the interference of the devil in mortal affairs (one of this mystically inclined writer's favorite themes), and it would later be included in the first collection of his *Evenings on a Farm Near Dikan'ka* (Vechera na khutore bliz Dikan'ki). At about this same time, Gogol made the acquaintance of Zhukovsky, and a bit later of Pushkin and joined their literary "party," which was at that time sparring with F. V. Bulgarin (1789–1859), a successful journalist and author of edifying novels and stories.

1831–2 saw the appearance of the two parts of "Evenings." For the Russian, particularly the Petersburg reader, these books were quite surprising: they were set in an exotic, but accessible place (Ukraine for the Russian reader was a bit like Scotland for an Englishman of Walter Scott's day or the Hudson Valley for a contemporary reader of Washington Irving), and they featured humor tinged with sadness, the fantastic mixed with a seemingly "ethnographic" portrayal of local color, vivid language, and the attractive figure of the narrator, the beekeeper Rudy Panko – Gogol's literary mask. In the stories one finds the influence not only of European Romanticism, but also of the Ukrainian puppet theatre with its comedy, its jesting dialogue, and its tendency to have no more than two characters in a single scene (two marionettes in the hand of a single puppeteer). Although the stories contained scenes that were sad and even horrifying, Gogol was received as a comic author. The writer himself, who always took his work completely seriously, would later assert that the humorous side of his stories was only a mask, hiding the deeper sadness evoked by the recognition of the imperfection of humankind and the world. Be that as it may, the combination of humor and sadness ("laughter through tears") became a Gogolian trademark.

In 1835 Gogol wrote two new story cycles: *Mirgorod* (including "How Ivan Ivanovich Quarreled with Ivan Nikiforich," "Vii," "A Terrible Vengeance," "Taras Bulba") and *Arabeski* (the latter included not only some of his Petersburg stories but also essays on a variety of topics ranging from history to geography, from poetry to theatre). In the second half of the 1830s, following a European Romantic mode, Gogol began to occupy himself with history. His plans, as always, were amazingly ambitious: to write the history of Ukraine, or better yet a universal history of the world. Friends arranged for him to receive an adjunct professorship in history at Saint Petersburg University and he wrote detailed outlines about history texts, produced syllabi and the texts of some lectures. His pedagogical work, nevertheless, ended in failure and Gogol decided to concentrate full time on literature.

He developed another grandiose plan – the complete reformation of Russian drama through a reform of the genre of comedy. Gogol sneered at the vaudevilles and light comedies that were the stock-in-trade of the capital's theatres. He believed that a modern comic intrigue should involve all the characters and be based not on a love plot but rather on things of far greater importance to his contemporaries – rank and money. In 1832 he began work on a comedy drawn from the life of bureaucrats entitled "The Order of Vladimir, Third Class." The hero of the play tries with all his might to be awarded this distinction and fails to do so. In the final scene, he was supposed to go insane: imagining himself the figure on the Vladimir cross, he was to stand in front of a mirror with his hands outstretched, as if crucified. Gogol did not finish the comedy, though he would later publish a few excerpts from it.

In 1835, Gogol wrote his comedy *The Inspector General* (Revizor) one of the Ur-texts of Russian literature. At its base is a simple story that Pushkin arguably recounted to Gogol: some local bribe-taking bureaucrats take a young government official from Petersburg who happens to come accidentally to their town as an auditor sent by the central government. They try to bribe the supposed auditor, who at first has no idea what they are doing but then figures it out and takes full advantage of the situation. Just after he leaves town, it is discovered that the real auditor has arrived. In the context of the 1820s and 1830s such audits were a characteristic phenomenon of Russian life. The young Tsar, having suppressed the Decembrist revolt, decided to tackle what he felt to be the main source of internal discontent: corruption. Nicholas sent auditors to all corners of the empire, and many legends circulated about the terror such visits instilled in provincial bureaucrats. Nevertheless, this program did not yield the desired results. After each local "apocalypse" bribe-taking would be renewed with equal vigor. Given this manifest political failure, in the 1830s Russian society began to think that perhaps literary satire should play the role of a "moral auditor," throwing light on the activities of dishonest officials.

Gogol imagined *The Inspector General* as a social comedy that would reveal all the faults of Russian bureaucratic life in the microcosm of a single town. He called laughter the positive hero of his comedy, and hoped it would have the power to deal with social flaws. In later years he would write a number of commentaries about the play (including some in dramatic form where the actors disagree about the author's goals). Gogol considered the key to his comedy to be the final "dumb scene," in which the local officials, paralyzed by the news of the real auditor's arrival, freeze on the stage, grouping themselves around the town's mayor, who stands "like a column" with outstretched arms and bowed head. The Christological subtext of this scene, which took its final form in the 1840 version of the play, was apparently meant by the mystically inclined Gogol to remind the Russian bureaucracy that every sin crucifies once more him who gave his life for humankind.

The comedy was first performed at Easter in 1836 at the Aleksandrisky Theatre in the presence of the Emperor himself. Despite clear signs that it was a success, Gogol decided that the play had been a fiasco, or, more importantly, that it had been improperly performed and received by the audience. As he had after the failure of "Hans Kiuchelgarten," he immediately fled abroad. He would spend much of the rest of his life in Italy, observing Russia "from a beautiful distance," as he put it.

Starting in 1836 and continuing into the 1840s, Gogol worked on his chef d'oeuvre, the "poem" *Dead Souls*. The first volume appeared in 1842 under a title revised by the censors: "The Adventures of Chichikov, or Dead Souls." The subject of the work, Gogol himself asserted, had again been a "gift" from Pushkin (Gogol constantly emphasized his debt to the poet): it describes the business trip of a talented crook who uses a loophole in the Russian legal system to buy up serfs who are actually dead or who have disappeared but still remain on the census rolls which, in those days, were revised only every decade. Landowners, who were required to pay a yearly tax on each male serf, were happy to get rid of these, and the hero proposes to turn them into real capital by mortgaging them as if they were alive and absconding with the money. In Gogol's mind, the hero's journey to various grotesquely depicted landowners was to illustrate "all of Russia" or, more precisely, the Russian soul in all its vulgar reality. The satirical poem in prose ends with a lyrical scene of the bird-troika, an image Gogol used to depict the national fate of Russia in the circle of European nations. The symbol of the troika racing into the unknown distance would be taken up by many other Russian authors, and became one of the most popular figures of Russian national mythology (Dostoevsky, for example, uses it in the culmination of his last novel *The Brothers Karamazov*).

As with all of Gogol's major work, however, what is most valuable about *Dead Souls* from a modern perspective is not the plot but rather the exceptional brilliance of the author's linguistic invention. As opposed to the classical prose of his erstwhile mentor Pushkin, Gogol's prose exhibits a baroque ebullience that takes on a life of its own and drags the reader along willy-nilly to a series of absurd and hilarious situations, which exfoliate extravagantly outside the apparent story line.

Dead Souls was a gigantic success. Gogol was immediately declared the "head" of Russian literature (Pushkin had been killed in a duel in 1837, so the post was temporarily vacant), and his poem was declared to be the national epic that Russian literature had been trying to produce for one hundred years. *Dead Souls* led to widespread discussions about the particularity of Russia, her mission, the national character, and the potential of literature to illustrate and correct the faults of the modern Russian character. The Slavophile critic K. S. Aksakov compared *Dead Souls* with the works of Homer and Shakespeare, finding in it a completely objective narration, a deep understanding of the national character, "universality, truth and at the same time that full expression of life . . . that is the secret of great art." The Westernizer Belinsky, welcomed the book, but did not agree with such an exalted and idealistic evaluation: *"Dead Souls* is a social novel, which analyzes life as it is and scourges the failures of contemporary society." Gogol himself took an active part in the discussion, publishing a number of articles about the work in which he tried to control its reception by explaining its higher meaning. It turned out that he was not describing Russia at all, but only his own diseased soul and, therefore, the comic and vulgar heroes were merely avatars of his own weaknesses and sins. He also intimated that this comic volume was only the first part of a broader work that would have earth-shattering transformative power, and many of his admirers awaited not merely a second volume but the second coming.

Gogol understood his recovery from a disease of the nerves in 1840 as a sign from on high, and he began to view his work on the second volume of his poem as a mission vouchsafed him by Providence demanding of him ascetic service and constant self-improvement: "My work is enormous, my feat is salvific; from henceforward I am dead to all things trivial." He began to perceive art as a means for the transformation of humanity, for the resurrection of the race. But at the same time he feared becoming an instrument of the devil, who was trying to use him for his own purposes (this theme had appeared for the first time in his story "The Portrait" of 1835).

In 1847 Gogol published his *Selected Passages from Correspondence with Friends* (Vybrannye mesta iz perepiski s druz'iami), a collection of didactic letters and articles of a religious-moral and aesthetic character. The work begins with a "Last Will and Testament," in which the author asks later generations not to build a monument to him after his death. His true reward will be the moral perfection of the Russian nation, which is the goal of his earthly existence. The central theme of the book, which is permeated with horror in the face of the devil's wiles, is salvation (personal, national, universal). Such salvation is only possible if everyone follows God's plan according to which everyone and everything in the world needs to occupy its proper place and do its duty. Gogol creates a mystical utopia for Russia as God's land, a state-monastery in which everyone works in his appointed place conscientiously and in holy fear of God (and the devil).

The publication of this work was an enormous shock for many of Gogol's admirers. Many decided that the author's rejection of his wonderful earlier comic literature was a sign that he had gone insane. Belinsky, who had promoted Gogol as the leader of a new Russian realist school, wrote his famous open letter in which he expressed his dismay over how the new Gogol, a mystic and reactionary, understood Russia and the Russian people. This letter was a kind of political testament (for Belinsky would soon die of tuberculosis) and can be seen as one of the first socialist proclamations in Russia. Reading this letter in a group of young men was among the reasons given for the 1848 arrest of the young Dostoevsky, who, along with his fellows, was sentenced to death for sedition (at the last minute the sentence was commuted and the author sent into imprisonment and Siberian exile).

In answer to his critics, Gogol wrote his "Confession," in which he described himself as an author-martyr continually tormented by a mystical yearning for his motherland and trying to understand and incarnate his mission for the Russian people. The notion that literature has a theurgic (transformative) mission, which lies at the foundation of Gogol's later creative work, was mocked by his contemporaries, but it had great resonance with later generations of Russian writers and philosophers from Dostoevsky and Tolstoy (see, for example, the latter's *Confession* [Ispoved'] of 1879) to Vladimir Solovev and the so-called younger symbolists (Alexander Blok, Viacheslav Ivanov).

Gogol's work on the second volume of *Dead Souls*, which he saw as a kind of Danteesque "Purgatory" for his sinner heroes, was indeed tortuous. Gogol felt that his own moral failures were the cause of his inability to realize his vision. In 1845 he burned all the chapters written to that point and began again. In 1848 he set off on a pilgrimage to the Holy Land. At the Tomb of the Savior he prayed for the strength to finish his work. And in the period from 1848 to the early 1850s he read some chapters of the second volume to his friends. Finally, he announced that the work was finished, but in February 1852, in a fit of mystic horror (caused, he claimed, by the devil), he burned the manuscript. On February 21, 1852, Gogol died. On his tombstone were engraved words from the book of the prophet Jeremiah: "I will laugh with my bitter word..."

Literary Work – Ivan Turgenev, *Notes of a Hunter* (Zapiski okhotnika)

The accession of Alexander II to the Russian throne in 1855 ushered in a period of reform unprecedented since the age of Peter the Great. In the course of fifteen years, Alexander issued decrees that completely altered Russia's judicial system (including, among other things, a new penal code, and the introduction of jury trials), created a new system for limited local self-government, and significantly reorganized Russia's military. By far the most significant of his decrees, however, was that of February 19, 1861, which announced the liberation of Russia's serfs (to take place in 1863). Given that enserfed peasants made up some 80 percent of Russia's population and that Russia's economy was highly dependent on this institution, emancipation was an exceptionally difficult undertaking. The question, of course, is why Alexander chose to undertake this effort, particularly given the fact that there was no clear compulsion to do so. A number of theories have been advanced: economic historians point out that the system was inefficient, and claim that Alexander recognized this, though he appears to have had only a limited understanding of economics; historians inclined to Freudianism have noted a desire to take the country in a direction diametrically opposed to that of his father; and it has also been noted that the emancipation simply followed a trend that had been occurring in most other European countries from the late eighteenth century.

Within Russian society, however, there was another explanation that, while perhaps apocryphal, indicates the exceptional status of serious literature in Russia. Alexander chose to free Russia's serfs, the story goes, because of the impression that had been made on him by *Notes of a Hunter* a book of short stories published by Ivan Turgenev in 1852.[20] Russian literature, in this view, differs from other European literatures both in its willingness to deal directly with the "accursed questions" of society and in the extent to which readers, even readers who are not members of the almost automatically oppositionist intelligentsia, form their political and social opinions based on their reading of literary texts. In this view, then, literature is at the core of Russia's national identity, putting on the agenda the most important issues facing the country and proposing a variety of solutions to them.

Turgenev came from the sort of aristocratic background typical for many Russian writers. His was an ancient gentry family that, in the early part of the nineteenth century, had produced a number of renowned men. Ivan's father, a relatively poor army officer, was less remarkable, and died when the future writer was sixteen. Thereafter, he was brought up on the estate of his mother in Orel province, not far from Tolstoy's Iasnaia Poliana. Unlike the mythological mothers in most gentry accounts of childhood, Ivan's was renowned for cruelty to her serfs. Ivan himself spoke rarely of his childhood. He was educated for the most part at home until the age of fifteen, and then enrolled in Moscow University, at that time a hotbed for student activism and intellectual activity.

Turgenev started writing early, first producing poetry in imitation of the current Romantic trends, particularly the work of Pushkin. His background ensured that he could have entrée into the best circles, and he quickly made the acquaintance of leading Russian writers and intellectuals in Moscow and Petersburg. The literary scene of the late 1830s and early 1840s was exceptionally unstable. The 1820s and early 1830s had been dominated by aristocratic writers from backgrounds similar to Turgenev's, and poetry had been the most important literary form. By the late 1830s, however, prose fiction had become dominant, and the literary field began to democratize with the appearance of the so-called *raznochintsy* (from the root words *razny* [various] and *chin* [ranks]) intellectuals, university educated men who were the sons of priests, merchants, and other non-noble parents. Among the most important of these men was the literary critic and theorist Vissarion Belinsky. While today Belinsky's interpretations of literary texts often seem rather arbitrary, he was a critic with an exceptional nose for talent (the first to appreciate Gogol, Goncharov, and Dostoevsky, for example), and his championing of realism in literature had an enormous influence on Russian writing in this period and beyond.

Turgenev unquestionably admired Belinsky and, although their backgrounds could not have been more different, the two men got along well. At this point, Turgenev gravitated toward those circles in which gentry and raznochintsy writers and thinkers gathered, and began to contribute to their literary enterprises and periodical publications. For, if literary life of the 1820s had revolved around salons and occasional almanacs, the increasingly professionalized literary world of the 1840s was organized around regular publication in the thick journals, which included multiple sections – politics, history, social and cultural criticism, as well as original literature. The majority of the famous Russian novels of the 1850s through the 1880s were published serially in such journals, including all the major works of Tolstoy and Dostoevsky. Each journal had a particular political profile, which reflected the views of the editor and his or her close associates.

From 1847 and until the mid-1860s, the most famous radical-leaning journal was *The Contemporary*, edited for most of this period by the poet Nikolai Nekrasov. The journal itself had a brilliant pedigree. It was founded by Alexander Pushkin, and, after a fallow period following his death in 1837, from the late 1840s until the early 1860s it brought out some of the most important contemporary Russian fiction, including most of the stories that would go into *Notes of a Hunter* and Tolstoy's *Childhood*. Beginning in the late 1850s, it became the home to the second generation of influential Russian left-wing literary critics, particularly Nikolai Chernyshevsky, Nikolai Dobroliubov, and Dmitry Pisarev. The journal was suppressed in 1866, accused unfairly of inciting student unrest.

It was in *The Contemporary*, beginning in 1847 that the first of the stories that would eventually go into the collection *Notes of a Hunter* were published. In the journal, these stories appeared side-by-side with a variety of short fictional works, often called "ocherki" (sketches), a fairly amorphous genre that had come to Russia by way of the fabulously successful French writer Eugene Sue, who had written a series of short literary pieces exploring the seamier sides of Parisian reality – the lives of rag-pickers, prostitutes, and so forth. The genre was picked up in Russia by Nekrasov himself, whose *Petersburg Sketches* explored urban life in the Russian capital. As a rule, through the persona of a "neutral observer," the creators of such sketches strove to show readers the "typical," presenting composite characters who were the quintessence of their type. Turgenev himself described his method as "distilling the essence" of his characters. In *Notes of a Hunter*, Turgenev extended the sketch genre to the countryside, focusing his attention on the life of the enserfed Russian *muzhik* (peasant), who, despite constituting the vast majority of the population, had been an almost invisible presence in Russian literature to this point. Most important, Turgenev showed his readers a broad variety of peasant types and he did so with an enormous amount of sympathy but without sentimentality.

The stories are linked by the figure of the narrator, who shares the predilections and opinions of Turgenev himself (and also of the majority of his readers). As a hunter, he has the opportunity to travel through the Russian countryside observing the life and habits of the peasant as well as the rural aristocracy. Having grown up on a country estate, the narrator, like Turgenev, does of course possess a wealth of first-hand knowledge of peasant life, though he is also aware that his presence among the peasants lends to a certain artificiality to their behavior.

The first story in the collection entitled *Khor and Kalinych* sets the tone for the work as a whole. "Anyone who has happened to go from the Bolkhov to the Zhizdrin district has probably noticed the sharp differences between the men of the Orel province and that of Kaluga." It is critical from the outset in this form of realist fiction to set the scene exactly. These are not generic Russian *muzhiks*, but very specific types from a particular place and time. The story indeed will turn out to be about contrasts, not between peasants of these two provinces but rather between two inhabitants of the Zhizdrin district, Khor and Kalinych. We also meet the men's owner Polutykin, whom the narrator reveals to be a limited, foolish man.

We first see the family of Khor, a collection of strapping young lads whom the narrator meets when he and Polutykin stop at their farmstead to rest. Although they remain human chattel tied to the land and in principle the property of Polutykin, Khor and his family live well; by agreement with their landlord they pay a fixed cash rent yearly and beyond that are free to live as they please. By contrast, Kalinych is poor and spends most of his time accompanying his master on hunting trips. Nevertheless, the two peasants are close friends, and the narrator observes them closely and with great sympathy. "Khor was a positive, practical person with an administrative cast of mind, a rationalist. Kalinych, by contrast, belonged to the idealists, the romantics, dreamers, and easily exalted folk."

The only overtly ideological moment in the story comes after the narrator recounts the questions that Khor and Kalinych ask him about life abroad. Having described Khor's interest in various useful innovations, the narrator concludes: "Peter the Great was a real Russian, Russian precisely in his transformations. A Russian is so confident of his strength and might that he is not opposed even to break himself: he isn't all that concerned with his past and looks eagerly into the future. Whatever is good he will like, whatever makes sense, bring it on, and he doesn't care where it comes from." Here Turgenev stakes out a difficult ideological position in the already bitter battle between Westernizers and Slavophiles. He is clearly a Westernizer in his praise of Peter and innovation, yet as opposed to most

Westernizers, who felt that the *muzhik* with his traditional ways and old fashioned life was a problem to be fixed, Turgenev identifies precisely the peasant with Peter's cast of mind, practically idealizing him. Almost, but not quite, as the narrator is quick to point out some of Khor's deficiencies: "Even so, no matter how smart he was, he had a lot of superstitions and presumptions. For example, he despised women to the depths of his soul, and constantly mocked them."

Although Turgenev's narrator avoids drawing overt conclusions about the morality of serfdom, the contrast between his depiction of the brutish stupidity of the local landowners and the talents of the peasants, as well as his self-irony, led to the assumption that Turgenev was opposed to serfdom and that his stories constituted an ideological tract in opposition to it and to the serf-owning members of the gentry class. As Nicholas I was said to have complained: "the bulk of the articles in the work have a clear tendency to humiliate the landowners, who are presented for the most part as silly caricatures, or in ways that make them look unpleasant." Be that as it may, Turgenev's narrator is careful not to draw conclusions from these implied comparisons and the best of these stories are perfect miniature works of art.

Perhaps the greatest single story in the collection is *Singers* (Pevtsy). Like so many stories in *Notes of a Hunter*, it opens with the narrator describing his approach to a situation in which he will encounter peasants; he comes upon a country tavern on a broiling hot day. Of all Russian authors, Turgenev is unsurpassed as a portraitist of nature, remarkable for his ability in a short paragraph or two to create the illusion of the living, breathing Russian countryside. He enters the tavern to slake his thirst and discovers that a singing contest is about to begin. Again, we have a contrast between two peasants, the contestants in the contest: a street vendor from Zhizdra, a short stout man of about thirty and Iakov (Yashka), a lithe, thin man of about twenty-three.

At a high point of tension, just as the contest is to begin, Turgenev breaks off the story to provide thumbnail sketches of the various peasants observing the contest. Each portrait is deft and perfectly individualized, providing a panoramic view of the kinds of people one might find in such a tavern while simultaneously holding the reader in suspense. The contest itself is presented masterfully. It is hard enough to describe a landscape or a person in words, but music is perhaps even more difficult to capture. Turgenev does this with exceptional skill, focusing not just on the sound of the voices, but on the movements of the singers and, most of all, on the effect the music has on the listeners. Again, Turgenev is willing to make comparisons that might have seemed surprising to his readers, comparing the untrained peasant to a professional European singer by calling him a "Russian tenore di grazia, tenor léger." When the street vendor has finished, all the listeners congratulate him in the local dialect, far removed from the elegant Russian of the narrator.

It is now Yashka's turn and he hesitates, seemingly unwilling to compete, but finally he begins: "The first sound of his voice was weak and wavering and it sounded as if it did not come from his chest but from some far-away place, as if it had wafted accidentally into the room. That quavering, plangent sound had a strange affect on us all." Over the next page and a half the narrator describes masterfully the emotions stirred up in him and the other listeners by Yashka's voice in which a "Russian, true, and ardent soul could be heard, breathed inside it and grabbed you by the heart, grabbed you by your Russian heartstrings." Having registered Yashka's victory, the narrator departs, not wanting to spoil the artistic moment by watching the celebration that is sure to follow.

But, brilliantly, Turgenev does not end the story here. The narrator leaves the tavern, naps in the late afternoon heat, and wakes up only in the early evening. He hears sounds coming from the tavern and goes up to the window through which he sees "a sad, though motley and lively scene: everyone was drunk – everyone beginning with Iakov." The moment of artistic inspiration has passed, as it must for any artist. No longer the brilliant singer of the contest, the drunken Iakov sits and sings "in a hoarse voice some village dancing song while lazily plucking the strings of a guitar." The narrator departs a second time but even here the story does not end. It concludes instead with the brutal side of peasant life and a different kind of voice, as a peasant boy calls across the village, presumably to his brother, to come home because his father wants to beat him.

Event – Dostoevsky's "Pushkin Speech"

On June 8, 1880, Fedor Mikhailovich Dostoevsky delivered an address to a raptly attentive audience containing the flower of the Russian intelligentsia. It was the high point of the three-day extravaganza organized to coincide with the unveiling of a sculptural monument to Alexander Pushkin (see above). The festivities surrounding this event marked the apotheosis of the attempt by the nineteenth-century intelligentsia to use literature, specifically the work of Pushkin, as a vehicle to create a robust conception of Russia's national identity. Building on almost half a century of cultural/literary exegesis, in his "Pushkin Speech," Dostoevsky laid out a messianic vision of and for Russia, which in his view was prepared to say a "new word" to a faltering Europe.

Before turning to Dostoevsky's particular conception of Russia's identity and destiny, it is necessary to go back some fifty years. As we noted previously, early in the reign of Nicholas I, the state had made an effort to define Russian identity on the basis of three pillars: orthodoxy, autocracy, and nationality. Given the actual composition of the Russian empire as well as its imperial aspirations, however, none of these categories was unproblematic. Large numbers of the Tsar's subjects were not Orthodox Christians. Devotion to autocracy as a basis for citizenship was, to say the least, not a modern concept. Finally, nationality, which "was at the time and has remained the most obscure, puzzling, and debatable member of the official trinity,"[21] assumed the existence of precisely what needed to be defined by any nationalist project – that is, the nation itself.

Though few Russians took the state's efforts at nation building seriously and most probably did not worry much about the issue, a loosely defined group of cultural figures, mostly writers and literary critics, did work assiduously between the 1830s and the 1880s to create a viable Russian national identity, imagined on the basis of a few carefully chosen qualities of Russian culture and the Russian language in particular. Although in general the Russian intelligentsia defined itself in opposition to the state, this was not the case regarding the project of national identity creation. Indeed, to a surprising extent, many writers and critics accepted the three pillars proposed by the state, though they sought to provide their own definitions. Specifically, they developed an original view according to which Russia's destiny was to absorb all world civilization into itself. Taking the idea of Moscow as the Third Rome seriously, they modeled modern Russia on classical Rome, seeing both as cultures of translation and imperial absorption.

Russia's manifest destiny was to be built not on any inherent quality of Russian culture itself, but rather on its ability to absorb and perfect what it has taken from outside. This universality was seen to reside, first and foremost in the language itself. As early as the 1750s, even before Russian had been the vehicle for any internationally recognized work, Lomonosov had proclaimed: "The Holy Roman Emperor Carl the Fifth used to say that one should speak Spanish with God, French with one's friends, German with one's enemies, and Italian with the fair sex. But had he been skilled in Russian he would of course have added that it would be appropriate to speak with all of these in it, for he would have found in it the greatness of Spanish, the liveliness of French, the force of German, the tenderness of Italian, and, in addition, the richness and strong terse descriptiveness of Greek and Latin."[22] The important point here is not that Russian is conceived as the universal language (many other languages have understood themselves in this way), but that it includes within itself the best qualities of the world's major languages. This lends it a flexibility and capaciousness that makes it an ideal vehicle for universal cultural translation.

By the 1820s and 1830s the leaders of Russian cultural opinion began to recognize that their views on the qualities of the Russian language could be projected onto the culture as a whole, and that Russia's national project could be defined by her ability to synthesize both European and non-European cultures. We can see hints of a realization of this kind in an article on Romantic poetry (1823) by the writer and critic Orest Somov: "But how many diverse peoples have merged under the single name of Russians or depend on Russia, separated neither by the expanse of alien lands nor by wide seas! There are so many diverse appearances, mores, customs which present themselves to the searching eye in the one volume of aggregate Russia! . . . And thus, Russian poets, without leaving the boundaries of their motherland, can fly across from the stern and somber legends of the North to the opulent and brilliant fancies of the East; from the educated mind and taste of Europeans to the crude and unaffected mores of hunting and nomadic peoples."[23]

A recognition of the essentially synthetic nature of the Russian national project, and therefore of Russian national identity, during this period was perhaps aided by the highly improbable but nevertheless true circumstance that practically none of Russia's major Romantic writers was a pure ethnic Russian. Zhukovsky was the son of a Turkish women. Pushkin was descended from an Ethiopian prince on his mother's side, a fact that played a central role in his personal biographical myth and in his poetic persona.[24] Gogol's father was Ukrainian, and so, like Zhukovsky, he was only half Russian. And, finally, Lermontov's ancestry was Scottish on his father's side.

In any case, the connection between the culture's peculiar synthetic essence and Russia's manifest destiny was already clear in Gogol's essays on Pushkin and translation written only a decade or so after Somov's essay. Gogol emphasized what he saw as Pushkin's protean nature, declaring him to have been a perfect instrument for poetic translation and, as a result, the model Russian: "In Spain he is a Spaniard, with a Greek, a Greek – in the Caucasus – a free mountaineer, in the full sense of the term; with an older person he breathes the passage of time in olden days; should he glance toward a peasant in his hut – he is completely Russian from head to toe:

all the features of our nature were echoed in him . . . Our poetry has tried all the chords, was nurtured by the poetry of all the people, listened to the lyres of all the poets, attained some sort of world-wide language, so that it could prepare everyone for a more meaningful service."[25]

Dostoevsky begins his short speech with a nod to Gogol, making it clear that he is following in the latter's footsteps. The focus, he tells his audience is to be on the prophetic and revelatory side of Pushkin's significance. Although he specifically disavows the role of literary critic, he spends the bulk of his time discussing *Eugene Onegin*. Specifically, he follows a trend of Russian criticism in which the line between literary characters and real individuals is blurry, such that he can imagine for Pushkin's characters motivations and actions beyond those described in the text. In his view, in the character of Onegin, Pushkin identified the quintessential type of the alienated Westernized Russian, cut off from the Russian people and its traditions and doomed to wander endlessly until he can reconnect to them. Onegin's foil is Tatiana, completely identified with the Russian people and their messianic destiny in Dostoevsky's reading. It is the creation of this positive figure that Dostoevsky counts as Pushkin's most significant achievement: "had Pushkin not existed, it might well be that our faith in our Russian individuality, our now conscious hope in the strength of our People, and with it our faith in our future independent mission in the family of European peoples would not have been formulated with such unshakeable force."[26]

That mission, in Dostoevsky's view, was to become the saviors of a decaying Western civilization on the verge of collapse. Russia could fulfill this mission, just as Lomonosov had intuited, because of its civilizational capacity to enfold within itself all that had been created elsewhere. This gene, as it were, for universal openness he finds already expressed in Pushkin. Even if this be a misreading, it tells us a great deal about how the nineteenth-century Russian intelligentsia attempted to define the essence of the Russian nation.

> The European literatures had artistic geniuses of immense magnitude – the Shakespeares, Cervanteses, and Schillers. But show me even one of these great geniuses who possessed the capacity to respond to the whole world that our Pushkin had. And it is this capacity, the principal capacity of our nationality, that he shares with our People, and it is this, above all, that makes him a national poet. The very greatest of these European poets could never exemplify as intensely as Pushkin the genius of another people . . . Pushkin alone, of all the poets of the world, possesses the quality of embodying himself fully within another nationality.[27]

Thus, Dostoevsky presents Pushkin as a precursor to the views he had been expressing for many years in his monthly *Diary of a Writer*, a work which was far better known to his contemporaries than were the great novels most readers of Russian literature treasure today. The *Diary* is a generic hodge-podge, containing essays, cultural criticism, and literary works. It is concerned primarily with two central and related historical themes: the development of European civilization; and Slavdom's (read Russia's) relation to that development. Both are discussed within a millenarian framework. Contemporary Europe, in Dostoevsky's view, was on the verge of collapse. Of course, this had been the contention of the Slavophiles as early as the 1830s. But Kireevsky, Khomiakov, and the Aksakovs, for all their idealization of the Russian past and Russia's potential, realized that Russia had a great deal of internal work to do before it could even fantasize about a place on the world-historical stage. As far as Dostoevsky was concerned, however, the Russians were ready to take the leading, world-historical role from a faltering Europe in his own day.

And what is the "word" that the Russians possess and that will allow theirs to become the ultimate word? "Our mission and our role are not at all like those of other nations, for there each separate people lives exclusively for itself and in itself, while we will begin, now that the time has come, precisely by becoming the servants of all for universal peace-making. And this is in no way something to be ashamed of; on the contrary, this constitutes our greatness because it all leads to the ultimate unity of humankind."[28] Here Dostoevsky's historical system takes a definite turn toward millenarianism; for if the meaning of history is the harmonious union of all humankind and if the Russian Orthodox ideal (which is about to be realized) is identical to it, it follows that history is about to come to an end.

As early as 1877, Dostoevsky had begun to connect Pushkin to these notions. Writing in the July / August number for 1877 he stated:

> There are two main ideas in Pushkin and both contain within themselves the prototype of our entire future mission and of Russia's entire future goal; that is of our entire future fate. The first idea is that of Russia's universality, her sympathy toward and the real, unquestionable, and deep kinship of her genius with the geniuses of all times and all the world's peoples . . . Pushkin's other idea is his turn to the people and his trust in their strength alone, the testament of the fact that in the people ["narod" – the simple people, A.W.] and only in the people do we find in toto our Russian genius and the recognition of its mission.[29]

The "Pushkin Speech," then, can be seen as Dostoevsky's last word on the theme of Russian national identity and Russian literature. One contemporary described the affect as follows: "It was a fever, an intoxication, an explosion . . . The exalted gathering did not have enough means to express its ecstasy, and people simply flung themselves all over the hall . . . [Dostoevsky's] fanatical, bottomless faith in the truth, beauty, and grandeur of his ideals reigned supreme . . . Its gleam and glitter burned and blinded . . ."[30]

Though Dostoevsky would die less than a year after the speech, his ideas regarding Russia's manifest destiny would outlive him. Starting with the thought of the Russian philosopher Vladimir Solovev and culminating in the so-called Eurasian historical theories of Nikolai Trubetskoy, the view that Russian civilization was a counterweight to that of Europe flourished in the late nineteenth and early twentieth centuries. A transformed version of this ideology is transparent in one of the final poems of Alexander Blok, entitled "Scythians" (1918), which begins as follows:

> You have your millions. We are numberless,
> numberless, numberless. Try doing
> battle with us! Yes, we are Scythians! Yes,
> Asiatics with greedy eyes slanting!
>
> For you, the centuries; for us, one hour.
> We, like obedient lackeys, have held up
> a shield dividing two embattled powers –
> the Mongol hordes and Europe!
>
> Russia is a sphinx. Grieving, jubilant,
> and covering herself with blood
> she looks. she looks, she looks at you – her slant
> eyes lit with hatred and with love.
>
> All things we love – the mystic's divine gift,
> the fever of cold calculus;
> all we appreciate – the Frenchman's shaft
> of wit, the German's genius . . .[31]

Echoes of this same messianic view of Russian national identity can also be heard in the claim that Soviet Socialist Realist was the heir to all of the greatest that had been produced in world culture.

5

Russian Psychology: The Quest for Personal Identity in Nineteenth-Century Russian Culture

I

It is by now a commonplace that the classic Russian realists – Dostoevsky, Turgenev, Tolstoy, Chekhov – are distinguished by their unparalleled ability to portray the complex inner mental states of their characters. As early as 1856, the critic Nikolai Chernyshevsky praised Tolstoy for his superlative rendering of the "dialectics of the soul," by which he meant Tolstoy's painstaking dissection of the inner life of his heroes. And in the English-speaking world, Virginia Woolf summed up a review of Tolstoy's *The Cossacks* by remarking: "They do not rival us in the comedy of manners, but after reading Tolstoy we always feel that we could sacrifice our skill in that direction for something of the profound psychology and superb sincerity of the Russian writers."[1]

In this chapter, we focus on a number of questions that relate to the depiction of inner life in Russian literature and its relation to Russian notions of the individual and the collective. Our central points will be two. First, Russian novelists, with few exceptions, are concerned with individual psychology because it provides a window onto what might be called social psychology; that is, the individual is crucial not primarily for him or herself, but as representative of a larger group. Although this is sometimes the case in the works of non-Russian novelists as well, we would assert that George Eliot, Thomas Hardy, Henry James, Gustave Flaubert, and other masters of European psychological prose are more usually interested in portraying individuals as individuals than are their Russian counterparts. Second, psychological portraiture is usually associated with disease or, at least, with distress; to paraphrase Tolstoy, all happy individuals have the same psychology, but all unhappy individuals have unique and fascinating psychologies worth exploring. In practice, this means that psychological analysis in the classic Russian novel tends to disappear if and when a major character finds happiness and to be foregrounded at those moments when he is most diseased. By disease, however, we do not mean having a bona fide mental illness – schizophrenia, manic depression, and the like – although characters suffering such maladies can be identified in Russian literature.[2] Rather, the novels tend to present astute portrayals of general human psychological problems – pride, doubt, lassitude, spite, envy.

Thus, on the whole, Russian psychological prose is concerned with exploring the ramifications of fairly common human failings through the analysis of the mental states of characters who are seen to be representative of Russians (or types of Russians) in general. The analysis can be carried out in one of two ways: either the character himself is the narrator, in which case he must be sufficiently self-aware to recognize at least dimly his own affliction, or else a third-person narrator able to penetrate, present, and weigh the character's inner thoughts is employed. The characters treated here are almost exclusively male. This is not accidental: the classic Russian psychological novel generally deals with a weak (read psychologically diseased) male character who is provided with a foil in the person of a healthy woman (who is, therefore, not treated psychologically). The exceptions to this rule are precisely those Russian novels that transcend this as well as most other models: *The Idiot* and *The Brothers Karamazov* of Dostoevsky and Tolstoy's *Anna Karenina*, about which there will be more below.

II

The concatenation of psychological analysis with a presentation of a character seen as a portrait of his age comes together in the first Russian psychological novel, Mikhail Lermontov's *A Hero of Our Time* (Geroi nashego vremeni, 1840). It is worth noting that Russia's earlier great writers of prose fiction, Pushkin and Gogol, practically eschewed psychological portraiture altogether, and showed little interest in portraying an inner essential self. This was despite the fact that Pushkin at least was well aware of French late eighteenth-century and early nineteenth-century fiction with its intense psychological portraiture. Nevertheless, in the brilliant novel in verse *Eugene Onegin*, Pushkin's narrator rarely makes his reader privy to the characters' inner states. Instead, he provides highly nuanced external description, which the reader, who has long been sure that these states must exist within the characters, can use to intuit convincing psychological explanation. Gogol's famous short stories from the 1830s and his epic *Dead Souls* avoid psychology even more thoroughly than do Pushkin's works. While Gogol does tell us what his heroes are thinking, this disclosure yields no knowledge about a given character's inner life because the thoughts presented are either empty or so metaphorically extravagant that they tell us nothing. The absence of psychological analysis is particularly striking in Gogol's "Notes of a Madman." The entire story is composed of the diary of a certain Poprishchin who goes progressively insane. But the narrator has no understanding of what is happening, and thus the story cannot be considered psychological prose of the type that will become so characteristic for Russian literature.

By the end of the 1830s, however, the situation slowly began to change, particularly in the work of those writers born after 1815. At first, a burgeoning interest in psychological analysis appeared not in fiction, but rather in the life of the newly appearing intelligentsia. As the Russian critic Lydia Ginzburg demonstrated in her broad-ranging analysis *On Psychological Prose*, all the narrative techniques that would be used later in the Russian psychological novel, as well as the tendency to link personal and social analysis, can already be found in the letters and diaries of such men as Herzen, Bakunin, and Belinsky well before any psychological novels had appeared.[3]

The first novel in which the incipient interest in the psyche is manifested is *A Hero of Our Time*. Lermontov's work is composed of five loosely related stories which revolve around a single individual, Grigory Pechorin. What sustains our interest in *A Hero of Our Time* as a novel is not the plot (which is fragmentary) but rather the gradual unveiling of Pechorin's personality. The novel's eponymous protagonist appears for the first time triply distanced from the reader – in time, space, and narrative frame: we hear about him in the chapter called "Bela" through a story told to the narrator by an old veteran of the Caucasus about events that occurred a number of years previously in another location. The veteran's insistence on and description of Pechorin's remarkable qualities pique our interest. The rest of the novel gradually brings this mysterious figure into focus, first through a meeting with him in the present (the story "Maksim Maksimych"), and then through three stories supposedly taken from Pechorin's own diary ("Taman," "Princess Mary," and "The Fatalist").

In this final trio of stories Lermontov unveils, for the first time in Russian literature, the complex inner life of a character. Pechorin indeed possesses remarkable abilities, yet he is bored, bilious, and a scoundrel. The novel's central concern is to explain why and how such a paradoxical combination has come into existence. What is remarkable about Pechorin is the contrast between, on the one hand, his seemingly highly developed self-understanding and evident talent and, on the other, his inability to accomplish anything except the production of misery for himself and those around him. This occurs because the only psychological categories Pechorin possesses for self-understanding are the polarities of Byronic Romanticism – either/or, an angel or a demon. Through Pechorin's pitiless self-analysis we come to recognize the mechanism of psychological development in which he believes. A person possesses certain internal, clearly defined qualities; depending on how they are received by society, they can either be developed to their full potential or turned into their opposite.

What makes the novel work is not Pechorin's outdated Byronism (which is even parodied by Lermontov through the presence of Pechorin's "double" Grushnitsky in the story "Princess Mary"), but our recognition that the limited poles provided by Romantic psychology are not sufficient to compass him. As the novel progresses, we begin to recognize that although Pechorin seems filled with self-knowledge, something is missing. He is trying too hard to fit his life into the Byronic poles that are all he possesses for self-understanding. Byronism is a mask, a disease, which ultimately makes him incapable of understanding himself, despite what seem to be valiant efforts. Something of the same problem afflicted Lermontov himself, whose attempts to live the Romantic life climaxed in his own death in a duel at the age of twenty-six.

From our perspective, however, Pechorin's psychology is less important than Lermontov's characterization of his own novel, which he provided in an authorial introduction to the second edition (1841). Here, ostensibly in response to those who had criticized the book by asserting that the main character was nothing but a self-portrait, Lermontov makes the counter-claim that Pechorin is best understood not as an individual but as a social portrait: "*A Hero of Our Time* . . . is a portrait composed of all the vices of our generation in the fullness of their development."[4] The novel, says Lermontov, is not meant to cure the disease he has portrayed, only to diagnose it. These parallel claims, that psychological analysis serves to portray disease and that what seems to be a nuanced portrait of a unique individual's psychology is best understood as a presentation of the psychology of a group or type, were destined to have a long history in Russian culture.

III

The character of the "superfluous man," as the Pechorin-type figure came to be dubbed, was treated in a realist rather than Romantic key in the novel *Oblomov* (1859) by Ivan Goncharov (1812–91). This outstanding work belies the belief that the Russian novel is necessarily characterized by grand passions and exciting plots. For what is remarkable about *Oblomov* is that practically nothing whatsoever happens in it; the first 150 pages or so describe neither more nor less than the main character's attempt to get out of bed in the morning. What saves the novel from being as boring as its title character is its subtle focus on Oblomov's inner life. Goncharov's ability to explore the hidden recesses of his hero's mind, to ferret out the wellsprings of his action (or inaction as the case may be) is light years ahead of Lermontov's. In place of the Romantic dualist view of the mind that dominated Pechorin's (and Lermontov's own) vision of self, Goncharov recognizes that the mind is a complex instrument, and that human motivation falls primarily in a prosaic gray area rather than in black-and-white.

The following passage illustrates Goncharov's ability to reproduce the complex associative mechanisms of human thought. It appears in the first part of the novel immediately after Oblomov's manservant Zakhar has offended his master by having the temerity to compare him to others, suggesting that if they can move to other apartments so can he: "He tried to grasp the whole meaning of that comparison and analyze what *the others* were and what he was, and to what extent a parallel between him and other people was justified, and how gravely Zakhar had insulted him. Finally, he wondered whether Zakhar had insulted him consciously, that is to say, whether he was convinced that he, Oblomov, was the same as 'another', or whether the words had escaped him without thinking."[5] These thoughts lead Oblomov to question the very nature of his own being. And in so doing, he must face the fact that he is incapable of accomplishing anything, in short that he is a superfluous man.

> Oh, how dreadful he felt when there arose in his mind a clear and vivid idea of human destiny and the purpose of a man's life, and when he compared this purpose with his own life . . . He felt sad and sorry at the thought of his own lack of education, at the arrested development of his spiritual powers, at the feeling of heaviness that interfered with everything he planned to do; and was overcome with envy of those whose lives were rich and full, while a huge rock seemed to have been thrown across the narrow and pitiful path of his own existence. Slowly there arose in his mind the realization that many sides of his nature had never been awakened, that others were barely touched, that none had developed fully.
>
> (101–2)

As opposed to Pechorin, who had a convenient theory to account for his superfluity, Oblomov cannot fully explain his inability to realize his own potential. The remainder of the novel can be seen as Oblomov's struggle first to answer the question he asks immediately after this moment of insight: "Why am I like this?" and then to escape the deadening weight of his own psychological complexes.

Of these prongs, the most interesting from our point of view is the former, because Goncharov provides, in the famous section called "Oblomov's Dream" an overtly psychological (as opposed to a political or sociological) explanation. The "Dream" (the first section of the novel to be published, a decade before the rest) transports Oblomov back to the idyllic world of his childhood, to the family estate of Oblomovka, an earthly paradise characterized by a cocoon-like softness and safety. And the narrator suggests that precisely the childhood impressions Oblomov drew from this bucolic paradise are what made him what he has become. Because no one around him ever did anything, the boy came to believe that lassitude was the natural order of things. Goncharov suggests that our basic psychological makeup is set in earliest infancy, never to change thereafter no matter what external circumstances might arise.

The rest of the novel, deals with Oblomov's ultimately unsuccessful attempts to escape from his torpor, but it need not concern us here. What is of cardinal importance, is the history of the novel's reception. Immediately after its publication, one of Russia's leading literary critics, Nikolai Dobroliubov (1836–61), wrote an appreciative essay entitled "What is Oblomovitis?" (Chto takoe Oblomovshchina?), which forever fixed Russian critical opinion of *Oblomov*. Despite the fact that Oblomov is drawn with a realist's fine brush and seems, at first glance, to be quite a specific character, Dobroliubov saw him not as an individual but as a social portrait.

> The story of how Oblomov, a lazy Mr. Nice Guy, lies around and sleeps and can be roused neither by friendship nor love is not much of a story. But Russian life is reflected in it, we see in it a vivid contemporary Russian type, sculpted with pitiless severity and accuracy. A new word in our social development has been pronounced here clearly and firmly without despair or childish hope, but with full knowledge of the truth. The word is Oblomovitis and it serves as a key to the solution of many phenomena of Russian life.[6]

The expectation that a carefully drawn psychological portrait of a literary character is actually meant to be a criticism of Russian society is one that Goncharov may well have shared, for he was on record as having said that the novel can only depict types.[7] Be that as it may, Dobroliubov's article fixed in the mind of the reading public the belief that literary characters were interchangeable with real people, and that the diseased fictional psychologies described by novelists could and should be seen as social psychologies.

IV

The Russian novelist whose works provide the most comprehensive attempt to fix through the portrayal of individual psyches the stages of Russian social development is Ivan Turgenev. Although his characters may lack the shattering power of Dostoevsky's greatest portraits and the astoundingly fine-grained detailing typical of Tolstoy's heroes, Turgenev's central fictional creations provide the best examples of psycho-social types in Russian literature. In the course of a series of novels starting with *Rudin* (1856) and culminating with *Fathers and Children*, Turgenev perfected his own psychological method, one fully in accord with the Russian expectation that individual characters should reflect general truths about the nation. Thus, any problem of personal identity in a Turgenev novel can be (and generally was) read as a problem of national self-definition.

Turgenev's main characters (as well as many of Tolstoy and Dostoevsky) are, in attempting to discover their essence, standing in for an entire country that was desperately trying to do the same. Perhaps the best Turgenevan hero to examine in this regard is his most controversial creation, Bazarov, the central character of *Fathers and Children*. Bazarov is an angry young man from a relatively poor background. He believes in nothing except physiology (symbolized in the novel by his constant desire to dissect frogs), convinced that the dualism of body and mind is specious, and that the way to all understanding is through a thorough knowledge of the workings of the nervous system. In the course of the novel, Turgenev gradually, lovingly, and gently, shows us the breakdown of Bazarov's system in the face of human life, which turns out, in essential ways, to be different from the amphibian.

In particular, Bazarov's system crumbles under the onslaught of love, an emotion whose existence he had never acknowledged. Turgenev carefully prepares to show us the developments that are occurring in Bazarov's mind by first describing external changes. "Bazarov, whom Anna Sergeevna [Odintsova] obviously favored, although she seldom agreed with him, had begun to show signs of unprecedented perturbation: he was easily irritated, reluctant to talk, he gazed around angrily, and couldn't sit still in one place, as though he were being swept away by some irresistible force."[8] The metaphors Turgenev uses here, of elemental forces and illness, hint that love has softened up Bazarov to such an extent that he has become a candidate to be treated psychologically; that is, he is sufficiently diseased that his formerly impregnable psychic defenses have been breached.

Bazarov's friend and disciple, Arkady Kirsanov, notices that something has changed in his formerly rock-solid mentor, and Turgenev's narrator, employing to great effect what has become known as the "free indirect style" of discourse hastens to add:

> The real cause of this "'change" was the feeling Mrs. Odintsov inspired in Bazarov, a feeling that tortured and maddened him, one that he would have instantly denied with scornful laughter and cynical derision if anyone had even remotely hinted at the possibility that it existed inside him. Bazarov was a great admirer of women and of female beauty, but love in the ideal or, as he put it, romantic sense he termed lunacy, unpardonable imbecility. He regarded chivalrous sentiments as something on the order of a deformity or disease . . . In his conversations with Anna Sergeevna, he expressed calm contempt for everything romantic more firmly than ever; when he was alone, though, he indignantly perceived the romantic in himself.[9]

The psychology Turgenev dissects here is infinitely more complex than that described by Lermontov or Goncharov; whereas their central figures were characterized by either/or, Bazarov suffers from the disease of both/and. His conscious mind struggles to avoid the conclusions that his subconscious is drawing, and as a result, contradictory world-views exist within him simultaneously. Worse yet, when Bazarov finally allows his subconscious feelings to come to the surface in a confession of love, the widowed Mme. Odintsov rejects him. He realizes, therefore, that he had not only misunderstood himself, but that his analysis of her character has been flawed. His response is to control himself through flight, but it is clear from his actions in the rest of the novel that this temporarily successful effort to bridle his emotions has so weakened him as to lead to his destruction.

The case of Bazarov is not different from that of most of Turgenev's male heroes. The conscious mind, Turgenev says, functions to protect us from the trauma that unbridled emotion would cause. This view of the mind's workings is part and parcel of Turgenev's overall view of human nature. In the words of one of Turgenev's most sensitive recent readers: "As Turgenev represents human nature in his works, he contributes to a venerable tradition – going back at least to the stoics in the West and continuing through Freud – that dwells on the susceptibility of human beings to suffering . . . Turgenev's psychology [as manifested in his characters], and the ethics derived from it, anticipated Freud in that Turgenev too could be said to have reduced the sources of suffering to three, not so different from Freud's: nature, other people, and the irrational."[10] This observation leads us to the further conclusion that the novel was, in fact, a substitute for scientific study of the mind in Russia in the nineteenth century. As has been pointed out by the historian David Joravsky, most Russian novelists had nothing but contempt for academic psychology and psychiatry, perhaps because they realized that their own powers of psychological observation and explanation far outstripped anything that contemporary science had achieved.[11]

V

While in the novels of Turgenev internal psychological analysis is always balanced by external narrative description (as in the passage describing Bazarov falling in love), in the work of Fedor Dostoevsky the psychological takes pride of place. Dostoevsky's primary concern, throughout all his great novels, is to explore the psychology of individuals possessed by an idea. Each of Dostoevsky's major works has at its center a character whose task is to comprehend the mystery of his own personality. Dostoevsky, like Freud who so admired him, believed that the human mind was an enigma begging to be solved; his central artistic concern was to show, by a process of unparalleled artistic intuition, the ways in which the human mind attempts to hide from itself and then, when this becomes intolerable, discovers its own inner workings. This concern was already apparent in his 1846 novella *The Double*. Dostoevsky borrows the popular Romantic theme of the Doppelgänger but characteristically shifts the center of interest from the eerie and supernatural to the psychological. The entire narrative interest of the piece comes from our observation of the gradual mental breakdown of the hero, Mr. Goliadkin, as he tries desperately to escape his self-created double.

What sets *The Double* apart from the novels that Dostoevsky wrote later in his career is that Goliadkin's obsession is primarily personal, while the ideas that possess Dostoevsky's greatest heroes are social and philosophical. They are refracted through the very specific characters Dostoevsky creates (which is why his heroes seem far more like individuals than like types). Nevertheless, the notion that the obsessions Dostoevsky portrays are meant to be read as portraits of his age, lies at the very foundation of all his ideological novels. In *Notes from Underground* (Zapiski iz podpolia, 1864) the link between the diseased individual and the overall state of society (or at least part of it) is explicit from the outset. In his brief authorial preface, Dostoevsky makes the following startling claim for the inner veracity of his fiction: "Both the author of the *Notes* and the *Notes* themselves are, of course, fictitious. Nonetheless, such persons as the author of such memoirs not only may, but must exist in our society, if we take into consideration the circumstances that led to the formation of our society."[12]

The hundred-odd pages of rambling first-person narrative that follow provide us with a more than adequate self-portrait of the underground man himself. From the mesmerizing first lines: "I am a sick man. I am a spiteful man. I am an unattractive man. I think my liver is diseased"[13] – we see a person who has literally been devoured by an idea, in this case a hypertrophied belief in determinism which seemed to follow from nineteenth-century materialism. The only impulse as strong as the underground man's belief in determinism, it turns out, is his hopeless desire to preserve some kind of freedom of action. All of the degrading, masochistic, and pitiful actions he describes are rooted in his paradoxical attempts to find an outlet for his free will. With supreme mastery, Dostoevsky shows us the psychological dialectic by which the underground man, in his hopeless fight against his own belief, has constructed a prison from which there can be no escape.

In *Crime and Punishment*, the author again focuses on an individual consumed by an idea. Originally, the novel was to have been written in confessional form and it was to be the psychological account of a crime . . . A young man, who was expelled from the university, of petit-bourgeois origins and living in utter poverty, through irresponsible thinking, through shaky notions, having fallen under the influence of those strange, 'incomplete' ideas which are floating about in the air, has decided to break out of his horrible position in a single stroke. He has decided to kill an old woman."[14] As Dostoevsky rewrote, he abandoned first-person narrative, but the new third-person perspective did not prevent him from depicting the inner workings of his confused hero's mind.

In its final version *Crime and Punishment* is a detective story with a twist; from the first pages we know that the murderer is the book's central character, the poor student Rodion Raskolnikov. The mystery is why he murdered and what psychological changes his having done so will effect in him. A further twist is that Raskolnikov himself does not fully know why he acted as he did. In this sense the novel is a psychological thriller, for it depicts, with frightening analytic depth, the process by which Raskolnikov discovers his own motivations. Dostoevsky gradually unveils the complex ideas that have taken possession of his hero. The first is the modish utilitarian calculus, which tells him that because he would do wonderful things with the money while the old pawnbroker he murders does nothing but hoard, the greatest good for the greatest number will be produced if he were to kill her and steal the money. This theory is overlapped and partially contradicted by another, the "idea of Napoleon" the notion that there exists in the world a class of human beings who do not have to follow the moral laws that bind everyone else. Raskolnikov suspects that he belongs to this group, and in part he murders in order to prove this to himself. In the aftermath of the crime, however, confronted by the enormity of his deeds, Raskolnikov slowly begins to recognize the speciousness of his theories. When he finally chooses to confess to his crime, he does so primarily because the psychological weight of his guilt becomes heavier than he can bear.

Crime and Punishment also brings up the fascinating issue of when psychology does not appear in the Russian psychological novel. As noted before, its primary function is to make clear the illness of individuals who are suffering from ailments which beset an entire generation or class. Thus, it should not be surprising that the psychological approach is abandoned precisely at those moments when Dostoevsky wishes to show that his character is either healthy or no longer representative (or both, since the two often overlap). The most obvious example of this different method of writing comes in the novel's epilogue. Raskolnikov confesses his crime, is convicted and exiled to Siberia. Sonia Marmeladova, whose moral purity inspired him to confession in the first place, joins him. At first, Raskolnikov seems not to have changed much, but after a serious illness, he recognizes the possibility of happiness, of an escape from the psychological demons that have tortured him. Raskolnikov lies in his bunk thinking of Sonia:

> He remembered how continually he had tormented her and wounded her heart. He remembered her pale and thin little face. But these recollections scarcely troubled him now; he knew with what infinite love he would now repay all her sufferings. And what were all, *all* the agonies of the past! Everything, even his crime, his sentence and imprisonment, seemed to him now in the first rush of feeling an external strange fact with which he had no concern. But he could not think for long together of anything that evening, and he could not have analyzed anything consciously; he was simply feeling. Life had stepped into the place of theory and something quite different would work itself out in his mind.[15]

Psychological self-analysis is a sign of illness, and health can only be reached at those moments when it is overcome. The underground man, Raskolnikov, Stavrogin in *The Devils*, and Ivan Karamazov are all ill. Of these striking creations, only Raskolnikov is vouchsafed the ultimate happiness of an escape from self-analysis; the underground man apparently continues to rave, Stavrogin commits suicide when the secrets of his mind are pierced by Father Tikhon (whom Stavrogin calls a "damned psychologist"), and Ivan lapses into brain fever at the close of *The Brothers Karamazov*.[16]

VI

When we turn from Dostoevsky to the other master of Russian psychological prose, Lev Tolstoy, we move from a world characterized by tension, extremes of emotion, and psychological obsession to one whose concerns are more quotidian and prosaic. While Tolstoy does provide the occasional character who seems to be a refugee from a Dostoevsky novel (Anna Karenina being the most prominent example), the majority of his characters are portraits of normal human beings with normal human emotions. This does not mean, however, that Tolstoy's analysis is any less subtle or penetrating than Dostoevsky's; they are simply describing different types of worlds. What it does mean, however, is that Tolstoy uses psychology in his novels for different purposes. Where all the great Russian novelists discussed above based their characters on the concept of type (even if Turgenev's and Dostoevsky's greatest creations rise above it), Tolstoy is fascinated by the uniqueness of each individual. "To say about a person: he is original, good, intelligent, stupid, logical, and so forth . . . such words do not give any idea about a person but they pretend to describe him while only throwing you off," wrote Tolstoy in an early diary entry.[17] What Tolstoy attempted to do in all his novels was to show how the human personality, which looks like a smooth and finished whole from the outside, is in fact constructed of a mass of frequently self-contradictory elements held in unstable equilibrium by the self.

Tolstoy's interest in and talent for dissecting individual psychological motivations was already apparent in his earliest work, the pseudo-autobiographical novel *Childhood*, (Detstvo, 1853). The hero of this short work, Nikolai Irten'ev, is the first of the line of Tolstoyan heroes that includes Olenin of *The Cossacks* (Kazaki, 1863), Pierre Bezukhov of *War and Peace* and Konstantin Levin of *Anna Karenina*. Through constant self-analysis, these questing heroes attempt to achieve happiness by means of self-understanding. In this they function as autobiographical avatars, for Tolstoy's copious diaries reveal that he himself employed pitiless self-analysis as a tool for improvement and development. As opposed to the heroes of Dostoevsky's novels (who are prevented from reaching self-knowledge because they have been possessed by an external idea), Tolstoy's central characters are held back by far more mundane and realistic enemies: doubt, self-pity, illusion, physical desire. These enemies, however, are no less dangerous for being quotidian, and in the Tolstoyan universe the heroes successfully navigate the path to self-knowledge, avoiding the diseases of everyday life to which others fall prey. Paradoxically, however, self-knowledge, when achieved, allows the Tolstoyan hero to stop thinking. In this respect, Tolstoy may be seen as a precursor to Freud, for he, like Dostoevsky, believes that the sign of a cure is the overcoming of the need to analyze.

Probably the best illustration of how Tolstoy uses his unparalleled ability to explore the inner life of his characters is *Anna Karenina*. From a psychological point of view, *Anna Karenina* can be read as a contrast between two starkly different ways of perceiving the world. On the one hand, we have Konstantin Levin, something of a provincial boor, simply unable to grasp the ways and wiles of the city. Tolstoy constantly analyzes Levin's thoughts, but the curious thing about the character is that the more he thinks the less he understands. We are told instead that he truly feels at home only when he is working on his farm, which also happens to be the one place where he is able, for the most part, not to think. Levin's battle throughout the novel will be to learn to trust the instinctual, non-thinking parts of his nature. When he can do this, he is happy, although the strength of his mind's desire to understand renders this happiness is unstable. Such famous scenes as the hay mowing (part 3, chapter 4), in which Levin gets so caught up in the physical exertion of the task at hand that he forgets to think, echo the epilogue of *Crime and Punishment* with their shared assertion that thinking too much is a disease which can be cured only by unconscious epiphany.

By contrast with Levin, Anna is introduced at the beginning of the novel as an entirely natural person. She is able to comfort her sister-in-law precisely because of the natural, unthinking, goodness that radiates from her. As she falls in love with Vronsky her naturalness begins to disappear. She has been infected with a particularly virulent form of the disease of self-consciousness. Her marriage, which had given her satisfaction before she began to think about it, turns bitter. We are meant to recognize that this change in feelings reflects not the truth about her life, but rather her attempts to justify her affair with Vronsky. As Anna gradually becomes more psychologically aware she becomes a more interesting, even a heroic character (despite the fact that Tolstoy did not wish for this). Self awareness, however, leads slowly to a kind of solipsism in Anna and by the end of the novel, she lives in an inner world of her own creation; indeed, as is the case with most of the characters discussed here, we can say that self awareness is itself Anna's disease. The last scenes of book seven of the novel depict in pitiless detail, the results of self-absorption. Anna travels in a railway carriage listening to the innocuous conversations around her. Functioning like a psychological black hole, she swallows and internalizes everything she hears, reinterpreting it to apply to herself and her own condition. For the first time in world literature, Tolstoy applies the method that has come to be known as stream of consciousness to depict the disjointed patterns of Anna's thought. Unfortunately for Anna, by the end of book seven the disease of self-analysis has advanced to a critical stage. The self-created world of her thoughts becomes an all-encompassing prison, and the only escape is suicide.

VII

The early 1880s brought about a crisis in the Russian novel. With the death of Dostoevsky in 1881, of Turgenev in 1883, and Tolstoy's public rejection of literature at about the same time, the giants of the Russian psychological novel had disappeared. It was unclear whether further development of psychology in the framework of the novel would be possible or even whether the genre itself had a future. And indeed, the period from the 1880s through the 1910s proved unpropitious for the Russian novel. Smaller genres dominated at this time. But, in a series of brief gems written in the second half of the 1890s and first years of the new century (including *Dushechka* [1898] and culminating in the brilliant and chilling novella *In the Ravine* (V ovrage [1902]) Anton Chekhov demonstrated that deep and complex psychological analysis could be achieved in small packages. Even more important, Chekhov expanded a concern with analysis of the mental states of characters into the world of the drama, creating in *The Seagull* (Chaika, 1896), *Three Sisters* (Tri sestry, 1899), *Uncle Vanya* (Diadia Vania, 1901), and *The Cherry Orchard* (Vishnevyi sad, 1903) unprecedented masterpieces of psychological drama.

The period from the late 1870s to the turn of the century saw psychological portraiture enter Russian visual art in the work of the painters who called themselves peredvizhniki (The Wanderers). Having broken with the tradition of Russian academic painting in the late 1860s, these artists drew their inspiration from Russian nature, the lower stratum of Russian society, and Russian history. Many of their best canvases, such as Vasily

Surikov's *Boyarina Morozova* (1887), which depicts dramatically the arrest of an Old Believer during the great schism of the Russian church at the time of Avvakum, Nikolai Ge's *Peter the Great Interrogating his Son Alexei* (1871), and Ivan Kramskoi's *Portrait of an Unknown Woman* (1883), seem the painterly equivalent of exceptionally legible snapshots taken in the midst of fully formed narratives. They demand to be read psychologically, which is what contemporaries did, in analogy with the classic Russian novels. Perhaps the greatest example of such "psychological narrative" painting is Ilya Repin's painting *They Did not Expect Him* (Ne zhdali, 1884–8). The painting depicts the return of a political exile to his upper-middle-class family and captures all the drama of what is clearly an unexpected meeting. The contrast between the man's shabby garb and emaciated features and the well-dressed members of his family captures our attention immediately, as do the exceptionally varied responses of his wife, mother and children. The viewer is invited to imagine the complex emotions evoked by this event, as well as to speculate on the background and the future of the family. In short, though it freezes only a single imagined moment in time, the painting functions as a kind of novelistic scene that leads us to reconstruct the absent psychological narrative.

The first writer to come out of the long shadow of Dostoevsky, Turgenev, and Tolstoy and to chart a new course for the depiction of psychology in the Russian novel was Andrei Bely (pseudonym for Boris Bugaev, 1880–1934) in *Petersburg* (1916, revised 1922). Bely's novel flamboyantly avoids the conventions of Realist narrative, foregrounding narrative play, intertextual reference, and symbolic organization. In terms of psychology, it breaks new ground in its attempt to show that all actions (including narrative gestures) proceed from psychological states rather than the other way around. The central psychological concept in the novel is what Bely calls "cerebral play," which is indulged in by the narrator (to create characters), by the characters themselves (to create their own internal and external worlds), and by the reader (to make sense of and derive pleasure from the narrative). The characters whose minds are depicted are Apollon Apollonovich Ableukhov (a high-ranking government official), his son, Nikolai Apollonovich, and Nikolai's erstwhile friend, the revolutionary Dudkin. Each is remarkable for his ability to create entire worlds via mental processes. Thus, although Apollon Apollonovich is physically unprepossessing, we are told that from his cranium gigantic forces pour forth, both forces that seek to control the growing anarchy and chaos that are enveloping Russian society around the year 1905 and those that create this disorder. "Apollon Apollonovich was like Zeus: out of his head flowed goddesses and genii."[18]

9 Ilya Repin, *They Did not Expect Him*, 1884–8. Repin was a prolific and wide-ranging painter who excelled in portraiture and in narrative genre painting. The original version of this painting featured a returning female ex-convict, but in the final version, now in Moscow's Tretiakov Gallery, she has been replaced by a male.

For all his efforts at control, however, Apollon Apollonovich is not even able to keep his own son in line. Nikolai Apollonovich's head becomes identified with revolutionary chaos through its equation with the bomb he agrees to store for Dudkin. When he absentmindedly winds the bomb up, we know that an explosion will take place in the senator's house within twenty-four hours. In some of the most brilliant passages of the novel, we read in horror as the ticking of the bomb is registered inside Nikolai Apollonovich's head, the mind and the bomb becoming one. In this framework, the narrative becomes an arena for psychological discovery. The narrator encloses us in cerebral games, which distract us from the awful events about to unfold, but leave our minds, too, in a state of expectation that can only be relieved by an explosion. Instead of viewing the characters objectively (as we are encouraged to do by the conventions of Realism), in Bely's novel we are meant to think as if we were one of the characters; that is, the reader becomes part of the novel's psychological universe rather than an observer.

The connection of psychology with disease, and the identification of individual characters with psycho-social types is, however, preserved in Belyi's novel, despite all its modernist trappings. Apollon Apollonovich is an incarnation of the bureaucratic state, his mind a microcosm of its collapsing ideology. The hallucinating terrorist Dudkin, who loses his mind by the novel's end, is, for all his individuality, meant to be representative of the Russian revolutionary class. Finally, Nikolai Apollonovich himself objectifies the confused and divided loyalties of the younger generation of the Russian intelligentsia. All three are profoundly ill, as is Russian society as a whole, and Bely's narrator, with his vaguely out of control cerebral play, is part of the same collapsing universe. Thus, although the narrative techniques for depicting psychology have changed, its function in Bely's great novel remains the same as in its nineteenth-century predecessors.

Biography – Mikhail Iurevich Lermontov (1814–1841)

Like his idol Lord Byron, Lermontov understood poetry as the by-product of life experience, and the biography of the poet as an artistic text in keeping with Romantic norms and expressing Romantic values and notions. In fact, his short but eventful life reads like a Romantic poem: the early death of his mother and his forced separation from his father; disappointment in love and revenge against society for his dashed hopes; political opposition and exile; participation in military action in the exotic Caucasus; brilliant literary success; the jealousy and intrigues of high society; and death in a duel at the age of twenty-six. And when appropriately Romantic facts were lacking, Lermontov did not hesitate to invent them. Thus, in his youth he claimed to be descended from Thomas Learmonth the Rhymer, a Scottish poet of the thirteenth century or from the Spanish seventeenth-century earl and minister Francisco Lerma. At the same time, for Lermontov, to live according to the laws of Romanticism did not mean merely writing his life story according to received models, it also meant testing those models. The artificiality of Romantic behavior, its lack of connection with "natural" life, which develops according to inexplicable laws uncontrollable by the will of the Romantic, is one of his most important artistic themes. It is no accident that Russian realist writers saw Lermontov as their direct ancestor.

Lermontov was born on October 3, 1814 in Moscow to the army officer Iury Lermontov and his wife Maria. After his mother's death (1817), he was brought up by his grandmother, the rich and noble landowner Arsen'eva. She blamed his father for the early death of her daughter and forbade him contact with his son. The boy took this family tragedy to heart, and it would leave an impression on his literary work. In 1828, Lermontov began his studies at the University Pension for Noblemen, the same institution where the poets Vasily Zhukovsky, Alexander Griboedov, and Fedor Tiutchev had been educated. In 1830 he matriculated first in the political and then the literary faculty of Moscow University. At this time (after the Decembrist uprising and consequent clampdown on liberal thought) this was perhaps the only place in Russia still able to nurture any form of free thinking. The future idols of the "realist epoch," Belinsky, Herzen, and Goncharov, overlapped with Lermontov here at this time.

An interest in German idealist philosophy was characteristic for the intellectual atmosphere of the 1830s, particularly one of its most important branches, psychology, which was understood as the science of life and the history of the soul. Various theories about the relationship between psychology and physiology were popular as well (the physiognomy of Johann Kaspar Lavater; the phrenology of Franz Joseph Gall; the magnetism of Franz Mesmer; the pneumatology of Justinus Kerner), and they had a significant influence on Russian literary developments. From "unmediated" expressions of feeling (early Romanticism), Russian literature moved to the analysis of these feelings, from "dreamy lyrics" to metaphysical poetry and psychological-physiological prose.

In his student years Lermontov experimented with a variety of literary genres. In quest of his hero, he tried on and mixed various literary masks and voices (Byron, Pushkin, André Chenier), attempted to get inside various Romantic models following in the footsteps of authors of the French Romantic school of the 1810s and 1820s (from Benjamin de Constant to Alfred de Musset), and blended psychological analysis of the hero with social critique of contemporary society. Gradually the theme of a sick, "lost" generation came to the fore in his poetry. Suffering from unbelief, anomie, and hopeless yearning, the poetic narrators express a Russian analogue to the Weltschmerz of Western Romantics. The classic expression of this theme would be found in his later works – the meditative elegy "Thought" (Duma, 1838) and *A Hero of Our Time*. Many of his poems are titled only with the date of their composition: "July 10," "1831 on the 11th of June," "September 28" and so forth. Practically all are constructed around antitheses taken from the Romantic repertoire: good:evil, heavenly:earthly, love:hate, angel:demon, past:present. Characteristic features of Lermontov's work in this time are his constant confessional mode and his frequent repetition and deepening of the same stock of themes as well as his endless rewriting of his earlier poems. At this early period two central themes for the poet and his work (and two models of literary behavior) had already appeared: the suffering demon and the rebellious hero.

From the beginning, love lyrics played a major part in Lermontov's oeuvre, based to a great extent on his Romantic experiments with his own life. Typical in this respect is the history of Lermontov's relations with Ekaterina Sushkova. According to his own account (in a letter to another woman!) because Sushkova had ignored him when he was a youth and had "mocked" his pure feelings, he decided to revenge himself on her a number of years later. He induced her to fall in love with him, destroyed her marriage, then dumped her. In Lermontov's lyrics, love is presented as mutual suffering and dreams of happiness as an unrealizable ideal.

In 1832, at the urging of his family, Lermontov left the university and embarked on a military career, transferring to the school of Guards' Officers and Cavalry Junkers in Petersburg. Three years later he finished his studies and was commissioned as a Cornet in the prestigious Hussar Guards Regiment. In 1837, he experienced his first literary triumph, a poem on the death of Alexander Pushkin "Death of a Poet" (Smert' poeta), in which the young poet, in the voice of his generation, accused haughty foreigners, the "new" Russian aristocracy, and the "executioners" who "stand by the throne" of harassing and killing Russia's poetic genius. Filled with references to Pushkin's poetry, this passionate work was received by the public not only as a requiem for the dead Pushkin and not only as a threatening address to his persecutors but also as a symbolic act of inheritance: a "new Pushkin" had appeared. In general, the idea of direct inheritance (Lomonosov begat Derzhavin, Derzhavin begat Pushkin, Pushkin begat Lermontov, and so forth) became a typical feature of Russian poetic mythology through the late twentieth century (Joseph Brodsky [see chapter 9] was the last in this line of "direct" poetic heirs, having accepted the mantle from Anna Akhmatova).

For his "impertinent verses" on the death of the older poet, which quickly circulated in manuscript though they remained unpublished, Lermontov was arrested, demoted from the Guards to the Dragoons, and transferred to the Caucasus where a new war with the highland tribes led by the famous Imam Shamil was just getting underway. The Caucasus, which thanks to Pushkin's narrative poem *Prisoner of the Caucasus* and the stories of Alexander Bestuzhev-Marlinsky (1797–1837) had become the Russian equivalent of the Romantic East, would become the setting for many of Lermontov's works – a symbolic arena in which key themes such as escape from boring and cold Russian reality, the clash of civilizations (Russia and the East), fate, and the testing of personality, would play themselves out.

Having received forgiveness from "the most high," Lermontov returned to the capital in 1838. The young author was met as the rising star of Russian poetry. He was received in the most glittering literary salons and published in the prestigious journal *Notes of the Fatherland*. In the period after 1838 Lermontov wrote most of his best work, including his jocular poem *The Tambov Treasurer's Wife* (Tambovskaia kaznacheisha; about a husband who loses his wife in a card game and what ensues), his Eastern poem *The Demon* (Demon; about the love of a demon for a mortal woman and the consequences of this tragic romance), his *Fairy-Tale for Children* (Skazka dlia detei; a sort of ironic postscript to the demonic theme in his work), and his best long poem *The Novice* (Mtsyri; the confession of a young highlander who runs away from a Georgian monastery and is fatally wounded in a fight with a mountain lion). He also obsessively wrote and rewrote his great tragic drama in verse, *Masquerade*. Finally, he wrote stories about a "contemporary demon," the victimizing and victimized young officer Grigory Pechorin, that he would collect under the title *A Hero of Our Time* and publish as a novel in the spring of 1840. Belinsky, the most influential ideologue of the post-Pushkin "realist" era of Russian literature, greeted the work as a new word in Russian literature, an objective analysis of the inner world of a modern man. But Emperor Nicholas I believed that Pechorin and the novel as a whole propagated amoralism. Lermontov not only "introduced an element of psychological contradiction into Russian literature"[19] here, but presented man's contradictory inner world as a product of history and culture. The following fragment illustrates Lermontov's historical (or cultural) psychologism:

> I was walking home along the empty alleys of the settlement. The moon, full and red, like the glow of a conflagration, began to appear from behind the uneven line of roofs; the stars shone calmly upon the dark-blue vault, and it amused me to recall that, once upon a time, there were sages who thought that the heavenly bodies took part in our trivial conflicts for some piece of land or some imaginary rights. And what happened? These lampads, lit, in the opinion of those sages, merely to illiminate their battles and festivals, were burning as brightly as ever, while their passions and hopes had long been extinguished with them, like a small fire lit on the edge of the forest by a carefree wayfarer! But on the other hand, what strength of will they derived from the certitude that the entire sky with its countless inhabitants was looking upon them with mute but permanent sympathy! Whereas we, their miserable descendants, who roam the earth without convictions or pride, withour rapture or fear (except for that instinctive dread that compresses our hearts at the thought of the inevitable end), we are no longer capable of great sacrifice, neither for the good or mankind, nor even for our own happiness, because we know its impossibility, and pass with indifference from doubt to doubt, just as our ancesors rushed from one delusion to another.[20]

In March 1840 Lermontov was arrested for fighting a duel with the son of the French ambassador (the duel was over a woman, but rumors circulated in society that Lermontov was defending the honor of his country). At this time Lermontov was visited by Belinsky who left what became the "official" description of the young poet: "A deep and powerful soul! How well he understands art, what a deep and pure unmediated taste for the refined . . . I argued with him and I was happy to see in his rational, cool, and angry view of life and people the seeds of a deep belief in the value of both. I told him this and he answered: "Let it be God's will" . . . Every word of his is an expression of himself, his whole nature in all its depth and coherence" (XI, 508–9).

By the Tsar's command, Lermontov was sent to join the regular army in the Caucasus, in order "to teach him a moral lesson." In June of 1840 he fought bravely in a bloody skirmish with the highlanders near the River Valerik. In early February 1841 he was given a short leave and went to Petersburg, but by April he was back in the North Caucasus in the town of Piatigorsk. While there he created a whole series of lyric chefs d'oeuvres, including "A Dream" (Son), "The Cliff" (Utes), "Alone I Go Out on the Road" (Vykhozhu odin ia na dorogu), "The Sea Princess" (Morskaia tsarevna), and "The Prophet" (Prorok). One evening at the house of some friends Lermontov angered one of his old classmates at the Junker Academy, N. S. Martynov, a vain man with a high opinion of himself. Martynov challenged him to a duel, which took place on July 15, 1841. The conditions almost guaranteed a fatal outcome for one of the participants – they were to fire up to three shots from fifteen paces (some accounts say ten). Martynov shot first and Lermontov was killed instantly. According to legend, Martynov had seen that Lermontov was purposely aiming to the side.

Lermontov's death was perceived by Russian society not only as a tragic event, but as a symbol of the tragic fate of Russian poets. Working off Lermontov's poem on the death of Pushkin, the Countess E. P. Rostopchina wrote:

> Not simply, not in tranquility, not peacefully
> But before their time, by an enemy hand
> Russian poets fulfill their destiny,
> Leaving their swan song unfinished.
>
> ("To Our Future Poets")[21]

The biography of Lermontov, or rather his biographical legend became one of the most influential literary myths of Russian culture. At the basis of this myth is the idea of the mystery of the life and personality of the poet, which writers, philosophers, and artists attempt to solve. Among works connected with the "Lermontov text" of Russian culture one could cite the "Nietzschean" articles of the religious philosopher and mystic Vladimir Solovev (*Lermontov*, 1899), Dmitry Merezhkovsky's *M. Iu. Lermontov. Poet of the Superhuman* (1909), Vasily Rozanov's *Pushkin and Lermontov* (1914), and, later, Daniil Andreev's *The Rose of the World* (1947–57). Lermontov's literary work, which was closely linked for Russian authors with his biographical legend, also played an enormous role in the history of Russian art: in poetry in the lyrics of Alexander Blok in particular, though few of the major twentieth-century Russian poets were not indebted to Lermontov; in visual art, particularly in the works of Mikhail Vrubel; in music (the romances of Glinka and Tchaikovsky, in the orientalist opera *The Demon* of Anton Rubinstein, and in symphonic music in the tone poem "Tamara" of Mily Balakirev); in theatre (the modernist ballet "Tamar" choreographed by Mikhail Fokine for the Diaghilev troupe (1912) and in Vsevolod Meyerhold's famous production of *Masquerade* at the Aleksandrinsky Theatre in 1917); and in film, where one of the first successes in the history of Russian cinema was V. Goncharov's *Song of the Merchant Kalashnikov* (1909).

Literary Work – Childhood by Lev Tolstoy

In the summer of 1851, when Tolstoy began writing the work that was to become *Childhood*, he was not quite twenty three. Although he had harbored vague literary plans for years, there was as yet no sign that he would become a professional writer. The publication of the work in 1853 brought the budding writer instant success. Tolstoy's exceptional ability to capture psychological nuance was already clear in *Childhood*, and his interpretation of childhood as a particular kind of golden age resonated powerfully with Russian gentry readers. Ultimately, *Childhood* would turn out to be one of Tolstoy's most influential works, and it illustrates beautifully two central issues for the Russian psychological novel: the complex interplay between the personal and the collective, and the complex feedback loop between literature and reality in nineteenth-century Russia.

Childhood is a lyrical and almost plotless work. The first-person narrator, Nikolai Irten'ev, recalls a few days from his childhood, describing for the most part apparently trivial events (though filled with meaning for the child) and freely digressing from accounts of activity to recollections of his family situation. The first chapters take place on the Irten'ev's country estate over several days around the time of the child's tenth birthday. The second section takes place in Moscow a few months later, providing a sharp contrast between country and city mores. The third, traumatic section, recounts the death of Irten'ev's mother, which is understood as the ending point of his childhood for it precipitates a final move from the idyllic estate to the city and school.

Tolstoy's deceptively simple narrative is presented through three distinct voices. First is the unmediated voice of the child, who recalls events as if they were happening to him here and now without any ex post facto knowledge. The second is a more conventional autobiographical narrator whose recollections of childhood occurrences are colored by his adult perspective. Finally, there is a third, authorial voice. The actual author, of course, is the person who writes the text as a whole, and the reader knows that he is the ultimate source of all the voices in the text. However, as producer of the entire text, the author remains outside it. What we call the authorial voice within the text, on the other hand, appears at those moments when neither the adult narrator nor the child is speaking, characteristically to make general statements that go well beyond what the narrator or child can say. Such statements would become a Tolstoyan trademark; recall the famous opening lines of *Anna Karenina*: "All happy families are alike, all unhappy families are unhappy in their own way."

In the final version of *Childhood* two conflicting impulses are held in delicate equipoise: they might be called the personal and collective. On the one hand, the narrative is particular and individualized; Irten'ev recounts experiences that he claims relate to him alone. On the other, the pervasive lyrical tone, coupled with the fact that Irten'ev is clearly a fictional creation lends the text a feeling of generality: Irten'ev's childhood, it seems, could have belonged to anyone. A work of this sort can be called a pseudo-autobiography, and the Russian literary scene of the second half of the nineteenth century was particularly conducive to the production of this form. As Boris Eikhenbaum and Lydia Ginzburg pointed out, the period just before the publication of *Childhood* was marked by a flowering of previously marginal literary genres: autobiography, the journal, letters, and so forth. The demand on the part of literary critics (the all-important taste-makers of this period) for autobiographies was particularly strong. Paradoxically, however, the most prestigious literary form remained the novel, which was expected to be a vehicle for telling the truth about society. In these circumstances the appearance of the pseudo-autobiography was completely logical. Written in the style of an autobiography and on the basis of autobiographical material, it met the demand for works in marginal, personal genres. Yet, simultaneously, pseudo-autobiographies contained fictional narrators, which allowed them to be included in the prestigious category of prose fiction. As novels they could make more general statements on the human condition than would be appropriate for the more subjective autobiography.

The kinds of experiences Irten'ev describes were typical of a gentry childhood. In this sense Tolstoy was a historian of sorts. But these sorts of experiences had not been expressed in Russia previously, nor had they been given an overarching interpretation. In his overall conception, in his descriptions and interpretation of Irten'ev's surroundings, his parents, and of Irten'ev himself, Tolstoy can be said to have invented a Russian gentry attitude toward childhood. His personal myths of childhood became the foundation on which practically all future Russian works on the subject were constructed. In this sense he was not the historian of gentry childhood, but rather its creator.

The single over-arching message in *Childhood* is that childhood is and should be a happy time. This does not exclude moments of sadness, but the overall impression is one of joyous innocence. It is well known that Tolstoy borrowed his theoretical conception of childhood from Rousseau, but Tolstoy applied Rousseau's concept more thoroughly than did its inventor. Though Rousseau may have had a happy childhood, he devoted scarcely twenty pages of *The Confessions* to it. When Tolstoy provided Irten'ev with a happy childhood he was clearly making an ideological choice. For the author's own childhood could not have been happy, at least in any conventional sense. His mother died before he was two, he was orphaned at eight after his father's death and thereafter he was shuttled around between the homes of grandmothers and aunts.

That childhood is a golden age is asserted at various points in the work. Most notable, however, is the opening to chapter 15: "Happy, happy irretrievable time of childhood! How can one not love, not cherish its memories?" For the Russian cultural mind these were among Tolstoy's most unforgettable sentences. Over the next eighty years, practically every first-person description of childhood in Russia, whether in fictional or in non-fictional form, was oriented to them. As is typical of authorial statements throughout *Childhood*, these lines are unmotivated by anything which precedes them and are not modified by a personal pronoun or time marker. Rather, they are meant to express an abstract, universal truth. The state of childhood happiness recreated through narrative cannot be sustained, however. It is destroyed by the same mind that resurrected it, as soon as that mind begins to question and analyze its own recollections. The adult narrator's hope that he can recreate it disappears as soon as time and space intrude. For the child, only the here and now exist. The adult narrator, on the other hand, is conscious of the spatial and temporal abyss separating him from his past self.

In addition to the central myth of happy childhood, Tolstoy's work introduces a series of other myths that would become part and parcel of how Russian autobiographers and novelists understood the meaning of this period of life. These include traits of the ideal mother, father, and the surroundings in which the child lives. Irten'ev's mother plays the piano, embroiders, and speaks fluent French and German, treats her serfs well and is loved by them, and embodies more ineffable qualities such as "kindness and love," a smile that makes everyone who sees it happier, and religiosity without fanaticism. While the portrait of Irten'ev's mother is quite simply that of "an angel," his father is a more complicated figure. His most important trait is "razgul," a kind of devil-may-care insouciance coupled with the ability to do nothing at all. Indeed, we never see the father do anything in *Childhood*. He does not work and he never did (he was formerly an army officer). He manages his estates but has little control over or interest in agricultural production.

A particularly influential feature of *Childhood* was the child's attitude toward the physical world. The estate where Irten'ev grows up, typical for the estates of the middle rank of the Russian gentry, is an isolated self-sufficient enclave understood as a latter-day Garden of Eden. The natural world is a good that opposes both social evils and personal problems. Here the influence of Rousseau on the young Tolstoy is felt most strongly. It is not only that nature opposes the baneful influence of civilization. For Tolstoy, nature stands against time and space; its beauty, which changes at every season but always returns, recalls a time before the child understood the meaning of death and decay. The intense nostalgia evoked by memories of nature on the estate is not merely personal. By the 1850s it was already clear that an era was ending; not only would Irten'ev not experience his childhood again, no one would grow up as he had. With the liberation of the serfs in 1863, the system that had been in place since the days of Catherine the Great was passing. The novel's combination of personal and collective loss lent the nature scenes a powerful resonance for Russian gentry readers.

In the course of the second half of the nineteenth century the interpretation of childhood proposed by Tolstoy became canonized in the Russian cultural mind. The canonization of myths of childhood derived from literary texts was undoubtedly an ideological process. The Russian gentry class was subject to constant pressure from below from the 1860s through the Revolution. Members of other social classes (particularly the *raznochintsy*) assertively demanded a share of social and political power. From the point of view purely of intellectual and administrative ability it was, of course, difficult to deny that the "new men and women" were the equals of the gentry. If the gentry were to defend their position in Russian society, it became extremely important for them to discover virtues that non-nobles did not possess. A gentry childhood, as understood through the prism of *Childhood*, endowed a person with certain positive principles that were retained for a lifetime and became just such a possession. While ambitious "upstarts" from among the *raznochintsy* could, and did, make up for the deficiencies in their early education, they could never close the childhood gap. In a sense then, for many gentry autobiographers a "proper" childhood became a substitute for the "blue blood" in which the positivist nineteenth century no longer believed. Childhood became a mark of class solidarity, a way to differentiate the gentry from other classes.

There is abundant evidence to indicate that gentry autobiographers drew heavily on Tolstoy when writing their own accounts of childhood, incorporating typically Tolstoyan situations and turns of phrase into their own ostensibly non-fictional work. That Russians perceived their childhoods as happy can perhaps be explained by social conditions, the national psyche, or other causes. However, the manner in which they chose to express this perception and the consistency with which they did so can be explained only by recourse to the literary tradition. Indeed, the first response one has after reading a number of gentry autobiographies is a Tolstoyan paraphrase: All gentry childhoods are happy in the same way. The following excerpt, for example, ostensibly non-fictional, invokes the myth of the happy childhood, while employing the iterative present-tense narrative style and many of Tolstoy's key words: "My childhood was happy, joyous; it was passed in an atmosphere of deep motherly love, and was filled with the most tender attention."

We are not suggesting that Russian autobiographers necessarily had to modify large portions of their childhood memories in order to conform to the gentry myths. Nevertheless, it is clear is that they selected, organized, interpreted, and even verbalized their memories of childhood experience in accordance with patterns drawn from literary works. Because there were practically no gentry autobiographical accounts of childhood published before the 1860s, it is hard to determine whether the patterns of childhood proposed by Tolstoy reflected pre-existing cultural myths or whether they created them. Most probably, both processes were at work. At the very least, however, the pseudo-autobiography of Tolstoy crystallized the myths relating to happy childhood in literary form and made it available for generations of Russians.

Event – The "Spiritualist Season" of 1875–1876

The 1850s through the 1870s, though generally known in Russia as the Age of Realism and dominated by materialist and positivist tendencies, was also a time that saw the flourishing of various spiritualist and mystical circles, opposed to both materialism and the official Church. The most influential (and most ridiculed) spiritualist movement of the period was Modern Spiritualism (or spiritism), a doctrine which espouses individual immortality and the possibility of communication with the souls of the dead through mediums – people gifted with special psychic talents. Spiritualism was born in America in 1848 and reached Russia in the 1850s. The adepts of this doctrine understood it not simply as an alternative to materialist science, the Church, and philosophy, but as a synthesis of science and faith, psychology and mystical understanding, empiricism and idealism – a shortcut to the final answer to each and every question.

The synthetic claim of spiritualism is especially attractive to the student of the fierce polemics regarding mind / body / problem in Russian culture of the 1860s-1870s. One of the major issues of the time concerned the reality of the soul, its dependence on the body (matter), the means of acquiring knowledge about it, and the possibility of its existence after death. These intense and passionate debates were in essence a battle among various "experts in human souls" (as Dostoevsky put it) for the souls of contemporaries, who were seeking someone to believe, something to have faith in. The attempt of spiritualists to "resolve" this debate by radical means – summoning and interrogating the dead! – created a fascinating and ideologically rich public scandal.[22]

On April 1, 1875, the prestigious journal *Herald of Europe* printed a letter from the Saint Petersburg University Professor of Zoology (and popular author of children's tales) Nikolai Vagner (1829–1907) entitled "On the Subject of Modern Spiritualism." In it the renowned scholar enthusiastically described mediumistic phenomena (rapping, sounds, partial materialization of spirits, and so on) that he had heard and seen at séances in 1874. These phenomena, asserted the zoologist, not only bear witness to the fact that life beyond the grave is a reality, but at the same time open new horizons for science, which should now address the study of manifestations from the spiritual world. Vagner's letter drew an indignant reaction from journalists on both the left and the right, but was supported by another well-known scientist, the chemist Alexander Butlerov (1828–86), who had long been interested in Modern Spiritualism.

On May 6, 1875, Vagner and Butlerov's famous colleague Dmitry Mendeleev (inventor of the Periodic Table of Elements) presented a lecture at the Physics Society of St. Petersburg University about the urgency of scientific examinations of so-called mediumistic (spiritualist) phenomena. The promotion of Modern Spiritualism by authoritative naturalists was taken by Mendeleev and his colleagues as a violation of academic ethics: Vagner and Butlerov did not present their hypotheses in scientific societies "where analysis and verification of new, still unknown facts take place, where an investigation is conducted and regulated with methods based in science," but bypassed this route and appealed directly to society. Mendeleev perceived as his mission the unmasking of modern superstition, the exorcism of spirits from the cathedral of science, and the attraction of society – especially its youth – to the exploration of the *real* mysteries of nature (he himself was occupied at that time with problems of meteorology).

In spite of Mendeleev's patently anti-spiritualist attitude, his opponents agreed to collaborate with his Commission, which was made up of twelve scholars. In the "interests of science," the spiritualists first called in the professional English medium brothers Joseph and William Petty, and then, after failing with the professionals – they appealed to the amateur English medium Madame Claire, who arrived in Petersburg on January 7, 1876. Throughout this period controversy over Modern Spiritualism was unceasing in journals, salons, drawing rooms, and private correspondence. Séances for some time became a socially significant experience, and to take part in them was practically a ritual task for the modern thinking man, who sought to "come to a conclusion" (or at least to "form an impression") about mysterious phenomena.

On Friday February 13, 1876, in the apartment of the philosopher and prominent figure in the international spiritualist movement Alexander Aksakov on Nevsky Prospekt 6, a séance took place under the guidance of Madame Claire. The renowned writers Petr Boborykin (1836–1921), author of the best-seller *Vespertine Sacrifice* (Zhertva vecherniaia), Nikolai Leskov, and Fedor Dostoevsky took part, as did the host and his spiritualist followers, Professors Vagner and Butlerov. Aksakov, Butlerov, and Vagner, who were continually being criticized in journals, were extremely interested in the potentially sympathetic opinion of the influential literary men. The writers, in turn, came to the séance not only with an interest in spiritualist phenomena (to be sure, all of them were concerned with this issue), but also, in a sense, on a professional assignment: to attempt to express the position of the *writers' guild* with respect to this issue so engrossing to society as a whole. This was essentially an attempt at a writers' conference – one contending with Mendeleev's scientific commission.

We find descriptions of the séance in three sources: the detailed "factual" accounts of Leskov (February 29) and Boborykin (March 16) and Dostoevsky's April article about Modern Spiritualism (as well as his preparatory materials for it) in his *Diary of a Writer*. First, the medium Claire, using the English alphabet which Aksakov recited, discovered from the "unseen presences" that of all the attendees the "most convenient for mediumistic intercourse" was Dostoevsky. The presences also indicated through rapping "that this evening the table might be lifted into the air, that chosen dates and names might be guessed; that little bells placed under the table might ring; an accordion placed under the table might play; and that those present might be touched by the unseen presences." The presences apparently tried to fulfill their promises. However, at some point in the middle of the experiment, Dostoevsky joked that he "refused to account for such phenomenon as anything but the dexterity of the medium." Although "it was said in such a way that, had Madame Claire understood Russian she would only have laughed at this perfectly harmless joke," upon hearing Dostoevsky's words translated into English she for some reason "instantly took offence, blushed, her eyes began to flash," and Boborykin "quite clearly heard a violent phrase, in English, which plainly showed her anger."

The participants of the séance tried in vain to calm the medium. She "stubbornly withdrew into her dignity, which no one had wounded, took her hands off the table" and "ceased all mediumistic participation." "I made the medium angry," observed Dostoevsky in his notebook (24: 150). As a result, the séance ended in a minor scandal, the initiator of which was the "most suitable" participant from the point of view of the "unseen presences" – Dostoevsky.

Still, the general opinion of the writers who participated in the February 13th séance went against the "mocking" conclusions of Mendeleev, which the latter made haste to proclaim before the completion of the commission's work on December 15, 1875. Leskov, Boborykin and Dostoevsky all acknowledged (to Mendeleev's displeasure) that some unexplained phenomena had taken place, but also agreed that their meaning and the means by which they were produced, had not been determined. They were also united in the conviction that the conclusions of Mendeleev's academic commission would not change anyone's mind, insofar as the matter was one of faith and not of scientific truth. At the same time, the writers also did not fully accept the hypotheses of the spiritualists. Each of the writers understood the "evidence" in his own way, according to his own convictions and aspirations and, as a result, reacted in his own way to the "wonders" that took place before his eyes, with mystical curiosity, rational skepticism, or religious fear. Simplifying a little, one may call the positions of Leskov, Boborykin, and Dostoevsky, as they took shape around the medium's table, mystical, positivist, and demonological respectively.

The mystically minded Leskov was attracted at the séance by the opportunity to penetrate into the spiritual world and to communicate with the dead. The writer believed in providential coincidences, omens, and visions. He regarded the spiritual manifestations at Aksakov's very seriously and, as Boborykin indicates, even somewhat exaggerated their scale afterwards. He would return frequently to the theme of spiritualist phenomena in his work, regarding them as hints at a secret life of the spirit, and opposing vulgar materialistic spiritualism (*spiritizm*) to true spiritualism (*spiritualizm*) based on deep moral feeling and a belief in the final triumph of the soul over impotent substance.

For the "empiricist" Boborykin (a translator and follower of Auguste Comte, the father of positivism), the séance was interesting first and foremost from a sociological and psychological point of view. His attention was focused on the medium – her appearance, the aspects of her national character: in a word, the *"habitus* of this mediumistic figure." At the same time, Boborykin emphasized the impossibility, using available empirical methods, for science or external observation to "arrive at the absolute truth" about what had been seen (one could not, for example, ask the lady to undress in order to find out whether she was concealing any "devices").

Dostoevsky came to the séance having already published an essay on Modern Spiritualism in the January 1876 issue of *Diary of a Writer* – "Something about Devils. The Extraordinary Cleverness of Devils, If Only These Are Devils." In this essay he mused that if these phenomena are real, then they are produced by enemies of the human race who are driving society to schism, religious wars, disbelief, and, as a result, to the reign of the Antichrist. At the same time – as a man of the secular nineteenth century – Dostoevsky had doubts about the reality of these phenomena, and, consequently, about their origins. The January article on devils offered, so to speak, a literary and theoretical examination of this unresolved question.

It seems that Dostoevsky went to the February séance in order to verify his conjectures with personal experience. Instead of fleeing from temptation (or from the utter foolishness of contemporaries who had been taken in – if it indeed was all a matter of deception), he willingly exposed himself to it. It would not be an exaggeration to say that the spiritualist séance was for Dostoevsky a psychological and religious experiment, a test of his own beliefs and doubts. In the article, "Just a Bit More about Spiritualism," in the April issue of his *Diary*, the writer explains that one result of this moral experiment was his discovery of the "law of disbelief":

> [A]fter that remarkable séance I suddenly surmised – or rather, I suddenly discovered – not only that I do not believe in spiritualism but that I haven't the least wish to believe in it, so that there is no evidence that will ever cause me to change my views. [. . .] I have a sense of some special law of human nature, common to all and pertaining specifically to faith and disbelief in general. I somehow came to understand then – specifically through this experience, specifically through this séance – what power disbelief can uncover and develop within you at a given moment, absolutely despite your own will, although it may be in accordance with your secret desire . . . The same thing is probably true of faith.[23]

Religious stubbornness, based on moral conviction (later a theme of Alesha Karamazov) and not on miracles (a theme of Ivan and the Grand Inquisitor) acts here as a means against temptation by spiritualist evidence. Dostoevsky's notebooks and letters of this time also reveal that he interpreted the séance as one of the staging grounds for the spiritual battle he repeatedly depicted in his works. Later he would compare this spiritualist collision with the poetics of Alexander Pushkin's "Queen of Spades."

For Dostoevsky, these are not the souls of the dead making their presence known, but the soul of contemporary Russian man testing itself and uncovering its doubts, contradictions, and dangerous secrets (its inner devils). In other words, as a result of personal experience Dostoevsky came to the conclusion that the true séance (a contemporary mystery play) was inside of us. In turn, the true medium turns out to be the author who, through the painful and spiritually dangerous act of writing, "materializes" (objectifies, verbalizes) in his work the "unknown forces" of man's inner world. In fact, it is the writing desk, rather than the levitating spiritualist table, that serves as the true means of communication with the unknown. For Dostoevsky, the séance becomes a metaphor for the writing process.

6

Life as Theatre: Russian Modernism

I

In the first decade of the twentieth century a pleiad of young writers, composers, stage directors, and visual artists burst onto the Russian and then the European artistic scene. From the turn of the century until the late 1920s these figures (including writers Anna Akhmatova, Alexander Blok, Osip Mandelstam, Vladimir Mayakovsky, Boris Pasternak, and Marina Tsvetaeva, composers Alexander Scriabin, Igor Stravinsky, Sergei Prokofiev, and Dmitry Shostakovich, visual artists Natalia Goncharova, Vasily Kandinsky, Kazimir Malevich, and Vladimir Tatlin, theatre directors Konstantin Stanislavsky, Vsevelod Meyerhold, and Alexander Tairov, and film directors Sergei Eisenstein and Dziga Vertov), for the most part born between 1880 and 1900, created works that captured the attention of their cultured European contemporaries and that retain enormous power and appeal to this day. This period of spectacular artistic achievement has come to be called the Silver Age, following but in no way artistically inferior to the Golden Age of the 1820s and 1830s. Living in a tumultuous period that spanned the apocalyptic expectations of the *fin de siècle*, the disappointment of the failed Russian Revolution of 1905, the wanton destruction of the First World War, the Revolution of 1917 and the Civil War that followed in its wake, and the consolidation of the Soviet state, these artists, generally grouped under the heading "modernists," were inevitably witnesses to their epoch, even as they struggled to preserve their artistic autonomy.

As was true of each previous cultural movement since neo-classicism, modernism did not originate in Russia, but rather arrived as an "import product" with a definite time lag. The earliest works of French modernism date to the 1860s and 1870s (Charles Baudelaire, generally acknowledged to be the "father" of modernism, died in 1867), but it is impossible to speak of a Russian modernism before the mid-1890s. However, Russian artists caught up to their European predecessors before the end of the first decade of the twentieth century and, by the 1910s and 1920s, took a significant "exporter" role in this trans-European movement, which is distinguished less by the similarity of the artistic work produced by various "modernists" than by the broadly shared mindset or world-view these disparate artists held.

There is no generally accepted definition of what constitutes modernism, nor which works and artists should be accounted modernist. The confusion is certainly not for lack of trying, as the scholarly literature on modernism and its various national incarnations is vast, but rather it results from the enormous variety of work that might be considered modernist and the attempts by critics to classify this work based on many different criteria. For the purposes of definition it is perhaps best to take a middle ground, examining works that share key features which distinguish them from their predecessors and successors (as well as from the copious non-modernist work of their contemporaries). Although not every one of these characteristics can be found in each work, in broad strokes one can identify the following as key features of Russian modernism:

1. Rather than attempting to reflect or comment on the phenomenal reality of the world as perceived by a "normal" (read bourgeois or aristocratic) viewer, the modernist work focuses on the idiosyncratic perspective of the artist which is frequently claimed to reflect the world as "it really is" (hidden or noumenal reality). In the most extreme cases art creates its own universe, divorced from the apparent reality of our world. As a corollary, the modernist work often foregrounds mystical, irrational, or spiritual elements that had rarely been treated (except satirically) in the literature of the second half of the nineteenth century.
2. The modernist work strives for originality, particularly formal originality.
3. The modernist work often displays a disdain for traditional "good taste," and is not immediately comprehensible to the uninitiated reader or spectator. Even when certain groups of modernists make use of "popular" or "mass" culture, they refigure this material in ways that make it incomprehensible to the masses. As a result, modernist art takes on a certain hermetic quality and must be explicated if it is to be understood and appreciated. The manifesto therefore is of central importance, and theory becomes inseparable from creative work.
4. Although there were many great individual modernist artists, modernism as a whole displays a strong penchant for collective / collaborative artistic expression in almanacs, journals, exhibitions, manifestos, and especially theatrical productions.
5. Intermediality was a particular feature of Russian modernism. Many leading writers had tried their hand at visual art or musical composition,

rare was the visual artist who did not produce literary or manifesto texts, and so forth. The ideal was seen as a *Gesamtkunstwerk* (total work of art) that could synthesize all artistic modes into a harmonious whole. A feverish desire for synthesis can also be felt in many of the theoretical statements that flowed in a seemingly endless stream from the pens of artists in this period. Andrei Bely, a leading theorist of symbolism, called for "a conjunction of music and poetry,"[1] and created verbal symphonies that were meant to bring the principles of musical composition to literature. A few years later, the painter Vasily Kandinsky predicted the appearance of a kind of monumental art which would represent "the unification of all the arts in a single work."[2] In a 1912 article, the futurist poet Velimir Khlebnikov announced: "We want the word bravely to follow painting."[3]
6. Russian modernism often exhibits a strong utopian streak. This is related to its goal of remaking rather than describing the world.
7. The modernist artist often attempts to blur the distinction between art and life. This was often an uncomfortable mix, responsible for a host of broken lives and suicides; at the same time it created a hothouse environment conducive to artistic creativity.

II

In their intensive search for synthetic forms and as a result of their theatricalized personal lives, it was only to be expected that the Russian modernists would find the theatre, with its potential for a mixture of text, music, gesture, and visual art particularly attractive. And indeed, discussions of the theatre and its function played a central role in the frequently opaque theoretical discourse of Russian modernism. As Bely put it: "The drama represents the dynamic principle of creative energy in art. The drama enshrines the synthetic principle."[4] The weightiest voice calling for a revival of drama as synthetic art, however, belonged to Viacheslav Ivanov (1866–1949), the leading theoretician of Russian symbolism. He saw the theatre as "capable of replacing religion and the Church for a humanity which had lost its faith,"[5] and he envisioned a return to the Greek roots of theatre, to its Dionysian origins. Similar beliefs could be seen all across the theoretical spectrum; Anatoly Lunacharsky (1875–1933), for example, who would eventually become the first Soviet cultural arbiter and who was no adept of symbolism, waited eagerly for the day when a "free, artistic, and constantly creative cult will transform temples into theaters and theaters into temples."[6]

Nor was theory the only realm in which thinking about theatre occurred in this period. Indeed, the period from the late 1890s until the early 1930s can be considered one of the rare instances in world cultural history of a theatrical golden age, rivaling such periods as Classical Athens, Elizabethan England, and seventeenth-century France. Beginning with Stanislavsky's earliest productions at the Moscow Art Theatre (particularly his path-breaking stagings of the works of Chekhov), Russian artists produced an unprecedented string of dazzling theatrical events including the 1906 premiere of *The Fairground Booth* (Balaganchik; text by Blok, sets and costumes by Nikolai Sapunov, music by Mikhail Kuzmin, directed by Meyerhold), Sergei Diaghilev's 1911 Parisian production of *Petrushka* (music by Stravinsky, sets by Alexandre Benois, text by Stravinsky, Benois, and Michel Fokine), the 1913 staging of the futurist opera *Victory over the Sun* (Pobeda nad solntsem; text by Alexei Kruchenykh and Khlebnikov, music by Mikhail Matiushin, sets and costumes by Malevich), and the 1929 performance of *The Bedbug* (Klop; text by Mayakovsky, sets by Alexander Rodchenko, and music by Shostakovich). Contemporary audiences were meant to experience a kind of total theatre. Each production was an embodiment of the ideals of a whole (more or less coherent) artistic movement whose ideals were manifested on the level of text, design, music, and stagecraft.

III

A mere half century before the founding of the Moscow Art Theatre, however, it would have been difficult to predict that Russia would become the site for one of the great flowerings of theatrical and dramatic art. For the path to a specifically Russian theatre was long and difficult. Traditionally, dramatic literature did not exist in Russia, although it would be incorrect to say that pre-Petrine Russian culture lacked a theatrical element. In the villages many rites of passage were marked with ritualized performances, which included singing, dancing, and conventional role-playing by the participants. Wandering minstrels called *skomorokhi*, performed a variety of acts, to the extreme displeasure of church authorities, who regularly called for banning them. By the era of Ivan the Terrible, Russian court ritual had evolved into an elaborate spectacle as well, as noted by a number of European travelers. Finally, the Orthodox Church service (particularly on festive days) was itself a highly choreographed spectacle with marked theatrical elements.

In Western Europe during the Renaissance the various elements of traditional street performance, peasant rituals, liturgy, and court spectacle slowly evolved into the pre-modern dramatic theatre, complete with the requisite professional actors, dramatic conventions and then texts, and eventually theatre buildings and rules of theatrical etiquette that separated performers from spectators. As a result primarily of the anti-theatre position of the Orthodox Church, no such evolution took place in Russia, which as was explained in chapter 1, remained in crucial respects an essentially medieval culture well into the seventeenth century. A change in attitudes toward theatre finally arrived, however, through a confluence of interests of the Russian church hierarchy and the royal court. The church's attitude to theatre began to soften in the course of the seventeenth century when the hierarchy began to recognize that it was losing believers to the hated Catholics in Russia's western territories. One cause was that people were attracted by the dramatic works of religious content that the Jesuits used as a tool of conversion. In response, the Orthodox sponsored the creation and production of their own liturgically based dramatic works, which comprise Russia's first dramatic literature. At approximately the same time Tsar Alexei Mikhailovich encouraged the formation of a theatre at his court. Peter himself was also interested in developing a Russian theatrical tradition, seeing it as one more sign of Westernization, and he created the first public theatre on Red Square. But Peter's interests were never centrally focused on culture and the theatre failed to catch on.

It was up to Peter's immediate heirs, three empresses with a definite flair for the dramatic, to develop a modern secular theatre in Russia. During the reign of Elizaveta (Peter's daughter, 1741–62), the first professional Russian theatre troupe was formed and the first plays in Russian (for the most part feeble imitations of French neo-classical plays) were written and performed. Theatre and drama continued to develop during the reign of Catherine the Great. The empress herself was a prolific author of dramas (both historical and comic) and during her long reign Russian spectators could enjoy drama in European languages, translations of European plays into Russian, and original Russian dramas including Denis Fonvizin's satiric comedy *The Minor, 1782* (Nedorosl'), the earliest Russian play to remain in the modern theatrical repertoire. The first Russian performances of opera and ballet, two forms that would become something of a Russian specialty in the course of the next century, also took place during Catherine's reign. A mania for theatre spread from the royal court to the houses of the grandees at this period as well, and a number of Russian nobles created exquisite theatres, staffed entirely by serfs, on their estates. Although from the perspective of a serf the prospect of spending one's life as an actor might have been more appealing than working the fields, the practice of exploiting unfree human labor for artistic purposes was rife with cruelty and exploitation, as later described in such stories as in "Birthday" (Imeniny) by N. F. Pavlov (1803–64) and "The Toupee Artist" (Tupeinyi khudozhnik) by Leskov.

It was during this period, as well as during the reigns of Catherine's grandsons, Alexander I and Nicholas I, that a real audience was built for theatre in Russia such that drama moved from being a pet project of the court and the highest grandees to a permanent feature of the Russian cultural landscape. In a famous passage in *Eugene Onegin*, Pushkin describes his hero's arrival at the theatre, which was seen more as a social than an aesthetic exercise:

> As all applaud Onegin enters –
> And treads on toes to reach his seat;
> His double glass he calmly centers
> On ladies he has yet to meet.
> He takes a single glance to measure
> These clothes and faces with displeasure;
> Then trading bows on every side
> With men he knew or friends he spied,
> He turned at last and vaguely fluttered
> His eyes toward the stage and play –
> Then yawned and turned his head away . . .
>
> (I, 21)[7]

For the first time, Russian performers began to make major names for themselves. By far the most famous was the actor Mikhail Shchepkin (1788–1863). Born a serf, Shchepkin got his start on the provincial stage and was eventually able to buy freedom for himself and his family in 1821. Having moved soon after to Moscow, Shchepkin would exert an enormous influence over the Russian stage, leading the transformation from a Romantic to a realist style of acting. His most famous role was the Mayor in Nikolai Gogol's *Inspector General*, but he played more than six hundred different parts during his career including Shylock in *The Merchant of Venice*, and the Fool in *King Lear*. Shchepkin was also an outsized personality who earned the friendship and admiration of practically all the major writers of his day.

More often than not in this period, Russian theatres presented translations of foreign plays. Nevertheless, original works by the most important Russian authors also appeared both for the operatic and dramatic stages – perhaps the most significant of these were Glinka's operas *Ruslan and Liudmila* and *A Life for the Tsar* (Zhizn' za Tsaria, 1842), and Gogol's *The Marriage* (Zhenit'ba) and *The Inspector General*. Other important works written in the period but not staged, generally for reasons of censorship which was particularly tight for dramatic works given their public nature, included Alexander Griboedov's *Woe from Wit* (written 1824 but not performed publicly until long after the author's death), Pushkin's *Boris Godunov*, and Lermontov's *Masquerade*.

Through much of the mid to late nineteenth century, there was a lively theatrical scene in the Russian provinces. Nevertheless, the most important developments took place in St. Petersburg and Moscow. In those cities no private theatres were permitted (until 1882) and all activity was concentrated in the five imperial theatres. The Alexandrinsky in Petersburg and the Maly in Moscow specialized in drama, while ballet and opera were performed, as they are to this day, in Petersburg's Mariinsky and Moscow's Bolshoi theatres. Finally, the Mikhailovsky Theatre in the capital was generally reserved for touring companies from Western Europe.

IV

Although there were important Russian plays written in the first half of the nineteenth century, the Russian theatre did not truly develop a solid core repertory of plays until the second half of the century. This period is best known in Russian literature as the age of the great realist novel, but realism was not confined to prose fiction. By far the dominant figure in Russian theatrical life during this period was the playwright and director Alexander Ostrovsky. To this day many of Ostrovsky's more than fifty plays, most famously comedies set in a merchant milieu but also some important tragedies, are frequently performed in Russia, although his work has never received its due in the West. As Turgenev (himself the author of a number of excellent comedies including *A Month in the Country* [Mesiats v derevne, 1850], a precursor to the plays of Chekhov) put it in a letter to the dramatist: "You have completed the building for which Fonvizin, Griboedov, and Gogol laid the foundation stones. It is only after you that we Russians can proudly claim to possess a national theatre of our own – a theatre that can justly be called the Theatre of Ostrovsky."[8] Ostrovsky was closely connected to the Maly Theatre in Moscow, where he directed a number of path-breaking productions of his own plays. His life-long dream, one he was never to realize, was the creation of a "people's theater" that would express the full range of Russian reality.

Ostrovsky and a number of other realist playwrights including Alexei Pisemsky (1821–81) and Alexei Potekhin (1829–1908), provided fare for serious Russian theatre goers in the middle decades of the nineteenth century, but by far the most glittering performances in Russia in this period took place in the classical ballet. Ballet had appeared in Russia as early as the first half of the eighteenth century. In the first quarter of the nineteenth century the French dancing master Charles-Louis Didelot created a series of successful and popular ballets, making use both of imported and Russian dancers. But the highpoint of the Russian Imperial ballet came during the tenure of the French-born Marius Petipa (1818–1910). In a career as dancer and ballet master that spanned more than fifty years, Petipa created a number of choreographic chefs-d'oeuvres. Probably the most famous were three ballets to the music of Tchaikovsky – *Sleeping Beauty* (1890), *The Nutcracker* (1892), and *Swan Lake* (1895).

In this same period, Russian opera also came into its own, with the vast majority of librettos based on works of Russian literature. Successful operas were written both by composers whose orientation was more toward Western Europe and the more nationalist composers who belonged to the so-called Mighty Handful. Chief among the former were Anton Rubinstein (whose 1875 opera *The Demon*, based on Lermontov's Romantic narrative poem of the same title, is still occasionally performed) the Tchaikovsky (whose best-known operas are a duo based on works by Pushkin – *Eugene Onegin* (1878) and *The Queen of Spades* (1890). Among the latter were Modest Musorgsky, whose *Boris Godunov* remains probably the best-known Russian opera, Alexander Borodin (*Prince Igor*), and Nikolai Rimsky-Korsakov, who composed fifteen operas including *May Night* (1890) and *Christmas Eve* (1895), both based on short stories by Gogol, and *The Tale of Tsar Saltan* (1900) and *The Golden Cockerel* (1909), based on Pushkin fairy tales.

V

In 1882 Tsar Alexander III finally abolished the monopoly held by the Imperial theatres in the Petersburg and Moscow. But private entrepreneurs were relatively slow to take advantage of the new possibilities. The state-subsidized Imperial theatres continued to dominate the theatrical scene, although there were a few adventurous souls who succeeded in establishing commercially successful theatres catering to Russia's growing urban bourgeoisie. A number of these were owned by actresses, perhaps inspired by the enormous financial success of foreign women actress / entrepreneurs such as Sarah Bernhardt who made multiple tours of Russia in the 1880s. Nevertheless, The Moscow Art Theatre (MAT), the most successful of Russia's private theatres, and unquestionably the most famous and influential Russian theatre throughout the world, did not begin to operate until 1898.

MAT was founded by two strong and very different personalities – Stanislavsky (1863–1938, whose real name was Konstantin Alekseev), the scion of a wealthy merchant family who had been involved in semi-professional theatre for more than a decade, and Vladimir Nemirovich-Danchenko (1858–1943), himself a well-known dramatic writer, theatre critic, and head of the drama section of the School of the Moscow Philharmonic. An enormous mythology has grown up around the founding and early years of MAT, much of it propagated by Stanislavsky in his well-known memoir *My Life in Art*. According to Stanislavsky, everything about MAT was new, a complete break with the entire past of the Russian theatre. In fact, it might be better to see MAT, at least in its early years, as the culmination of the long realist tradition in Russian theatre, both in terms of its acting style and its concern to found a "people's theatre." There is no doubt, however, that MAT raised the standards for acting, for directing, and for general theatrical professionalism to a level that had never before been seen in Russia and provided a springboard for an unsurpassed flowering of theatre in Russia during the first decades of the century. Though never exceptionally friendly, Stanislavsky and Nemirovich-Danchenko collaborated closely in the early years, with the latter acting primarily as dramaturg while the former prepared exceptionally detailed stagings.

The original MAT troupe was drawn mostly from Stanislavsky's semi-professional Society for Art and Literature and from Nemirovich-Danchenko's school. Rehearsals began in the summer of 1898 in Pushkino outside of Moscow. The repertoire for the first season was quite varied, and included Sophocles, Shakespeare, Goldoni, Hauptmann, Alexei K. Tolstoy, and Chekhov's *Seagull*. The last had premiered a mere two years before in St. Petersburg, where it had been a qualified success, with the nymph-like Vera Komissarzhevskaia in the role of Nina Zarechnaia. The season opened successfully with Tolstoy's 1868 *Tsar Fedor Ivanovich*, a richly detailed historical drama. Other productions that first year did not fare particularly well, with the exception of *The Seagull*: Stanislavsky himself took the role of Trigorin, the brilliant young actor and future director Vsevelod Meyerhold played Treplev, and Olga Knipper (who would marry Chekhov a few years later), took the role of Arkadina. Although it took a few performances for audiences to warm to the production, it was eventually recognized as a triumph for both MAT and for Chekhov. Over the next five years MAT would stage the premieres of Chekhov's final three plays *Uncle Vanya*, *Three Sisters*, and *The Cherry Orchard*. In addition to Chekhov, MAT became closely identified with the work of Maksim Gorky (real name Alexei Maksimovich Peshkov, 1868–1936), and the production of his play *The Lower Depths*, (Na dne 1902) marked the culmination of Stanislavsky's naturalist theatre method.

MAT was best known for its realistic productions of Chekhov, Ibsen, and Gorky, but Stanislavsky did not limit himself to such plays. MAT also had success with symbolist works such as *The Bluebird* by the Belgian Maurice Maeterlinck and *The Life of Man* (Zhizn' cheloveka, 1907) by Leonid Andreev (1871–1919), as well as with adaptations of Russian literary classics such as Dostoevsky's *Brothers Karamazov*. Although in the early years success was mixed with failure, MAT nevertheless quickly became the standard by which all theatrical performances in Russia were judged. As the artist and critic Alexandre Benois would put it a few years later: "You can criticize him [Stanislavsky] as much as you want (in particular the design element of the 'Art Theatre' is poorly handled), but you have face the fact that this man of action, and not of words, has managed in our time of total collapse to create a grandiose and lasting whole, a true monument with a true style. The only Russian theatre that can impress, elate, and convince today is the 'Art Theatre.'"[9] Over the decades, MAT would become an icon of Russian, then Soviet cultural life. Although severely hemmed in by Stalinist cultural policies of the 1930s, which favored a highly formulaic "realism" that reflected only one part of MAT's heritage, the theatre lived on past the deaths of its founders, and it remains a vital part of the Russian cultural landscape in the twenty-first century.

VI

If the nineteenth-century Russian theatre tended to be focused on the actor, twentieth-century Russian theatre, following in the footsteps of Stanislavsky, was highly director oriented. In the first decades of the century, a number of exceptionally talented directors appeared. Although all imitated Stanislavsky in their minute attention to theatrical detail and their desire to control all aspects of the production, most of them rejected his naturalist leanings and his "method acting" in favor of less mimetic and more flamboyantly theatrical modes. The most significant of the new generation was Stanislavsky's earstwhile protégée Vsevolod Meyerhold (1874–1940), whose career will be treated in detail below. Another Stanislavsky protégée was Evgeny Vakhtangov (1883–1922), who staged two exceptional productions in 1922. The first was *The Dybbuk* by the Yiddish writer S. Ansky (real name Shloyme Rappaport, 1863–1920) staged at the "Habima" Jewish theatre in Moscow. The range of Vakhtangov's talent can perhaps best be appreciated by the contrast between the expressionistic, grotesque style in which he staged *The Dybbuk* and the ironic fairy tale version of Carlo Gozzi's *Princess Turandot*, put on to enormous acclaim at MAT's Third Studio a few months later.

By no means, however, were all the important Russian directors pupils of Stanislavsky. Nikolai Evreinov (1879–1953) was a tireless theatrical experimenter and theoretician. He was particularly interested in reviving medieval and Renaissance drama as well as cabaret theatre for which he produced many short plays. His treatise *The Theatre as Such* makes the argument that theatre is humankind's oldest and most natural form of artistic expression. After the Revolution, Evreinov immigrated to Paris where he continued to write plays as well as a history of the Russian theatre. Alexander Tairov (1885–1950) opened his Chamber Theatre just before the Bolshevik Revolution of 1917. Through the late teens and early twenties, Tairov staged a string of significant productions, usually with his wife, the talented Alisa Koonen, in the lead roles. These included three extraordinary "cubist" productions designed by Alexandra Ekster (Innokenty Annesky's *Famira Kifared* [1916], Oscar Wilde's *Salomé* [1917], and Shakespeare's *Romeo and Juliet* [1921]) as well as E. T. A. Hoffman's fable *Princess Brambilla* (1920) and Racine's *Phèdre* (1923). Like Meyerhold, Tairov became enamored of Constructivism in the early 1920s, and his production of G. K. Chesterton's *The Man Who Was Thursday* (1923) employed a complex constructivist set designed by the architect Alexander Vesnin.

Although he would become much better known for his work in film, Sergei Eisenstein got his start in the dramatic theatre, working as an assistant to Meyerhold on a number of his constructivist productions of the early 1920s. Eisenstein staged a revised version of Ostrovsky's play *Even a Wise Man Slips Up* (Na vsiakogo mudretsa dovolno prostoty) in 1923, and it was in the course of his work on this production that he formulated his concept of montage, the sudden juxtaposition of two or more dramatic units meant to produce "shock" in the spectator. He would later develop this idea in such classic films as *The Battleship Potemkin* (Bronenosets Potemkin, 1925), *Alexander Nevsky* (1938), and *Ivan the Terrible* (Ivan Grozny, 1944–6).

During and immediately following the period of the so-called New Economic Policy (NEP) of the mid 1920s (when the state made a tactical decision to allow some independent economic activity), a number of original satirical plays by Soviet writers were written and staged. These included *The Warrant* (Mandat, 1926) by Nikolai Erdman (1900–70), Valentin Kataev's (1897–1986) *Squaring the Circle* (Kvadratura Kruga, 1928), Mayakovsky's *The Bedbug* (1929), and Mikhail Bulgakov's *Zoya's Apartment* (Zoikina kvartira, 1926). Bulgakov (1891–1940) was also the author of the Civil War drama *The Days of the Turbins* (Dni Turbinykh, 1926), said to have been Stalin's favorite play and unquestionably the most successful post-revolutionary drama staged by MAT. Later he would write *The Master and Margarita* (Master i Margarita), arguably the greatest Russian novel of the 1930s.

Not all post-revolutionary theatre, however, consisted of director dominated high culture. From the beginning of the Soviet period, there was a strong tradition of theatrical events for and by a mass public. In 1920, for example, on the third anniversary of the Revolution, Evreinov and the designer Iuri Annenkov produced a mass spectacle entitled *The Storming of the Winter Palace*. According to Annenkov, the right side of the "stage" alone required 125 ballet dancers, 100 circus performers, 1750 students and supernumeraries, 200 women, 260 other actors, and 150 assistants. This cast was nothing, however, in comparison to one proposed for an unrealized spectacle of 1921 entitled *The Struggle and Victory of the Soviets* that called for 200 cavalry, 2300 infantry, artillery batteries, tanks, motorcycles, and five airplanes.[10]

The 1920s thus saw an exceptional number of path-breaking theatrical productions in a great variety of styles. Throughout the period, however, various cultural groupings attempted on the one hand, to enlist the support of the Soviet state for their version of socialist art and, on the other, to suppress other artistic tendencies. Nevertheless, under the leadership of Commissar for the People's Enlightenment Anatoly Lunacharsky, himself a well-respected playwright, the Soviet state refrained from making its cultural preferences overly transparent. By the end of the 1920s and certainly in the early 1930s, however, the period of cultural pluralism gradually came to an end and the state began to limit the possibilities for expression. Suspicious both of the spontaneous efforts of workers and of avant-garde work that was difficult to comprehend, cultural authorities gradually settled on an artistic mode that came to be called Socialist Realism (see chapter 8).

Vladimir Kirshon's (1902–38) play *Grain* (Khleb, staged by MAT in 1931) is perhaps the best example of a Socialist Realist drama. Set during the period of collectivization, the play depicts, in a seemingly realistic way, the conflict in a village between those willing to join the newly formed collectives and provide the grain needed by the Soviet state to support its industrial leap forward and the kulaks (rich peasants) who resist. Simultaneously, it charts the conflict between two types of revolutionaries. Raevsky and Mikhailov had been companions in arms during the Civil War, a time when, according to Soviet mythology, spontaneous feats of daring had been both necessary and frequent. The latter, however, has come to recognize that things have changed and that the new period requires a far more deliberate approach. The former, just returned from Germany where he was overly impressed by Western technology, holds on to a romantic and heroic vision and attempts single-handedly to force the peasants to provide grain to the Soviet state. He is supported by Mikhailov's wife Olga, who instinctively sides with the dashing romantic. In the play's denouement, Mikhailov simultaneously rescues his former comrade, whose hotheaded approach has created disaster, and unmasks the evil plotting of the kulak farmer, allowing for the triumph of the Soviet state and pointing the way toward the inevitable bright future of socialist agriculture.

By the 1930s, however, the theatre lost its position as the central locus for drama in the Soviet Union. Though theatres continued to operate, the central site for drama by the high Stalinist period became the courtroom, where elaborate show trials of formerly powerful Soviet figures provided a chilling spectacle. Beginning already with the so-called Shakhty trial of 1928, the courtroom became the locus for a ritualized, theatrical spectacle where those accused of crimes against the state were allowed to confess and where appropriate poetic justice was meted out. By the time of the Great Purges of the late 1930s, this spectacle had been rehearsed to almost clockwork perfection.

Equally powerful as dramatic site was the top of the Lenin Mausoleum on solemn Soviet holidays. Here is the scene as described by British diplomat Fitzroy Maclean:

> At least twice a year Stalin would appear in public, on May 1st and November 7th, when standing on Lenin's tomb, he would take the salute at ceremonial parades of the Red Army . . . Unobtrusively he would emerge from a little side door in the Kremlin wall, followed by the other members of the supreme Politburo of the Party, and, clambering up to the top of the Mausoleum, would take up his position, a little in front of the others, looking out over the great expanse of the Red Square, a squat Asiatic figure in a peaked cap and drab, semi-military greatcoat: narrow eyes close set under heavy brows, the downward sweep of his moustache ponderous beneath a hawk-like nose, his

expression alternating between benignity and bored inscrutability. Infantry, cavalry, tanks would sweep past while fighters and bombers roared overhead. Every now and then he would raise his hand, palm outstretched, with a little gesture that was at once a friendly wave, a benediction, and a salute. But most of the time he would chat affably with those around him, while they, for their part, grinned nervously and moved uneasily from one foot to the other, forgetting the parade and the high office they held and everything else in their mingled joy and terror at being spoken to by him.[11]

Biography – Vsevolod Meyerhold

If any one figure was emblematic of the exceptional wealth of Russian theatrical culture from the turn of the twentieth century until the 1930s, that would be Vsevelod Meyerhold. A passionate and tireless innovator, Meyerhold tried his hand at practically every theatrical genre and in almost every milieu from tiny cabarets to the grand stages of the Imperial theatres in the pre-revolutionary period and from the mass spectacles to avant-garde productions after the Revolution. Along the way he interacted with practically every significant director, actor, writer, composer, and visual artist of the time, often enlisting their assistance in his daring theatrical enterprises.

Meyerhold was born Kasimir Theodore Karl Meyerhold in the provincial town of Penza in 1874. His father, a fairly wealthy German businessman, left his son to be educated by his mother, who despite her German origins was well connected to the local cultural and particularly theatrical scene. Meyerhold's father died in 1892, and soon thereafter the future director moved to Moscow to study law. He was quickly drawn away from the legal profession and joined Nemirovich-Danchenko's acting school from which he was recruited into the original MAT troupe. Like Stanislavsky, however, Meyerhold was not satisfied to be an actor, no matter how talented. He dreamed of directing his own theatre company. Initially Stanislavsky hoped to keep Meyerhold within his orbit, and in 1904 allowed him to create a theatre studio in parallel to the work of MAT. Here Meyerhold began his attempts to find a suitable method for staging modernist works that could not be successfully presented employing the realistic acting techniques that were MAT's bread and butter. But the two headstrong directors could not see eye-to-eye, and Stanislavsky would not allow public performances of the plays that Meyerhold had so painstakingly rehearsed with his studio actors. Although the two would retain a lifelong admiration, by 1905 Meyerhold decided to strike off on his own.

Probably the most significant production of Meyerhold's early years was of Blok's short play *The Fairground Booth* in 1906. Mikhail Kuzmin (1872–1936, an important symbolist writer as well, and the author of *Wings* [Kryl'ia, 1907], the first openly gay Russian literary work) provided a musical score, and the talented artist Nikolai Sapunov designed the costumes and sets. In addition to directing, Meyerhold also played the lead role of Pierrot. Blok's play was one of three "lyrical dramas" the poet wrote just after the Russian revolution of 1905. Filled with self-directed irony, written in an aggressively non-realist idiom and employing the conventional theatrical masks of Pierrot, Harlequin, and Columbine, *The Fairground Booth* can be seen as a sharp satire on the symbolist movement with which Blok had been closely associated. It opens with a group of puppet-like figures waiting unsuccessfully for the end of the world and devolves into a grotesque *commedia dell'arte*-derived love triangle. The production caused a scandal, both because of its satirical treatment of the apocalyptic dreams of Blok's symbolist colleagues, and because the love triangle could be interpreted as a literary recasting of the overheated relationship between Blok, Andrei Bely, and Blok's wife Liubov Mendeleeva. As such it was a dramatic illustration of one of the central tenets of modernism – the belief that art and life, rather than being separate realms of activity, should be merged as much as possible.

The production was notable for Meyerhold's embrace of non-realist stylization. An eyewitness commented: "The entire stage is hung at the sides and rear with blue drapes; this expanse of blue serves as a background as well as reflecting the color of the settings in the little booth erected on the stage. This booth has its own stage, curtain, prompter's box, and proscenium opening. Instead of being masked with the conventional border, the flies, together with all the ropes and wires, are visible to the audience. When the entire set in the booth is hauled aloft, the audience in the actual theatre sees the whole process."[12]

In 1908 Meyerhold was unexpectedly offered a post with the Imperial theatres in St. Petersburg. Even more unexpectedly the bad boy of Russian directing accepted, and over the next decade he would stage a number of brilliant productions of drama and opera (including Molière, Calderon, Ostrovsky, and Lermontov at the Alexandrinsky and Wagner, and Gluck, at the Mariinsky) often working in close collaboration with the artist Alexander Golovin. Although his contract with the Imperial theatres forbade him to work elsewhere, Meyerhold continued to work actively in small-scale, experimental, and cabaret theatre projects under the pseudonym of Dr. Dapertutto (Dr. Everywhere). Among the influential works staged by Dr. Dapertutto was Arthur Schnitzler's pantomime *Columbine's Scarf*, an important source text for the ballet *Petrushka*.

From the beginning of his theatrical activity, Meyerhold had always considered pedagogy to be at least as important as productions for an audience, and in the period between 1913 and 1917 Dr. Dapertutto operated a school at which budding young actors were given courses on an exceptionally broad range of subjects including: "musical reading in drama," "the history and technique of the commedia dell' arte," "stage movement" (taught by Meyerhold himself), as well as on the material elements of performance (props, costumes, and so forth). In addition to practical classes, Meyerhold expected his students to be familiar with an astonishing array of theoretical topics, among them the role of popular theatre in theatrical regeneration, mimesis, performance methods, Russian dramatic works from the 1830s and 1840s, the circus and the theatre, Carlo Gozzi and his theatre; Spanish theatre, stage and performance methods in Japanese, Chinese, and Indian theatre, contemporary theatrical theories, the role of the director and the artist in the theatre. As opposed to Stanislavsky's insistence on the importance of creating a convincing character from the inside out through a deep study of his putative psychology and the actions he could be expected to perform in "real life," Meyerhold worked from the outside in, focusing on body control, the ability to recite poetry, improvise, perform acrobatic or circus stunts, appreciate and play music so as to create a wide variety of possible characters.

Although Meyerhold had not been identified with radical politics in the pre-revolutionary period, he threw in his lot with the Bolsheviks immediately after the revolution of 1917, and quickly became a leading theoretician and practitioner of "revolutionary theatre." Appointed deputy head of the drama section in the Commissariat for Education, Meyerhold staged Mayakovsky's allegorical *Mystery-Bouffe* (Misteriia buff) in 1918. Especially as restaged in 1921, this play, which Mayakovsky characterized as "the movement of crowds, the conflict between classes, and the struggle of ideas – a microcosm of the world within the walls of a circus"[13] allowed Meyerhold enormous scope for experimentation. Meyerhold's staging broke down the separation of spectators and performers, and circus performers mixed with actors in a rollicking performance that took place on a series of gangways and staircases rather than within traditional scenery.

Meyerhold continued his experiments with stage construction and action in a series of constructivist productions in the early 1920s. The most fully realized was the 1923 staging of Fernand von Crommelynck's play *The Magnificent Cuckold*. In place of the realistic evocation of bourgeois Belgium described in the stage directions, designer Liubov Popova created a series of interlocking wheels, machines, and ladders that served as "a springboard for the actor, comparable to those contraptions and devices used by circus acrobats."[14] The actors, trained carefully in Meyerhold's system of "biomechanics" and provided with an almost balletic choreography, created a brilliant, rhythmic dynamic in, on, and around Popova's construction.

By the late 1920s, Meyerhold's relentless innovation began to come under increasing attack in the Soviet press. In the theatre, as elsewhere in the cultural world, conservatism became the order to the day and Meyerhold's restless avant-garde desire for new forms of theatrical expression did not sit well with a cultural bureaucracy increasingly interested in preservation and consolidation rather than innovation. In particular, despite his stated desire to stage theatrical works that would reflect the realities of the USSR, Meyerhold had great difficulties in finding and presenting contemporary plays. Two aborted productions, *I Want a Child* (Khochu rebenka) by Sergei Tretiakov (1892–1937) and Erdman's *The Suicide* (Samoubiitsa), illustrate the difficulties of Meyerhold's position at this time. Tretiakov's play was designed as a theatrical discussion bringing up themes of eugenics and socialist sexual morality. Erdman's is a black comedy whose hero Podsekal'nikov, despairing at his inability to find a place for himself in Soviet society, decides to commit suicide, only to have a wide variety of disaffected fellow citizens ask him to do so in the name of their various causes. The weak-willed hero agrees with all of them, only to realize in the end that he really wishes to live. Meyerhold and his actors brought both of these plays through long production processes, only to see them banned by the authorities before they could be performed. Among contemporary works, he was only able to realize productions of Mayakovsky's final two plays: *The Bedbug* in 1929 (see discussion of this play in the next chapter) and *The Bathhouse* (Bania, 1930).

The director had more luck in staging some classics of Russian and world theatre at this time. His 1926 production of Gogol's *Inspector General* and his 1928 version of Griboedov's *Woe from Wit* are widely acknowledged as his masterworks of this period. The mise-en-scène for the former production was one of Meyerhold's most innovative attempts to break down the division between performer and spectator. Not only were the footlights and curtain gone, but Meyerhold's rewriting of Gogol into fifteen episodes was mirrored in a fragmented stage space with fifteen sets of double doors from which characters as well as individual platform stages could emerge. For almost every episode, tableaux of characters and carefully arranged furniture would appear from one of the sets of side doors and glide up to the audience before the action began. The space between stage and auditorium thus shifted constantly and unexpectedly, forcing the spectator to remain active and expectant.

Though Meyerhold managed to stage a few acclaimed productions during the 1930s, particularly his 1934 *Lady of the Camelias*, in which his wife and former student Zinaida Raikh starred, the decade was littered with unrealized projects, retreats under storms of criticism against "formalism," and "left deviationism" (both code words for modernism), and attacks from former friends and associates. By the beginning of 1938, Meyerhold's theatre was closed. His former mentor Stanislavsky stood by him, however, and offered him a position, but after Stanislavsky's death in the summer of that year Meyerhold was adrift. Arrested in 1939, the director was shot as an "enemy of the people" in 1940 and his legacy, at least in the Soviet Union, was forgotten until the 1960s.

Literary Work – *Petrushka*

Beginning in 1907, the Russian impresario Sergei Diaghilev (1872–1929) organized performances of opera and ballet in Paris under the general title "saisons Russes." Despite war, revolution, and frequent financial chaos, these would continue, with a kaleidoscopically changing cast of composers, designers, and dancers until Diaghilev's death. Though Diaghilev's troupe did not perform in Russia, its theatrical activity was Russian to the core, and its iconic production, the ballet *Petrushka*, can be seen to stand in for the entire modernist period of Russian culture.

For the Russian modernist esthetic, ballet occupied a special place. Its synthesis of music, motion, costumes, and pantomime fascinated many of the leading theatrical theoreticians and practitioners in Russia, not merely the members of Diaghilev's circle. The theatre director Alexander Tairov, for example, wrote: "ballet productions are the *only* productions in the contemporary theater in which I can still experience true creative joy and excitement."[15] This statement was made in 1921, but it exudes the same excitement about ballet's potential that Stravinsky expressed in a letter written a month after *Petrushka's* premiere: "It [ballet] is not applied arts – it is a union of arts, they strengthen and complement each other."[16] That *Petrushka* did indeed fulfill the Russian modernist ideal of the total work of art can be seen from a contemporary Russian review: "but all of these [criticisms] are trivial when compared with the amazing wholeness of the entire production. Precisely, wholeness, for despite the barbaric disharmony of the orchestra, the gaudy and wildly varied costumes, the seeming dissonance of an intimate 'Blokian' puppet drama seen against the coarse background of a drunken Mardi Gras celebration – one feels here a kind of endlessly familiar, deeply Russian harmony."[17]

True to the collaborative principles that animated Russian modernism in general and theatre in particular throughout this period, *Petrushka* was a multi-authored project. The music was by Igor Stravinsky (1882–1971), still a young composer at the beginning of what would be a long transnational career. The production was designed by the veteran artist and critic Alexandre Benois, who had been involved in Russian modernist circles from the 1890s. It was choreographed by Mikhail Fokine (1880–1942), and the premiere starred the legendary Vaclav Nijinsky in the title role and Tamara Karsavina as the Ballerina. The libretto is credited to Stravinsky and Benois, but in fact all of the collaborators played roles in shaping the story.

The ballet takes place in St. Petersburg in the 1830s during the traditional Shrovetide (Mardi Gras) festivals. Its plot, which unfolds over four short scenes (the whole ballet lasts no longer than forty minutes), is deceptively simple. As Russians of all ages and classes mill about during the festivities, a mysterious magician shows three puppets, which he animates by playing a tune on his flute. In scenes 2 and 3 we are taken to the rooms of two of the puppets – Petrushka and the Moor (fairground versions of Pierrot and Harlequin) – and see their competition for the love of the Ballerina (Columbine). Petrushka adores her but she falls for the gaudy Moor. In scene 4 the conflict spills out of the back rooms and back into the Shrovetide festivities. As the horrified passersby watch, the Moor kills Petrushka. The Magician emerges to show that this whole action was merely a trompe d'oeil and that Petrushka is nothing more than a puppet. But as he drags the puppet off the stage, Petrushka's ghost appears, threatening and terrifying him.

Stravinsky's bravura music, with its striking synthesis of tawdry urban Russian street songs and sophisticated modernist harmonies has become a classic score and is still performed frequently as a stand-alone work at orchestral concerts. It is perhaps his most famous piece, rivaled only by *The Rite of Spring*, which he would produce two years later for an even more controversial *Ballets Russes*' premiere. In its day, however, the music produced enormous debate. Complaining about the mix of Russian folk music with more modernist harmonies (and hinting that the whole thing was merely pandering to the poor taste of the Europeans), a contemporary critic called *Petrushka* a cocktail "mixed of Russian moonshine and French perfume."[18]

Though he designed ballet and opera productions for more than fifty years, the sets and costumes that Benois created for this production are unquestionably the highpoint of his career and have become famous in the their own right. Benois was particularly challenged by the possibility of evoking memories of the old Shrovetide fair that had, by the early twentieth century, pretty much petered out of existence and contrasting these scenes (acts 1 and 4) with the two that take place inside the rooms (and souls) of the male protagonists.

As for the libretto, its synthesis of sources is perhaps the most complex of all. Essentially the creators drew on four different kinds of sources for this short but exceptionally pithy work – Russian accounts and in certain cases personal memories of the Shrovetide fair, the tradition of *commedia dell'arte*, the modernist reinterpretation of that tradition, and hackneyed plot items from (mostly) Russian operas, ballets, and literary works that are generally parodied in the ballet. It is not surprising that a text produced by committee would show less unity than the product of a single artist. Indeed, a collaboration of this sort could easily have led to complete chaos. That chaos did not result was in part a happy accident, born of the fact that each of the ballet's separate layers (music, design, dance) was already marked by syncretism. The libretto merely took the syncretic aesthetic to the next level. Each of the individual collaborators juxtaposed cultural material from different registers in his own field of expertise for his own artistic purposes. The resulting synthesis led to an intensely theatrical combination of personalized "Petrushkas" layered one on top of another and constantly interacting and amplifying one another.

Petrushka points to a number of sources and meanings simultaneously, and each contributes to what could be called a field of expectations for the spectator. Each time a motif appears that can clearly be defined as belonging to one field or another, the audience expects that line of development to be developed further. Of course, for a knowledgeable audience, it takes only a bit of cultural material to evoke a large field of expectations. In *Petrushka*, the line suggested is generally not developed straightforwardly but it is modified or distorted through contact with other motifs, carrying different expectational fields. Sometimes the layers mesh smoothly, while at others jarring ambiguity results. For the most part, the ballet's expectational fields are drawn from both sides of what are often seen as binary oppositions such as high culture / popular culture, comedy / tragedy, realism / grotesque, serious drama / parody. By invoking both sides of the opposition simultaneously, *Petrushka* aims to question the very nature of such binaries.

The ballet echoed a number of the central concerns of contemporary Russian theatre. Primarily these had to do with two interrelated concepts: the call for a more imaginative use of theatrical space and a heightened interest in the spectator, in particular, a desire to break down traditional audience expectations. Diaghilev's Russian collaborators were all aware of the advances that had been made by the Moscow Art Theatre. They were also aware of the sharp critiques, both theoretical and practical, that had been leveled at Stanislavsky's methods by adepts of Russian symbolism as well as by Stanislavsky's erstwhile student Meyerhold.

Petrushka synthesizes theatrical theories and practices characteristic of these seemingly incompatible schools. According to Lyn Garafola, Fokine's staging of the ballet, and indeed his entire choreographic orientation, was marked by a Stanislavskian concern with theatrical naturalism.[19] But here the frames in which this naturalism operated were provided not by Fokine, but by Benois, who was far more interested in the then avant-garde theories and practices of symbolism. If we examine more closely the theatrical frame of the ballet, we see that its concerns were those of Stanislavsky's critics rather than those of the Moscow Art Theatre.

In the final version of the ballet the action occurs on at least three different levels. The first is the street where the carnival is in full swing. The little theatre of the Magician fronts onto this street, but when he opens the curtain of his theatre to reveal the three puppets, the audience becomes, as it were, doubled. That is, the characters that had been wandering about the stage become spectators of the puppets' dance. The theatre audience watches them watch the dance and it watches the dance as well. As a result the audience is watching two ballets simultaneously. The doubling of the fourth wall causes it to disappear, and unsettles spectators' expectations about their relationship to the on-stage action.

The second and third scenes call into question the conclusions to which the audience has been led in the first. Theoretically, the action takes place far backstage. That is to say, the theatre audience is transported behind the wings of the Magician's theatre to see what the on-stage audience does not see: the private drama of Petrushka, the Moor and the Ballerina. The change in perspective from the first to the second and third scenes throws into high relief the ways in which the libretto manipulates the audience's fields of expectation. If the expectations evoked by the first scene are primarily connected with the carnival, the Petrushka play in its folk incarnation, naturalist theatre, distance (as emphasized by placing the audience at double remove from the action) and comedy, then the second and third scenes evoke unmistakably the symbolist lyrical chamber drama, intimacy and tragedy. But what makes juxtaposition such an effective theatrical device is that the new expectations do not eliminate those that had been evoked earlier. Instead, these seemingly incompatible theatrical perspectives coexist and amplify one another.

The fourth scene does not so much resolve this conflict as sharpen it. The expectational fields, which had been segregated, are put on stage simultaneously in the finale. Thus, the fourth scene begins on the same level as the first but now, unexpectedly, the hierarchy that had been carefully preserved breaks down. First, both the audience on stage and the theatre audience hear cries from behind the closed curtain of the theatre. Then Petrushka, the Moor and the Ballerina come out of their rooms and intermingle with the "real" world. In the first scene, they danced among the revelers as puppets, but now the human qualities, which they seemed to possess when they were backstage, turn out to coexist with their puppet status, at least momentarily. The tension is temporarily dissipated by the appearance of the Magician, but the appearance of Petrushka's ghost (or the real Petrushka) adds a final ambiguous touch.

The end result was captured best by Benois himself: "*Petrushka* lasts just ¾ of an hour, but, as if by a conjuring trick, not only does a single man's life pass by in that time, but so does the tragedy of the collision of the life of one with the life of everyone."[20] By combining and layering three separate groups of sources, all of which were part of the cultural memory of Russian audiences, the authors of *Petrushka* created a Russian *Gesamtkunstwerk* that was both true to the ideals of modernist theatre and tremendously effective on stage.

Event – Publication of Anna Akhmatova's *Rosary* (Chetki, 1914)

Poem without a Hero (Poema bez geroia), begun in the early 1940s but revised by Akhmatova until her death in 1965, begins with the "author" expecting New Year's Eve visitors but instead visited by "spirits from 1913 who arrive as mummers." This theatricalized memory should be connected to Akhmatova's acclaimed second collection of poetry, *Rosary*, which though published in 1914 was mostly written in 1913, the last full year before the beginning of the Great War. This slim book of poems cemented the image of Akhmatova as the leading Russian woman poet (in an era in which there were no shortage of talented peers). The poetry of *Rosary* reveals a great deal not merely about Akhmatova's work, but about the entire atmosphere of Russian cultural modernism, particularly its linkage of life and art in a seamless web of interconnections.

The image of "Anna Akhmatova" had already begun to be created in her first collection of poetry, *Evening* (Vecher, 1912). That collection introduced to the Russian reading public a poet of love and loss, whose favored tropes pointed simultaneously to a strong heritage from the symbolist movement as personified in the poetry of Blok and Innokenty Annensky (1855–1909) as well as to new prosaic notes that would become central to the group of poets who called themselves Acmeists (including most notably Akhmatova's husband Nikolai Gumilev [1886–1921], and her close friend Osip Mandelstam, and whose debut as a group would come in 1913. The following poem, entitled "Song of Final Meeting," is typical of Akhmatova's poetic self-presentation in this period:

> My breast grew helplessly cold,
> But my steps were light.
> I pulled the glove from my left hand
> Mistakenly onto my right.
>
> It seemed there were so many steps,
> But I knew there were only three!
> Amidst the maples an autumn whisper
> Pleaded: "Die with me!
>
> I'm led astray by evil
> Fate, so black and so untrue."
> I answered: "I, too, dear one!
> I, too, will die with you . . ."
>
> This is a song of the final meeting.
> I glanced at the house's dark frame.
> Only bedroom candles burning
> With an indifferent yellow flame.

The first quatrain provides a beautiful illustration of Akhmatova's almost Tolstoyan ability to capture a psychological state through a depiction of a physical action. The second two quatrains, while perhaps poetically less successful (the linkage of autumn leaves and death and the characterization of fate are neither original nor striking), are important for creating the image of "Akhmatova" that would dominate the early collections. The focus is on her romantic life, she is vulnerable and prone to thoughts of death and suicide. Finally, in the fourth quatrain, Akhmatova redeems the clichés that dominated the middle of the poem, by avoiding the image of a candle going out (with its tempting allusion to Anna Karenina's final thoughts) and instead using the prosaic candle to indicate a recognition that for all the personal weight of her romantic agony, the broader world is indifferent to her fate.

The poem "In the Evening," written in 1913 and published in *Rosary*, indicates the continuity of that collection with her earlier work as well as her poetic development.

> The garden rang with music
> Of inexpressible despair.
> A dish of oysters spread on ice
> Smelled like the ocean, fresh and sharp.
>
> He told me: "I'm a faithful friend!" –
> And lightly touched my dress.
> How different from embraces
> The touch of those two hands.
>
> That's how one strokes a cat or bird
> Or looks at slender lady riders . . .
> Just laughter in his quiet eyes,
> Beneath his light gold lashes.
>
> And the despondent voices of the violins
> Sing out beyond the hanging smoke:
> "Give blessings to heaven above
> At last you're alone with your beloved."

Again the theme is love, though in this case the beginning rather than the end of the affair. Once more, the prosaic details stand out – the dish of oysters and the specificity of the lover's touch. Notable here is the poem's synaesthetic quality (in the four quatrains Akhmatova references the senses of smell, hearing, sight, and touch). Nor is the emotion of the poem entirely straightforward. While the experience of happiness should be unalloyed, the fragility of the poetic narrator's position is indicated by the "despondent voices of the violins," and the ambiguity of her lover's attitude hinted at by the inappropriate associations his touch recalls.

Contemporary readers were happy to link Akhmatova herself to the poetic speaker of the poem and a determination to create a linkage of this sort was unquestionably part of Akhmatova's exercise in poetic self-fashioning. Though not all of the details of the poems in her first collections can be taken at face value as biographically accurate, Akhmatova included sufficient autobiographical material to create a presumption of autobiographicality in the minds of her readers, and as a result these first books of poems could be and frequently were seen as a pseudo-autobiography whose heroine is Akhmatova herself.

Dubbed the "Sappho of the North," Akhmatova presented herself as a combination of fragile, vulnerable womanhood and *femme fatale*. The famous 1914 portrait of her by Natan Altman captures this image visually, and serves as a reminder of the hothouse environment in which much modernist poetry was created, a world in which artists, poets, and musicians mingled on an almost daily basis. Akhmatova, slender and elegant, sits regally and is shown in three-quarters profile. Her most characteristic features are her bangs, her prominent, slightly crooked nose, and her long fingers. In those days her favorite haunt was the Stray Dog Café, a hybrid Petersburg institution that attracted most of the city's leading artists from its founding in 1911 through the beginning of the war. Describing the scene, the critic Andrei Levinson recalled: "a precarious stage in the center of a smoke-filled room" and " the supple specter of Akhmatova, the Tatar princess."[21]

But for other readers, especially perhaps for those who did not know her personally, Akhmatova's importance was greater even than her personal image. She became a symbol of Russian womanhood itself, "Anna of all the Russias" as she would sometimes be called later in life. *Rosary* was seen to reveal "the essence of the female soul, the female element."[22] Or, as another critic put it: Anna Akhmatova's book [*Rosary*], in addition to its purely literary qualities, is interesting as illustrative material of the psychological crisis, the breakdown, through which the modern woman is living as she attempts to achieve inner freedom."[23]

Rosary then, is a work that in many ways captures the essence of Russian modernist culture of the fin de siècle. Lyric in its essence, presenting a highly theatricalized portrait of a woman living in a highly theatricalized society, it attests to the vitality of Russia's so-called Silver Age, and it still speaks to readers at the turn of the twenty-first century. It cemented the image of Akhmatova both as Russia's greatest woman poet (a title for which only her contemporary Marina Tsvetaeva could conceivably compete) and as a symbol for Russian womanhood. Later in life, Akhmatova would consciously draw on this metonym, as in the famous prose opening to her *Requiem*, a poetic monument to all who suffered in the Stalin-era camps: "In the terrible years of the Yezhov terror, I spent seventeen months in the prison lines of Leningrad. Once, someone 'recognized' me. Then a woman with bluish lips standing behind me, who, of course, had never heard me called by name before, woke up from the stupor to which everyone had succumbed and whispered in my ear (everyone spoke in whispers there): 'Can you describe this?' And I answered: 'Yes, I can.'"[24]

7

The Art of the Future: The Russian Avant-Garde

I

Let us imagine we have discovered a manuscript from a hypothetical Russian avant-garde artist born – let us say – in 1890. The manuscript is dated 1919, at the very height of the Russian Civil War (1918–23) between the supporters of the Bolsheviks, who came to power in the October Revolution of 1917, and their numerous unrelenting enemies. The country's economy has been destroyed, and a significant part of the country is suffering from famine.

Owing to the lack of proper writing paper, our artist has written his lines on an old scrap of wallpaper. In the centre of the page is a detailed sketch of a new bridge connecting Moscow and Mars. The bridge is labeled both as the arrow of the world and as a practical application of abstract (geometrical) art. Scribbled notes show the estimated costs of constructing the bridge. Next to it, there is a plan for entering the Red Army Club, which involves a project for using hollows in tree trunks as a rational solution to the acute housing problem (our imaginary artist was the head of the artistic section in his local revolutionary government organization). On one side, there is a poem about the project. At the very bottom, there are a few aphorisms about poetry and painting, written in the form of "military" instructions, characterized by frequent use of imperatives and exclamation marks, as well as swear words to describe reactionary (i.e. bourgeois) art.

This hypothetical (or, we might say, potential) manuscript can be seen as illustrative of the cultural and historical phenomenon that was the Russian avant-garde. "Fragments" of this sort can be found in museums, albums, or poetry anthologies. The defining characteristics of this consciousness, found in varying degrees in the various schools of "Leftist" art of the early twentieth century include a total refusal to accept "dead tradition," an orientation to the future, global-scale thinking, and a combination of the most fantastic ideas with the most pedantic rationalism, aesthetic maximalism, and utilitarianism. Artistic production was considered a means of creating a draft for the future, expressing anticipation for it, or temporarily realizing it on paper. Art was a unique kind of factory whose product was "tomorrow."

The Utopian ideas of the Russian avant-garde were directly influenced by the "apocalyptic events" of the first twenty years of the century: the Russo-Japanese War and the Revolution of 1905, the First World War (then called "The German War," 1914–18), the two revolutions of 1917 – the liberal February Revolution and the Bolshevik October Revolution – the Civil War, and the social revolutions which shook the world from Germany to Persia and China. The Russian avant-gardists thought of these contemporary events as stages of a total transformation of the world. They wanted to participate in the creation of this new world and a new kind of man. In such an era, it seemed possible to achieve the incredible.

II

The Russian avant-garde was part of the broader international movement of modernism in the early twentieth century. Cultural relations between the Russian avant-gardists and their Western counterparts were exceptionally close and productive. At the same time, a new nationalist and millenarianist tendency was emerging in Russia: Russian art was considered by its creators to be the pinnacle of the Western aesthetic project, and the apocalypse of the Western aesthetic imagination. In this, the Russian modernists were building on a long tradition according to which Russia is a chosen country that will eventually enlighten the world (see chapters 1, 2, and 5).

The immediate goal of the art of the new world involved a radicalization of the Symbolist aesthetic, which had spanned the late nineteenth and early twentieth centuries. Symbolism was characterized by a rejection of the academism and monotonous socially conscious moralizing realism of the nineteenth century. Symbolists imagined that they were living on the cusp of a new era, and envisaged themselves as involved in a "Nietzschean" revolt against anything that restricted the freedom of the artist. They were interested in folk magic and myth, and were involved in a search for an "art of synthesis" that would unite literature, painting, and music. Their work was forward-looking and experimental, and they believed that the future was the unique domain of the artist (Valery Briusov, one of the founding fathers of Russian symbolism asserted that "the future alone is the field of the poet"). Both Symbolism and the avant-garde conceived the artist as a demi-god, a creator of the new world, with his own life influenced by his creative work. Thus, the composer Alexander Skriabin (1872–1915) planned a universal production, the Mystery, which would unite not only music and poetry, but also odors, touch, color, and light. He suggested that the ideal place to perform this Mystery would be a temple on the banks of a lake in the Himalayas. The columns of the temple should be "sweet-smelling" and the cupola "sky blue." The Mystery should not be performed by professional musicians, but rather by people "of all races and from all corners of the earth" summoned by a composer-prophet in a single outburst of creativity. The Mystery would be performed over a period of seven days, and during that time the souls of the people would be cleansed and the world transformed according to the laws of Beauty.

While the symbolists based their thinking on the mystical teachings of Vladimir Solovev on the theurgical mission of art (an aesthetic re-creation of the world), the avant-garde artists were closer to the scientistic utopia of the philosophy of Nikolai Fedorov, a contemporary of Solov'ev, and the author of *The Philosophy of the Common Task* (Filosofiia obshchego dela, 1906, 1913). Fedorov thought artistic production could provide a design for the transformation of life. Fedorov's utopia – a paradoxical blend of the positivism of the latter half of the nineteenth century and Christianity, of materialism and spiritualism – declared the major tasks of humankind to be the acquisition of a knowledge of the laws of nature and proper regulation of their functions, directed toward solving the global problems of humankind. This included the resurrection of the dead – to be achieved with the aid of science – and the colonization of the cosmos. Fedorov (and, following him, other Utopian visionaries) considered time and entropy to be the true enemies of this universal project. His ideas – directly or indirectly – appear in the work of Futurist poets Velimir Khlebnikov (real name Viktor Khlebnikov, 1885–1922) and Vladimir Mayakovsky, the "analytic" paintings of Pavel Filonov (1883–1941), the novels and theological tracts of the ideologue of god-building and "proletarian culture," Alexander Bogdanov (pseudonym for Alexander Malinouski, 1873–1928), the natural-philosophical poems of Nikolai Zabolotsky (1903–58) and the tragic Utopian prose of Andrei Platonov (1899–1951).

III

The Russian avant-garde was a broad movement, including various directions and schools from the "New Art" of the 1910s and 1920s: cubo-futurism, rayonism, suprematism, analytism, futurism, constructivism, transrationalism [zaum'], imagism, 'real art'. According to the key tenet of avant-garde aesthetics, art must not reflect life, but rather create a new reality in line with the individual vision of the artist (or group of artists who share similar principles). The new art was publicized and propagated through various methods: manifestos and leaflets, slogans and posters, exhibitions, debates, shows which included the work of artists, writers, and composers, noisy conferences with delegates of the new art and public performances. Their favored method of appealing to the public was through épatage (provocation). For example, the Futurists used shocking slogans such as "I like a pregnant man" or "poetry is a defiled virgin and beauty is blasphemous rubbish!" Conservative critics of this new art called them savages, hooligans, nihilists, vandals, and lunatics. The artists proudly accepted these labels, considering it better to be lunatics, savages, or louts than sensible philistines.

The Futurists (or *budetliane*, as they sometimes styled themselves, from the Russian verb '*budet*,' meaning 'will be''') played a particularly important role in the development of the Russian literary avant-garde. The Russian Futurists, together with their Italian counterparts (Filippo-Tommaso Marinetti and his followers) set themselves the task of establishing the theory and practice of a new poetry which would express the human consciousness of the new era: an era of airplanes, cars, cinema, great scientific and technological advances. They believed that the new era would be one of free will and action rather than quiet meditation, spirituality, psychology, or materialism and envisioned this change as a sudden and radical transformation, not a slow progression.

The leader and organizer of the Futurist movement was David Burliuk (1882–1967), who boldly attacked the "old-fashioned" aesthetic tastes in the literary debates of the 1910s: "Art is not a stuffed sausage! . . . An artist is not a tradesman selling sausages! The right of an artist is the right of a creator, a thinker, master of his own tools. And it is the right of the viewer to look at a new work of art with the new eyes of a modern man."[1] Burliuk saw Futurism not merely as another literary "school" born from symbolism, but as a new way of experiencing the world. Others who shared this vision included Velimir Khlebnikov, who aimed to reform poetic language, the iconoclastic poet Vladimir Mayakovsky, who declared himself the "thirteenth apostle" and a prophet of the New Man, and Aleksei Kruchenykh (1886–1968), a theoretician of transrationalism, who insisted on the poet's right to create his own language. The Futurists also included the poet and artist Elena Guro (1877–1913), who represented the impressionistic and emotional side of early Futurism, her husband Mikhail Matiushin (1861–1934), who developed a theory of "expanded vision," the poet Vasily Kamensky (1884–1961) of the "anarchist" wing, and the poet and translator Benedikt Livshits (1887–1939). Many visual artists actively worked together with the Futurist writers, including Natalia Goncharova (1881–1962) and Mikhail Larionov (1881–1964), as well as the founding fathers of abstract art, Vasily Kandinsky (1866–1944), Kazimir Malevich (1878–1935) and Pavel Filonov. A group of young innovative philologists (who would later develop the theory of Russian Formalism) were also close to the Futurists: Viktor Shklovsky (1893–1984), Iury Tynianov, Osip Brik (1888–1945), Roman Jakobson (1896–1982).

The appearance of the collection *A Trap for Judges* (Sadok sudei) in 1910 prepared by Burliuk, Kamensky, Khlebnikov, and Kruchenykh became a prologue to the Futurist movement. The book was printed on wallpaper, used a variety of typefaces and contained deliberate spelling errors, all of which publicly demonstrated the Futurists' rejection of the Symbolists, whose work had been printed in elegant and expensive volumes. In 1912, Khlebnikov and Kruchenykh printed the experimental poem "A Game in Hell" (Igra v adu), which was illustrated by Goncharova. In late 1912, the Futurists produced the collection "A Slap in the Public's Taste" (Poshchechina obshchestvennomu vkusu) which opened with a manifesto of that title. This was probably the most famous manifesto of the Russian avant-garde. The authors of "Slap" loudly declared their intention to throw Pushkin, Dostoevsky, and Tolstoy off the boat of Modernity. Here they formulated their key artistic beliefs: the need to broaden the poetic lexicon through the creation of new words; hatred of the existing language; a stubborn determination to continue their work despite "the sea of cat-calls and indignation."[2]

The public performances of the Futurists in the early 1910s were staged as farces, in which each participant had his own emploi and signature trait. The one-eyed Burliuk looked at the audience through a monocle, the pilot Kamensky had an airplane painted on his face, Mayakovsky wore a yellow blouse on stage, which itself became a banner for the Russian avant-garde. "The newspapers were filled with stories about Futurism," Mayakovsky later recalled when speaking of the early days, "their tone was less than polite. For example, I was often simply labeled a 'son of a bitch.'"

The infamy of the Futurists reached in its zenith in 1913. In January of that year, a mentally ill student who had no connection whatsoever to Futurism, slashed Ilya Repin's monumental masterpiece "Ivan the Terrible and his son Ivan." Several newspapers accused the Futurists of providing

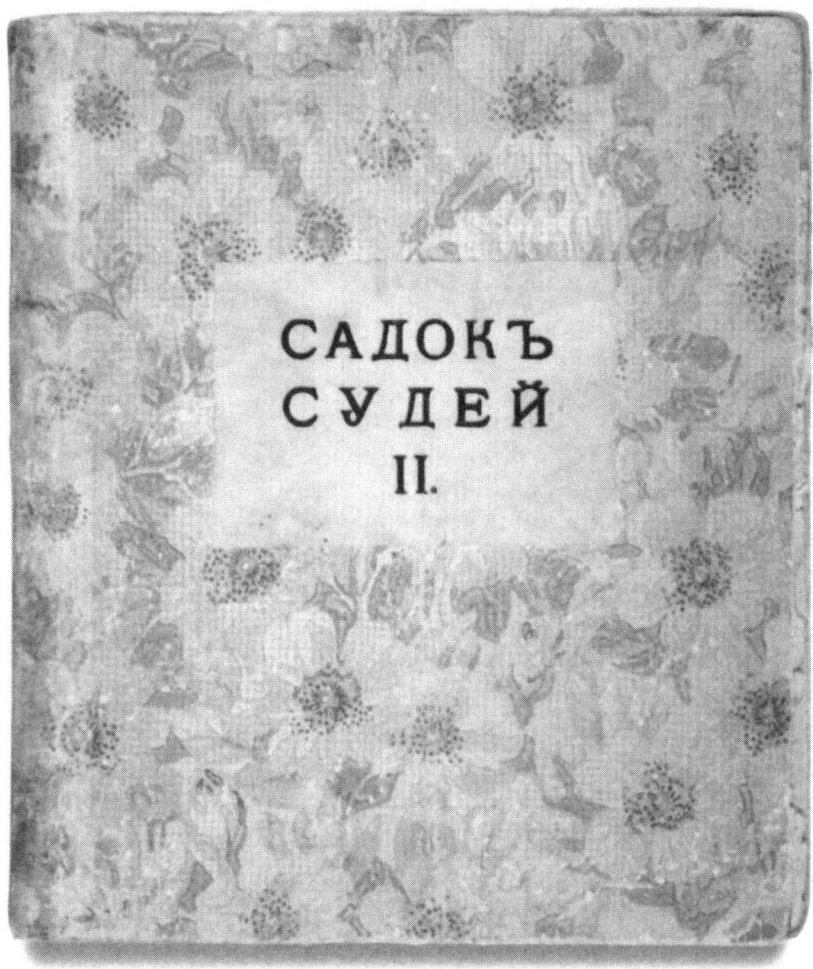

10 Cover from *A Trap for Judges II*, 1913. This Futurist almanac of 1913 came out in an edition of 800 copies. The cover was printed on wallpaper, and the interior featured art work by David and Vladimir Burliuk, Natalia Goncharova, Mikhail Larionov, and Elena Guro.

the ideology that had prompted this act of vandalism. During the debates surrounding the "responsibility" of the Futurists in this affair, the young poets rejected both the accusations of guilt and the "old' art," of which they considered Repin a representative. That year also saw the release of Kruchenykh's collection *Lipstick* (Pomada), which included probably the most notorious Futurist poem of all:

Dyr bul shchyl
ubeshchur
skum
vy so bu
r l ez

The text was written in the poet's "personal language," and it aimed to provide "an extract of the sounds of the Russian language, with all its dissonance and its scraping and roaring sounds." Kruchenykh, commenting on the Utopian task of creating an entirely new language, said of his project: "The artist has seen the world in a new way, and like Adam, is giving names to everything in that world. Lilies are beautiful, but the word 'lily' is ugly, abused, and 'defiled'. Therefore I call the lily not 'lily' but 'euy'. This name restores the primordial purity of language." Even more flamboyantly, he asserted: "there is more of the Russian national character in this poem than in all the works of Pushkin."[3]

In 1913 the "First All-Russian Congress" of Futurist Poets was held, which announced a new field of activity: reforming the theatre. Two emblematic works were staged: Vladimir Mayakovsky's tragedy *Vladimir Mayakovsky*, in which the author himself played the leading role (the set was designed by Filonov) and the first avant-garde opera in history: *Victory Over the Sun*. The latter was the fruit of combined efforts between the Futurists and their allies. The prologue was written by Khlebnikov, the libretto – including "arias" in transrational language – by Kruchenykh, the music by Matiushin, and the set and costumes were designed by Malevich. The protagonists of the opera are Futurist strongmen who defeat the old aesthetic, symbolized by their victory in a duel with the sun. Kruchenykh declared that this opera, probably the first without female characters, would "make way for an era of manliness, sweeping away the age of effeminate Apollos and filthy Aphrodites of old [here 'decadent'] art." Malevich's innovative set design, which included a curtain with the image of a black square, anticipated the new non-figurative directions art would take in the twentieth century. In 1915, Malevich gave a name to this new trend of using colorful geometric shapes against a neutral background: "New Realism" or "Suprematism."

During the early stages of the war with Germany, the Futurists and their allies rode the popular wave of patriotism and produced a number of anti-German works. However, they soon began to adopt a pacifist position. In 1915, Mayakovsky shocked his audience in the Petersburg cafe "The Stray Dog" with his poem "To You!" [Vam!]. In this poem he shouted that it would be better to give pineapple soda to prostitutes in a bar than entertain the well-fed bourgeoisie who had closed their eyes and ears to the quagmire of war. The cafe was closed down after this performance.

The Futurists took the momentous events of 1917 – the February and October revolutions – to be the beginning of a process of world regeneration. They considered the leaders of the Bolshevik uprising – Vladimir Lenin and Lev Trotsky – to be great architects of history. They thought of the Communist hymn "The International" – which extolled the destruction of the old world and birth of the new – as expressing a certain kind of political Futurism. Immediately after the first revolution, Khlebnikov called for a world government that would reform the entire globe. In 1918, Mayakovsky summoned the "proletariat of the factories and the land to a third revolution – bloodless but cruel – a revolution of the soul." This would cleanse the human psyche and everyday life of the vestiges of the old world. The Futurists ("the Bolsheviks of art") should become a social force who would "go out on the street" and bring art to the toiling masses.

Mayakovsky attempted to realize this Communist-Futurist vision in his 'cosmic' agitational play *Mystery-Bouffe*, which was staged for the first anniversary of the October Revolution. It was directed by Meyerhold and Mayakovsky himself; the set was designed by Malevich. The mystery invoked biblical and apocalyptic allegories to depict the destruction of the old bourgeois world and the birth of the new proletarian world. In this new world, there would be no room for exploiters (tsars, nobles, capitalists, and priests), nor indeed those who supported political compromise.

In the early 1920s, Mayakovsky became the leader of the Neo-Futurist organization "The Left Front of Art" (Levyi Front Iskusstva), known by the acronym LEF. This organization proclaimed itself – without much success, it must be said – the literary avant-garde of the victorious proletariat. LEF claimed that poetry should fulfill the social demands of the revolution: in practice, this meant producing agitational texts to serve the interests of the Bolsheviks. The first edition of the journal *LEF* set out the goals for Left art: "not to teach, not to spread information, not to prophesy, not to give blessings, not to give out patents, but only to finish off the destruction, clear away the left-over fragments and rubbish, and leave a wide, clear space for new builders," who were bound to arrive and start building soon. For the members of LEF, the heroic present was the place from which the beautiful future would spring.

What did the actual future hold for the avant-garde "generation of twenty-two-year-olds"? In the Stalinist state, art was conceived as an instrument for improving (in fact, indoctrinating) the ill-educated masses. This did not depend on the idea of art as an egalitarian project of transformation of mankind, a notion that had become associated with the theory of permanent (international) revolution as formulated by Stalin's rival Trotsky, who would be exiled in 1929. While particular ideas and slogans of the avant-garde were appropriated and given new meanings by the school of Socialist Realism (which imagined art as a political force, bringing social order, criticizing the bourgeois way of life, and encouraging the cult of the builders of the new society; see chapter 8), the members of the avant-garde movement were for the most part thrown off the boat of Soviet reality. "The masters of the future" – such as the imaginary artist at the start of this article – had few options. They could keep silent, try to escape, attempt to come to terms with their new environment, or perish. As Khlebnikov had predicted in one of his moments of doubt, the "citizens of time" had become "firewood for the stoves of generations that would never come to be."[4]

As to particular individuals, Velimir Khlebnikov died in 1922. Mayakovsky, who had written numerous works of propaganda and several epic poems devoted to the revolution, committed suicide in 1930. His death symbolically coincided with the end of the Russian avant-garde as a historical and cultural phenomenon. Kazimir Malevich, who had founded a unique avant-garde university and an academic centre for Left art, had to leave his academic posts at the end at the 1920s because of the changing political environment. In 1931 he was arrested, but was released shortly afterwards. However, he remained in disfavor and died in poverty in 1935. In the years following the revolution, Pavel Filonov gave lectures in analytic art, painted his "formula pictures" without charging for them, and created his own artistic school, where he gave lessons free of charge. He was preparing a collection of his work for an exhibition in 1931 but it was canceled at the last minute. He died of starvation in 1941, during the Fascist siege of Leningrad. That other "knight of the avant-garde," Alexei Kruchenykh, refused to go against his convictions and declined to take any part in the public literary world by the end of the 1920s. He devoted himself to collecting and preserving the archives of the Russian avant-garde movement. He died in 1968.

The transrational poet Igor' Terent'ev, who had been a follower of Kruchenykh and a student of Malevich, tried to unite "Leftist" artists in a new kind of literary and artistic brotherhood in the 1920s. In 1927, he staged an ultra-experimental version of Gogol's classic comedy *The Inspector General* in Leningrad. The security services arrested him and accused him of using his transrational poetry to convey secret information to the enemies of the Soviet Union. He was shot in 1937. The purges also affected Terent'ev's allies, participants in the last Russian avant-garde society, OBERIU (The Association of Real Art [Ob"edinenie real'nogo iskusstva]). These included the poets Daniil Kharms (whose real surname was Iuvachev), Alexander Vvedensky and Nikolai Zabolotsky. Only Zabolotsky survived the late 1930s and early 1940s. The "young" futurists Nikolai Aseev and Selvinsky were able to adapt to Soviet life and accept the demands of the totalitarian state. They were officially recognized as forming the left wing of the Soviet "detachment of writers." David Burliuk, the "father of Futurism," immigrated to Japan in 1920 and settled in the USA in 1922. He continued to paint and gained an international recognition. In the Soviet Union, however, his work remained virtually unknown. He died in New York in 1967.

Biography – Velimir (real name Viktor) Vladimirovich Khlebnikov (1885–1922)

Khlebnikov the poet, one of the major figures in the Russian Modernist movement, stands out as a champion of Utopianism, even in this age characterized by Utopian ideas. Specifically, he planned to discover the laws of time, to make it possible to plan the future scientifically and to save humankind from future wars. He intended to create a "scientifically designed" world language, and to summon scholars and inventors to form a world government. He proposed the creation of new cities with hundreds of glass buildings. Apartments in these cities would be portable: they could be taken out of one building and carried to another. He believed that people would be able to broadcast art exhibitions through the air and project them onto the clouds. He proposed to solve the food crisis by chemically transforming soil into bread, and to develop an art which would "easily awaken us from dreams" and allow us to travel into space. His future world would extend "certain civil rights" to monkeys and other primates, establish "freedom for horses," and "equal rights for cows." The image of Khlebnikov – mad genius, "King of Time," visionary scientist, bewitched wanderer – who needed only "the sky and the clouds," occupies an important place in the cultural mythology of twentieth-century Russia.

Khlebnikov was born on October 28, 1885 in the steppe of Kalmykia, a coastal region of Russia near the mouth of Volga. His father was a natural scientist, a follower of Darwin, who had devoted his life to studying birds. Khlebnikov's mother had been a teacher in an orphanage before marrying, and had served as a nurse during the Russo-Turkish war (1877–8). This was a typical *intelligentsia* family from the "Realist" era: they held liberal convictions, believed in gradual social progress, possessed a strong work ethic, and had conservative (classical) artistic tastes. They were firm believers in science, in particular the exact and natural sciences. They had some admiration for the ordinary people, who were in need of their Enlightenment, but from whom something could occasionally be learned. The family completely rejected modernist ideas, and this would strain the relationship with their son in years to come. In 1898 the Khlebnikovs settled in Kazan, a university and market town on the crossroads between Europe and Asia.

As a young man, Khlebnikov was particularly interested in mathematics and ornithology. It appears that, while still in high school, he learned about Lobachevsky's non-Euclidean (imaginary) geometry, which would have an important influence on his world-view. In August 1903, he began studying mathematics and physics at Kazan University, but later switched to the natural sciences. Founded in 1803, Kazan University was one of the oldest in Russia and had a strong academic tradition. Several major figures had worked there over the years, including Lobachevsky, the chemist Alexander Butlerov, the zoologist Nikolai Vagner, and the linguist Jan Niecislaw Baudouin de Courtenay. Both Tolstoy and Lenin had been students there. At the beginning of the twentieth century, the university was seized by a growing wave of revolutionary sentiment. In 1903, Khlebnikov took part in a student demonstration to commemorate the death of a "revolutionary martyr." When the demonstration was broken up by the police, Khlebnikov was arrested and spent a month in prison. This ended his involvement in politics. Later on, he wrote defiantly: "A police station is a great thing: / this is the place / Where the State reminds [us] / that it still exists."

In 1905, Khlebnikov went on his first scientific expedition to the Central Urals. It was an ornithological expedition, and his sister recalled that he brought back "piles of notes, especially on the songs of woodland birds." In later years, transcribed birdsong became an important material for his "bird language," one of the major linguistic themes of his poetry. Khlebnikov proposed a new scientific term, "metabiosis" (by analogy with symbiosis) to describe the laws linking "two lives" taking place in the same physical space one after another. The problem of the link between time and space (and life and death) in nature is extremely important in Khlebnikov's scientific Utopian vision.

He declared his lifelong goal to establish laws of time, which would eventually allow humankind to overcome death. A moral dimension was added to this vision after the tragic destruction of the Russian fleet in the battle of Tsushima in the Russo-Japanese War. "I wanted to find a justification for the deaths," Khlebnikov stated. His creative work became focused on discovering a formula for time, which had roots in Pythagoreanism. However, Khlebnikov emphasized that, unlike Pythagoras, he was interested in living phenomena and life cycles which were subject to mathematical laws:

> I see right through you, Numbers.
> I see you dressed in animals, their skins,
> coolly propped against uprooted oaks.
> You offer us a gift: unity between the snaky movement
> of the backbone of the universe and Libra dancing
> overhead. You help us to see centuries in a flash
> of laughing teeth. See my wisdom-wizened eyes
> opening to recognize
> what my I
> will be
> when its dividend is one.
>
> ("Numbers," 1911; trans. Paul Schmidt)

The poet was proud of the fact that as early as 1912, he used his number theory to predict that the Russian Empire would fall in 1917.

Khlebnikov also started his bold experiments with artistic language in his student years. The Russian language in its current state did not satisfy the poet: it seemed to obscure and distort the "natural" link between sounds and concepts. For this reason, it was unable to serve as an instrument in Khlebnikov's great goal: the unification of people and the transformation of their lives. He considered it necessary to make drastic reforms to language, aimed at liberating the word from the dead chain of tradition. During the 1900s–1910s, the poet made various attempts at developing a universal language ("a single means for mortals to converse") using etymology, word-creation, transrational language, bird language, star language, and number language. Khlebnikov's linguistic theories informed his artistic practice: his theoretical discoveries were "played out" in his literary works; numerical and mathematical formulas appear on his manuscripts surrounded by his drawings. The experimental nature of Khlebnikov's work is undeniable, but it is also clear that his poetic program is rooted in the Russian cultural tradition: the "scientific" poetry of Mikhail Lomonosov, the linguistic theory of Alexander Shishkov, the social theorizing of the Slavophiles, the theurgy of the symbolists, and the cyclical historical theories of Danilevsky and Lev Tolstoy can all be seen as predecessors.

In 1908 Khlebnikov arrived in St. Petersburg to study natural sciences. He quickly transferred to the department of Oriental languages to study Sanskrit literature, and to the Russian and Slavic department. He did not graduate: in 1911 he was expelled for not paying his university fees. While in St. Petersburg, however, Khlebnikov became acquainted with famous writers and attended literary meetings in the apartment of Viacheslav Ivanov. He participated in the literary group that published the journal *Apollo* [Apollon] and became a regular at the Stray Dog cafe, where the intellectual and artistic elite of the city met. The older authors saw Khlebnikov as a talented eccentric, an author of "crazed but ingenious poetry."

Khlebnikov, however, soon decided that his period of poetic apprenticeship was over. In 1912 he published his manifesto dialogue "Teacher and Pupil. On Words, Cities and Peoples." The protagonist of this work – an alter ego of Khlebnikov himself – reports his success in achieving a number of goals. These include the creation of a linguistic theory of the "inner declension" of words, the discovery of "the law of the emergence of cities" by examining the distance between them; the discovery of the laws of history, which determine the fate of peoples, as well as the rise and fall of states (like Prometheus, the pupil "stole the secret supply of laws which direct fate").

In the early 1910s, Khlebnikov joined the Futurists and participated in creating the founding texts of the new movement. In the charged atmosphere of the time, young poets rebelling against the old masters called Khlebnikov a "genius," "the great poet of modernity," and "a latter-day Pushkin." Khlebnikov's contemporaries thought that his work – the poems "Incantation through Laughter" [Zakliatie smekhom] and "Bobeobi sang the lips" [Bobeovi pelis' guby]; the epic poem *The Crane* [Zhuravl']; the drama *The Marquise Dezes* [Markiza Dezes] and others – symbolized the New Art, and, of course, these same works aroused the indignation of traditionalists.

During the First World War, Khlebnikov and his friends were horrified to learn he had been drafted. He came up with a peculiar program of mathematical pacifism, declaring that his scientific research would allow humankind to remove war from the world like a "redundant appendix" (in Russian "izhitsa," a letter that was indeed removed from the Russian alphabet after the February revolution of 1917). In 1916, the poet established the society "Presidents of the Globe," a world government to establish universal peace and transform the world's nations into a "scientifically structured" organism. He invited his friends to staff this world government, as well as the Indian Nobel laureate Rabindranath Tagore, the Chinese revolutionary Sun Yat-sen, Woodrow Wilson and, later, the Head of Russian the Provisional Government, Alexander Kerensky. At the bottom of his "decree" for the creation of a union of inventors Khlebnikov signed himself "Velimir I, The King of Time" ("The Trumpet of Martians," 1916).

Like many apocalyptically minded colleagues from a variety of avant-garde persuasions, Khlebnikov thought of the revolution as bringing mankind one step closer to the glorious finale of history. This final stage would be characterized by the acquisition of knowledge of the laws that organized the world, the application of these laws in intelligent ways, and the world brotherhood of creative people. Even during the insanity and cruelty of the Civil War – when he wrote the powerful "realist" poems *Night Search* (Nochnoi obysk) and *The Cheka Chairman* (Predsedatel' Cheki) that described the horrors of the revolution – Khlebnikov believed he could foresee a perfect future for mankind. In his Utopian poem *Ladomir* (1920–1) – the title of which means "world harmony," referring to the harmony of the scientifically organized free society – Khlebnikov formulated his artistic credo: "Draw not with chalk, but with love, / That, which will be drafts. / And fate, having flown down to the headboard. / Will bend an intelligent ear of rye."

Khlebnikov's life after the revolution involved constant wandering and deprivation. He left starving Moscow for Ukraine, which was experiencing the worst of the Civil War. He avoided being conscripted into the White Army by feigning madness, checking himself into a psychiatric hospital near Kharkhov. According to the sympathetic doctor who assessed his case, the poet had suffered "a complete withdrawal into an interior world" and, like Strindberg and Van Gogh, "this made him seem like an eternal wanderer, separated from the world surrounding him, as though it was passing him by."

In 1920 Khlebnikov traveled to the Caucasus, where he took part in the First Congress of Eastern Peoples in Baku. The fate of the wise, sleeping (but waiting to arise) East was a constant source of interest for the poet. In Baku, Khlebnikov solemnly proclaimed that he had at last discovered the laws of time. In a state of euphoria, he addressed a group of revolutionary sailors on the subject of the laws of time in nature and society. From the Caucasus, Khlebnikov moved on to Central Asia where he worked with Communist forces in Persia to bring about a socialist revolution. The Persians nicknamed him "the Russian Dervish," of which he was very proud. On his return journey by train to Russia, Khlebnikov was attacked and robbed. Tragically, he lost many manuscripts during this attack (friends recall that he carried them in a pillowcase).

In 1922, Khlebnikov completed two of his major works. The "supersaga" *Zangezi* is a universal epic "poem-building," which is set in various mythopoetic "planes" or "realms": the realm of birds, the realm of people and the realm of numbers. In his historico-philosophical work "The

Tables of Fate," Khlebnikov summarized his discoveries on the mathematical laws of time. Khlebnikov came to Moscow for the last time in 1922 in order to visit friends. However, he unexpectedly left for the south again to wander. On his journey he became seriously ill. He lost the use of his legs and developed gangrene. He died a month later, on the June 28, at the age of thirty-seven, the same age at which Pushkin died, as Khlebnikov's friends loved to point out. Khlebnikov was buried in a forest by his friend and disciple, the artist Pavel Miturich. Miturich painted a blue globe on the coffin lid and inscribed the words: "Chairman of the World: Velimir I."

Work – *The Bedbug* (Klop) by Vladimir Mayakovsky

Perhaps no single figure was more closely involved with the evolving Russian avant-garde project than Vladimir Mayakovsky. He was one of the leaders of the pre-revolutionary Russian Futurists: one of the main authors of the notorious and brilliant manifesto "A Slap in the Public's Taste," a highly visible and provocative performance artist (known for his massive frame, bellowing voice and bright yellow blouse), and an exceptionally gifted poet. The following short lyric from 1913 provides a taste of the young Mayakovsky's inventive poetry, characterized by a larger-than-life and highly provocative poetic "I," bold metaphors, unexpected images, complex sound patterns, and innovative rhymes:[5]

> I suddenly smeared the weekday map
> splashing paint from a glass;
> On a plate of aspic
> I revealed
> the ocean's slanted cheek.
> On the scales of a tin fish
> I read the summons of new lips.
> And you
> could you perform
> a nocturne on a drainpipe flute?

As opposed to most of his fellow avant-garde writers, who had had little to do with politics before 1917, Mayakovsky identified himself with radical political activity as early as 1905, and immediately after the Revolution became a vocal advocate of the Bolshevik political and social project. His versified support of the revolution took many forms, from four-line advertising jingles to long poems such as *150,000,000* (1921), *Vladimir Ilich Lenin* (1924), and *Good* (Khorosho, 1927). In addition to creative work,

Mayakovsky was a leading theoretician of literature and culture in the 1920s, and the chief editor of the journal *LEF* (*Levyi Front Iskusstva*, The Left Front of Art, 1923–5).

An uncompromising individual by nature, Mayakovsky had increasing difficulties in the course of the 1920s reconciling his personal vision of the revolution with the actual course of events in the USSR as well as finding a balance between his public and private personae. Like many other pro-Bolshevik artists, he found the compromises of the NEP period extremely distasteful and was suspicious of the increasing conservatism of the Soviet state and particularly of its cultural policies. His late theatrical masterpiece *The Bedbug* reflects the complex situation in which he and the Russian avant-garde in general, found themselves in the late 1920s. The first production of this play also marked Meyerhold's final great, realized project. As was frequently true of his important productions, Meyerhold put together a stellar creative team to realize his and Mayakovsky's vision in 1929. Music was commissioned from the young Dmitri Shostakovich. Costumes and designs for the first half of the play were produced by a trio of artists who called themselves the Kukryniksy, while the veteran constructivist Alexander Rodchenko designed the second half.

The play begins during the height of the NEP period. Its protagonist is the former proletarian Ivan Prisypkin who is angling to join the NEP-era bourgeois elite. Having changed his name to the more fashionable Pierre Skrypkin, he hopes to marry Elzevir Renaissance, daughter of a successful NEP-era businessman. In turn, the Renaissance family will accept him because his proletarian background and union card will, they hope, help to legitimize them in Soviet society. Having jilted his true Communist girlfriend Zoia Berezkina, Prisypkin/Skrypkin goes ahead with his marriage, only to perish in a fire at his drunken wedding reception.

In writing a satire against the excesses of NEP and the embourgeoisement of Soviet society, Mayakovsky was not particularly original. This was the topic of a number of plays and novels of the mid to late 1920s. More original is the second half of the play, which is set fifty years in the future when perfect communism has apparently been achieved. Zoia, now a research assistant in a scientific laboratory, takes part in an experiment to revive someone who has been frozen for fifty years. This turns out to be Prisypkin/Skrypkin, who, like some sort of futuristic Frankenstein's monster, causes a number of unexpected problems. Having not participated in the process of social engineering that produced Communist society, he brings back to life a host of habits and thoughts that have ostensibly been eradicated. These atavisms prove peculiarly attractive, however, and Prisypkin rapidly infects all he meets with such 1920s "diseases" as alcoholism, love, dancing, and individuality. In the play's finale, to protect the perfect world of the future, he is locked in a zoo cage with only one companion from his former days to keep him company – a bedbug. In the final scene, in a theatrical trick fully in keeping with Meyerhold's theatrical vision, the caged Prisypkin turns away from the characters on the stage and toward the audience in the theatre, implicating them in the action: "Citizens! Brothers! My own people! Darlings! How did you get here? So many of you! When were you unfrozen? Why am I alone in the cage? Darlings, friends, come and join me! Why am I suffering? Citizens . . ."[6]

The sets and costumes for the first production set the story off perfectly but reveal a clear retrenchment from Meyerhold's experimental heyday. For the first half the Kukryniksy created a fully realistic 1920s backdrop; while this is justified by the script, the sets and costumes are a far cry from the constructivist vision Meyerhold had espoused only a few years earlier. The "futuristic" sets and costumes of Rodchenko, while again perfectly in keeping with the play, seem faintly menacing in their cold, black and white starkness. They do, however, perfectly set off the 1920 "refugee" Prisypkin. Even Shostakovich's music (certainly not his best nor his most extensive score) lacks the sonic modernism that was so powerfully evoked in his earlier opera *The Nose*, for example.

The play's message is ambiguous. In his comments on the play, Mayakovsky tended to focus on the satiric, at least in part because there was nothing contoversial about anti-NEP satire, especially by 1929 when the period had already come to an end. And it is undoubtedly true that in the context of 1920s Russia, Skrypkin appears as a selfish villain. But what makes the play more than a satire on contemporary life is that in the context of the "perfect Communist future" Skrypkin is suddenly transformed. This is not because he has changed; indeed it is precisely because he has not changed at all. But suddenly, in the context of the perfectly sanitized utopian society of the future, he begins to seem almost attractive. He has personality, verve, and life, whereas the rest of the figures on stage seem to be wooden and flat. Ultimately, audiences are unsure whether to sympathize with the hapless Prisypkin or to condemn him.

The play, then, can be seen as a double dystopia. On the one hand, it reflects Mayakovsky's disappointment with Soviet society of his own day, which he feared had turned away from the radically innovative project promised by the Revolution in favor of creating a new Red ruling class whose central goal was to recreate the middle-class comforts of the bourgeoisie. On the other hand, it suggests that the perfectly engineered future might also turn out to be problematic if humanity believes that technological progress can be counted on to solve complex human problems.

The Bedbug would turn out to be Mayakovsky's last major public success. His final play, *The Bathhouse*, was savagely criticized in the press and although Mayakovsky made vigorous efforts to defend it, the production was not seen as a success. Feeling increasingly trapped and isolated in a society whose goals he supported in principle but whose reality seemed ever more unpleasant, Mayakovsky took his own life in 1930. For many, the suicide of this key figure of the avant-garde marked the end of the Russian modernist period. Although many modernist artists would continue to live and work in the USSR, the public presence of the avant-garde, already much diminished by the late 1920s, would all but evaporate in the wake of Mayakovsky's death.

Event – The Meeting "Three Left Hours"

On January 24, 1928 a literary evening entitled "Three Left Hours" was held in the *Dom Pechati* (Press House) in Petersburg. This was last significant event in the history of the Russian avant-garde movement. The poets who participated were members of a group with the curious name of OBERIU (an acronym for Association of Real Art [Ob'edinenie real'nogo iskusstva]).

The founding members of OBERIU were the poet and prose-writer Daniil Kharms (1905–42), the poet and natural philosopher Nikolai Zabolotsky, and the "world authority on senselessness," the poet Alexander Vvedensky (1904–41). In a declaration composed on the eve of the *Dom Pechati* meeting, they stated: "We, the OBERIUTs are honest art workers. We are poets who offer new ways of experiencing the world and a new art. We are the creators not only of a new poetic language, but also of a new way of experiencing life and its objects." By this, the OBERIUTs meant "a widening and deepening of our understanding of the object and the word," "bringing together verbal meanings," exposing the specifics of art, which is alien to conventional logic, and also the principle of a new poetic vision. They placed particular emphasis on the pluralistic nature of this new union: "Our union is free and voluntary, it brings masters together, not apprentices; artists, not decorators. Each person understands himself and each person understands how he is connected to the others." Zabolotsky wrote part of the declaration, in which he outlines the key characteristics of the society's participants. The OBERIUTs thought of their meeting in

Dom Pechati as the birth of a new stage in the history of Russian "Left" art.

In modern artistic terminology, the event "Three Left Hours" might be called a "happening," a kind of performance practice that in Russia can be traced back to early Futurism in the beginning of the 1910s. "Three Left Hours" was heavily promoted: the OBERIUTs intended not only to attract the attention of Leningrad's cultural elite, but also to publicize the new group's artistic ideas. A billboard was placed in the city center with posters attached to it in such a way that only enormous individual letters and fragments of words were visible. This created a kind of *trompe l'oeil* effect, in the spirit of transrational language. Posters displayed throughout the city used various typefaces, with a few words or letters printed sideways or at right angles around corners, "in order to attract and maintain the attention of passers-by." Kharms, one of the main organizers of the evening, had posters sent to a great variety of addresses, from newspaper offices to banks and foreign embassies. Personal invitations were sent to the founding fathers of Left art: Malevich, Matiushin, and Filonov, as well as Terent'ev and any philologists interested in experimental art.

Dom Pechati was one of the few avant-garde islands remaining at the end of the 1920s. It was here that Terent'ev had directed his transrational version of Gogol's *Inspector General*, a performance that resulted in the director being hounded in the Leningrad press until his subsequent arrest. Generally, Left art had become unsafe by the late 1920s, as the Party was orienting itself towards a standardized, simplified art that would be comprehensible to a mass audience and remain under the control of the state.

"Three Left Hours" consisted of three parts. The first "hour" was devoted to poetry readings. That was followed a performance of Kharms' play *Elizaveta Bam*, written specially for the evening. Finally, the OBERIU film *The Meat Grinder* [Miasorubka] was shown, and the evening concluded with a debate. The evening was organized like a carnival. There was general buffoonery, conventions were turned upside-down, taboos were broken, and audience participation was actively encouraged. The evening was introduced by the young poet Bakhterev, who gave a "transrational" speech, which promptly led to general confusion among the audience. An enormous lacquered wardrobe was then brought onto the stage. Kharms sat on top with his legs crossed: "powdered and pale-faced, dressed in a long jacket with a red triangle, in his favorite golden hat with pendants." He looked like "a fantastic effigy or a minstrel from some unknown time." The poet read a selection of "phonetic" (transrational) poetry. As soon as he finished, he pulled a pocket-watch out of his jacket and declared that the OBERIU poet Nikolai Kropachev was about to begin his performance in the center of the city. Indeed, exactly at that moment Kropachev, whose appearance was listed in the program, began reading his poetry on the street, to the surprise of the passers-by. A specialist in OBERIU has described Kharms' actions as "an experiment in breaking down the unity of space."[7]

Bakhterev then re-appeared on stage. He read more poetry, and suddenly fell on his back, immobile. Workers appeared and carried his "body" off the candle-lit stage. Konstantin Vaginov's appearance was accompanied by a dancing ballerina; the poet paid no attention to her. Later Vaginov (1899–1934), one of the most original writers of this period, would describe this evening in his novel *The Works and Days of Svistonov* [Trudy i dni Svistonova]). Alexander Vvedensky rode on to the stage on a tricycle. He remained on the tricycle as he read his poems. Zabolotsky read his poem-manifesto "Movement" [Dvizhenie], which presented an OBERIU "view of the world through naked eyes." The poem brought together the dynamic poetics of early Futurism, Filonov's analytism, and the primitivism of the early avant-garde artists:

> The wretched horse waves his limbs
> Now stretching out like a fish,
> Now letting his eight legs sparkle
> Inside his shiny belly.

Elizaveta Bam, the staged manifesto of OBERIU, began after the intermission. Kharms' play, which has often been referred to by critics as a forerunner of Western absurdist theatre, continued the tradition of futurist and neo-futurist manifesto performances. Kharms' unusual play stands out because of its setting in a local and everyday context: the personal life of the heroine Elizaveta Bam. The play is characterized by an all-encompassing alogism: cause and effect relationships are broken down; the name and the age of the heroine suddenly change; the plot is interrupted by unnecessary scenes; the characters often forget what has just been said. Nevertheless, this dream-like kaleidoscope of senselessness is drawn together by a tragic theme: the heroine is being pursued for a crime she did not commit. The nature of the crime is not disclosed for most of the play: those who come to arrest her merely tell her that she already knows what she did and threaten "terrible punishments." However, at the very end, she is accused of the murder of a certain Petr Nikolaevich in the presence of the "murdered" man himself. The play closes with a soliloquy by Elizaveta Bam about a mysterious cottage in the mountains, where there are mice with moustaches and evil cockroaches "carrying axes."

The theme of being pursued for a crime one did not commit links Kharms' play with Franz Kafka's novel *The Trial* and Vladimir Nabokov's (1899–1977) *Invitation to a Beheading* [Priglashenie na kazn', 1936], though Kharms had certainly never heard of Kafka or the émigré Nabokov. The absurd accusations made against the heroine can be seen as a reference to the show trials in the USSR that were already beginning in the late 1920s. However, it appears that Kharms was more interested in the aesthetic, philosophical, and metaphysical potential of the absurd. Illogical art paved the way toward the depths of human consciousness, which remained inaccessible to the unwieldy tools of formal logic. At least for Kharms and Vvedensky, the essence of the Utopian program of OBERIU involved shaking the foundations of commonsense and seeing deep inside the "star of irrationality" to the point of absolute zero. The OBERIU members were not interested in the absurd "for its own sake," but rather as a means of uncovering truth.

The final item of the evening was the film *The Meat Grinder*. This montage film was created by OBERIU members Alexander Ramovsky and Klementy Mints who assembled it by putting old fragments of film together. The film has not survived, so we can assess its content only through personal recollections. "The screen came down and we saw the outline of a train speeding forward. What happened next? Nothing. The train keeps going forward and forward, like a woman rocking her thighs. The length of the train stretches on and on, like a ball of wool eternally unraveling. Wagon after wagon crawls out from the back of the screen and disappears into the darkness of the theatre." The endless motion of the train was reminiscent of the first film in the history of cinematography, *L'Arrivée d'un train en gare de La Ciotat* (1896), whose audience famously jumped out of their seats in terror when they saw the train moving toward them. "Perhaps the creators of *The Meat Grinder* intended the endless motion of the train to evoke the never-ending mincing motion that takes place in a meat grinder."[8]

The film was followed by an entr'acte with jazz dancing, and then the discussion began, led by Vvedensky. As a whole, the audience seemed satisfied. They left the next morning when the trams started running. The following day, however, *The Red Newspaper* (Krasnaia gazeta) printed a feuilleton with the mocking title of "Ytuirebo" (OBERIUTs written backwards). The evening was described as "gobbledegook, a cynically naked muddle" and "a circus without the humor." This feuilleton marked the start of the official media's scorn towards OBERIU. Even after the collapse of the society, this scornful attitude persisted to the time of the arrests of Kharms, Vvedensky, and Zabolotsky. Only the last survived the Stalinist terror.

"Three Left Hours" was intended to mark the re-birth of avant-garde art under new socio-historical conditions. Instead it became a carnivalesque funeral for the avant-garde art of the 1910s and 1920s.

8

The Future as Present: Soviet Culture

I

In his classic history *Russian Literature since the Revolution* (1963) Edward J. Brown wittily called the 1920s the Indian summer of Russian Modernism.¹ Indeed, this amazing period, which began with the end of the Civil War (1918–21) and the introduction of a relatively liberal New Economic Policy [NEP], marked the last outburst of Modernist creative energy in Russia. Unlike bohemian Modernist culture of the 1900s-1910s with its nostalgic portrayal of the past and utopian visions of the future, post-revolutionary culture was inseparable from politics and characterized by the millenarian cult of the present as a heroic era and the associated idea that artists were living witnesses who ought to express the historic times in which they lived. In the revolutionary language that was adopted by (and eventually imposed on) practically all writers to a greater or lesser extent, the present was a realization of the "future," or more accurately, a prelude to the triumphant finale of human history, and each and every contemporary action – whether an event of great public significance or some minor private occurrence – was automatically considered to be exceptional and momentous.

This cult of the heroic present is nicely illustrated in one of Mayakovsky's poems in which he alludes to two of Pushkin's major works, "Poltava" – which celebrated Peter the Great's historic triumph over the Swedes – and *Eugene Onegin*, which pre-revolutionary critics had praised as an exemplary love story. Mayakovsky proclaimed:

> The battles of the revolution
>   are more serious than "Poltava"
>   And our love
>   more marvelous
>   than the love of Onegin.

In general, nineteenth-century humanistic and individualist values seemed outdated and even suspicious for the proponents of the revolutionary art who, to cite from another poem by Mayakovsky, "learned their dialectics not from Hegel," but rather from their Civil War experience:

> In the heat of battles
> it broke into our verse
> When
> under fire
> the bourgeoisie fled from us
> Just as we
> had once
> fled from them.

Of course, revolutionary mythology considered the present to be marvelously heroic only within the borders of the new Soviet state. However, as it was only a matter of time before the revolution would spread internationally, "our" present, which had begun in October 1917, could be seen as representative of the future of the rest of the world. This mythologizing of Soviet space and time can be seen in Vladimir Tatlin's (1885–1953) design for the unrealized "Monument to the Third International" (1919–20), a magnificent tower intended to house the World Communist Government. The proposed tower was to be 400 meters tall and it was to be composed of cylinders that rotated at different speeds around a slanted central column. They would house the world parliament, the world government, and – at the very top – the world news offices. Tatlin conceived his tower as a monument to the glorious present of the new world.

The contemporary writer was expected to keep "in step" with the cosmic revolutionary transformations. The mythologized representation of contemporary history as a military march towards the great goals of mankind was so powerful that some writers began to develop peculiar anxieties about "getting left behind the times" and "not keeping pace with the collective." This particularly affected those writers who had come of age in pre-revolutionary Russia (Osip Mandelstam, for example) and those who expressed values considered old-fashioned or socially alien to the Soviet project (Sergei Esenin [1895–1925] and Iury Olesha [1899–1960]).

II

According to the Bolshevik political mythology (which was loosely based on a Marxist interpretation of history), socio-economic revolution would pave the way for the cultural – or spiritual – revolution, in which literature was

11 Vladimir Tatlin's "Monument to the Third International" (model), 1919–20. Tatlin's tower was to be a 1200-foot steel symbol of modernity. Though it was never built (and was certainly not remotely realizable given the economic situation of the early Soviet Union), its conception was an important marker of the utopian thrust of the Soviet project.

required to play an active part. The importance of individual writers began to diminish as groups of writers sprang up, composed of members who shared similar views on major politico-aesthetic questions of the day. There were many such groups, and they were often engaged in open conflict. The major questions raised in the public disputes of the time were as follows: What kind of literature was and was not required in the new era? Who could (and who could not) write it? Could writers from the pre-revolutionary period be relied upon to create a new kind of literature? What should be done about the literature of the past and the classics: should they be re-appropriated or "destroyed"? What was the proper relationship between writers, the

Communist Party and the state? To what extent was artistic freedom possible in a proletarian state that was surrounded by enemies? How important was the quality of creative work for the new proletarian literature? Would satire be allowed in the new literature: should the proletariat laugh?

Critics addressed these questions – together with many others – in their readings of the major literary works of this period. These included the epic poems of Blok (*The Twelve* [Dvenadsat'], 1918) and Mayakovsky (*150000000*, 1921; *Good!* [Khorosho!], 1927), the short-story cycles *Red Cavalry* (Konarmiia, 1926) by Isaac Babel (1894–1940) and *The Stories of Nazar Il'ich, Mr. Sinebriukhov* (Rasskazy Nazara Il'icha, gospodina Sinebriukhova, 1921–2) by Mikhail Zoshchenko (1895–1958), and novels such as *The Naked Year* (Golyi god, 1922) by Boris Pilniak (real surname Vogau, 1894–1938), *Cement* (Tsement, 1925) by Fedor Gladkov (1883–1958), *The Rout* (Razgrom, 1926) by Alexander Fadeev (1901–56), the poetry of Boris Pasternak (1890–1960) – *My Sister-Life* (Sestra moia, zhizn', 1922); *Lieutenant Schmidt* (Leitenant Shmidt, 1926–7) – Ilya Selvinsky (1899–1968) – *Ulialiaevshina*, 1924, – the satirical novels of Ilya Ilf (1897–1937) and Evgeny Petrov (1903–42) – *The Twelve Chairs* (Dvenadtsat' stul'ev, 1928) and *The Little Golden Calf* (Zolotoi telenok, 1931).

The literature wars of the 1920s were fought on the pages of journals and newspapers, inside artistic clubs and cafés – which enjoyed a flowering during the economic chaos of the Civil War years – and in political meetings and agitational street performances. While there was a great diversity of views on the questions of the day, a number of different literary groups claimed that they alone had the only right answer, and that the opinions of others were flawed and dangerous. In some ways, this situation was not new for Russia: one might recall a similar doggedness in the battles fought in the journals of the 1860s and 1870s, or in the "War on Parnassus" in the early nineteenth century. However, the literary-ideological battles of the 1920s were unique because this was the first time that the state – or, more precisely, the Communist Party – held the position of supreme arbiter. This position was adopted in accordance with the new Communist religion that upheld the state as the creator and guardian of a just and righteous world.

Literature was assigned a particularly important role in this project because the Bolshevik government saw it as the most effective way of influencing the masses (according to Lenin, films could rival literature as an effective means of propaganda, but cinema was not yet sophisticated enough to fulfill its potential). Hence the main objectives of the Bolsheviks' cultural policy were to stimulate and support pro-Soviet literature as well as to prevent any counter-revolutionary expression of thought. In 1919, the monolithic state publisher Gosizdat was set up to provide ideological leadership on literary matters to all of Soviet Russia. Gosizdat exercised strict controls on private publishing firms, which were still allowed during the NEP, and drastically reduced their numbers. Finally, in 1922 the censorship agency Glavlit was established (it continued to exist until 1991); it was responsible for pre-publication political surveillance over periodicals, books, radio broadcasts and advertising. The distribution of library funds also fell under its purview.

However, in the early 1920s, the Party leadership had no consensus on what the literature for the new world should be. At least two conflicting visions of the cultural revolution were held by Party ideologues: class-war conception and conciliation. Various sides in the literature wars often took their cues from different wings of the Party leadership. As the Greek gods had sometimes intervened on behalf of one side or the other in the Trojan War, so the leading political figures in the Soviet Union – Trotsky, Lenin, Stalin, Lunacharsky, and Bukharin – attacked and defended particular authors. So long as there were a variety of political positions in the Party during the NEP period, it seemed the fiercely fought literature wars were destined to continue. Indeed, they came to an end only after the abolishment of NEP and the consolidation of Stalin's power in the late 1920s.

III

Let us briefly outline the trajectory of literary processes of the first decade following the October (Bolshevik) Revolution. This stormy period saw a number of schisms and endless ideological battles in the Soviet cultural world. The first schism occurred almost immediately after the Bolshevik seizure of power in 1917 and the dissolution of the Constituent Assembly. It divided those who recognized the Bolsheviks as the rightful leaders of the country, and those who considered them destructive usurpers.

Few major artists responded to the Bolsheviks' initial loud demand that they support the new state. The fact that the "left-wing" poet Mayakovsky and the director Meyerhold immediately counted themselves among the ranks was hardly surprising: they thought of the revolution as the political realization of their avant-garde dream. More surprising was the involvement of Alexander Blok, whose willingness to cooperate with the new regime came as a great shock to the old intelligentsia. Blok's support for the revolution grew out of his mystical, historical and philosophical ideas: he imagined the revolution as a wild poetic force that would destroy the washed-out bourgeois world. As the barbarians had destroyed Roman civilization, but in so doing had paved the way for the rise of Christianity, so the revolution would lead to the construction of a new world in Blok's view. He called on the intelligentsia to "listen to the music of revolution" and to participate in the process of building this world. In his apocalyptic poem *The Twelve*, written as early as January 1918, Blok depicts a Red Army patrol operating in a city gripped by fear. "Dark evil" surrounds the twelve soldiers on all sides: behind them is a hungry dog, symbolizing the old world; in front an invisible figure carrying a "blood-stained flag": Jesus Christ. Although this poem has attracted a great variety of contradictory readings, the symbolic association of the twelve godless Red Army soldiers with the twelve apostles of the new (or long-forgotten?) faith seems clear.

The years 1918–1919 saw the new regime come under intense criticism from liberal writers (Ivan Bunin [1870–1953], Alexander Kuprin [1870–1938], Leonid Andreev, Dmitry Merezhkovsky, and Zinaida Gippius [1869–1945]). They accused the Bolsheviks of founding a state based on lies and violence. While Gorky – the "father of proletarian literature" – had strong socialist convictions, he also opposed the Bolsheviks in this period. Having quarreled with his old friend Lenin, in 1922 Gorky followed in the footsteps of many other major cultural figures and left the country. However, once in the West he distanced himself from the anti-Soviet mood prevalent in much of the émigré world.

The Bolsheviks responded to their critics not only by closing down the oppositional press (between November 1917 and June 1918 they shut down more than 400 newspapers considered hostile), but also by purges of the "counter-revolutionary intelligentsia." Hence, in 1921, the renowned poet Nikolai Gumilev was shot. In 1922, the Soviet government exiled or deported "active counter-revolutionaries." These included philosophers, lecturers, doctors, writers, and journalists. Among those exiled were the philosophers Nikolai Berdiaev (1874–1948), Sergei Bulgakov (1871–1944), Ivan Ilin (1882–1954), Semen Frank (1877–1950), and Nikolai Lossky (1870–1965). The image of the "steamship of philosophers" became one of the enduring symbols of the purges of the early years of the Bolshevik state, a grotesque replay of the medieval Ship of Fools.

This schism led to the development of two Russian literatures in the 1920s: a Diaspora literature (based in Paris, Berlin, Prague, Riga, and the city of Harbin in northern China) and the new Soviet literature, produced by writers who accepted the revolution and who participated in the construction of the new Russia. Among the émigrés were the writers Bunin, Gippius, Merezhkovsky, Ivan Shmelev (1873–1950), Boris Zaitsev

(1881–1972), Marina Tsvetaeva, and Vladimir Nabokov, composers Igor Stravinsky, Sergei Prokofiev, and Sergei Rakhmaninov (1873–1943), and visual artists Alexandre Benois, Aleksandra Exter (1882–1949), Natalia Goncharova and Mikhail Larionov. The outstanding opera singer Fedor Shaliapin (1873–1938) also emigrated, as did many renowned scientists. Official Soviet criticism labeled the émigré writers as "Whites" and bourgeois counter-revolutionaries. In the thirties, some of them were also labeled Fascists. However, in the relatively liberal years of NEP there was still significant contact between the Soviet and émigré literary worlds. The major point of contact was Berlin, capital of Weimar Germany, where an active Russian-language publishing industry flourished.

IV

The next "dialectical schism" occurred within Soviet literature itself in the early 1920s. It divided "proletarian" – by virtue or birth or viewpoint – from "non-proletarian" writers. The latter were dismissed as "fellow travelers" of the revolution, a term that had been introduced by Trotsky. The ideologues of proletarian culture applied the Marxist theory of historical development to the arts. They supposed that just as the proletariat had replaced the bourgeoisie, so proletarian culture should replace bourgeois.

As early as September 1917 – just one month before the Revolution – the Marxist philosopher Alexander Bogdanov established the organization Proletkul't, which aimed to develop proletarian art as a means of activating of the creative potential of the working masses. Bogdanov believed that workers' art, based on the collective and production, would replace the decaying individualistic art of the exploiting classes. This would represent the final stage of humankind's cultural development. The early members of Proletkul't imagined the future society as a massive factory, "where there would be no knowledge of the lyrical or the intimate" (as the proletarian poet Alexei Gastev [1882–1939] put it) and the future person as a flawless machine, able to control and regulate the laws of nature. Proletkul't theorists considered workers' theatre to be particularly important, as it was "founded with the aim of allowing the proletariat to express their workers 'I' in dramatic works." To realize their goals, they encouraged theatre studios and workers' clubs all around the country. In 1920, the membership roll of Proletkul't exceeded 400,000.

Bogdanov's idea of art leading to Utopian Enlightenment became more directly political in the 1920s with the rise of a new generation of proletarian critics, who belonged to the MAPP (The Moscow Association of Proletarian Writers). This organization was later renamed VAPP (The All-Union Association of Proletarian Writers) and finally RAPP (The Russian Association of Proletarian Writers). Just as the proletariat had become the hegemonic class in the new society, proletarian literature, in their view, should claim a monopoly in the sphere of literary production. "In literature, art, and culture there is not a left front and right front, but rather a reactionary and revolutionary front. Every writer, every poet, everyone in the literary world must openly declare what he stands for and whom he stands with" (1923).[2]

Unlike Bogdanov, the RAPP theorists understood proletarian art not to mean art necessarily created by workers, but rather art loyal to the Communist Party and that upheld its role as the vanguard of the proletariat. RAPP members appointed themselves as "watchdogs" who worked to preserve the purity of the new art from the "bourgeois" influence of non-proletarian writers. They regularly criticized fellow travelers for their ideological errors and demanded public repentance from them. The leaders of RAPP – G. Lelevich, Iury Libedinsky, Semen Rodov, Leonid Averbakh – actively participated in the literary "purges" of the 1920s, the rhetoric and practice of which anticipated the political show-trials of the "enemies of the people" of the thirties (in their turn, many of these men would fall during the great purges at the end of the 1930s). The RAPP critics considered "their own" those writers who stoutly maintained "a proletarian point of view" – meaning those who favorably depicted Party leaders, "Old Bolsheviks" or young educated Commissars in their fiction, such as Dmitry Furmanov (1891–1926) in his novel *Chapaev*, Fedor Gladkov in *Cement*, or Alexander Fadeev in *The Rout*. In these works, model Communists taught political "consciousness" to the peasants and workers who remained politically immature, and were hated by villainous enemies of the Soviet regime and by those pitiful intellectuals who were weak in their socialist convictions.

V

The Fellow Travelers – that is, all those whom RAPP did not consider proletarian writers – were represented in the literature wars of the twenties by two active forces – the "Left Art" movement grouped around the organization LEF (Left Front of Art 1919–28) and the "traditional" writers and critics, associated with the journal *Red Virgin Soil* (Krasnaia nov', [1921–8]), edited by the Marxist critic Alexander Voronsky (1884–1937). In the early

1920s, Voronsky enjoyed the support of Trotsky, who theorized that professional fellow traveler writers were better able to cope with the task of creating the new Soviet literature than the as-yet-uneducated proletariat.

The Left Front artists saw themselves, rather than RAPP, as the true literary avant-garde. They aimed to create a new art that would serve the interests of the revolution and which was founded on the effective technology of persuasion. "Old art"- by which they meant psychological and humanistic writing and *belles-lettres,* advocated by Voronsky and his group – was rejected in favor of "the art of bare facts," which they understood as art that depicted the rapidly changing momentous events of modernity. The Left Critics – and their ideological allies, the philologists who have come be be called the Formalists [see chapter 7] – saw art as a device and deformation of material, and the artist as a master or constructor, who possessed a particular set of necessary skills. The theory of social command, which the writers had inherited from the party, was crucial to the project of LEF. This is how Mayakovsky – the group's leader – controversially described the group's conception of the perfect poetic work:

> The best poetic work would be one written according to the principles of the social command of the Comintern [The Communist International, an organization founded in 1919] with the specific purpose of supporting the victory of the proletariat. It would use new, expressive language that would be intelligible to everyone. It would be assembled on a table and built according to Taylor's principles of scientific management; it would then be delivered by airplane to the editor.[3]

LEF's functionalist aesthetic theory exerted a powerful influence on the development of Soviet cinema (Dziga Vertov [1896–1954], Lev Kuleshov [1899–1970], Sergei Eisenstein), theatre (Vsevolod Meyerhold, members of FEKS [The Factory of the Eccentric Actor] such as Grigory Kozintsev [1905–73] and Leonid Trauberg [1902–90]), experimental art (Vladimir Tatlin and the Vesnin Brothers) and photography and design (Alexander Rodchenko [1891–1956], El Lissitzky [1890–1941]).

Voronsky's journal *Red Virgin Soil* took a stand against both the class fanaticism of RAPP and the aesthetic nihilism of the Left Front. The members of "Pereval" [The Pass], a group founded by Voronsky in 1922, emphasized the continuity between contemporary literature and the nineteenth-century Russian classics. They also declared the beginning of a new (socialist) humanism and insisted on the right of the writer to find "truth" and express his own individuality, as long as he broadly supported the Party's mission of socialist construction. The work of the greatest writers of this period – Isaac Babel, Sergei Esenin, Vsevolod Ivanov (1895–1963), Boris Pasternak, Boris Pil'niak, and Alexei N. Tolstoy (1883–1945) – appeared in *Red Virgin Soil*.

Other groups and circles existed in the 1920s too, but these were normally sub-divisions or allies of the major movements. For example, constructivists and "transrationalists" associated themselves with LEF. RAPP nurtured several groups of peasant writers, while Voronsky supported a curious group named "The Serapion Brothers," who were somewhat anomalous amid the politicized atmosphere of the 1920s. The members of this group – Lev Lunts (1901–24), Mikhail Zoshchenko, Veniamin Kaverin (1902–89), Vsevolod Ivanov, and others – tried to realize the Romantic ideal of a brotherhood of creative individuals who had divergent interests and opinions.

Finally, there were a few authors actively writing in the 1920s who attempted to position themselves *above* the literature wars (Boris Pasternak) or *outside* group battles (the poets Anna Akhmatova and Osip Mandelstam and the novelist and dramatist Mikhail Bulgakov. This type of writer received the harshest criticism from vigilant proletarian "watchdogs." By the end of the twenties, most of them found themselves in a critical situation. Not only were they hounded by the proletarian press, but they also struggled to publish their work, making it difficult for them to earn a living. Ironically, however, most of these writers managed to avoid being killed during the great purges at the end of the 1930s, while many of their most outspoken critics perished.

VI

The literature wars of the 1920s took place under the watchful eye and episodically active intervention of the Party. In 1920 Lenin put an end to the hegemonic thrust of the Prolet'kult, criticizing the "lefty dreams of the Proletkul't ideologues" and refusing, in effect, to break definitively with the "bourgeois" art of the pre-revolutionary era. In 1923, Trotsky defended the fellow travelers, and in 1925 the Party adopted a resolution against those proletarian associations that were claiming to be the sole legitimate artistic voice of the Revolution. This was quite frustrating to many artists who considered themselves Communists. Finally, in 1932 the Party adopted a resolution to dissolve RAPP and create a single union of Soviet writers whose work would follow a specific program of socialist art as defined by the Party. Ironically, this resolution, welcomed by most non-proletarian writers as liberation from the tyranny of RAPP's watchdogs, put an end to the very idea of Soviet literature as pluralism within the borders of the acceptable. The Communist "non-Hegelian" dialectic, which Mayakovsky had praised shortly before his death, led to a systematic attempt to erase all contradictions. This resulted in the quasi-synthesis of Socialist Realism, which attempted to unite RAPP's demand for party loyalty, LEF's idea of social command, and the traditionalism of "The Pass."

By the mid-1930s Soviet art had been redefined as an integral (and extremely important) part of the state's central project: the construction of communism. The author was no longer an "independent contractor," but rather a state employee, "an engineer of human souls" as Stalin put it, who should follow norms formulated by the Party. The Soviet artist should reflect in his or her works the great achievements of socialist construction and educate Soviet readers in the spirit of party consciousness and socialist patriotism. Unlike "critical realism" of the second half of the nineteenth century, Socialist Realism was not supposed to focus on the drawbacks of contemporary society. Instead, using their knowledge of the inexorable march of Soviet society toward the perfect Communist future as revealed in the works of Marx, Engels, Lenin, and Stalin, authors were to discern the "true reality" that was often hidden behind a façade of imperfection. Paradoxically, insofar as it discovers the noumenal reality hiding behind phenomenal appearances, this ostensibly materialist theory of art appears profoundly idealistic, harking back to Plato and the Russian medieval tradition. As formulated by Lunacharsky, the Socialist Realist writer "not only understands the world, he tries to change it." He is "completely goal oriented, he knows what is good and what is evil, he can see those forces that hinder development and those that stimulate powerful forward motion toward the great goal [the creation of Communism, ABW, IV]."[4]

During the Cold War era, Socialist Realism was seen as a monolithic top-down approach to literary production imposed on Soviet writers by a totalitarian state. Recent research, however, has called into question the extent to which Socialist Realism can be seen as a top-down process and has indicated that a certain amount of plurality continued to exist beneath the apparently monolithic façade. To be sure, Party bureaucrats did play an enormous role in systematizing and synthesizing the overall direction of Soviet literature after 1934, but the central models on which they build their synthesis had all been produced in the period before the state asserted its right to control literary and artistic production.

Regardless of its origins, however, Socialist Realism played a crucial role in forming and nurturing the Soviet myth, or more accurately the Soviet religion focused on transforming the world.[5] At the center of this myth was Joseph Stalin, the heir to the work of Lenin, or, better, his reincarnation. Stalin knew everything and thought about everyone, he was the best friend of women and children, never slept, and could foretell the future. The Soviet people were his happy and grateful children – workers, peasants, Red Army soldiers, the Soviet intelligentsia. Their loving mother was the Socialist motherland herself. The office of "the father of the nation" in the Moscow Kremlin was the holy of holies in the USSR. The entire country, "rotating" around the Kremlin, was sacred space: from the sky, where Soviet pilots were conquering the heavens, to the earth, where builders were racing to erect new cities and factories, and even below the earth where miners were setting records digging coal. The Moscow metro played an important symbolic role in the Soviet picture of the world (beginning in 1934): its palace-like stations were adorned with allegorical sculptures of Soviet military personnel, workers and peasants, mosaics on the walls and arches depicted the great triumphs of socialism. All of this created the paradoxical image of an underground heaven. On the surface, the monumental architecture that came to be known as Stalin Gothic, expressed the greatness and power of the land of the Soviets.

Next to Stalin in the socialist pantheon were his co-workers, the political leadership of the country. They carried out his commands effectively, administered the grandiose construction projects of socialism, and executed Soviet policy at home and abroad. Among these co-workers a special role was played by the noble and grim defenders of the USSR – the military officers and the secret police (Chekists), whose exploits were constantly sung in verse, prose, and in the works of Soviet visual artists. The USSR itself was the bastion of the new world, surrounded by capitalist enemies. These enemies were constantly attempting to sneak into the Soviet world and to corrupt the weakest and most unreliable elements of Soviet society – particularly the "old" creative and technical intelligentsia (i.e. those who had had their world-view formulated before the Revolution) and the wealthy peasants. But the Enemy did not operate exclusively externally, but also within the soul of each individual who had not yet conquered his own internal bourgeois tendencies. The signs of this sort of spiritual corruption were manifold: doubts in the triumph of communism, dissatisfaction with the present state of affairs, depression, individualism. That is why the Soviet regime had to be alert at all times and each individual needed to watch for external enemies and be ready to engage in self-criticism to root out his internal demons. This mytho-poetic war for the happy future served as a kind of camouflage for the cruel political repressions of the 1930s that eventually caught up citizens from all walks of Soviet life.

The normative art of Socialist Realism, served as a kind of catechism for the social and moral development of the Soviet citizen. The most illustrative example is the Socialist Realist novel of re-education in which the protagonist, who had been brought up in the conditions of the old (pre-revolutionary) world, undergoes a ritual series of trials and, despite the cunning attempts of the enemies of socialism, and with the help of a wise Communist (a stand-in for Stalin), comes to understand the historical inevitability of the Communist Party and his own place in the ranks of those constructing Communism.[6] Some famous examples of this type of novel are *How the Steel was Tempered* (Kak zakalialas' stal', 1932) by Nikolai Ostrovsky (1904–36), *The Pedagogical Epic* (Pedagogicheskaia poema, 1935) by Anton Makarenko (1888–1939), and *Quite Flows the Don* (Tikhii Don, 1927–40) by Mikhail Sholokhov (1905–84). Another popular Socialist Realist novel type was the so-called construction novel, which featured heroes of socialist construction successfully completing their assigned tasks, again despite various efforts by "wreckers" to sabotage these efforts (*The Hydroelectric Plant* [Gidrotsentral, 1932] by Marietta Shaginian (1888–1982), and *Time Forward!* [Vremia vpered!, 1932] by Valentin Kataev. Simultaneously, the ideal Soviet peasant was "grown" in works devoted to the collectivization of agriculture between 1929 and 1932 (Sholokhov's novel *Virgin Soil Upturned* [Podniataya tselina, vol. 1, 1932] and Kirshon's 1931 play *Grain*. The Soviet historical novel (as well as the historical film) portrayed the entire history of Russia as a progressive way from the dark past (briefly illumined, however, by historical prototypes of Stalin: Alexander Nevsky, Ivan the Terrible, and Peter the Great) toward the glorious present and even more gorgeous future. The Soviet historical theodicy was formulated in Stalin's *Concise History of The Communist Party of the Soviet Union* (1938).

Film played a particularly important role in the Soviet religion, especially musical comedy which served as an illustration of Stalin's famous claim that life in the land of the Soviets had become "better and more joyful." The world of the Soviet musical film (Grigory Alexandrov's *Happy Guys* (Veselye rebiata, 1934), *The Circus* (Tsirk, 1936), *Volga-Volga* (1938), *The Bright Path* (Svetlyi put', 1940), *Spring* (Vesna, 1947) as well as Ivan Pyrev's *The Kuban Cossacks* (Kubanskie kazaki, 1949)) is festive and collective: we see sunny Moscow streets, parades of athletes, circus tricks, collective farm feasts. The heroes are young enthusiasts who find personal happiness in serving their country. Their main enemies are hypocritical Soviet bureaucrats who turn out to have a secret animus against the state. Victory over these comically inept enemies is achieved easily and it all ends with the ritual performance of a triumphal song glorifying the present-day Soviet citizen, his beautiful motherland and the incredible future toward which the entire country is marching under the tutelage of its Wise Leader. The most representative of these is "Song of the Motherland" (music by Isaak Dunaevsky, words by Vasily Lebedev-Kumach) from the film *Circus* – it is an enthusiastic summa summarum of the ideology that permeated Socialist Realism as the myth of glorious, heroic, and eternal Soviet Present (to achieve the ideological purity and artistic effectiveness, the authors created thirty-five drafts of the song):

> *My fatherland is broad and wide*
> *It's filled with rivers, woods and fields*
> *I know of no such other land*
> *Where people breathe so freely.*
>
> From Moscow to the far frontiers
> From southern mounts to northern seas
> A man can travel like the ruler
> of unencompassable Rus'.
>
> Life everywhere is free and clear
> It's flowing like the Volga.
> There's room to spare for all the young
> The old respected everywhere.
>
> *Refrain*
>
> A spring breeze wafts across the land
> Each day is better than the last
> And no one else throughout the world
> Can laugh or love as we.
>
> But we will knit our brows in care
> Should any enemy contest us.
> We love our Russia like a bride
> Protect her like a mother.
>
> *Refrain*

Biography – Alexei Nikolaevich Tolstoy (1882–1945)

The life of Count A. N. Tolstoy is reminiscent of an adventure story, replete with scandals, mysteries and unpredictable twists. As a general rule, the protagonist of the adventure story comes to a bad end, and Tolstoy's own work includes several examples of failed adventurers. However, in spite of this tradition, and in defiance of the strict historical determinism that characterized the era, the Count managed to live his life as a rich, successful man in the country of the victorious proletariat.

The illicit encounters that led to Alexei Tolstoy's birth on December 29, 1882 recall the kind of affairs depicted in *Anna Karenina*, the high-society adultery novel written by Tolstoy's namesake. Alexei Tolstoy's mother, a writer and prominent society figure, left her tyrannical husband, Count Nikolai Tolstoy for her lover Alexei Bostrom, a petty landowner and member of the *intelligentsia*. In a fit of jealous rage, the spurned Count shot the lover, but was acquitted in court less than a month before the birth of Alexei Junior. The marriage between the Count and his wife was annulled, but she was forbidden to marry again for having committed "adulterous acts which breached the sanctity of matrimony."

Alexei Tolstoy's mother fought an eighteen-year battle to gain the right for her son to take the Count's hereditary title. While she was eventually successful, the authenticity of Alexei Tolstoy's lineage always remained in doubt among his contemporaries, as he was presumed to be the son of Bostrom. Tolstoy spent his childhood and adolescence on Bostrom's small estate in the Samara region. His recollections of this period were later recorded in the novel *Nikita's Childhood* [Detstvo Nikity] (1923). This is perhaps his best work and it should be seen as part of the important tradition of the happy childhood in Russian literature (see chapter 5).

In 1901 Tolstoy commenced studies at St. Petersburg Technological Institute. In 1902, he married a woman from Samara, whom he left in 1907 for the young Jewish artist Sofia Dymshits. Sofia was already married, but by that time she was separated from her husband. Tolstoy married for the third time in 1917 to the writer Natalia Krandievskaia, but this was not to be his final marriage.

Tolstoy began his literary career with decadent poetry, publishing *Lyrics* in 1907. However, by 1910 he had moved to prose and published a collection of short stories in 1911. In 1908, Tolstoy visited Paris, the cultural capital of Europe and became acquainted with the leading figures of Russian modernism: Valery Briusov (1873–1924), Andrei Bely, Maximilian Voloshin (1877–1932) and Nikolai Gumilev. On returning to St. Petersburg, he began to spend time at Viacheslav Ivanov's apartment, then the most influential literary salon in the capital, known by its habitués as "The Tower." Tolstoy was involved in one of the most famous scandals of the Bohemian literary world: he acted as a Voloshin's second in his duel with Gumilev (the duel was caused by a literary hoax in which Voloshin deceived Gumilev).

Tolstoy's role in the artistic world of the 1910s was that of a pagan savage filled with *joie de vivre*. In the early stages of his literary career, his jovial vitality was interpreted as a challenge to the melancholy spiritualism of the symbolists. The young poet's role was related to the 'paganism' of the Acmeist poet Sergei Gorodetsky (1884–1967), the celebratory bodily aesthetic of the avant-garde group "Jack of Diamonds" and, to a certain extent, the mythologizing of Stravinsky. Tolstoy invested much energy in building up his personal image: from the rosy-cheeked *enfant terrible* in the artistic club *Stray Dog*, he grew into a Russian Gargantua, such a "pale-pink, fresh, indestructibly healthy body that it seemed as if nature had spent a thousand years thinking him up" (Chukovsky).

The young Tolstoy experimented with several different genres. However, all of his early work is characterized by a peculiar sense of vitality and a hint of the occult, in which he had an active interest. "Art," he opined, "should smell of flesh and be more material than everyday life." His passion for the historical genre can be linked to this idea: he strove to create the illusion of resurrecting the past. Tolstoy identified both the First World War and his marriage to Krandievskaia, a "real Russian woman," as key turning points in his life. He now adopted the role of a Russian patriot, becoming a correspondent for one of the major Petersburg newspapers and writing both articles on the war and short stories.

Tolstoy welcomed the liberal February revolution, but fled from the Bolshevik October revolution. He first went to Ukraine, and from there took the well-trodden émigré path to Constantinople and Paris. In Paris, he began working on *The Road to Calvary* [Khozhdenie po mukam, 1922–42], a sprawling trilogy chronicling the fate of the Russian intelligentsia amid the maelstrom of events in early twentieth-century Russia: The First World War, the Revolution and the Civil War. The Russian title of the novel – which translates literally as "walking through torments" – is taken from a medieval Russian apocryphal tale in which the Virgin Mary visits hell and prays to God on behalf of sinners. Tolstoy was one of many writers of the twenties who represented the contemporary chaos in Russia as an eschatological drama (from Blok's *The Twelve* to Mikhail Bulgakov's *The White Guard*, 1925–7 (Belaia gvardiia)).

The originality of Tolstoy's approach comes from the strict historical determinism evident in his novel's plot: at the cost of enormous privation and suffering, the honorable nobles of the intelligentsia gradually come to realize that the old Russia is doomed and the new Russia must be welcomed. Tolstoy essentially created a new type of historical novel in which the characters had to undergo certain trials, a formula that was to become popular in the Soviet era. Tolstoy's odyssey of the Russian intelligentsia would later be closely mirrored by Mikhail Sholokhov's epic of peasants and Cossacks *Quiet Flows the Don*.

In 1921 Tolstoy moved to Berlin, another important European centre for Russian émigrés (there were some 100,000 Russians then living in the city): the writers Maxim Gorky, Alexei Remizov (1877–1957) and Boris Zaitsev (1881–1972), the philosopher Lev Shestov, the poets Andrei Bely, Igor Severianin, and Vladislav Khodasevich were all living in Berlin at this time. After April 1922, when Weimar Germany formally recognized Soviet Russia, more famous writers began to arrive: Boris Pilniak, Konstantin Fedin (1892–1977), Iury Tynianov, Viktor Shklovsky, and Sergei Esenin.

In Berlin, Tolstoy grew close to the supporters of the ideology of "National Bolshevism," who published the journal *Change of Signposts* [Smena vekh] and the daily newspaper *On the Eve* [Nakanune]. The *Smenovekhovtsy*, as this group became known, called on the intelligentsia to end their hopeless war against the Bolsheviks, as they were the only ones who could save Russia and guarantee her future stability and power. The title of their newspaper *On the Eve* was not merely a reference to the famous political novel by Turgenev, but it also hinted at the possible reunification of the two Russias that had separated during the Civil War. A symbolic pro-Soviet move on the part of the newspaper was its adoption of the simplified Russian orthographic system which had been introduced by the Bolsheviks in 1918. Tolstoy accepted a position as editor of this newspaper's literary supplement.

Tolstoy's decision to work for a pro-Soviet newspaper made him appear a turncoat to the émigré intelligentsia community. They demanded he state decisively which side he was on. He answered in an open letter where he laid out his new political beliefs. He argued that the intelligentsia would have to accept the reality of the Bolshevik government in Russia, help them foster all that was good and just in the revolution and likewise oppose all that was unjust. It was true, he said, that their seizure of power had been followed by terror. However, that was now in the past. Furthermore, everyone in Russia – including the intelligentsia – had to accept some of the blame for the tragedy that had swept the country. "I see myself as a real Russian émigré, by which I mean a person who has walked along the sorrowful road to Calvary . . . But my conscience tells me that I must not spend my life in some cellar, but travel back to Russia and help to mend the sails of the ship that has been tossed and damaged by storms. In so doing, I follow the example of Peter [the Great]."[7]

Tolstoy returned to Russia in 1923. The Soviet propaganda system publicized his return as evidence that the very best of the *intelligentsia* were coming to accept that the Bolsheviks had been right. (If official Soviet statistics are to be believed, more than 180,000 émigrés returned to Soviet Russia in the period between 1921 and 1931.) Tolstoy now adopted the new role of Soviet writer. Even before his departure from Germany, he had written a fantastic "Martian" novel with the beautiful and mysterious title *Aelita* designed to appeal to the Soviet reader. The "Red Planet" is a recurring motif in much esoteric and futuristic literature of the late nineteenth and early twentieth century, from the work of Camille Flammarion to H. G. Wells and the Russian Utopian writer Alexander Bodganov. In Tolstoy's novel, Mars is visited by Los, an engineer from the intelligentsia (upset by the recent death of his wife), who has managed to build a spaceship, and Gusev, a former Red Army soldier. Los falls in love with Aelita, the daughter of the ruler of Mars. Gusev attempts to start a revolution, but it fails. The story can be read simply as a science-fiction adventure novel, a popular genre which sold well in the 1920s. However, it can also be considered a political allegory. Tolstoy's despairing Mars is the rotting Western world, while the Earth is Soviet Russia. Los running away from Earth is the Russian émigré. Gusev is the spontaneous revolutionary attempting to incite world revolution. Gor, a character in the story who opposes the Martian government, is the Western Communist celebrated by the Earthlings (i.e. the Russians). The novel was published in installments in 1922–3 in *Red Virgin Soil*.

In 1924, the prominent Russian film director Iakov Protazanov (who, like Tolstoy, had just returned from emigration) adapted the novel into a silent film that was destined to become a classic. The film used elements of both the psychological – if not psychoanalytical – melodrama and the detective story: a dream sequence is used to explore Los's jealousy and a detective suspects that Los has murdered his wife. In the film, the Martian Revolution is successful, but Princess Aelita betrays the Earthlings and gives orders to open fire on the workers. The film concludes with Los waking up and discovering that his adventures on Mars were all a dream and his wife is still alive. He burns his plans to build a spaceship: there is little point in dreaming of space when there is so much to be done on Earth. Both the set design for Mars and the Martian costumes are in the constructivist style.

In Russia, Tolstoy wrote a second science-fiction novel, *The Hyperboloid of Engineer Garin* (Giperboloid inzhenera Garina, 1925). The protagonist of this work is again an inventor from the intelligentsia, a great scientist and individualist named Garin. Garin invents an amazing weapon which he intends to use to get rich quick. However, Tolstoy's novel is most remarkable for its depiction of the Soviet detective. The brave, honorable, strong and honest Shel'ga from the Cheka, who travels across world in search of Garin, became a literary model for secret agents in Soviet detective stories and films.

Tolstoy arrived in Russia at the very height of the Literature Wars. The proletarian journal *On Guard* [Na postu] immediately attacked him as a class enemy. "He is an artistic stylist of the old days, whose title 'Count' remains not only in his passport, but also in his inkwell."[8] The Left Front critics also attacked Tolstoy as a traditionalist. However, Tolstoy quickly shed his conservative skin and outwitted his opponents. By the 1930s, he had accepted the mantle of socialist realism. In the late 1920s and early 1930s, Tolstoy's work extolled the virtues of socialist construction, including the digging of the White Sea Canal, built almost exclusively by convict labor. He wrote the script for the play *The Revolt of the Cars* [Bunt mashin], the satirical adventure stories *Ibicus, or Nevzorov's Adventures* [Pokhozhdeniia Nevzorova, ili Ibikus] and *Black Friday* [Chernaia piatnitsa] and continued to work on *The Road to Calvary*, which transformed into a politically informed work on how honest Russian émigrés had come to accept the Russian Revolution and its leaders. In 1928–30, a fifteen-volume set of Tolstoy's collected works was published, ensuring his status as a classic Soviet writer.

Tolstoy continued to joust for position in the literary hall of fame with his namesake Lev Tolstoy. The latter had planned to write a historical novel set in the era of Peter the Great. Alexei Tolstoy had also long been interested in Peter: he had published a story "Peter's Day" [Den' Petra] in 1919 and adapted it as a play in 1929. Now he began working on a monumental historical novel about the Tsar's life and his great reforms. The novel was an attempt to re-kindle the spirit of the Age of Peter and it aimed to extol the reforming Tsar as a prototype for Russia's new leader, Joseph Stalin.[9] In 1944, the orthodox literary critic Kornely Zelinisky described the political conception of the novel in tune with the contemporary campaigns against real and imaginary opposition to Stalin's regime: "Peter is portrayed as the builder of a new progressive statehood which established itself in the struggle with the aristocrats' sectionalism."[10] Tolstoy later turned his attentions to another of Stalin's forebears, Ivan the Terrible, whom he depicted in a play. Stalin was also the hero of Tolstoy's novel *Bread* (1938), which explored the history of the Civil War. Here Stalin, the "voice of the will and reason of the people" is directly juxtaposed with the villainous and treacherous Trotsky.

Count Tolstoy had managed to become part of the Soviet literary establishment. In 1932, he joined the Organizational Committee for the First Congress of Soviet Writers, and in 1934 made a speech at the Congress and became one of the leaders of the Writers' Union. Before long, the "Red

Count" gained the status of the foremost voice of socialist realism, a position that had been left vacant by Gorky's death in 1936. In the late 1930s, he represented the USSR at international congresses and writers' conferences. In 1941, he received his first Stalin Prize, and a second followed in 1943 for *The Road to Calvary*.

During the Second World War, Tolstoy wrote several short stories, the most interesting of which is probably "The Russian Character" [Russkii kharakter], which manifested the shift in Soviet ideology towards Russian nationalism. In 1944 he became ill with lung cancer and died on February 23, 1945.

Throughout his life, Tolstoy freely changed his ideological convictions and political affiliations, apparently without experiencing any pangs of conscience. He constantly re-invented himself in ways that would allow him the opportunity to write and increase his material well being. In 1941, the artist Petr Konchalovsky (1876–1956), one of the founders of the avant-garde "Jack of Diamonds" group painted him not as an all-powerful Soviet dignitary or poet laureate, but as a welcoming host and gourmand, sitting at a well-stocked table. In this painting, Tolstoy almost appears a part of the still life: he and the food seem to form a single brilliant whole. "We eat well," Tolstoy wrote to his wife in 1930, "Sturgeon, pike-perch, sometimes sterlet, caviar, and *balyk*. Yesterday I got through a whole kilogram of raspberries served with baked milk."[11] Indeed, it is possible that a belief in the "appreciation of the corporal pleasures in life" (K. Fedin), that Tolstoy associated with the Russian soul and with which he endowed many of his protagonists, was his only constant conviction.

Event – The First Congress of Soviet Writers

The First Congress of Soviet Writers opened on August 17, 1934 in Moscow. It was a showy event convened to illustrate the unity of the country's writers – and their adherence to the objectives of the Party – to the country and the world at large. As early as April 1932, the Party had issued a resolution entitled "On the Restructuring of Literary and Artistic Organizations." This decree ended the proletarian literary associations' attempts to establish a monopoly in the literary arena and set a new direction toward uniting all the writers who had pledged support to the Soviet state into a single union of Soviet writers. As a parallel measure, the "Ministry of censorship," Glavlit, had received new administrative functions. The chief of the agency put it bluntly: "Until the present time we have been a repressive agency par excellence, a kind of GPU [i.e. the Soviet security service] in literature. Now we are turning in a new direction. Without diminishing our previous functions, we must also pursue the management [rukovodstvo] of all literary activity. The Central Committee of the Party has authorized Glavlit not only to watch books in print but also to reveal all tendencies, which originate in various fields of literature, in order to learn in advance about upcoming danger."[12]

A simple and ruthless system was used by the party to establish ideological control over the new, indivisible union of writers. Any attempts at creating "bottom-up" ideology from the writers were crushed. Effectively, writers had become incorporated into the state sector. This reform can be seen as part of the broader drive towards totalitarianism that occurred under Stalin. The command to consolidate literature directly followed the state's violent consolidation of the economy through collectivization and the establishment of the foundations of socialism, which had been triumphantly declared at the Seventeenth Party Congress in 1934.

In typical Soviet style, the Congress of Soviet Writers was a magnificent and somewhat pompous affair, stretching over two weeks and including no less than twenty-six different sessions. The Congress included 377 full delegates, 220 consultative delegates and forty foreign visitors. More than fifty-two nationalities were represented. Sixty percent of the participants represented the "Communist Fraction" – i.e. they were members of the Communist Party, candidates for membership, or members of Communist Youth Movement. The average age of the writers was thirty-six, meaning that the majority of them had come of age after the Revolution. Keynote speeches were devoted to Soviet literature as a whole, children's literature, the literatures of the non-Russian peoples of the Soviet Union, contemporary world literature and the proper role of proletarian art, Soviet drama, poetry, and publishing. Like many other Soviet congresses, the delegates' speeches were interspersed with dramatic interludes when writers from diverse backgrounds – the Young Pioneers, the Red Army, the Navy, the collective farms, the workers – were brought on stage to address the audience. The minutes of the Congress run to over seven hundred pages.

As was the case with other political events of that time, from the Party Congresses to public trials of enemies of the people, the Writers' Congress was carefully choreographed by Stalin and his closest aides. It was a mythologized event, which would have its own over-arching plot and heroes. Publicized as an historic occasion of monumental importance, both for the country and for the progressive world at large, it was styled the "first ever Congress in the many centuries of the history of literature." The participants imagined that the world beyond the borders of the Soviet Union was still living in the Dark Ages, and that the bourgeois literature of the West had gone into terminal decline. In Germany, the Nazi government was attempting to create its own "New Art" which extolled race theory and called on the German people to wage a bloody war. Soviet writers perceived themselves as fair judges of the bourgeoisie – who were doomed to perish – and as true humanists who "professed the humanism of the revolutionary proletariat." The presence of foreign "progressive" writers at the Congress was of particular symbolic significance. According to Soviet mythology, they had come to Moscow to see for themselves the center of the new, happy world.

Although he remained invisible, the central protagonist of the Congress was the great leader and father of the Soviet people, Joseph Stalin. The speakers at the Congress constantly referred to him as the embodiment of Party wisdom, and the rightful heir to Lenin. They made references not only to Stalin himself, but also frequently alluded to his recent statement that Soviet writers should be "engineers of human souls." Andrei Zhdanov, a leading communist ideologue, took on the role of officially interpreting the leader's words. To be an "engineer of human souls" meant to "express reality in its revolutionary development," in accordance with the tasks of "bringing radical ideological change and educating the working people in the spirit of socialism."[13] Comrade Zhdanov called this approach to literature "Socialist Realism," which should be the fundamental (read "only acceptable") method of Soviet art. The only permissible differences of opinion would involve technical questions as to how this method would best be realized.

According to Zhdanov, the writer needed to stand on the soil of real life, possess professional knowledge of language (technical ability), struggle to produce good-quality literary writing, and work on his personal development, constantly striving to perfect his socialist Party consciousness. The Party had created all the right conditions in order to help writers achieve that goal, just as they helped all responsible workers. Moreover, he stressed that "only in our country do literature and the writer play such a crucial role." To put it more simply, the Party was allowing writers to take charge of the mission of ideologically developing Soviet citizens. In exchange, the Party was willing to promise cooperative writers material support and high social status.

After completing his brief but portentous speech, the Party emissary Zhdanov handed the floor to Maxim Gorky, chairman of the organizing committee of the Congress. Gorky was the foremost writer in the Soviet literary world at this time, having written the proto-socialist novel *Mother* (Mat', 1907) and the Romantic revolutionary "Song of the Stormy Petrel"

(Pesnia o burevestnike, 1901). In emigration for most of the 1920s, Gorky had returned to the Soviet Union in 1931, having been asked by Stalin to "lead" Soviet literature. Gorky's works were published in millions of copies (according to official statistics, some 8 percent of the books printed in the Soviet Union between 1929–34 were by him).[14] Speeches by Gorky opened and concluded the Congress, beginning with a heroic Prologue and ending with a majestic Epilogue.

As the Party had planned, all kinds of writers expressed their allegiance to the achievements of socialism and committed to working towards the specific goals of the Party. This included writers of different aesthetic convictions, Party members and non-Party members, writers of proletarian and non-proletarian backgrounds, and representatives from many different nationalities. In other words, the Congress was a mythologized initiation rite for writers and a staged reconciliation. It was understood that certain important writers would participate in certain debates, especially those who had been actively involved in the literature wars of the 1920s (a few were not invited to the Congress, such as Gorky's enemy, the incorrigible ideologue Averbakh of RAPP).

In this context, it is particularly revealing to examine Iury Olesha's speech. Olesha was an archetypical Fellow Traveler, clearly sympathetic to the overall goals of the Communist state but unwilling or unable to abandon his carnivalesque, satirical and morally ambiguous literary approach. Olesha recognized and struggled enormously with the "social command" to subordinate his individuality to the needs of the state. In his speech, Olesha compared himself to the dreamer-hero of his brilliant and famous novel *Envy* [*Zavist'* 1927)]. He explained how he gradually came to reject proud and resentful individualism, completely unnecessary in Soviet society, to recognize the need for spiritual unity with the people, and how this realization had brought back his lost youth and granted him long-sought happiness. For all that, Olesha ultimately found it impossible to work publicly within the context of Socialist Realism, and published almost nothing between the Congress and his death in 1960. He did, however, produce "for the desk drawer" a unique autobiography entitled *No Day without a Line* (Ne dnia bez strochki), which was published posthumously in 1965.

The appearances of the delegates were carefully choreographed by the Party, which wished to create an impression of happy reconciliation among Soviet writers, as well as the sense that they were engaged in brotherly collective work. Nevertheless, a few controversial areas remained. Nikolai Bukharin's paper on contemporary Soviet poetry dealt with particularly thorny issues. Bukharin was then a member of the Central Committee and Editor-in-Chief of the newspaper *Izvestiia*. In 1934, the position of this long-time "Party favorite" (in Lenin's words) was called into question (four years later he would be fired from his positions and tried and executed as an "enemy of the people"). Bukharin's central thesis was that further development of Soviet poetry demanded "a great improvement in our poetic culture generally." This would require more erudition, an acquaintance with the best works of Western literature, and a rejection of the parochial and primitive nature of agitational poetry, which had long since outlived its purpose.

Socialist Realism, Bukharin argued, should not demand fanatical asceticism from the writer, but should rather unveil the endless diversity of human development: "There is a richness in everything in life: all tragedies and conflicts, all twists and turns, all battles . . . All of these things can serve as material for creative poetic work." Bukharin extrapolated from this the necessity to develop a wide variety of poetic forms, which would dialectically unite "great style" with the method of Socialist Realism. Soviet poetry would therefore be "multi-layered."

Unlike Zhdanov, who did not mention individual names, Bukharin gave specific examples of writers in his speech: he favored Boris Pasternak and Ilya Selvinsky, and disdained the agitational poet Demian Bedny (pseudonym for Efim Pridvorov, 1883–1945). The writers whom Bukharin attacked gave fierce rebuttals to his speech, knowing that he did not have the same level of power as Stalin in the Party. One of his opponents attacked Bukharin's naive view of literary pluralism, arguing that literature should not be concerned with cultivating emotions, but should rather be the means of mobilizing the nation for war, clearly defining friend from foe. Bukharin ridiculed his opponents when he next rose to the podium, but at the end of the Congress he was made to write a conciliatory speech which apologized for his fierce criticism of certain writers and emphasized that his opinions were not representative of the Party at large. The hopes some writers had entertained for a relatively liberal attitude towards literature following the liquidation of the Leftist association of Proletarian writers went unfulfilled. Subsequent events demonstrated that the idea of Soviet literature as a military and bureaucratic instrument had been victorious.

The Congress closed with the unanimous acceptance of the Statutes of the Union of Soviet Writers, which declared Socialist Realism to be the fundamental method of Soviet literature. Soon, this universal method would also be applied to art, music, theatre, cinema and architecture. The general aim of the Union was declared to be the creation of works of great artistic significance, worthy of the great era of socialism. A board of directors was constituted to lead the Union, and writers began to be defined by their position in the bureaucratic hierarchy. This meant a new era in the history of Russian literature, an era of "state literature" which ritualistically repeated the same myth of the happy Soviet reality. According to Soviet mythology, this literature was written by self-sacrificing conscious writers who worked under the wise guardianship of the Party, and it existed in spite constant threats to its very existence from cunning and malicious enemies who operated both inside and outside the Soviet Union.

Literary Work – Andrei Platonov, *The Foundation Pit* (Kotlovan)

Andrei Platonov (1899–1951) should have been the ideal Soviet writer. He was born in a working-class family in the provincial town of Voronezh. By his early teens he had joined the industrial proletariat, working in a locomotive building factory where his father was also employed. He joined the Red Army in 1919 and saw action in the Civil War. After the war was over he studied for an engineering degree and in the 1920s worked actively on a number of agricultural and hydrological projects. Simultaneously, he published actively, beginning in the late 1910s. He was, therefore, of unimpeachable background and he clearly wished to serve the Soviet state. As it happened, however, his greatest works (the novels *The Foundation Pit* and *Chevengur*), written in the mid to late 1920s, could not be published in the USSR until the late 1980s. This failure helps to illustrate the great tragedy of those writers and artists sympathetic to the revolution and the professed goals of the Soviet state who attempted to find an authentic mode of artistic expression to depict the reality of the Soviet experience.

In the aftermath of the Revolution, there was a fairly broadly held belief that the task of art was to be the depiction (or even the creation) of the new Soviet person. This "new man" would differ from those who had come before in a variety of ways but perhaps most important was his relationship with the collective. Osip Mandelstam, another great artist who proved unable to answer the "social command" of the Soviet state despite a sincere desire to do so, set the parameters of the literary discussion of this problem in an essay called "The End of the Novel" (published in 1928 in *On Poetry*, but most likely written starting in 1923):

> this suggests a connection between the fate of the novel and the status at a given time of the problem of the individual's fate in history ... It is clear that when we entered the epoch of powerful social movements and organized mass actions, both the stock value of the individual in history and the power and influence of the novel declined, for the generally accepted role of the

> individual in history serves as a kind of monometer indicating the pressure of the social atmosphere. The measure of the novel is human biography or a system of biographies . . . Thus the novel always suggests to us a system of phenomena controlled by a biographical connection and measured by a biographical measure . . . The future development of the novel will be no less than the history of the atomization of biography as a form of personal existence; what is more, we shall witness the catastrophic collapse of biography . . . A human life is not in itself a biography, nor does it provide a backbone for the novel. A man functioning in the time system of the old European novel serves as a pivot for the entire system of phenomena that cluster around him. Today, Europeans are plucked out of their own biographies, like balls out of the pockets of billiard tables, and the same principle that governs the collision of billiard balls governs the laws of their actions: the angle of incidence is equal to the angle of reflection. A man devoid of biography cannot be the thematic pivot of the novel, while the novel is meaningless if it lacks interest in an individual, human fate, in a plot and all its auxiliary motifs. What is more, the interest in psychological motivation (by which the declining novel so skillfully sought to escape, already sensing its impending doom) is being radically undermined and discredited by the growing impotence of psychological motives in the confrontation with the forces of reality, forces whose reprisals against psychological motivation become more cruel by the hour. The modern novel was thus simultaneously deprived of both plot, that is, of the individual acting in accord with his sense of time, and psychology, since it could no longer support action of any sort.[15]

In his essay Mandelstam was talking about the reality of the revolutionary period, but his words apply even more aptly to the Stalinist Soviet Union which, with its increasingly faceless and terrifying bureaucracy, its mass actions, five-year plans and collectivization efforts, was certainly a place in which the individual was being "radically undermined and discredited by the growing impotence of psychological motives in the confrontation with the forces of reality." The task of prose writers, in this view, was to find a way to construct fictional texts without psychology, or, at the very least, to produce successful works of fiction that would undermine the central position of individual psychology in the world of the novel. And this is precisely what Platonov does in his major novels. In *The Foundation Pit* we find two important elements: (1) a consistent linkage of future socialist happiness with psychological emptiness and (2) an avoidance of the devices of traditional psychological prose.

The result, in Platonov's novel, is not merely a formal break with the expected narrative conventions of the chosen genre, but an even more vertiginous refusal to allow the reader to identify with the characters, and, thereby, to discover his or her own self. The contrast between how Platonov's characters act and what readers do has also been noted: "The Platonov gaze externalizes any event, even those that by their nature must belong only to inner measurements of the world and of human beings. Even the most thoughtful of Platonov's characters are more akin to sage-automatons than to living, sensible people who are responsible for their actions – like us, the 'normal' readers."[16]

The main character in *The Foundation Pit* is Voshchev, a man whose central trouble is thinking too much. When we first meet Voshchev, he has just been fired from his job for "the growth of weakliness in him and for thoughtfulness amidst the general tempo of labor."[17] He wanders off to discover the meaning of life, and his travels bring him first to a group of workers who are digging a gigantic foundation pit for the future house of the proletariat, and then to a farm in the process of collectivization. Ultimately, he returns to the pit and, apparently, becomes a kind of leader of the working masses in their increasingly futile effort at "socialist construction." What is significant for us is the extent to which happiness in the novel is identified with psychological emptiness. In the passage that follows, Voshchev observes a group of workers eating. The men are seen as a generalized mass, distinguished by no particular features, as opposed to the observing Voshchev: "Although they knew the meaning of life, which is equivalent to eternal happiness, their faces were nevertheless gloomy and thin, and instead of the peace of life, they possessed exhaustion." (13) Of cardinal importance is the oxymoronic character of the description; instead of the joy or at least the tranquillity we might expect to see on the faces of these men, there is a chillingly empty blankness. And the narrator simply refuses to enter into their minds, to show us what they are thinking, as a way to resolve this contradiction. It should be noted that, in contradistinction to the practice of nineteenth-century novels, this refusal cannot be chalked up to the status of the men as secondary characters. Rather, it appears that they simply do not have any psychology to treat.

The correlation between happiness and emptiness is repeated in a passage that appears somewhat later in the novel. Here, Chiklin (one of the workers from the construction brigade) and Voshchev have gone to the countryside to help collectivize a village.

- Is everything good now, comrades? – Chiklin asked.
- It is, replied the entire Org-courtyard. – We don't feel anything now. Only dust remains in us.

> Voshchev was lying to one side and he just could not go to sleep lacking the tranquillity of truth within his own life, and then he stood up from the snow and went amidst the people.
> – Hello! – he said joyfully to the kolkhoz. – You have now become like me. I am also nothing.
>
> (83)

The Soviet men of the future, it appears, reach happiness by draining themselves of all desire, leaving nothing but matter – "only dust remains in us." Again, the collective is identified with happiness and blankness simultaneously.

The position of Voshchev is curious. He has been searching for the meaning of life not by emptying his mind, but by intense thought. At this point, it appears that he has reached the same level of happiness as the collective, but by a diametrically opposite path; he has literally thought his way through to emptiness. *The Foundation Pit* can thus be seen as a novella in which a psychologized individual is brought into contact with a world lacking psychology. Voshchev's paradoxical quest, therefore, has been to achieve the level of happiness, equivalent to psychological emptiness, that the masses appear to possess naturally. At the end of the novel, however, Voshchev's route to happiness is called into question. Nastya, the child who has symbolized that ideal future world for which the foundations are being dug, dies, and the building task of the collective becomes transformed from construction to burial. As Voshchev parts with the child, the narrator tells us: "Voshchev would have agreed to know nothing again and to live without hope and in the nebulous desires of a vain mind, if only the girl were to be whole again, ready for life, even if she did need to suffer in the course of time. Voshchev lifted Nastya into his arms, kissed her swollen lips and hugged her with the greediness of happiness, finding more than he had searched for" (113). This passage again indicates that Voshchev has indeed found what he had taken to be happiness – before, he had known nothing but now, presumably, he knows something of importance. The death of the child calls the value of this knowledge into question. The opaque final gestures – the hug of happiness and the final kiss – along with the cryptic hint of the attainment of a new level of knowledge, beyond what Voshchev had ever consciously sought, hint that he has perhaps achieved a final stage of unconscious happiness. He has merged with the collective of diggers, no longer alienated from them because of his psychological fullness. But if he has finally drained his mind completely and found happiness, he has found it in death, a state that is not (cannot be?) expressed.

From the description we provided earlier of the central thrust of the Socialist Realist novel, it is fairly easy to see why on a thematic and narrative level *The Foundation Pit* could not possibly be seen as an appropriate work of Soviet fiction (not even to mention the problem of Platonov's extremely complex style, which stands in opposition to the felt need of the Soviet novel to be accessible to the mass reader). Although it does deal directly with the process of Socialist Construction (indeed it has sometimes been read as a grotesque parody of a construction novel) its intensely philosophical tone and its ambiguous rather than up-lifting conclusion rendered it completely unacceptable. From a position of hindsight, however, it seems clear that *The Foundation Pit*, as well as analogous works by artists similarly sympathetic to the Soviet project but unable to create work in the acceptable Socialist Realist mode (most notably Kazimir Malevich's famous series of faceless portraits from the late 1920s and early 1930s) successfully rises to the challenge Mandelstam had set in his essay. Platonov's non-psychological human portraits are a devastatingly accurate portrayal of a populace that had, after years of war and ideological struggle, been deprived of individuality. They are, in the deepest sense, realist works, insofar as they reflect a world in which individual psychology had lost its place. Because they depict a time in which many people were willing to abandon the individual as a step toward to the creation of a utopia, we now recognize these works as tragic, both in their subject matter and in their revelation of their creators' psychology. On the one hand we have to do with artists who supported and continued to support the revolution and its goals, who wished to be part of Soviet art, and who included echoes of its ideals in their work. But on the other, either consciously or unconsciously, they sensed that the void the revolution had created, its destruction of the possibility for individual action (and therefore the futility of psychology as an artistic device), was leading to misery rather than utopia. The depression and deep sadness produced in the viewer or reader by these faceless portraits is the result of their ability (most likely despite their authors' conscious desires) to capture what was perhaps the greatest tragedy of our century – the blindness of those who hoped for happiness built on the abnegation of their own individuality, of people who "stepped on the throat of their own song," and who in so doing helped to bring unheard of misery to themselves and to millions of others.

9

After the Future: Russian Thaw Culture

I

On June 22, 1941 Nazi troops poured across the Soviet border meeting little resistance from the Red Army. The inability of Soviet forces to repulse the invasion was not merely a matter of equipment and munitions, which had to some extent been modernized and upgraded in the course of the crash industrialization program of the late 1920s and 1930s. Much more serious were deficiencies in leadership, decimated during the great purges of the late 1930s, and Stalin's refusal to listen to those of his advisors brave enough to tell him that the Germans were preparing a surprise attack. But the military's lack of preparedness was nothing compared to that of the civilian population. After years of upbeat propaganda announcing that "life had gotten better, life had gotten happier" and insisting that the Soviet system was far stronger than anything the decadent West had to offer, it was difficult for many to fathom that practically the entire European portion of the USSR could be under Nazi occupation in a matter of months.

An effective military response to the invasion took time to organize, and signs of success were difficult to discern before 1942. On the civilian front, however, the government, realizing that the support of the entire society was going to be necessary if the USSR was to survive, a certain loosening in the tight controls that had been imposed during the 1930s was quickly apparent. Long-shuttered churches were opened and the state showed a glimmer of tolerance toward religious belief. Some writers who had disappeared from public view were allowed to publish and many more volunteered to go to the front as war correspondents. Stories about Soviet heroes and heroism by such writers as Vasily Grossman (1905–64), Konstantin Simonov (1915–79), and Alexander Tvardovsky (1910–71) played an important role in nurturing the belief that the heroic Red Army could and would eventually emerge victorious.

When the war ended, many believed that the worst of Stalin's excesses were over and that victorious Soviet society would be allowed to enjoy the fruits of its bitter triumphs. That this was not to be the case in the cultural sphere became chillingly apparent in 1946, when Leningrad party boss Andrei Zhdanov, employing the worst 1930s invective, led a campaign against a number of leading writers and journals. Most memorably, Zhdanov attacked Anna Akhmatova ("half nun and half harlot") and Mikhail Zoshchenko ("a vile hooligan"). In the wake of this speech, a number of leading Leningrad journals were closed, Zoshchenko was expelled from the Writers Union, and Akhmatova reduced to public silence. For the next seven years, published Soviet literature was at its most mind-numbingly conformist, as writers such as Alexander Chakovsky (1913–94), Semen Babaevsky (1909–2000) and Simonov vied to produce the most acceptable narratives lauding the state, its organs, and the Soviet collective, while vilifying enemies, real and mostly imagined.

II

In March 1953, Joseph Stalin died at his dacha outside Moscow. The secretive ruler had, at least to the public eye, been the absolute leader of the Soviet State since the late 1920s. Though it is conservatively estimated that his policies led directly and indirectly to the deaths of some thirty million Soviet citizens, his own death produced widespread confusion and emotional tension. Typical are the reminiscences of the Azeri Vagif Samadoghlu (1939–): "I remember I was at home and had been awakened by the neighbor's radio announcing that Stalin had died. I jumped up and ran to my father and told him that Stalin was dead. He shouted at me: 'Shut up. That's impossible.' Then he turned on the radio and heard it for himself. He looked at me with tears in his eyes. Almost everyone felt lost; nobody knew what would happen next. Everybody was in shock."[1]

In the ensuing power struggle Nikita Khrushchev managed to oust other Kremlin insiders, including the Minister of Internal Affairs Lavrenty Beria, and assume the title of First Secretary of the Communist Party. For reasons that still stir scholarly debate, Khrushchev decided quite quickly to ease the terror Stalin had imposed on the country and to demolish the "cult of personality" that had surrounded the dead leader. Most famously, in his "secret speech" (leaked almost immediately) to the 20th Communist Party Congress in 1956, Khrushchev castigated his predecessor, providing information about the terror of the 1930s, failures of military preparation on the eve of the Second World War, and tactical blunders during the war itself. Of the once all-powerful leader himself, Khrushchev said, "Stalin acted not through persuasion, explanation, and patient cooperation with people, but by imposing his concepts and demanding absolute submission to his opinion. Whoever opposed this concept or tried to prove his viewpoint, and the correctness of his position, was doomed to removal from the leading collective and to subsequent moral and physical annihilation."[2]

III

Even before the speech, however, Soviet writers, artists, and filmmakers had begun to test the waters to see whether the heavy-handed censorship of the Stalinist era might be lightening. Indeed, the entire cultural and social period spanning from the death of Stalin until the mid-1960s, generally known as "the thaw," took its name from a novel by that name (in Russian Ottepel') published by Ilya Ehrenburg (1891–1967) in the thick journal *The Banner* (Znamia) in 1954. Although Ehrenburg's novel followed in many respects the canons of Socialist Realism, the work was notable for touching on a few previously taboo topics and for its hints that personal happiness should not always be trumped by collective values. Ehrenburg was quickly attacked by a number of leading orthodox Soviet writers, including Mikhail Sholokhov and Simonov (known for his heroic portrayals of the Red Army and its soldiers in his war-time reportage and his celebrated novel *Days and Nights* (Dni i nochi, 1944). But, in a sign that things really had changed in the USSR, rather than being forced to recant his work and be expelled from the Writers Union (or worse), Ehrenburg was given the opportunity to respond publicly to the criticism his novel had received. In a rousing speech to the Second Congress of Soviet Writers, Ehrenburg deplored the insincerity of much Soviet writing and the tendency of Soviet writers and critics to see the world in black and white terms, choosing as heroes "primitive creatures, good little waxen children having nothing in common with Soviet people, with their complicated, deep internal life." Over the next few years "sincerity" would become a watchword used as shorthand for all that had been lost during the high Stalinist era.

By the mid-1950s, the small chink in the wall of Socialist Realism that Ehrenburg had opened widened considerably. Of course, in a society that remained as tightly controlled as the USSR, this liberalization could occur only because it served the interests of the authorities. Nevertheless, writers and other artists frequently took a leading role in exploring what was and was not possible to discuss. The 1956 novel by Vladimir Dudintsev (1918–98) *Not By Bread Alone* (Ne khlebom edinym), for example, and the 1957 film *The Cranes are Flying* (Letiat zhuravli) directed by Mikhail Kalatozov (1903–1973) opened important new vistas: the former dealt more or less forthrightly with the issue of abuse of power by the bureaucracy, while the latter attempted to give the treatment of the sacred subject of the Second World War some depth and complexity.

By the late 1950s, a new generation of Soviet writers had emerged, whose members were young enough to have never had to try to publish under the strict censorship of the Stalinist period. The brashest and freshest voices of this generation were poets Andrei Voznesensky (1933–), Evgeny Evtushenko (1933–), and Bella Akhmadulina (1937–), who became sufficiently popular that they could on occasion draw audiences of up to 50,000 for public poetry readings. The raw energy of their writing and performances linked them with the American 'beat" poets, whom they would befriend in the course of the 1960s. Evtushenko's 1961 poem "Babii Iar," memorializing the thousands of Jews murdered by the Nazis and castigating the Soviet authorities for their Anti-Semitism as expressed by their unwillingness to commemorate this and other Holocaust sites shows this generation of poets at their best. The fully Russian Evtushenko identifies himself with the Jewish victims in a poem that is simultaneously highly personal yet politically engaged:

> No monument stands over Babii Iar.
> A drop sheer as a crude gravestone.
> I am afraid.
> 	Today I am as old in years
> as all the Jewish people.
> Now I seem to be
> 			a Jew.
>
> . . .
>
> I am behind bars.
> 			Beset on every side.
> Hounded
> 	spat on,
> 		slandered.[4]

IV

Khrushchev, however, was mercurial, and by no means a partisan of artistic liberalism for its own sake. Rather, he used his power as cultural arbiter selectively, choosing to allow literature that exposed flaws in the Stalinist project, while preventing the appearance of work that was overly modernist or likely to weaken the Soviet system. As a result, even at the height of the Thaw, movement away from Stalinist cultural and social norms was by no means universal. This was illustrated by the furor surrounding the publication of Boris Pasternak's novel *Doctor Zhivago* in 1958. Pasternak had been one of Russia's leading modernist poets in the 1920s, but like so many Soviet artists he had been reduced to almost complete silence during the Stalinist period. Unable to publish his original work, he had survived as a translator (his translations of Shakespeare and Goethe are literary masterpieces in their own right). Throughout the 1930s and 1940s, however, Pasternak had tinkered with a historical novel whose protagonist, Iuri Zhivago, was a poet / physician living through the Revolution and Civil War. Pasternak's unorthodox treatment of these iconic Soviet experiences ensured that his novel would be unpublishable in the Stalinist period, but by the mid to late 1950s he began to hope that a Soviet publisher might take the work on. Ultimately, however, *Zhivago* was deemed too dangerous to make available to Soviet readers, and in 1958, fearing that his book would never see the light of day in the USSR, Pasternak authorized the Italian Communist publisher Feltrinelli to bring it out in Italy. Translated almost immediately into a number of major European languages, this intensely poetic novel made an artistic and political splash. The award of the Nobel Prize for Literature to Pasternak in 1958 in the wake of the novel's publication infuriated the Soviet leadership. An enormous campaign against the author, reminiscent of the worst excesses of the Stalin era, was initiated and the author was prevented from leaving the USSR to accept the prize.

Still, the overall arc of cultural development during this period was in the direction of greater liberalism, albeit under strict state supervision. The early 1960s saw the appearance of a new generation of young prose writers who grouped themselves around the journal *Iunost'* (Youth). Including Vasily Aksenov (1935–), Anatoly Gladilin (1935–) and Vladimir Voinovich (1932–), and heavily influenced by American contemporary fiction, particularly the work of J. D. Salinger that was translated at this time into Russian, they explored previously taboo themes and ignored the traditional socio-political conflicts that had been the bedrock of Socialist Realist fiction. Aksenov's 1961 novel *A Ticket to the Stars* (Zvezdnyi bilet) can be seen as emblematic of Youth Prose. The work focuses on two brothers, twenty-eight-year-old Viktor Denisov, who is finishing dissertation research connected to the Soviet space program, and Dmitry (Dima), a rebellious seventeen-year-old. The slangy Westernized language of Dima and his young friends, their rejection (at least initially) of the paths provided for them by the Soviet state in favor of an apolitical, even anti-social journey to the liberating beaches of Estonia indicated that at least some Soviet writers had moved well beyond the conventions of Socialist Realism by this point. Nevertheless, at the end of the novel Dima and his friends find happiness in a commitment to making socialism in the ranks of a fishing cooperative, so it would be impossible to claim that Aksenev has fully rejected Soviet ideals.

Writers unconnected to the *Iunost'* group began to explore even more taboo subjects, including the Stalinist camps. With the explicit permission of Khrushchev, the journal *New World* (Novyi mir) published Alexander Solzhenitsyn's novella "One Day in the Life of Ivan Denisovich" (Odin den' Ivana Denisovicha) in 1962 (see the detailed discussion of this event below). Poets began to experiment once more with formally difficult work and to explore erotic and highly personal themes. Artists working in other art forms also gravitated to more personal, lyrical forms of expression. Film in particular became far more daring led by the efforts of the young director Andrei Tarkovsky, whose exceptionally poetic and visually stunning film *Ivan's Childhood* (Ivanovo detstvo) was awarded a major prize at the Venice Film Festival in 1962. Nevertheless, even at the height of the Thaw, artistic expression was carefully monitored by the state, which never gave up the prerogatives of pre-publication censorship or control over the various artists' unions which determined who had the right to work officially as an artist. On a number of occasions, Khrushchev himself, born a peasant with a personal taste in art that was quite unsophisticated, clashed publicly with writers and artists whose work he disliked. Most memorable was an extended public shouting match with the sculptor Ernst Neizvestny (born 1926) during an exhibition in Moscow during which the premier described Neizvestny's work as "dog shit." Ironically, it was Neizvestny who would eventually sculpt the headstone that stands over Khrushchev's grave in Moscow.

V

The Thaw slowly ended as Khrushchev's grip on power loosened in 1963–4. No two events illustrated that the USSR was heading back into a period of conformism than the trials of Iosif Brodsky (1940–96) in 1964 and that of Andrei Siniavsky (1925–97) and Iuli Daniel (1925–88) in 1965. The former will be discussed below in the context of Brodsky's biography, but the latter is perhaps more interesting as an illustration of Soviet cultural practice. Siniavsky was a respected literary critic who had written his dissertation on socialist literary icon Maxim Gorky. But while pursuing a scholarly career in Moscow, Siniavsky was simultaneously creating much less conventional literary work under the pseudonym Abram Terts. Recognizing that this writing could not be published in the USSR, Siniavsky/Terts began to smuggle his work abroad, where both his critical study *On Socialist Realism* and his fictional work (the collection *Fantastic Tales* and a novella *The Trial Begins* [Sud idet]) appeared beginning in 1959. Almost immediately the KGB attempted to figure out who Terts was, but it took five years before they discovered that Terts and Siniavsky were one and the same person.

In 1965, Siniavsky and co-defendant Daniel, a minor but talented writer who had also had the temerity to publish his work abroad, appeared in a Moscow courtroom to answer to charges of anti-Soviet activity. The trial record forms a compelling literary work in its own right, complete with almost farcical exchanges between the judge, who insisted that every word in a literary text could and should be construed to be the opinion of the author himself, and Siniavsky, who insisted on the autonomy of the literary text. The result of the trial was tragic, however, as both writers were sentenced to prison terms of between five and seven years.

Nevertheless, even after the fall of Khrushchev in 1964 and the rise of the far stodgier Leonid Brezhnev to power in the USSR, the worst excesses of Stalinism never returned. Instead, through the rest of the 1960s and until the mid-1980s a complex three-tiered system developed in Soviet literature. In one camp were official writers willing to follow the canons of Socialist Realist orthodoxy. Most had come of age during the period of high Stalinism, and they occupied important posts in the cultural bureaucracy, as editors-in-chief of leading publishing houses and journals, and officials of the Writers' Union. Their works were published in enormous editions, and they formed a privileged caste, living in luxurious apartments and country houses (at least by Soviet standards), and chosen to travel abroad as part of official state delegations. But the blandishments offered to official writers came at a price, for choosing this path meant accepting a moral and ethical position of dependence that many could not condone. Particularly in the post-Stalinist period, there was in fact a certain opprobrium attached to official writers; seen as lackeys and opportunists, they were often perceived to be mediocre writers at best.

At the other end of the spectrum were dissident writers, a phenomenon that had been unheard of in the Stalinist period. Unable or unwilling to work within the Soviet literary establishment, they existed on the fringes of society. As they were not members of the Writers Union, they were for the most part unable to publish their work for the state controlled all publishing houses and journals. Dissident writing can be seen as part and parcel of a larger phenomenon in the USSR and its satellites – the inevitability, given the construction of the system, of a parallel economy in every sphere of life. As Katherine Verdery notes in her discussion of socialist economies: "since the center would not supply what people needed, they struggled to do so themselves, developing in the process a huge repertoire of strategies for obtaining consumer goods and services."[5] Literary production is not identical to the production of shoes or coats, but an analogous argument can be made about the culture "industry." Works of official literature poured out of state publishing houses in enormous editions but they did not satisfy the cultural needs of the population. Dissident literature, produced on typewriters, laboriously retyped in carbon copies, and circulated clandestinely (samizdat), came to fill the needs of that portion of the population dissatisfied with what the state provided. As with the black market, the state tacitly agreed to tolerate this activity as long as dissident writers did not attempt to challenge state power in an overly confrontational way. The quip of Venichka, the narrator of Venedikt Erofeev's (1938–90) classic novel *Moscow Circles* (Moskva-Petushki), originally published in samizdat, gives a flavor of the way the medium functioned: "The first edition of *Moscow Circles* disappeared quickly – thanks to the fact that it consisted of a single copy."[6]

VI

There was and still is a commonly held belief that the worlds of the dissident author and the official writer were completely segregated. Furthermore, it is often believed that the quality of samizdat literature was far better than that of works that were published in the USSR. A typical expression of this notion can be found in the introduction to the nine-volume *Blue Lagoon Anthology of Modern Russian Poetry*, which came out in the United States during the height of the Cold War. Each of these approximately 600-page "loose and baggy monsters" presented the work of Russian "dissident, unofficial or nonconformist writers" as John Bowlt characterized them. Continuing, Bowlt noted: "these terms carry an implied value judgment according to which 'unofficial work' means 'good work' and 'official work' means 'bad work.'"[7] This view was widely shared inside the USSR as well. Thus, the novelist Georgy Vladimov (1931–2003) wrote in an open letter to the Soviet Writers' Union that "creative freedom ... is being realized ... in the activity of the so-called *samizdat* ... There are now two kinds of art in the country. One is free and uninhibited ... [its] distribution and influence depend only it its genuinely artistic qualities. And the other one, commanded and paid for ... is badly mutilated, suppressed, and oppressed."[8]

Indeed, one could say that despite official oppression, underground writing and writers achieved something like cult status in the USSR and in the West from the late 1960s through the mid-1980s. A character in Solzhenitsyn's novel *The First Circle* (V kruge pervom, 1968) called writers a kind of "second government" in the Soviet Union, and the view that such writers formed the conscience of the nation, the voice of truth amidst oppression, was deeply held, at least among the urban intelligentsia. Furthermore, unlike the status accorded official writers, the prestige of unofficial writers, especially the best known, was international. From the 1960s on, foreign publishers vied to produce editions of leading underground writers, such influential publications as *The New York Review of Books* devoted frequent columns to their books, and even the Nobel Committee helped out by awarding the literature prize to Solzhenitsyn in 1970 and Brodsky in 1987. Now, some twenty years after the collapse of the system, the black-and-white view of the relationship between the official and unofficial spheres, as well as the question of the relative quality of the art produced in them, should be seen in a different light. There was in fact significant traffic back and forth between official and unofficial literature, and their relationship fluctuated depending on the internal situation in the USSR. Many writers, including some of the best, spanned both camps. Aksenov, Solzhenitsyn, and Voinovich, for example, all started out as officially accepted writers during the Thaw period before becoming leading dissidents in the 1970s. Many others, including Voznesensky, the popular "bards" (who sang their verse accompanied by the guitar) Alexander Galich (1918–77), Bulat Okudzhava (1924–97), and Vladimir Vysotsky, practitioners of so-called Village Prose such as Valentin Rasputin (1937–), Fedor Abramov (1920–83), as well as writers such as Vladimir Makanin (1937–) and Iuri Trifonov (1925–81), whose underappreciated novels explored the psyche of everyday Muscovites, existed in a difficult grey space between fully accepted orthodox writers and full-blown dissidents. Some of their work was acceptable to the State and made available to the public, while other pieces were deemed overly sensitive and suppressed. As for quality, while a few major works appeared in samizdat or were smuggled abroad for publication, the vast majority of unofficial literary texts were not of very high quality.

There are a number of reasons for the wide range of quality in samizdat. First of all, it was generally produced by the author him or herself; it was by definition amateur work, something like today's internet. That is, there was no intermediary of literary agent, editor, or publishing house to make choices based on quality. Rather, an author could say whatever he or she wanted to say, albeit to a limited audience. Furthermore, readers also did not pay much attention to quality when it came to samizdat. Instead, unofficial literature was valued as a symbol of the very possibility of dissent rather than, *pace* Vladimov, for its literary quality. Even a semi-public enunciation of "the truth" was a kind of scandal, and audiences felt vicariously brave just by reading it.

Regardless of whether a writer was official or unofficial, the social and economic policies of the USSR provided a number of incentives that encouraged literary production. Whereas a young man or woman in the West might also have found the idea of being a writer attractive, the difficulties of making a living by the pen coupled with the relative ease of entry to and the high status and pay of other professions would usually tip the scales in their favor. Even for extremely creative individuals in the West, the allure of entrepeneurship is strong, and developing one's own successful business can satisfy the creative urge. In the USSR, state policy eliminated financial incentives for entering competing professions. As there was little or no private business, the possibility of earning large sums and satisfying the need to create by this means did not exist; the law was completely at the mercy of the state, so choosing the legal profession was rightfully seen as an even greater sell-out than becoming an official writer; doctors were woefully underpaid and overworked. The only relatively high paying professions were inside the state apparatus or in the top military, neither of which tended to attract would-be writers.

While one set of state policies eliminated incentives to take up non-literary professions, a complementary set softened the disincentives to choosing a literary career, even an unofficial one. Salaries – all of which were paid by the state – were set artificially low. In fact, state policy practically eliminated the cash economy, substituting for it a system in which connections, barter, and inter-personal networks predominated. In such a system there was little financial penalty for choosing to take a job that paid poorly because no job paid well. As the Communist era quip went, "they pretend to pay us and we pretend to work." Thus, even if unofficial writers could not earn the relatively large sums available to official writers, it was not difficult for them to find a job that paid more or less the national, artificially low average and that demanded little attention.

VII

The system outlined above endured for the entire period between the mid 1960s and the mid 1980s (a time that has come to be called the period of stagnation). At a number of points state repression loosened a bit, at others it increased, but the overall mood was of marking time, waiting for something to happen. Nevertheless, a number of interesting literary movements and individual writers did appear. Perhaps the strongest of the former was the so-called Village Prose movement. Throughout the Soviet period, one of the central imperatives was the modernization and urbanization of the country. Marx had commented on the "idiocy of rural life," and despite the claim that the USSR was a workers' and peasants' state, it often appeared that the latter were second or even third class citizens. During the era of high Stalinism, village life in literary work was considered almost exclusively in the context of collectivization, and the goal was to show the replacement of traditional mentalities by new Soviet values. For the authors identified with Village Prose, many of whom themselves hailed from rural areas, the headlong rush to modernity had come at too great a cost. While most if not all of them professed allegiance to the state and were members of the Writers Union, their literary work celebrated the timeless traditions, rhythms, and values of Russian peasant life. In time, a number of leading Village Prose writers became identified with neo-nationalist ideologies, Russian Orthodoxy, and environmental activism that put them at loggerheads with the Soviet state.

Although not a Village Prose writer per se, Alexander Solzhenitsyn produced one of the iconic texts of the movement in his early short story masterpiece "Matrena's House" (Matrenin dvor, written 1958, published 1963). The story is narrated through the eyes of a man who has recently been released from the Gulag (clearly a stand-in for the author). Unable by Soviet law to live within 100 kilometers of a major city, he takes a school teaching job in a tiny village where he rents a room from Matrena, an independent peasant woman whose thought and speech patterns reflect the values of Turgenev's Kalinych far more closely than they do Soviet ones. At first somewhat put off by Matrena, the narrator eventually comes to appreciate her. After her death, the narrator concludes his story with an encomium to this positive hero who embodies traits strikingly different than those espoused by the heroines of official Soviet literature:

By the mid-1960s and into the 1970s, many writers were working in the Village Prose vein. The popular short stories of Vasily Shukshin (1929–74) tended to focus on humorous or ironic situations, and were heavily larded with Russian peasant speech. The novels of Abramov, Viktor Astafev (1924–2001), and Valentin Rasputin were more epic in scope. Rasputin's *Farewell to Matera* (Proshchanie s Materoi, 1976) is the classic mature Village Prose novel. It chronicles the last year in the life of a traditional farming village on an island that is soon to be flooded by an artificial lake that will be created through the damming of a river for a hydroelectric plant. In a traditional Soviet novel, progress in the form of electrification would have the highest value, and the work would have celebrated the triumph of man over nature. Peasants clinging to their traditional existence would have been at best ignored and at worst would have appeared as "wreckers" whose absence of proletarian class-consciousness would lead them astray. In Rasputin's novel, however, we see the traditional world of Matera sympathetically, through the eyes of the old peasant woman Daria Pinigina, and we come to appreciate that the hydroelectric plant will break bonds between man and nature that cannot be reconstituted and will be lost to the detriment of Russian society.

Event – Publication of "One Day in the Life of Ivan Denisovich" in *Novyi mir*

In November 1962, the Moscow journal *Novyi mir* published a novella entitled "One Day in the Life of Ivan Denisovich" by the then unknown author Alexander Solzhenitsyn. The appearance of this simple story describing a single day in the life of an ordinary prisoner in the Gulag was the most spectacular publishing event in the history of the USSR. It catapulted the author to instant celebrity, affirmed the leading cultural position of *Novyi mir* and its editor Alexander Tvardovsky, and seemed to guarantee that the USSR, under the leadership of Nikolai Khrushchev (who had personally approved the publication of this work) was continuing to make progress in overcoming the evils of Stalinism. Although the liberal moment of 1962 would soon pass, "One Day" remains a vital text and the story of its publication provides an instructive lesson on the relationship between authorship and power in Russia.

Solzhenitsyn was an unlikely candidate for literary heroism. He was born in the North Caucasus, the son of a Tsarist-era artillery officer. After the accidental death of his father, he moved with his mother, the daughter of a relatively prosperous Ukrainian farmer, to Rostov-on-the-Don, where he grew up in difficult circumstances, both because of the general privations in the first years of Bolshevik rule and because of his unfortunate class background. As a youth, Solzhenitsyn showed talent in mathematics and physics, and he also enrolled as a distance student in a post-secondary literature program in Moscow. Called up during the Second World War, he fought with distinction but was arrested in 1945 for negative comments made about Stalin in a private letter to a friend. For this "political crime" he was sentenced to eight years of hard labor to be followed by internal exile within the USSR. As a prisoner, Solzhenitsyn experienced a variety of conditions, though he was fortunate to avoid the deadliest Siberian camps. After his release he was first exiled to Kazakhstan, where he miraculously survived cancer (a topic he writes brilliantly about in his novel *Cancer Ward* [*Rakovyi korpus*, 1968], then moved to a small village outside of Moscow and finally to the provincial city of Ryazan.

Throughout the time of his exile, Solzhenitsyn wrote obsessively, though he was well aware that his work was not publishable in the USSR. Not surprisingly, one of his central themes at this period was the reality of the Gulag, a subject that remained taboo in Soviet literature despite the more liberal atmosphere of the Thaw period. Years later the author provided his own account of how he developed the novella, which tells us a great deal about both his literary genealogy and his ambitions:

> On one long winter workday in camp, as I was lugging a handbarrow [filled with mortar] together with another man, I asked myself how one might portray the totality of our camp existence. In essence it should suffice to give a thorough description of a single day, providing minute detail and focusing on the most ordinary kind of worker; that would reflect our entire experience.[9]

Before he became a celebrated novelist and sage, Lev Tolstoy had tried and failed to write his first work, "A History of Yesterday" in which he wanted to describe a day in the life of his hero so as to capture, through myriad tiny details, the totality of his existence. Although he came to recognize that this was an impossible task, his first published work *Childhood*, with its focus on the ordinary details of the child's daily existence, clearly builds on the unrealized project of "A History of Yesterday" and the capacity to observe the tiniest details of life (both external and even more importantly internal) would remain a hallmark of Tolstoy's style even as he moved to epic projects such as *War and Peace*. Solzhenitsyn quite consciously follows in Tolstoy's footsteps, beginning with "One Day" and in his later monumental works, both those focused on the camps (in particular his *Gulag Archipelago*) and his *Red Wheel* cycle of historical novels.

Given the enormity of the Stalin-era terror, the deep trauma it left on Soviet society, and the seeming unwillingness of the state to address the issue, the desire to capture the "totality of our camp existence" would become an obsession for many writers, particularly but not exclusively for those who had experienced the reality of the camps directly. Although he was almost certainly unaware of the work's existence when he wrote "One Day," Solzhenitsyn's comments on his motivation for writing clearly echo the desire expressed by Akhmatova in her introduction to *Requiem* (see chapter 6). Many other writers would subsequently attempt to capture in whole or in part the experience of the camps, most notably Varlaam Shalamov (1907–82), whose almost Chekhovian stories are the most powerful literary works set in the camps, and Evgenia Ginzburg (1904–77), whose brilliant autobiography *Journey into the Whirlwind* (Krutoi marshrut) is one of the greatest non-fictional accounts of camp life; but "One Day" was the first to be published in the USSR and evoked the strongest reaction.

In face of the enormous importance of "One Day" as a literary fact, it is easy to overlook its literary qualities, which are considerable. It opens with a series of simple declarative sentences that set the time and place and indicate the narrative tone that will dominate the entire text. "As always reveille sounded at 5a.m. – a hammer banging on a rail near the barrack headquarters. The intermittent sound came faintly through the window, which was covered with an inch of ice and soon died away: it was cold and the warder didn't feel like waving his arm for long."[10] Quite quickly we recognize that the entire third-person narrative will be presented from the point of view of the protagonist Shukhov, a normal prisoner trying his best to survive his sentence. Solzhenitsyn made a brilliant decision in choosing for his protagonist an everyman, a semi-literate peasant not completely capable of understanding, let alone verbalizing his situation. An intellectual hero would have likely analyzed his position, much as the hero of Dostoevsky's semi-autobiographical account of his own prison experiences *Notes from the House of the Dead* (Zapiski iz mertvogo doma, 1862). Instead, Solzhenitsyn, through Shukhov's eyes and for the most part employing Shukhov's linguistic resources, shows simply and with little unnecessary verbiage the stark realities of camp life. Equally important is his choice of a completely "normal" camp day. Shukhov interacts with other inmates, works, eats, but most of all endures. When the day ends with Shukhov falling asleep to meet his awakening in the first paragraph, we feel we have come in contact with the rare literary work that successfully compresses reality into an image any reader will carry forever:

> Shukhov fell asleep completely satisfied. He'd had a lot of success today: he hadn't landed in solitary, his brigade hadn't been forced to work outside building Socialist City. He'd managed to get some extra kasha at lunch, the brigade leader had gotten them good rates, he'd gotten pleasure from

> building the wall, they'd missed his homemade blade when he'd been frisked, he'd made a bit of dough working for Cesar in the evening, and bought some tobacco. He'd gotten over feeling sick.
>
> The day had passed without a cloud, almost happily.
>
> From reveille to sleep there were three thousand six hundred fifty three days like this.
>
> The three extras were for leap years.
>
> (143)

That "One Day" came to be published at all is something of a miracle. Solzhenitsyn was by all accounts extremely reluctant to allow his literary work to be seen. Nevertheless, through the efforts of his wife, the manuscript was lent to friends who passed it on to other friends, all of whom told Solzhenitsyn that he had to try to publish the story. Encouraged by Khrushchev's public denunciation of Stalinism at the 22nd Party Congress in 1961 and by a speech given at the same event by Tvardovsky, Solzhenitsyn asked his friend Lev Kopelev to transmit the novella to *Novyi mir* for consideration. It took a fair amount of internal cloak and dagger work in the journal's editorial offices to get the manuscript in front of Tvardovsky, who was taken by both the subject matter and the presentation of Solzhenitsyn's work. It then took a great deal of further maneuvering to get the manuscript in front of Khrushchev. Nikita Sergeevich, however, was a peasant himself, and the simple tone of Solzhenitsyn's prose as well as its implicit indictment of the Stalinist system was fully in keeping with his literary tastes and political needs. He immediately issued a decree overriding the normal censorship apparatus and the novella appeared, to the amazement of practically all. Early criticism of the work was almost universally positive, as everyone was aware it had come out with the express approval of the First Secretary. Solzhenitsyn became a household name, and he followed up the publication of "One Day" with a number of short stories in *Novyi mir* the following year. But the Thaw was rapidly drawing to a close and Solzhenitsyn's plans to publish his more ambitious novels *Cancer Ward* and *The First Circle* came to naught. Soon, he would find himself the most famous dissident in the USSR, watched at every step by the KGB, until he was eventually sent into exile in the West in 1974.

Biography – Iosif Brodsky (1940–1996)

Iosif Brodsky, perhaps the most important Russian poet of the second half of the twentieth century, was born on May 24, 1940 in Leningrad. His father was a photographer, and his mother a book-keeper. Both were

Russian Jews. In August 1941 his father went to the front and in September Leningrad was besieged by Hitler's armies. In April 1942, mother and son were evacuated to the East and they did not return to the city until 1944. The blockade of Leningrad, one of the great humanitarian catastrophes of the century, turned the city into a ghost of its former self: more than half a million people died of starvation and part of the city was destroyed. In the opinion of Brodsky's friend, the poet Lev Losev, "early impressions of the destroyed city determined the central position of the elegy in his work."[11]

Brodsky spent the first eight years of his life without his father, who was not demobilized until 1948. Among his strongest early memories were screenings of "trophy films" that had been brought back home by the victorious Red Army. Adventure flicks about Tarzan and Zorro were seen by his generation as "tales about individualism." The absence of any ties with a particular time, he would recall later, "made them perfect symbols of the age, the beginning of the 1950s, the last years of Stalin's rule. The "Tarzan" series alone did more for de-Stalinization than all Khrushchev's speeches at the Twentieth Party Congress and after."[12] Another "American" childhood passion was jazz, which could be heard by tuning the radio to the Voice of America. "When we were twelve, the German names on our lips gradually began to be replaced by those of Louis Armstrong, Duke Ellington, Ella Fitzgerald, Clifford Brown, Sydney Bechet, Django Reinhardt, and Charlie Parker. Something began to happen, I remember, even to our walk: the joints of our highly inhibited Russian frames harkened to 'swing.'"[13] American jazz culture would have an important influence on Soviet culture of the 1950s and 1960s (the writing of Vasily Aksenov, the music of Rodion Shchedrin and Alfred Schnittke).

Individualism and a love of risk were trademarks of the post-war generation. The young Brodsky dreamed of becoming a submariner, but he did not end up enrolling in the naval academy (nevertheless, the theme of the sea, its broad expanse and depth, occupies an important place in his work). He left school at fifteen and began to work in a factory. In a short time he held thirteen different jobs, including stints in a morgue, a bathhouse, and a lighthouse. He took part in a number of geological expeditions as well. Such expeditions to distant parts of the country were a cultural phenomenon of Soviet life in this period. They were an expression of the Romanticism of the young generation, and allowed them to indulge a love of travel and nurture a cult of friendship as well as to test themselves in difficult conditions. They also made it possible to escape, at least for a short time, from the ideological control of an authoritarian system which was felt far more strongly in the major cities than in the far-flung reaches of the USSR.

Early on Brodsky began to organize his life as an aesthetic experiment. In a letter to a girl from his school he wrote: "I juggle my fate for no particular or stable purpose. That is to say, I have no intention of choosing some kind of hierarchical staircase and progressing up it . . . What I do is merely an experiment. New ideas, new images and, most important, new forms."[14] Brodsky began to write poetry fairly late for a literarily inclined Russian. He started at seventeen, but immediately set the goal of writing better than anyone else. Later, he would cite as particularly important sources of inspiration at this point Derzhavin, Baratynsky, Tsvetaeva, Mandelstam, and the Polish and English metaphysical poets (especially John Donne, whom he eventually translated and to whom he dedicated one of his greatest elegies). At the beginning of the 1960s, Brodsky discovered contemporary Anglo-American poetry (Robert Frost, T. S. Eliot, W. H. Auden – the last became his favorite poet). Brodsky's aesthetic experiment became the attempt to marry the classical Russian lyric with Anglo-American philosophical poetry.

By the end of the 1950s, Leningrad's cultural life was gradually beginning to emerge from the destruction that had been wrought by Stalin's culture satrap and Leningrad party boss Andrei Zhdanov. A host of literary groupings and small-scale salons emerged. Unofficial poetry included poets of a wide range of artistic and aesthetic persuasions, but all were united by their marginal status with reference to official art. It was a kind of Renaissance, but playing the role of classical poetry was the modernist poetry of Russia's "Silver Age." Some poets looked to the Acmeists for inspiration, while others turned to futurism. Of particular importance to this generation was the idea of the poetic torch, which was to be passed from one generation to another. At this time Akhmatova, Pasternak, and Kruchenykh were all still alive, and they had a strong poetic and moral influence on the new generation. For Leningrad poets the very place in which they lived – Petersburg-Petrograd – helped to motivate their dialogue with the past. They saw the city as a locus of memory which preserved the great cultural traditions that had been rejected and forbidden by the "Muscovite" authoritarian regime. This Petersburg-in-memory was also opposed to the official "cradle of October Revolution" Leningrad, with its overcrowded buses "carrying the barnacles of humanity to their factories and offices," and ugly new building constructions on the outskirts whose style was known popularly as "barrackko."[15] In this nostalgic vision, two old cultural myths merged: a medieval legend about the invisible holy city of Kitezh, which miraculously submerged into the lake to avoid being destroyed by the barbarians (this legend was later reanimated by the Slavophiles and canonized in Rimsky-Korsakov's 1905 opera), and the nineteenth-century myth of St. Petersburg as a haunted city.

Poetry was read aloud in the informal Leningrad circles of the 1950s and early 1960s. This orientation toward sound led to the formation of a culture that was "more oral than written": "We understood that we were living in a pre-Guttenberg age. What happened in Russia in the 1960s was very similar to what had occurred in Byzantium or in Alexandria, say, a thousand and a half years ago . . . For us, poetry became in a considerable degree a mnemonic art."[16] The historical analogy Brodsky cites here is quite typical for his historical philosophy: he "reads" the apparently mighty USSR against a background of ancient empires at the moment of their decadence.

Beginning in 1957, Brodsky began to appear in public, usually in front of student audiences. He attracted attention immediately both because of his unusual verses and his provocative behavior. His poetic credo at this time was openly rebellious: "a naked hymn to idealism" and extremely individualistic. One of his early readings ended in scandal when in the discussion afterwards he quoted Trotsky (it was, apparently, from then on that he began to be watched by the secret police). Brodsky's contemporaries immediately noticed his unusual manner of reading, which recalled the performance of a shaman or an oracle: "Brodsky was able to achieve such a level of intonational intensity that listeners could become physically ill – the pressure was simply too great. But that was not the real point. Brodsky's reading of his own work was *life in verse* . . . It was not a reproduction [of the written], a performance – even a great one. It was literally lived poetry."[17] This performance style was part of the poet's aesthetic program; the theme of the author's voice captured in verse is one of the most important in his metaphysical poetry. Among Brodsky's best works from the early 1960s are "A Christmas Romance," "Abraham and Isaac," "The Grand Elegy to John Donne," and "On the Death of Robert Frost."

As opposed to the public poets of the 1950s and 1960s (Robert Rozhdeshtvensky [1932–94], Evgeny Evtushenko, and others), who stepped out loudly onto the ideological territory that had recently been "demined" by the state, Brodsky wrote practically no political verse. His revolt, and he considered it much more courageous and important, was against the spoken and unspoken canons of Soviet literature: in his choice of topics (not civic but "metaphysical": time, space, God, the soul, the void), his style (extremely personal, experimental, with vertiginous shifts between "high" and "low" registers, exotic stanzaic forms, and eccentric rhymes), his models (those Russian and Western poets who had been "consigned to hell" by the socialist canon), and in his unacceptable authorial pose (a demonstrative distaste for the authorities, aesthetic provocation).

The culminating moment of Brodsky's poetic biography was his acquaintance with Anna Akhmatova in 1961. Akhmatova was a living symbol of the modernist teens and twenties, and she was surrounded at that time by a circle of young Leningrad poets ("Akhmatova's orphans" as one of them called the group). In Brodsky, Akhmatova saw a brilliant poet who could link two ages that had been violently split – the contemporary renaissance and the age of Russian modernism. Having thus been annointed by Akhmatova, Brodsky was symbolically raised from one among many excellent young poets of the late 1950s and early 1960s to the pantheon of eternal Russian poetry – the unbroken line of poetic succession that stretched from the Golden Age of Pushkin through Tiutchev and Fet in the latter half of the nineteenth century into the Silver Age.

The popularity of unofficial poetry among the youth did not escape the attention of the authorities. In 1963, as Khrushchev's hold on power weakened, a Communist Party plenum was devoted to the topic of the "ideological development" of the youth and the need for increased vigilance over literature and art. The party secretary in charge of ideology, L. Il'ichev, attacked "young and politically immature but extremely self-assured and exceptionally boastful" writers who had forgotten to "take joy from the heroic achievements of the people." They were dubbed "worthless whiners, moral cripples" who "to approving nods from over seas, attempt to dethrone the principles of ideological and national art and replace them with the magpie chattering of the ignorant and lazy."[18] This speech, which in general terms outlined the image of a new enemy, was a signal to the party, the Komsomol, writers' organizations and other "civil society" groups to begin a campaign against unofficial youth culture and its leaders.

As early as May 1961, the Party had issued an decree titled "Regarding Increased Vigilance against People Avoiding Socially Useful Labor and Leading an Antisocial Parasitic Life." Although in principle the law was aimed at those living off such activities as small-scale black marketeering, prostitution, and begging, it was used against a variety of dissidents, who were equated – as if illustrating Michel Foucault's *Histoire de la folie à l'âge classique,* published the same year – with the poor and the insane. In order to avoid being prosecuted under this statute, many dissident intellectuals in the 1960s and 1970s who had either been fired for their convictions or who simply refused to serve the state began to work as stevedores, janitors, coal shovelers and the like. Such unprestigious jobs gave them relative freedom from state control and generally provided sufficient free time to pursue their intellectual pursuits. This law "against parasitism" remained on the books until 1991. The first person to be charged under its provisions was the young Brodsky.

On November 29, 1963 the newspaper *Evening Leningrad* published an article entitled "A Pseudoliterary Drone" in which Brodsky was charged with antisocial behavior and anti-Soviet writing, specifically pornography and parasitism. The initiator of this campaign was a self-appointed guardian of public order who was attempting to improve his career opportunities. In order to save the poet from arrest, his friends checked him into a psychiatric hospital under the care of a sympathetic doctor. In the Soviet period mental hospitals were not merely medical but also political institutions. While in the mid-1960s some intellectuals feigned insanity in order to escape the authorities, beginning in the late 1960s, the mental institutions were used by those same authorities to incarcerate and forcibly medicate dissidents.[19] Brodsky considered his short stay in the mental hospital the worst experience of his life.[20]

In early January 1964 a new article with an even more threatening title appeared: "No Place for Parasites in our City": "No attempts by Brodsky and his defenders to escape from the court of public opinion will succeed. Our wonderful youth will say to them: Enough! Brodsky has been a drone living off society for long enough. Let him work. And if he doesn't want to, he'll have only himself to blame." He was arrested on February 13. The court met twice to hear his case, and in between these sessions he was required to undergo a psychiatric exam.

The trial record of the case against "the parasite Brodsky," set down by the journalist Frida Vigdorova, became one of the best-known pieces of dissident writing. It was read as political theatre, the collision between the proud poet and an ignorant and aggressive state. What follows is one of the best-known sections of the text. In answer to the judge's question as to his profession, Brodsky answered, "I'm a poet, a poet-translator."

> *Judge* And who said you were a poet? Who included you among the ranks of the poets?
> *Brodsky* No one. (*Without emphasis*). And who included me among the ranks of the human race?
> *Judge* Did you study this?
> *Brodsky* What?
> *Judge* To be a poet? You did not try to finish university where they prepare ... where they teach ...
> *Brodsky* I didn't think you could get this from school.

>Judge   How, then?
>Brodsky   I think that it . . . (confused) . . . comes from God[21]

The sentence was handed down on March 13:

>Brodsky has systematically refused to fulfill the obligations of a Soviet citizen to engage in productive labor and support himself, which can be seen from his frequent job changes . . . He promised to find a permanent job, but having done nothing about it, continued to avoid work and to write decadent poems and read them at various parties. Documents from the Commission of young writers tell us clearly that he is no poet. The readers of the newspaper *Evening Leningrad* have accused him. As a result the court invokes the Decree of May 5 1961: Brodsky is to be exiled to distant places for a period of five years during which he will be required to engage in forced labor.[22]

Brodsky was sent to a camp in the far north, to the village of Norenskaya. Akhmatova was heard to say: "What a biography they are creating for our red-head!" Indeed, Brodsky's sentence placed him in the company of poet-exiles from Ovid and Dante through Byron, Pushkin, Lermontov, and Mandelstam. Brodsky himself, however, took his "ideal" Romantic poetic biography with a grain of salt, not surprising given his basic philosophical attitude, which can be characterized as a view of the world and of himself from a distanced perspective, the point of view of eternity perhaps. "What can I say about life?" he would later ask in his most autobiographical poem ("I walked in a cage in place of a wild beast . . ."). And he answered: "That it was long." That length (the poem was written for his own fortieth birthday) was not measured in years but rather in the quantity of absurd events in his biography.

While the trial was ongoing, a campaign in defense of Brodsky was organized. Letters were written in his favor by the composer Dmitry Shostakovich, the editor and writer Alexander Tvardovsky, and the writers Samuil Marshak (1887–1964), Kornei Chukovsky (1882–1969), Iuri German (1910–67) and Akhmatova. On June 22, 1964 the American journal *New Leader* published the transcript of his trial and one of his poems. The subsequent publication of the same transcript in the French *Figaro Littéraire* and the English *Encounter* had the effect of a bombshell. Jean-Paul Sartre wrote an open letter in defense of Brodsky. At the end of 1965 the poet was released early, having spent eighteen months in exile.

Having demonstrated their "mercy," the authorities let Brodsky know that he could publish in the Soviet media as long as he agreed to follow certain rules. He refused. His first book, entitled simply *Lyrics and Longer Poems*, came out in New York in 1965. In 1970 his collection *A Stop in the Desert* (Ostanovka v pustyne) was released, also in the West. Many of his poems began to be translated into foreign languages. In May 1972 the American president Richard Nixon visited the USSR. One concrete result of this visit was that the Soviets began to allow Jews to immigrate to Israel. In 1972 Brodsky was called in to the KGB and told that he should emigrate if he wanted to avoid further problems. On the eve of his departure for Vienna, Brodsky wrote an open letter to Soviet leader Leonid Brezhnev: "Even if my people has no need of my body, my soul will still be valuable to them." In his poem "The Year 1972," written a few months after his forced exile, Brodsky compared himself to the Greek mythological hero Theseus, returning to his country after having slain the monstrous Minotaur. In his later work (1972–96) Brodsky developed a unique metaphysic of exile (in the words of the American Slavist David Bethea), a reworking of a theme traditional for classic Russian literature. On this view the poet is always an other, who combines within himself everything left behind and unexpectedly found; exile is the poet's natural milieu, not the result of his conflict with the powers that be:[23]

> Listen, lads, friends, and foes!
> All that I created I created not for the sake
> of fame in an era of cinema and radio,
> but for the sake of native speech, literature.
> For which solicitous priesthood
> (as is said to the doctor: let him heal himself),
> Deprived of a cup at the feast of the Fatherland,
> now I stand in an unfamiliar place
>
> (trans. David Bethea)

To an external glance at least, Brodsky's Western period was more than successful. He was invited to work at the University of Michigan in the United States. He also became acquainted with his poetic idol Auden, who took great pains to assist the poet-exile. Between 1972 and 1989 Brodsky taught Russian poetry at Michigan, Mount Holyoke College, Columbia, and other American universities and colleges. In 1977 he published his collections *The End of a Beautiful Era* (Konets prekrasnoi epokhi) and *A Part of Speech* (Chast' rechi). They were followed by *New Stanzas to Augusta* (Novye stansy k Avguste, [1983]), the play *Marble* (Mramor [1984]), and *Urania* (1987). His collection of essays in English *Less Than One* (1986) won the National Book Critics Circle's Award.

In 1987 Brodsky was awarded the Nobel Prize "for an all-embracing authorship, imbued with clarity of thought and poetic intensity." In his acceptance speech he spoke, in particular, about the cultural mission of poets of his generation:

> That generation – the generation born precisely at the time when the Auschwitz crematoria were working full blast, when Stalin was at the zenith of his Godlike, absolute power, which seemed sponsored by Mother Nature herself – that generation came into the world, it appears, in order to continue what, theoretically, was supposed to be interrupted in those crematoria and in the anonymous common graves of Stalin's archipelago. The fact that not everything got interrupted, at least not in Russia, can be credited in no small degree to my generation, and I am no less proud of belonging to it than I am of standing here today. And the fact that I am standing here is a recognition of the services that generation has rendered to culture.[24]

With perestroika, Brodsky's work began to appear in Soviet journals. Books, popular and scholarly articles, and dissertations were written about him. But, unlike many other émigré writers, he never returned to Russia (he did not want to come as a tourist and he had no wish to stay there).

Brodsky died of a heart attack in his study on the night of January 27–8, 1996. Once he had written: "The century is coming to an end but I will end first." His death marks the end of one of the most important myths of Russian "high" literature of the nineteenth and twentieth centuries – the myth of the Poet as the link between cultural epochs separated by time and space.

Literary Work – Andrei Voznesensky, Iunona i Avos'

Solzhenitsyn began his publishing career with *One Day* as a fully official writer supported by the First Secretary himself. Very quickly, however, he became an unofficial writer and dissident. In Western exile he was a mysterious figure, who chose to separate himself from society in his Vermont compound, writing an enormous cycle of historical novels that few would read. Throughout his career in the USSR Iosif Brodsky was a nonconformist artist for whom regular publication was impossible. In exile, he became an internationally renowned figure, mixing with a pleiad of major poets including Seamus Heaney, Czeslaw Milosz, and Derek Walcott. As opposed to Solzhenitsyn and Brodsky, Andrei Voznesensky chose throughout his career to work within the Soviet system. He walked the fine line between the officially acceptable and the avant-garde, deftly staying just close enough to the official line to avoid censure and just far enough away to remain challenging. While publishing openly in the USSR and frequently representing the state at international literary festivals and other public events, he managed to inspire and assist generations of younger poets. To be sure, there were those who despised him, either perceiving him as too cosy with the state and too willing to accept the perquisites that went with being a visible official writer or seeing him as a closet dissident, too willing to defend anti-Soviet writers and artists. Such is the lot of those who avoid extreme positions in a polarized society.

The poem "Avos'" is not one of Voznesensky's masterpieces. We have chosen to focus on it primarily because of its adaptation into the "rock opera," *Juno and Avos'* (Iunona i Avos'), which had its Moscow premier in 1981. Although *Juno and Avos'* is also not a masterpiece, it is a fascinating work for examination here both because it is representative of a phenomenon that has been widespread in Russian culture (the adaptation works from one medium into another) and because it illustrates the multiple ways in which an official writer could play at the edges of the acceptable in the USSR.

As we noted in chapter 6, one sign of the litero-centric nature of Russian culture is the tendency of Russian composers to use works of national literature as the basis for opera libretti. From Glinka's *Ruslan and Liudmila* through Rimsky-Korsakov's *Tsar Saltan* it is the rare nineteenth-century Russian opera that is not based on Russian literature, most frequently on a work of Pushkin or Gogol. The trend continued into the twentieth century, though the range of authors from whom composers borrowed expanded: Shostakovich's *Lady Macbeth of Mtsensk* (based on a story by Leskov) and *The Nose* (Gogol), Prokofiev's *Fiery Angel* (Briusov), *War and Peace* (Tolstoy) and *The Gambler* (Dostoevsky) and Shnitke's *Life with an Idiot* (Viktor Erofeev). For Russian opera-goers, part of the pleasure is clearly in the comparison of the original literary work with the operatic adaptation. In this respect, *Juno and Avos'* is a typical Russian opera.

"Avos'" is drawn from a fascinating and little-known episode of Russian history – the expedition led by Nikolai Petrovich Rezanov to California in 1806. Rezanov was born in St. Petersburg in 1764, scion of a poor gentry family, but grew up in Irkutsk where he showed a talent for languages. After a short stint in the military, Rezanov took a number of civilian posts in the government of Catherine the Great. In 1794 he was sent back to his home town to investigate the activities of Grigory Shelikhov, who had pioneered Russian settlement and trade in Alaska. Taking his duties seriously, Rezanov met and eventually married Shelikhov's daughter, and after Shelikhov's death in 1795 became one of the leading shareholders of what would become the Russian-American Company.

In 1802, Rezanov's wife died after the birth of their second child, and in 1803 he set off on an around-the-world mission to Japan and Russia's American territories. From the Russian government's perspective, the most important goal of the mission was to open trade relations with Japan, which was at that point almost completely off limits to foreigners. Rezanov, as Russian Ambassador to Japan, spent half a year cooling his heals in the tiny Dutch settlement near Nagasaki, but ultimately had to depart empty-handed as the Japanese refused to accredit his mission. Having left Japan, he went to the Russian Alaska colonies, where he bought the Juno (the Avos' was acquired a bit later) and outfitted it for a voyage to San Francisco, then controlled by Spain. Arriving in late March, Rezanov spent a few months in California, charming the Spanish governor Don Jose Dario Arguello and his fifteen-year-old daughter Concepcion. Before leaving San Francisco, Rezanov asked for Concepcion's hand in marriage and promised to return to marry her in two years time. On the return trip to European Russia, however, Rezanov fell ill and died in Krasnoyarsk in 1807. Concepcion remained faithful to her fiancé and, legend has it, refused for many years to believe that he was dead. Eventually she became a nun, dying in California in 1857.

Voznesensky created his "poema" Avos' in 1970. Although the ship Avos' was not central to Rezanov's story, Voznesensky seems to have used the name as his title because its connotations are perfect for what he wished to express. To do something "na avos'" means to do it in a stereotypically Russian way – impulsively, on faith, without too much calculation as to risks and rewards. The central themes Voznesensky explores here are typically Romantic and focus on Rezanov's search for something new and different than he can find in Russia: thus, the poema focuses on the joy of adventure, travel, mobility, the tragic disjunction of Russia and the West along with, of course, tragically unfulfilled love. In the post-Thaw USSR such themes resonated powerfully among an intelligentsia that felt stifled and isolated.

The generic tag "poema" has historically been used in the Russian tradition to describe longish narratives in verse. Some of the most famous such pieces include Pushkin's masterpieces *Ruslan and Liudmila*, *The Bronze Horseman*, and *Poltava*, Nekrasov's *Russian Women*, Mayakovsky's *Vladimir Ilich Lenin*, and Akhmatova's *Poem without a Hero*. This poem is certainly not on the same level as those distinguished predecessors, and it did not make an enormous impression. Nevertheless, it is noteworthy for its polyphonic use of various voices, including excerpts from original contemporary documents, lyrics from the perspective of Rezanov, Concepcion, a stylized sailors' ballad, poetic dialogues between the captains of Rezanov's ships, and meta-historical commentary on the historical material by some "archive rats." Perhaps the most interesting segment of the poem is the seventh section, an imagined letter in verse from Rezanov to Derzhavin (with whom Rezanov had worked in the early 1790s). Recalling the famous topic of the "poetic monument," Voznesensky begins his second stanza with a line that any Russian schoolboy would recognize as a partial quotation from Pushkin's "Exegi monumentum" (derived originally from Horace and transposed into Russian by Lomonosov and Derzhavin in the eighteenth century) – "I've raised myself a monument, amazing and eternal." Voznesensky continues:

> I am the last poet of civilization,
> Not our Roman one but civilization in general.
> In an age of spiritual crisis
> Culture is the most shameful thing.
>
> It is shameful to recognize injustice and not to name it,
> and, having named it, shameful not to eliminate it.
> It is shameful to call a funeral a wedding,
> and to make funny faces at a funeral.
>
> My contemporaries will kill me for these words,
> while some future afro-euro-americano-asian
> will rip my foundation from the ground
> and leave a gaping hole in the planet.[25]

Though in principle these lines are written by Rezanov, contemporary Russian readers of the 1970s and 1980s would have had little difficulty recognizing that they can also be read as Voznesensky's commentary on his own time and place. Reading between the lines was a time-honored tradition in a society in which information was carefully controlled, and Russian authors have frequently been skilled at the use of what they call "Aesopian language." In this case, one can plausibly see Voznesensky commenting on his own position – the last poet of world civilization who is constrained to see injustice but not comment (except in this coded form) and to pretend that things are their opposite. He recognizes that many of his contemporaries cannot accept this and looks to a time when a synthetic world culture (Afro-Euro-American-Asian) might come along to swallow up his Russian monument, though nevertheless leaving the trace of its absence behind.

Although the poema "Avos'" failed to make an enormous impression, the "opera-mystery" *Juno and Avos'* (1980, music by Alexei Rybnikov, libretto by Voznesensky) based on it was one of the most popular late Soviet theatrical productions, and has been performed more than 700 times since its premiere at the Lenin Komsomol Theatre in 1981. It can be difficult in the early twenty-first century to appreciate why this work, produced at the height of the Brezhnev "years of stagnation" not long after the Soviet invasion of Afghanistan had put an end to the so-called period of détente with the West, struck such a chord with Russian audiences. The music, though it does employ electric guitars and a synthesizer, seems decidedly tame, the story line is sentimental, and the lyrics generally fail to sparkle. Nevertheless, contemporaries perceived the production, by director Mark Zakharov, as daring, and they recognized that Voznesensky's libretto had pushed right up to the edge of what was allowable in the USSR (indeed, the censors demanded that a number of scenes be cut before they would authorize the performance). A contemporary dispatch filed by one of *Time* magazine's Russian correspondents helps capture some of the atmosphere:

> The roar throbbing through the rafters of Moscow's Lenin Komsomol Theater was loud enough to rouse the Soviet Union's founding father in his Kremlin mausoleum. After two decades of sparring with the Soviet authorities, hard rock had triumphantly taken the Lenin stage. The occasion was the premiere of the country's first rock opera, Juno and Avos, by Alexei Rybnikov, a popular composer of movie scores. In addition to guitars, violins, cellos, drum and a chorus of 16, Rybnikov called for electronic instruments – including a Multimoog synthesizer and a Roland paraphonic – rarely used before in the USSR. The opera was a bold blend of hard-rock rhythms, shimmering folk melodies and traditional Russian Orthodox Church chants.[26]

Some of Voznesensky's lines undoubtedly captured the emotions of the intelligentsia of his generation, which was deeply disappointed by the turn that Russia had taken in the post-Thaw years but were not happy with the West either: "The Russian empire is a jail, but its a mess abroad as well," sings Rezanov at one point.[27] Most poignant of all for listeners who knew how hard Voznesensky had worked to liberalize Soviet culture (he had, for example, befriended the Amercan "Beatnik" poets and publicized their work in Russia) were the last lines of the opera's second act, spoken one of Rezanov's officers: "Having taken the bit between his teeth he dreamed of bringing America and Russia close together. The attempt failed, but we're thankful he tried."[28]

Straddling the fine line between the official and the dissident, Voznesensky's work illustrates a relatively rare success of an author balancing at the knife's edge in the complex cultural environment of the waning years of the USSR. This was a balance that became distressingly difficult to achieve with failures on both sides. On one hand in this regard, it is worth mentioning the almanac *Metropol* (1979) produced by a number of leading former official writers as well as some young rising stars who hoped to publish the work officially. Their failure to convince the authorities to allow them to publish and the subsequent publication of the work abroad led to severe consequences for a number of the participants. On the other extreme, one might cite the almost universally reviled collection *Mama and the Neutron Bomb* by Evgeny Evtushenko, which showed that what the state would permit could increasingly not pass muster with unofficial circles.

10

Instead of the Apocalypse: Russian Culture Today

I

In 1985, after the death in rapid succession of three superannuated leaders, the Communist Party of the USSR appointed Mikhail Gorbachev to the position of First Secretary. Almost immediately, the new leader introduced a series of changes meant to solve the economic, social and cultural malaise that had been afflicting the country for the previous decade and a half. The two watchwords of Gorbachev's new deal for the USSR were "glasnost" (openness, transparency) and "perestroika" (restructuring). In the course of the next six years, these twin processes would lead not to Gorbachev's hoped for renewal of the USSR and its version of Marxist-Leninist society but rather to its collapse in 1991 under the leadership of Gorbachev's successor Boris Yeltsin.

The demise of the system that had directly controlled some one-sixth of the globe's surface and had both predicted and attempted to realize the triumph of communism throughout the world had enormous political, social, economic, and cultural repercussions both within and without the USSR. In the new conditions of post-communism, all the standards that had dominated the state for so long broke down, particularly in the anarchic years from 1991 to 1998. The former "republics" of the USSR declared and received their independence, creating fifteen sovereign national states, including Russia, which reappeared on the map as an independent country for the first time since 1918; within the Russian Federation itself, multi-party elections became the norm and the Communist Party fell from power; state control of the economy loosened and then all but disappeared allowing insiders to amass enormous fortunes through corrupt privatization schemes, while the evaporation of state-supported entitlement programs and services led to a sharp deterioration in the already low material standard of living for much of the population; the oppressive control over daily life vested in the state and enforced by the KGB disappeared, but in its absence petty crime and mafia-style protection rackets proliferated;

the monolithic state-sponsored ideology fragmented (as did that of its almost equally monolithic dissident opponents), and a confusing free-for-all followed in which Western-style popular culture, Russian Orthodox revivalism, strident nationalism, and entrepeneurship existed side-by-side with no seemingly dominant trend.

Beginning in the late 1990s, with the rise to power of Yeltsin's handpicked but democratically elected successor Vladimir Putin, the Russian state began gradually to reassert itself. Using income earned from the sale of Russia's enormous supply of raw materials (mostly oil and natural gas) the state began to exert ever-greater centralized control over the economy, effectively renationalizing much of Russia's industrial sector while allowing the private sector to flourish in the small business and the service sectors; the so-called oligarchs, who had amassed enormous wealth and power under Yeltsin and had lived largely outside the law, were brought to heel, either absorbed back into state structures or forced into exile or jail; Putin and his followers gradually eliminated political freedoms by a variety of means, most effectively through their takeover and muzzling of the independent media that had flourished under Yeltsin; although the monolithic value system of the Soviet era was not revived, the state and its agents engaged in sustained efforts to create a new, positive national image that would combine certain elements from the Soviet period with symbols and traditions from Tsarist Russia. By the middle of the first decade of the twenty-first century, Russia had come almost full circle, and while all observers would agree that contemporary Russia is not the USSR, in significant ways it looks far more like the USSR than like the Western democracies that were at least the ostensible model for many of the reformers who took power in the late 1980s and early 1990s.

II

Culture, and particularly literary culture, could not help but be enormously affected by the wild gyrations of the overall political and economic situation in the country. Literature and those who produced it had traditionally played an exceptionally important role in the USSR, which liked to boast that its citizens were the most avid readers on the planet. From the mid-1950s until the 1980s, as we described in the previous chapter, a relatively stable bi-polar cultural sphere had become the norm. On the one side were official writers, members of the Writers' Union and heirs to the "engineers of human souls" of the Stalinist period. They could publish in the major journals (which had large circulations and paid high honoraria) and with the state-owned publishing companies that controlled 100 percent of the book market. The best of them were household names throughout the USSR and had the privilege of representing the state in delegations abroad, terra incognita for the average Soviet citizen. In exchange, they were expected to uphold existing cultural norms, focusing in their novels, poems, and plays on presenting an optimistic view of society in accessible, formally unchallenging ways. In opposition were a relatively small group of so-called dissident writers, who lived at the margin of Soviet cultural life (though they were often indirectly supported by official state institutions) and who were united by their unwillingness or inability to comply with the expectations of the state's censorship apparatus. These writers could not generally publish their work openly, and they circulated it in hand-typed copies (samizdat) and/or smuggled it out of the country for publication abroad (tamizdat). Although there had been a fair amount of flexibility during the so-called thaw years of the late 1950s and early 1960s, by the late 1970s and early 1980s, the cultural system had become quite sclerotic. The lines between official and non-official writing became more clearly marked, the grey area between the two spheres harder to occupy, and the quality of writing, especially official writing, took a turn for the worse.

III

Between the late 1920s and the early 1970s, the borders of the USSR had been all but closed for the majority of citizens. By the mid-1970s, however, two categories of people were permitted to leave the country and this set the stage for a revival of Russian-language writing outside of Russia. The first category included those whom the authorities wished to remove from the body politic but who were too well known simply to jail – these included a number of leading writers: Alexander Solzhenitsyn, Andrei Siniavsky, Iosif Brodsky, and Vasily Aksenov as well as other outspoken cultural figures such as the great cellist Mstislav Rostropovich. In addition, Jews, who often felt discriminated against in the USSR were allowed to apply to leave for Israel and many, including many writers, took advantage of this opportunity. By the late 1970s and into the 1980s a lively literary life was underway in the United States and Western Europe. Journals such as the Paris-based *Kontinent* published important literary work, as did the US-based Ardis and Paris-based YMCA publishing houses. Among notable works by already well-known authors that appeared outside of Russia in this period were Aksenov's novels *The Burn* (Ozhog) and *The Island of Crimea* (Ostrov Krym), Siniavsky's *Good Night* (Spokoinoi nochi) and Voinovich's *Ivankiada*. Important younger writers, who had been practically or completely unknown in the USSR, including Sergei Dovlatov (1941–90), Eduard Limonov (born 1943), and Sasha Sokolov (born 1943), also captured the attention of émigré publishers and readers.

Meanwhile, in the late 1970s and early 1980s in the USSR a new generation of writers began to emerge. Having come of age after the end of the Thaw, they were never able to have the broad cultural and social impact of those who were born in the 1930s and 1940s. Nevertheless, many talented prose writers appeared, as did two important groups of poets. Perhaps the most important prose writers of the late 1970s and early 1980s were women including Liudmila Petrushevskaia (born 1938) and Tatiana Tolstaia (born 1951). Petrushevskaia is a master of short prose, and her laconic stories, usually told from a woman's point of view and concerning the particularly difficult position of Soviet women, were among the most effective literary works produced (though generally not published) in the late Soviet period.

Poetry in this period was dominated by two groups which came to be known as the Conceptualists and the Metarealists. The former grew out of a visual arts movement and took as its central principle the inescapability of Soviet language. Its practitioners attempted to use that language against itself (to deconstruct it) in order to attack its stultifying effects on society. Poetry by such writers as Dmitry Alexandrovich Prigov (1940–2007) and Lev Rubinstein (born 1947) tended to be constructed almost entirely of Soviet clichés deployed in such a way as to undermine and ridicule the verbal formulae by making them strange. The following Prigov poem, produced at the height of the Soviet Union's response to the Reagan administration's "evil empire" campaign, illustrates beautifully the methods of conceptualist poetry. Though the language is completely banal and formulaic, the way in which stock Soviet phrases are combined with a very small amount of other material creates an ironic twist on the sorts of commonplaces that appeared daily in the Soviet press:

> Reagan doesn't want to feed us
> Well, OK, it's really his mistake
> It's only over there that they believe
> You've got to eat to live.
>
> But we don't need his bread
> We'll live on our idea

It'll come to him quite suddenly: Hey, where are they?
But we've already gotten to his heart.

The Metarealist group, on the other hand, was concerned with exploring the possibilities of poetic form and language to create outside of the boring realities of Soviet life. The work of writers such as Alexei Parshchikov (born 1954), Ilya Kutik (born 1961), and Ivan Zhdanov (born 1948) bursts with creative energy and builds on the best traditions of Russian verse as seen in this short lyric by Kutik:

> From Catullus
>
> > *. . . but can a cat know about Catullus?*
>
> The sparrow died, and neither earth nor heaven
> can resurrect her . . . She twisted her head
> back, like the number 7,
> and turned into 0.
>
> And I thought, standing above the avian text,
> the splayed out sparrow,
> that – by the logic of the auspex –
> we should live to seventy.
>
> If it works out

IV

Most Russian writers, with the exception perhaps of the most conservative elite, welcomed Gorbachev's "glasnost" initiative and the eventual collapse of the USSR. Liberated by the fall of communism of demands to do the impossible, writers in the early 1990s dared to dream of life in a "normal society" in which they could become "just writers," free to create whatever and however they wished. Many looked forward to giving up what many had come to see as the heavy burden of being spokespeople for the nation, prophets, and gadflies. The psychological difficulty of this role was expressed beautifully by Prigov: "Here's me, an ordinary poet let's assume / But the thing is that by the whim of Russian fate / I have to be the conscience of the nation / But how to be that thing, if there is no conscience / Poems, maybe, there are, but a conscience – no / What is to be done?"[1] Prigov is a supreme ironist, and the poem is meant to poke fun at the self-importance of Russian writers. Nevertheless, the irony only works because of the more or less equal strength of the verbal reality expressed by the cliché (the demand to be the nation's conscience). Few if any writers recognized that in many respects, the situation for writers and writing would become significantly more difficult and complex than it had been under the Communist regime which had, for all its faults, supported an extraordinarily large number of writers (directly or indirectly), shielded them from outside competition (particularly from the competition of popular culture), and insulated them from market forces that had no interest in or appreciation for their work.

As the changes in Soviet society began with practically no warning, producers of literature required some time to react and thus new works taking advantage of the freedoms allowed took some time to appear. Even when they did, however, they were drowned out in a flood of publications and republications of "lost classics" that inundated the Russian literary market in the period from 1985–91. These included the works of émigré writers like Nabokov, whose novels had never been published in the USSR, the prose and poetry of Russian modernism, which had been suppressed since the early 1930s, novels that had been written in the 1950s and 1960s but that had moldered unpublished in the USSR such as Pasternak's *Doctor Zhivago* and Vasily Grossman's (1905–64) the Second World War epic *Life and Fate* (Zhizn' i sud'ba, completed in 1959, published in 1980), the works of such living exiles as Alexander Solzhenitsyn including his *Gulag Archipelago* with its encyclopedic treatment of Stalin's prison-camp system, as well as an eclectic selection of writings by nineteenth and early twentieth-century Russian thinkers who had been banned for their conservative or religious affiliation.

In this environment, the production and dissemination of newly composed Russian literature became difficult for a number of reasons. In the immediate aftermath of 1991, in its quest to institute market reforms, the state trimmed the substantial subsidies formerly available to writers and to literary publications. At the same time, the state controlled distribution networks that had guaranteed that what was published could be sent all over the country through a series of state-owned stores and libraries collapsed completely. Simultaneously, economic restructuring had a catastrophic impact on the cash flow of Russian citizens – whereas under communism money was generally available but there was nothing to purchase, post-communism saw goods of all kinds become available as cash became scarce. Finally, although private publishing houses multiplied, the newly open publishing market led to a segmentation of the audience for literature. After the market for lost classics had been sated, beginning in the late 1980s and accelerating enormously in the first years of the 1990s, average Russian readers abandoned serious literature. Instead, they turned in droves to generally hack, pirate translations of Western popular literature. These included detective novels and science fiction, both of which had existed at the margins of Soviet literary production, as well as genres that had never existed in the USSR: horror, romance, fantasy.

V

A few statistics help to illustrate the problems faced by writers of serious literature in Russia in the post-communist period. In the USSR in 1985, the average fee paid to an author for a novel was 8,000 rubles, or approximately four years' salary for an average Russian. Articles in the leading "fat journals" paid on the order of 200–300 rubles per signature (24 pages) for an article of 4–8 signatures. Thus, a 100-page critical article commanded almost a year's salary. Finally, translation, an activity in which even writers who were not members of the Union could engage, paid between 100 and 150 rubles for signature, meaning that a translation of a single short story could bring in the equivalent of a month's salary. And because members of the Writers' Union could access scarce consumer goods, including such big-ticket items as apartments and cars, at official state-subsidized prices (instead of having to resort to the black market like the majority of their fellow citizens), the fees they were paid were in effect even larger than they seem. In comparison, in the new market economy, the payment of fees is negotiated separately with each author – the value of an author to a publisher is in direct correlation to the success of his or her work, to popularity measured in sales. While a writer of detective or romance fiction can sell millions of copies in this market and make enormous amounts of money, the fees paid for serious novels are modest – averaging perhaps $1000 for a solid novel, while a major book by a famous author might reach $8,000–10,000.

The changes in the material position of non-official writers are more difficult to assess. They were, of course, unable to take advantage of the majority of perquisites available to official writers in the Soviet period. Nevertheless, they did benefit from the system in numerous ways; in terms of direct earnings from writing, many were able to earn at least an average salary from literary translations. Now, with the rates paid to translators having fallen as precipitously as all other fees for literary work, this method of earning a living has all but dried up. Unofficial writers also benefited from the over-employment characteristic of the USSR. Given that all publishing houses, editorial offices, and the like employed at least three times as many staff as they needed (at least by Western standards), those unofficial writers who were employed in the publishing sector did not have to work very hard for their paychecks. This afforded them significant free time for their writing, even if their work could not be published. Now, if they have not been laid off, they have to work to earn their salaries, leaving little time for writing. When they do write they now have the chance to see their work in print, but the fees paid are so small as to be almost laughable.

The book publishing industry reflects the enormous changes that have occurred in Russia since the collapse of communism. All told, in 1990 (a year in which the old state publishing plan was still effectively in place), some 41,000 titles were published in Russia in editions totaling more than one and a half billion copies. By 2000 the number of titles was 40,000, but the total number of books published had fallen to four hundred million. Overall, the number of books published per capita had fallen from ten to something like 2.8. In 1985, the large Russian publishing house *Sovremennik* brought out 365 titles with an average print run of 90,000 copies. Eighty percent of these were new with a large percentage in such high-prestige literary genres as poetry, fiction, and literary criticism. Books of poetry were published in editions of ten or 20,000 and fifty to 100,000 copy runs for novels were normal. Editions of this size ensured that the writer would receive a significant fee for his work. In 1999, however, *Sovremennik* published only twenty-eight titles with a total print run of 140,000 copies.

It would be incorrect to conclude, however, that all sectors of the Russian publishing industry are in the same dire straights as the traditional thick journals and the old-line publishing companies. New publishers, better attuned to the vagaries of the market, have appeared and have expanded rapidly. These publishers have come to recognize that the once almost monolithic audience has segmented rapidly and that no single author or type of literature can dominate public attention. Publishers, if they are to survive, must behave more like clothes manufacturers than arbiters of taste, and they can afford to support only those authors whose works reach a broad market. To some extent, then, the collapse of the old prestigious state firms (which have now been privatized) has been balanced by the rise of new firms with more flexible publishing ideas and a better feeling for the market. But that market will not bear fees for works of serious literature that are remotely sufficient to procure its producers even an average middle-class income.

VI

It is more difficult to measure fluctuations in the prestige attached to writing than it is to track changes in the material base. But it is nevertheless clear that the prestige of serious literature has fallen in Russia, albeit perhaps not as precipitously as the financial rewards available. One way to gauge the prestige attached to literature, at least in the public sphere, is to see how literary prizes are awarded and covered in the media. In the Soviet era the awards ceremony of prizes to Soviet authors took place in the Kremlin in a solemn event. Party leaders handed out medals, prizes, and other awards. The ceremonies were broadcast on State television and were noted on the evening TV news programs, on state radio, and in the major newspapers. By the year 2000 prizes in Russia had multiplied. Where once there had been only a few major prizes, some 600 literary prizes were offered in 2000. The numbers alone are an indication that no individual prize can capture the attention of the entire public.[2]

By the mid-1990s and into the twenty-first century Russian writers had begun to recognize the perils of the new society, and they began actively searching for solutions, starting with the accumulation of jobs, and ending with various forms of conversion of already acquired symbolic prestige into new positions, which, in turn, could bring more income and social visibility. Depending on circumstance, education, and reputation, writers have employed various strategies to convert their symbolic cultural capital into positions in politics, journalism, or the private sphere – some become free-lance writers, some editors, others are attracted to the relative safety of academic positions. However, as opposed to the Communist era, there is now an expectation that writers, editors, and professors will actually work for their salary, so available time for creative writing has drastically decreased. What is more, the salaries paid by academic and literary institutions are generally not high, so writers who choose this route must have one or two other jobs, and all this besides writing literature. Thus, although writing still carries sufficient prestige to attract new participants, the financial situation makes it increasingly likely that, for many, writing will become a hobby rather than a profession.

Perhaps the most difficult and intriguing question that arises after a consideration of the radical changes that have taken place in the material and social conditions of writing in Russia since 1989 is how they have affected literary production. While it is intuitively obvious that they must have had some effect, we want to avoid the kind of vulgar sociology (itself so prevalent in literary criticism of the Communist era) that would draw a straight line between material conditions of writing and literary output. Taking a broad look at Russian literary production of the past fifteen years, it is reasonable to say that two central, interrelated questions emerge: what is the role of the writer and of serious literature given that for the first time in more than 200 years literature cannot play the role of "the conscience of the nation" and what should the relationship be between contemporary Russian literature and a literary tradition, that, for all the enormous changes between the eighteenth century and the end of the USSR, embodied precisely those roles?

Event – The Return of the Repressed – Opening the KGB's Literary Archives

The Soviet state had the peculiar ability to make an unwanted person, event, or thing disappear. With complete control over all forms of media it was possible to ensure that "enemies of the state" could be broadly attacked and then, after their arrest or exile, never mentioned again. Furthermore, in the Stalinist period those who fell foul of the state could be and were removed from history – their images were airbrushed out of photographs, their deeds were expunged from histories, and the original documents that provided a record were buried deep in secret inaccessible archives. Perhaps the most famous such case was Leon Trotsky, after Lenin the most celebrated of the early Bolshevik leaders. After losing a power struggle with Stalin, he was vilified, exiled, and eventually murdered, his achievements as Commissar for Defense during the Civil War and as a Bolshevik theoretician were written out of Stalinist-era histories, and by the 1950s it would have been next to impossible to find his picture anywhere in the USSR.

In the cultural sphere, the situation was no different. Major Russian writers and artists – émigrés, religiously inclined, and especially the modernists of the 1910s and 1920s, simply evaporated from Russian culture – their works became bibliographical rarities known only to narrow groups of specialists, they were removed from library catalogues and shelves, even their names went unmentioned in literary histories. Nor was this fate reserved only for the dead or for those whom the Stalinist state imprisoned or executed – even major living figures such as Akhmatova, Pasternak, and Platonov became virtual non-persons during the 1930s, 1940s and early 1950s; although they continued to live in the USSR and in many cases to write, their new work was not published, their old work was unavailable, and they eked out a living through translation and journalism.

To be sure, given the relatively short time span between the 1920s and 1950s, it was impossible to wipe the memory of major cultural figures from those who had lived through the earlier period, and one of the signs of the post-Stalinist thaw in the cultural arena was a cautious attempt to recall the names and to some extent rehabilitate the work of repressed artists, writers, and composers. Ilya Ehrenburg, for example, who had somehow managed to survive the purge years despite a dubious political past and many years spent in the West, began to publish his *People, Years, Life* (Liudi, Gody, Zhizn') in 1960; here he discussed the contributions of many writers who, for younger generations, were at most legendary names and whose work, for all practical purposes, did not exist, and attempted to write them back into the historical record. In this period as well, state publishing houses brought out limited edition collections of Akhmatova, Pasternak, and other modernist poets, as well as some prose works that had been written "for the desk drawer" such as Mikhail Bulgakov's *The Master and Margarita*. The last, published in a limited edition and in somewhat expurgated form in 1966, caused a major sensation. Nevertheless, an enormous amount of significant work remained unpublished and unknown in the USSR, and when the thaw came to an end in the mid-1960s, no further efforts to make it available to Soviet readers were undertaken until the mid-1980s.[3]

As we noted earlier, one of the first signs of "glasnost" was the appearance in the major thick journals and soon thereafter in books brought out by independent publishers (which were allowed to open by the end of the 1980s) of an enormous quantity of previously suppressed literary work. For a few years contemporary Russian literature did not consist of works written in the 1980s, but rather of a mish-mash of texts from the 1880s through the 1970s which were linked only by the fact that Soviet censors had been unwilling to approve them for publication: cheek-by-jowl readers could find Konstantin Leontiev (1831–91, suppressed for his right-wing political views), Mikhail Kuzmin (1872–1936), the first openly gay Russian writer, Pavel Florensky (1882–1937) and Nikolai Berdiaev philosophers silenced for their religious orientation, Daniil Kharms, whose absurdist short stories had never seen the light of day in Russia though they had appeared in the west in the 1970s, Vasily Grossman, whose *Life and Fate* portrayed the Second World War in non-canonical form, Anatoly Pristavkin (born 1931), whose novel *A Golden Cloud Spent the Night* (Nochevala tuchka zolotaia) depicted the deportation of whole peoples during the Stalinist period, Solzhenitsyn, Brodsky, as well as the work of a younger generation of émigrés such as Eduard Limonov and Sasha Sokolov. Soon thereafter came the cautious return of some of the writers themselves, either for short visits, or in the case of Solzhenitsyn and Limonov, for good.

Amidst all these returns, one of the most fascinating was a series of essays by a then obscure poet and journalist Vitaly Shentalinsky that began to appear in the early 1990s in journals like *Ogonek* and *Novyi mir* (which still had hundreds of thousands of subscribers at this time). Collected under the title of *Raby svobody. V literaturnykh arkhivakh KGB*, this book, which also appeared almost immediately in various other languages, concerned the fates of many of the most celebrated Russian writers of the 1920s and 1930s who had subsequently disappeared, in most cases killed by Stalin's secret police.[4]

Shentalinsky's own biography is noteworthy. Born in 1939 he toiled in obscurity as a journalist in the Soviet Far East. In the 1980s Shentalinsky managed to publish a number of collections of his poetry in Russia. None of them made an impression, and it is safe to say that while he may have been a sincere poet, Shentalinsky was never a particularly talented one. His verse is filled with uplifting sentiments, as well as exhortations to fellow artists and writers to work for the good and the beautiful, all wrapped in nineteenth-century verse forms.

Unlike many other officially published poets, however, Shentalinsky had a hidden talent, one he was never able to exercise in a socially useful way. For, although he worked as a journalist in the Far East and North, in this period journalists were even less free than poets to express their mind. This all began to change by the mid-1980s. And at least in one area, it was Shentalinsky who both heroically and courageously forced that change to go much further than its original architects wished, and who was able successfully to present the fruits of that change to a broad public.

It is telling that the best way Shentalinsky could think of to serve society was by forcing open the KGB archives devoted specifically to writers of literature and not, say, to those of agronomists or geneticists or any of a number of other professions whose ranks were decimated by Stalinist persecution. On the one hand, this choice presumably reflects his personal conviction, as a writer, that writers are a particularly important group to be resurrected in the search for truth. At the same time, the resonance that Shentalinsky's articles and book made illustrates that in Russia's highly litero-centric society, writers and their fate were generally recognized to be of central symbolic value.

Shentalinsky presents the material in a highly effective manner by combining excerpts culled directly from archival documents with imagined scenes based on those materials. Thus, the chapter devoted to Isaac Babel, the first in the book, begins: "16 May 1939. It is early morning and Moscow is still fast asleep. The only sounds are the peaceful chirruping of the birds and the caretaker's broom sweeping the courtyard."[5] After a few short dramatic paragraphs describing Babel's arrest, Shentalinsky writes: "Perhaps that is how Isaac Babel would have described such an episode, had he been allowed to finish the book he was writing about the Cheka. Instead, that

May morning he himself became a helpless prisoner of the NKVD, arrested on the orders of Lavrenty Beria." This fictional scene is amplified by materials quoted directly from Babel's dossier, including excerpts from the records of his cross-examination, the hand-written testimony he provided under torture, and the last photograph of the condemned.

Although most of this information merely fills in a picture that had been outlined earlier in other books devoted to the machinery of Stalin's terror, Shentalinsky is sufficiently attuned to the specifically literary aspects of the material to make some shrewd comments about Babel's situation. Thus, at one point he quotes a long passage from Babel's confession in which the author discusses remarks he made at a meeting with Soviet writers and filmmakers who had solicited his advice. After the quotation, Shentalinsky comments: "We hardly find any theoretical reflections about art and the role of the writer in Babel's books. He thought in images, like a poet. How much more important then, is this enforced exposition of his artistic credo for which the interrogators could find no use at all. Perhaps he committed it to paper because he sensed there would be no other chance. Perhaps there was even a secret calculation that one day, suddenly, his notes might be read by another reader, and not just his interrogators" (51). Shentalinsky, in effect, becomes the posthumous amanuensis of his subjects, the whole panoply of writers repressed by Stalin's terror.

He also attempts, with investigative journalistic finality, to provide the details of the execution in all cases in which a given writer was killed: "Today we know the exact date and even the hour when Babel died: 1:30 am on January 27, 1940. Babel's name was first in a list of sixteen to be executed. His remains were cremated the same day" (70). Shentalinsky's text, for all its obvious (and unconcealed) use of fictional devices, is meant to stand as the last word on the fate of each writer, at least insofar as the materials in the KGB archives can provide such a word. Each essay is a cenotaph, solid in its fact-based foundations, and replacing the previously unmarked graves in which the victims were buried.

But Shentalinsky does not discuss only those writers who were actually murdered by the Stalinist regime. Thus, in addition to Babel, Florensky (the only non-literary writer in Shentalinsky's first volume), Boris Pilniak, Osip Mandelstam, and the poet Nikolai Kliuev (1884–1937), he also considers the fates of writers who died in their beds and were never arrested such as Mikhail Bulgakov, Andrei Platonov, and Maxim Gorky. Each case is presented in a literary format appropriate to the subject matter. Thus, the section on Bulgakov, who despite his fame as the author of the novel *The Master and Margarita* was primarily a playwright, is entitled: "Under the Heel. The File on Mikhail Bulgakov: A Story in Six Acts with an Epilogue." It includes, in addition to the fictional recreations and documentary evidence provided in other sections, a number of scenes presented in dramatic form.

When writers were arrested or even investigated by the NKVD, their manuscripts were frequently arrested as well. Quoting Woland's famous line in *The Master and Margarita*, "manuscripts don't burn," many Russians expected that with the opening of the KGB files a number of lost masterpieces would reappear. Unfortunately, for the most part it turned out that manuscripts did indeed burn because as opposed to depositions they were not generally considered crucial to the cases against writers (in the Stalin era writers were not as a rule arrested for any specific literary work; and even when they were, they usually ended up being charged with belonging to fantastic Trotskyite conspiracies rather than producing seditious literature). Nevertheless, Shentalinsky did succeed in making literary discoveries in the KGB archives, and he interpolates excerpts from these into his texts as well, most notably in the chapters devoted to Nikolai Kliuev and Platonov.

Framing the stories devoted to Soviet writers in Shentalinsky's book is the story of the volume's composition. It begins with an invocation of the author's dacha in the waning days of the Soviet Union: "Night. A tranquil dacha outside Moscow."[6] This opening would be echoed at the beginning of the description of Babel's Peredelkino dacha. But the first chapter is devoted to Shentalinsky's fight to get access to the documents that would make up the meat of the book, as well as the organization of the committee that eventually forced the KGB to hand them over. The final chapter, by contrast, takes place after the demise of the Soviet Union and that of the Soviet Writers Union (which outlasted it), a demise, it is implied, that Shentalinsky's truth-telling exercise helped to bring about. In the end then, Shentalinsky's book is as much the story of a mediocre poet who had once implicitly supported the Soviet Union by writing verses extolling the natural beauty of Kolyma and later transformed himself into a crusading journalist who helped to destroy the Soviet Union by writing the biographies of some of those who lost their lives in Kolyma as it is the story of those writers themselves.

Literary Work – Boris Akunin's F.M.

Communist regimes disliked Western popular culture. In his study of popular fiction, Clive Bloom lays out some of the reasons: "No really authoritarian states can stand pulp culture. It reeks of anarchy and nonconformity and subversion. Thus authoritarian states ban such corruption and condemn rock 'n' roll, alongside comic books, erotic literature, fast food, Levi jeans, James Bond, US soap operas and Coca Cola . . . For Marxist-Leninism, spiritualism and rock 'n' roll were one and the same thing, not surprising that authoritarians can find themselves in Shakespeare and Dante but cannot tolerate Batman comics read by the lightning flashes of rock technology."[7] The problem with truly popular culture was, it would seem, twofold. First, it was spontaneous and therefore difficult to control from above. Perhaps even more important, the plurality of cultural values these forms implied went against the ideal of a single national culture that was the sine qua non of Communist social and cultural engineering.

Like all forbidden fruit, however, many products of Western popular culture acquired an aura of attractiveness in the USSR. The best-known such products were musical, at least in part because music needed little or no translation. Thus, jazz, pop, and Western rock and roll were reasonably well known, at least among relatively educated groups in Moscow and Leningrad by the 1970s. Western popular literature, by contrast, was almost completely inaccessible to Russian readers. For official and unofficial writers, despite their differences, did agree on a number of things, one of which was that literature should provide a system of values for the public at large. Western popular literature, which either aggressively denies the need to propagate values or propagates values that neither Communists nor dissidents would have approved of, simply had no space in the mental universe of Soviet elites. Official state publishers could not accept popular literature for the ideological reasons enumerated by Clive Bloom above. Nor could dissidents accept the seeming frivolity and lack of moral purpose in popular literature. While music could be smuggled in on LPs and reproduced by local musicians on improvised instruments, popular literature needed to be translated and published before it could reach an audience.[8] And, although some dissidents were willing to work for years to translate a forbidden classic like James Joyce's *Ulysses*, no one wanted to translate, say, romance novels, and so these almost never appeared in samizdat. As a result, the public that might have wished to read these works, less-sophisticated Russian readers who did not know foreign languages, never even knew of their existence.

All of this changed swiftly in the 1990s. Censorship disappeared, publishers needed to sell books, and they quickly discovered that there was an enormous pent-up appetite for Western pop culture. One of the characteristic new sights in this period, remarked by natives and visitors alike, was the profusion of kiosks and tables selling hundreds of new titles in genres like criminal fiction, detective stories, horror, and romance, that had never existed before. Mostly pirated, translated from English by teams of hacks, these books rapidly overwhelmed the local cultural production, and, to the dismay of former Communists and dissidents alike, became the reading matter for the masses. More than a decade later, although some continue to decry the popular culture invasion, more and more writers and publishers have realized that it is better to switch than fight. Thus, while the big imported names continue to sell well, local writers have busily begun to carve out their own market share, producing works that naturalize the genres of popular literature.

The most interesting phenomena of this type, however, are not direct knock-offs of Western pulp fiction, but rather works that make use of the genres of Western popular fiction while simultaneously lending them new and interesting twists. This seems to occur in part because "classically trained" writers who turn to popular genres can still draw on a broad range of literary culture even as they produce books for a mass market. They possess the cultural resources to do so because their own literary training was heavily litero-centric. And, even more important, they know that their potential readers went through this same educational system and can thus appreciate a certain level of literary sophistication. Furthermore, they recognize that many readers want to enjoy the pleasures of popular fiction but would be embarrassed to be seen buying or reading a Harlequin romance or a novel by Steven King. Exploiting this niche, if they are sufficiently clever, this new breed of writer can satisfy the hunger of many Russian readers for popular and exciting genres while cloaking their writing in a halo of respectable literariness. Ultimately, the best of them produce works that blur the boundaries between popular and high-brow literature to create strangely attractive, extremely self-conscious hybrids. Among the most interesting writers of this type is Boris Akunin. Here, we will focus on his recent novel *F.M.*

Akunin's biography and his literary works provide a perfect example of the complex ways in which contemporary Russian culture has attempted to come to terms with the past. Akunin is a pseudonym for the Russified Georgian Grigory Chkhartishvili (born 1956). Chkhartishvili came of age in the midst of the period of stagnation, the second generation of Leonid Brezhnev's rule over an increasingly sclerotic USSR. After graduating from Moscow University's Institute for Asia and Africa, Chkhartishvili became one of Russia's leading experts on Japanese literature. Although he was known as a translator of writers such as Yukio Mishima and Kobe Abe, and became an editor at the prestigious journal *Foreign Literature* (Inostrannaia literatura) in the mid 1980s, he did not show any signs of creative talent.

Beginning in 1998, however, under his pseudonym (which evokes both the famous nineteenth-century Russian anarchist Mikhail Bakunin and the Japanese word for evil guy), Akunin has produced a string of detective novels that have enjoyed both critical acclaim and widespread popularity with Russian readers.

The novels of Akunin's best-known series, the so-called "Fandorin" cycle linked by the actions of the detective hero Erast Petrovich Fandorin, illustrate the keys to the author's success among the mass public. First there is the time period in which the novels are set: Russia in the second half of the nineteenth century. They are thus both detective novels and historical novels. The period they describe is one that Russian readers have come to see as a kind of golden age – the years just before the Bolshevik revolution. The novels project a definite nostalgia for a lost world of manners, aristocratic privilege, and order. Within this world, Erast Fandorin acts as a detective magician. With his knowledge of all world languages, his phenomenal physical strength and ability to disguise himself (i.e. his perfect control of his own body), his Sherlock-Holmes-like logical capacity, his personal charm combined with aloof independence, and his dogged determination, Fandorin embodies a number of the qualities that post-Soviet Russians admire and wish to emulate. What is more, the novels in this series are written in a style that, while by no means primitive, is readable for anyone with a Soviet high-school education. And, as all good detective novels do, Akunin's feature exciting plots, situations of high drama and intrigue, and the pleasant challenge of figuring out whodunit.

At the same time, the novels and their author offer a great deal more to the well-educated member of the intelligentsia, and this helps to explain their impressive "crossover" potential. To see what else they offer, we must turn to the category of intellectual and literary play. For this purpose, let us examine one of Akunin's most recent novels: *F.M.* (2006). This work is set in contemporary Moscow and the detective is Erast Fandorin's grandson, Nicholas, London-born and bred but who returned to Moscow in the mid-1990s to set up a private detective agency. The plot revolves around the discovery, loss, and ultimate recovery of a previously unknown manuscript of an early draft of Dostoevsky's *Crime and Punishment*. Akunin sets his novel on parallel tracks, one involving contemporary life in Moscow, and the other the world of Dostoevsky, although the two tend to bleed into each other at times.

The manuscript, we are told, was discovered by Boris Filipovich Morozov, a Dostoevsky specialist who, like many members of the Soviet intelligentsia, fell on hard times in the post Soviet period. He needs money to pay for the treatment of his son Iliusha (presumably named after the ill boy in *The Brothers Karamazov* [nomen ist omen]). Through a complex series of plot turns, the manuscript is divided into four pieces, each of which finds its way into the hands of a different sort of contemporary Muscovite (a drug addict, a dealer in old manuscripts, a fashionable literary agent, a book publisher). Morozov, who was hit over the head by the drug addict who stole the first portion of the manuscript, is in a rehabilitation hospital presided over by Mark Donatovich Zits-Korovin, whose patients also include Oleg, the son of a New Russian millionaire and parliamentarian Arkady Sergeevich Sivukha. Fandorin attempts to recover the manuscript for Sivukha by following clues provided by the insane Morozov, while Oleg, working in parallel, tries to do the same. In the end, the manuscript is recovered, in part by Fandorin and in part by Oleg, who is revealed to be a deranged murderer. Along the way, Akunin provides a running commentary on commercialized, everything goes contemporary Moscow, and weaves a complex and often compelling detective plot filled with unexpected twists.

Simultaneously, for the serious reader Akunin provides the "actual unknown Dostoevsky manuscript" in toto. This version of the story, entitled *Teoriika* (A Little Theory) follows the basic events of *Crime and Punishment* fairly closely, but the central focus is on the detective Porfiry Petrovich rather than on Raskolnikov. The text is written in pseudo-Dostoevskian style, far different from the hard-boiled and slang-laden contemporary Russian of the scenes set in contemporary Moscow. And, unexpectedly, the murderer turns out to be not Raskolnikov but Svidrigailov, who is aware of Raskolnikov's famous "Napoleonic" theory but has carried its calculus one step further. The manuscript ends with Svidrigailov about to commit suicide, but the passage is crossed out and followed by "Dostoevsky's" words: "I can't go on! This is all nonsense! It shouldn't be like this, or about this! Start it differently" (vol. 2, 240). This is followed immediately by the first paragraph of the canonical version of the novel. For greater authenticity, Akunin provides a facsimile of the "actual" page of Dostoevsky's hand-written manuscript on the facing page.

Given that *Crime and Punishment* was part of the required school literature curriculum, Akunin can be sure that even the least educated of his readers has some basic awareness of the ways in which this "new text" differs from the published version; but he clearly expects that his most educated readers will get the greatest enjoyment from noting all the little details he has put into this literary mystification. Nor is *Crime and Punishment* the only classical text to play a role in *F.M.* The discerning reader will, for example, recognize references to other works of Dostoevsky, and, in the relationship between

Fandorin, his wife Altyn, and her piano teacher, echoes of Tolstoy's "The Kreutzer Sonata" as well.

Akunin's novels, then, can be seen as an original solution for connecting contemporary Russian reality and the literary past. Building on the legacy of classical Russian literature, Akunin is creating space in Russian culture for a new kind of reader, one who is aware of the major achievements of the past but who reads primarily for enjoyment in a culture that is less literocentric and expects less from literature than at any time since the eighteenth century.

Biography – Eduard Limonov

Eduard Limonov was born Eduard Veniaminovich Savenko in Dzerzhinsk in 1943. He originally made his mark as a writer in emigration in New York but after the collapse of the Soviet Union he returned to Russia where he has thrown himself into politics as the leader of the opposition National Bolshevik party. Thus, his life trajectory provides an illustration of at least one writer's frustration with the limits of literature in post-Communist Russia.

Limonov spent his youth in Kharkov where his father was an officer in the local KGB. A rebel all his life, he says that between the ages of fifteen and twenty-one "[I was] a real criminal, breaking into stores and apartments. I stopped only when my close friend Konstantin B. was arrested and sentenced to death."[9] In 1967, he moved to Moscow where he rapidly made a name for himself among unofficial poets and writers. A glance at the poetry from that period published subsequently in emigration indicates just how restrictive the Soviet post-thaw censorship had become, for there is nothing in either form or content that is particularly dissident. Rather, most of his work is quite lyrical and, other than a youthful restlessness and arrogance, lacks any hint of an oppositionist political stance.

> Having broken with the shadows of his family
> why does he run from his homeland
>
> Why doesn't he just head to the store with a shopping bag
> Strolling unhurriedly
> A genius among dolts?
> But then his soul would fall silent.[10]

Nevertheless, as he was not willing to let his soul fall silent in the years of Brezhnevian stagnation, Limonov took the opportunity to leave the USSR when it was offered in 1974. He himself, however, has said: "I was never a dissident . . . I never expressed any opposition to the politics of the USSR or against its ideology. I simply struggled for the expansion of artistic freedom."[11]

There is some evidence that Limonov expected to be welcomed as a kind of savior in the West, at least if his poem "My – natsionalnyi geroi" (We are the National Hero) published only in 1977 but written earlier, can be taken as evidence of the author's own point of view. Here, Limonov imagines the ecstatic reception that he and his then-wife, the Moscow poet Elena Shchapova, will receive in the West. By 1975, having failed to make much of an impression in the "free world," Limonov was living in New York, where he developed a deep revulsion to the American way of life. Unlike such dissidents as Solzhenitsyn, however, who walled themselves off from day-to-day life in the United States and whose distaste for American civilization was based more on theoretical than observational grounds, Limonov lived among the poor Russian and other émigrés of New York, and he frequently and brilliantly wrote about that life in his pseudo-autobiographical novels and stories.

A polemical essay that Limonov wrote against fellow-immigrant Iosif Brodsky helps to define his position in the West. Brodsky, in Limonov's self-proclaimed non-conformist vision, should be seen as "a charlatan." Limonov attacks Brodsky's poetry as well as his life style in a series of provocative slaps: "More and more his poems recall catalogues . . . He is a poetic bureaucrat, a poetic bookkeeper . . . Brodsky's exile is the imposing, elegant, decadent exile of monied people. Geographically speaking, it encompasses Venice, Rome, and London, it includes museums, churches, and the streets of Europe's capitals, excellent hotels. Of the hundreds of Russian immigrant poets only Brodsky has managed to achieve a lifestyle that allows him to think and travel . . . Brodsky's poetry is destined to be the subject of doctoral dissertations written by conformists in the Slavic departments of American universities."[12]

By contrast one could define Limonov's entire literary output during his Western exile as an exercise in non-conformist self-fashioning. A Limonov alter-ego, generally called Edichka, appears as the main character in much of his work, some of which is narrated in the first person, and some in the third. It is impossible and unnecessary to know whether all the descriptions in the novels and stories are in fact autobiographical, but there is no question that readers are meant to see the whole package as a portrait of the artist as the hero of an on-going story. That is, Limonov's central topic is the creation of himself as a larger than life hero. His self-image is that of an iconoclast, a rebel with or without a cause, and a misunderstood genius.

In the Soviet Union, that hero could be an anti-establishment bohemian. In the United States he was an individualistic Russian who refused to succumb to the blandishments of Western-style capitalism. Until the beginning of the 1990s, readers could easily imagine that this was merely Limonov's literary persona, and that some other Limonov could conceivably be hiding behind it. However, events of the past decade would seem to indicate that Limonov took this posing seriously.

Limonov achieved lasting notoriety among Russian readers with the publication of his pseudo-autobiography *It's Me, Eddie* (Eto ia, Edichka) in New York in 1979. The book opens with a stunning scene describing a half-naked Edichka sitting on the balcony of his cheap long-term sixteenth-floor hotel room in Manhattan cooking cabbage soup, and musing on himself and his own unrecognized genius, the venality and stupidity of Americans, and the disappointment of a Russian émigré (and through him of all Russian émigrés) with American life. The tone is raw, the language a brilliant idiolect of Americanized Russian, and the book seems precisely designed to be as scandalous as possible. Russian émigré readers were horrified by its negativity and ingratitude toward the United States, its frank portrayal of the narrator's / author's bisexuality, and the implication that in escaping the USSR they had merely exchanged one form of exploitation for another. Limonov's raw hatred of those who have made it (in the Soviet, American, or post-Soviet Russian establishment) characterizes his life and work, and helps to explain the extreme political position he would eventually espouse in post-Soviet Russia.

Limonov's literary career continued with a string of novels and stories, two set in his native Ukraine (including his masterpiece *Adolescent Savenko, 1983* (Podrostok Savenko), and others set in the United States and Europe. A few were translated into English, but perhaps not surprisingly given his negative view of the United States, he never became as well known as some other émigré novelists. He did, however, make an impact in France, where he became a citizen in 1987 and began to spend the majority of his time in Europe. After the collapse of the USSR, however, Limonov became more and more active in the political life of post-Communist Russia.

As was the case with *Eddie*, what is most striking in the Kharkov-based autobiographical novels is the extravagant, epic, and theatrical nature of the self that Limonov projects. Limonov's persona is Mayakovskian in his grandeur and conceit. What is important, what is foregrounded is the transgressive, and this is flouted as publicly as possible. As Patricia Carden noted in an insightful essay on Limonov's Kharkov novels, "At fifteen he prides himself that 'he has fucked them all over,' that he has established his specialness and his dominance."[13]

Limonov's motivations for turning from literary work to politics are worth considering. His own public view, as expressed in interviews, is that the switch was not surprising. "Political work is the natural continuation of what I did when I was a writer. The writing of pamphlets and revolutionary articles provides just as much passionate pleasure as I once got writing poetry. Then and now I serve Russia. Don't forget, my first book of poems was called "Russianness." [14] His claim, then, is that in the days of the Soviet Union the best way to serve his country was as a writer of literature, but in conditions of post-communism direct political action is more necessary and appropriate. Less sympathetic observers agree that Limonov's post-Soviet political adventure is in a sense a natural continuation of his earlier work, but they view the work in progress in more personal and less altruistic terms. Thus, Evgeny Bunimovich, Moscow Duma deputy and poet said in a 1999 interview: "Limonov is connected not to the creation of a Russian national idea, but to the creation of a personal literary myth.[15] An even more cynical observer might suspect that, given the falling visibility of literature in post-Communist times, the switch to politics was motivated first and foremost by Limonov's ongoing desire to be in the public eye, to be a hero, and to shock. This desire, one might guess, was one of the motivations for taking up the most extreme positions he could find, regardless of whether they had the support of a significant portion of the population. The uncalculating nature of Limonov's politics can be gauged by his abject failure at the ballot box, where, for example, he received exactly 1.84 percent of the votes cast for a seat in the State Duma in the 1995 elections.

It took a while for Limonov to find his place in political life. Rather than beginning immediately, he edged into politics through journalism. As he puts it in his 2002 "political biography," the goal of his immediate post-Soviet articles was "to explain to my countrymen that they were insane and that they should stop the insanity. That European prosperity had been achieved gradually, over hundreds of years, at the cost of the pitiless exploitation of colonies. That projects like 'Five Hundred Days' were completely unrealistic."[16] At the same time he began to travel to Russia and renewed his Russian citizenship in 1992. From the beginning, he sided with Russian nationalist political forces, at first joining Vladimir Zhirinovsky's Liberal-Democratic Party (LDP) where for a time he was announced as a member of its shadow cabinet. Quite quickly, however, he fell out with Zhirinovsky and attempted to form his own party. He burnished his credentials as a defender of Russia's historical interests by traveling to the former

Yugoslavia where he had himself photographed with Bosnian Serb forces in a variety of warlike poses.

In 1994, after returning once again to Russia, he became one of the founders of the National Bolshevik Party. The party's program, couched in highly inflammatory rhetoric, can be characterized as communitarian, conservative, authoritarian, and nationalist, a mix of fascist and Communist ideologies. The preamble announces that "the basis of national-bolshevism is a fiery hatred to the anti-human trinity of liberalism / democracy / capitalism," and it promises to "construct a traditional, hierarchical society."[17] This will be realized in an "empire that stretches from Vladivostok to Gibraltar on the foundation of Russian civilization." The party's economic policy is one of strict economic autarchy. Within the country the NBP promises to realize the Soviet ideals of collective ownership of all the major means of production, along with guaranteed minimum living standards.

Limonov's own heroes are a curious amalgam of Russian conservatives like Konstantin Leontiev, anarchists such as Mikhail Bakunin, and leftists such as Lenin. Describing the men and women who joined the party, Limonov writes: "You are young. You are disgusted by the Russia of priests, moneybags, and the KGB. You experience a feeling of protest, your heroes are Che, or Mussolini, or Lenin, or Baader, or even Timothy McVeigh (he got his revenge on the system!), you are a nats-bol."[18] The only trace of the irony and humor that once characterized Limonov's literary work is the National Bolshevik Party symbol, an apparently about-to-explode grenade of a type called "Limonka" (little lemon) in Russian, which is simultaneously a play on the author's literary pseudonym.

When Limonov first entered politics, it is safe to say that many saw his engagement as a kind of stunt, the actions of a publicity-seeking writer who could no longer attract attention through his literary work. Limonov's fate since Vladimir Putin took over as President of Russia indicates that, whatever his initial motivations, he has come to take himself seriously, at least if a willingness to suffer for the cause can be understood as seriousness of purpose. Limonov and his Party had already run into a certain amount of legal hot water during the later years of Yeltsin's presidential term. Thus, in 1996 his newspaper was accused of fanning hatred against various nations, which is a crime in Russia. Much more serious, however, were the accusations brought against Limonov in October, 2001, when he was arrested and accused of "organizing an illegal armed formation." On February 3, 2003 (the wheels of justice in Russia turn slowly), in Saratov district court, Limonov was found guilty of most of the charges brought against him and the state prosecutor recommended a fourteen-year prison sentence for the writer turned politician. According to the *RFE/RL Newsline*, in a subsequent interview with a Saratov television station, "Limonov said that he is being prosecuted in the same way as the nineteenth-century writer Nikolai Chernyshevskii. 'After Soviet power, after seventy years of the dictatorship of the proletariat, we see that our valiant special services have turned to the methods of 140 years ago and the time of Chernyshevskii.'"[19] Perhaps Limonov's invocation of the famous Russian radical novelist and literary critic is an indication that he will eventually return to literature. Whether or not he chooses that path, he has certainly come to understand that one difference between literature and politics is that powerful enemies in the latter sphere have far more power than those of the former. Limonov's life story, then, illustrates the high risks of attempting to transpose a literary mode of being directly into a political, and his fate indicates that farce can indeed turn into tragedy.[20]

Conclusion
Whither Russian Literature

Over an almost 250-year period, from the late eighteenth century until the end of the Soviet experiment in 1991, Russian literature held a uniquely powerful position in society. In the almost complete absence of Western liberal democracy in the political sphere, literature came to be the locus of discussion for many of society's most burning issues and a central vehicle for the development of social values. The reading public, tiny at the beginning of this period and quite large by the end, looked to writers for definitions of Russia's national identity as well as for models of personal behavior. Although writers sometimes chafed at society's expectation to produce literature relevant to everyday concerns and at the desire of critics to search for social and political meaning in every work, the phenomenon of an individual writer or literary movement that completely ignored the social command was rare.

The overwhelming majority of Russian writers, regardless of literary orientation, shared a belief in the possibility and desirability of a single unifying discourse (though they often disagreed fiercely about its content), a "grand narrative" to use the phrase of Jean-François Lyotard,[1] in which literature functioned as the definer and arbiter of values. An illustrative example of the similarities in expectation shared by writers of very differing profiles can be seen by comparing excerpts from the Nobel Prize acceptance speeches of two Russian laureates who received the award in a five-year span: Mikhail Sholokhov (in 1965) and Alexander Solzhenitsyn (in 1970). It would be natural to expect stark differences in the attitude and rhetoric of a leading icon of socialist realism and the Soviet Union's most famous dissident. However, when they speak of the role and purpose of literature, the two men sound remarkably alike.

Sholokhov couches his comments in the typical false modesty of the vanguard Communist Party: " Mankind is not broken up into a host of individuals moving in a state of weightlessness, like cosmonauts when they have gone beyond the limit of terrestrial gravitation. We live on earth, we obey terrestrial laws. Huge strata of the earth's population have common interests and aspire for the same goals, and the pursuit of these goals unites rather than disunites them.

These strata are working people who create everything with their hands and their brain. I belong to those writers who regard it as the highest privilege and the highest freedom to be able to serve unreservedly the working people."[2]

Five years later, Solzhenitsyn, prevented by the Soviet State from traveling to Stockholm to receive his prize, sent a speech that asserted in equally powerful terms the belief that there could and should be a single system of values for humankind. He proclaimed, albeit less modestly than Sholokhov: "Who will give mankind one single system for reading its instruments, both for wrongdoing and for doing good, for the intolerable and the tolerable as they are distinguished from each other today? Who will make clear for mankind what is really oppressive and unbearable and what, for being so near, rubs us raw – and thus direct our anger against what is in fact terrible and not merely near at hand? Who is capable of extending such an understanding across the boundaries of his own personal experience? . . . Propaganda, coercion, and scientific proofs are all powerless. But, happily, in our world there is a way. It is art, and it is literature."[3]

The advent of democratization and the appearance of market economies after the fall of communism created a crisis for literature, one that threatened permanently to displace it from its pre-eminent position in Russia. In the words of the Serbian critic Mihailo Pantić: "from what had been an elite art form, which in a synthetic way recapitulated the general truths of people's experience and which deepened their understanding of reality . . . artistic literature in the post-socialist cultural model has become socially unnecessary, an almost completely private affair which lacks any social importance and which is interesting only to narrow academic circles, to writers, and to rare dedicated readers who nurture their passion as other marginal groups nurture theirs." Although Russian society appeared in the 1990s to be moving down the same path as the societies of Eastern Europe, the consolidation of state authority that took place under the regime of president Vladimir Putin changed the equation substantially. Russian writers, many of whom, as we saw in the previous chapter, retained a belief in literature as the proper locus for a discussion of major social and political matters, had for the most part never abandoned the attempt to create literary work that would address the burning issues of the day. As the state reconsolidated its control over the public sphere, limiting democratic political participation and squeezing if not fully eliminating pluralistic discourse in the media, writers of literature, especially younger writers who had come of age in the very late Soviet period, again began to publish work that asserted literature's traditional functions.

In this concluding section, we propose a brief examination of three works published between 1999 and 2006, each of which asserts a strong connection to the classic Russian literary tradition: Vladimir Makanin's (born 1937) *Underground, or A Hero of Our Time* (Andergraund, ili Geroi nashego vremeni, 1999), Viktor Pelevin's (born 1962) *Homo Zapiens* (the translator's English title for *Generation "P"*, 1999) and Sergei Minaev's (born 1975) *Soulless: The Story of an Unreal Person* (Dukhless. Povest' o nenastoiashchem cheloveke, 2006). Each of these novels confronts what the implied authors appear to believe is the collapse of the traditional Russian cultural value system and attempts to answer a question posed by Makanin's narrator: "What would happen if, in our days, people were really to learn to live without literature?" Simultaneously, building on the introduction to Lermontov's famous 1840 novel *A Hero of Our Time*, each of the works considered here presents a "diagnosis" of new Russian society rather than a cure for it.

Makanin's novel is a long (500-page plus) first-person narrative presented by a character called Petrovich who had been an author of literary work during the Communist era but who claims to have renounced his profession in the post-Communist period. To be sure, this claim clearly needs to be taken with a grain of salt, as the existence of the first-person narrative in the reader's hands demonstrates. Petrovich spends a large percentage of the work, which is structured as kaleidoscopic picaresque rather than a conventionally plotted novel, in an alcohol-induced haze, and he writes in a traditional realist style (though his lexicon displays a large number of colloquialisms), building his narrative quite consciously on the nineteenth-century Russian tradition.

The hero of Pelevin's novel is Vavilen Tatarsky a writer of slogans for the post-Soviet advertising industry. In the waning days of the Soviet Union, the young Tatarsky had dreamed of a different career: he had hoped to become a poet, writing for "eternity." By the early 1990s, however, he came to understand that "the eternity in which he formerly believed could exist only through state subsidy – or, and this was the same thing, as something forbidden by the state . . . He stopped writing poems: with the collapse of Soviet power they had lost all meaning and value. The last words he wrote just after these events were shot through with influences from a song by the group DDT ("What is fall – it is leaves . . .") and allusions to the late work of Dostoevsky. The poem ended as follows: "What is eternity – it is a jar. / Eternity is a jar of spiders. / If some simple Masha / forgets about the jar / What will happen to our Fatherland and to us?"[4]

The question posed by this jejeune poem echoes the thoughts of Makanin's narrator: "What would happen if, in our days, people were really to learn to live without literature?" Living without literature would mean no longer using it as the basic medium for asking existential questions. It would mean that the "Mashas" of this world would no longer be likely to use allusions from classic works like *The Brothers Karamazov* to formulate their answers, and it might lead would-be Dostoevskys to realize that literary work had lost its centrality as the motor of meaning creation in their societies.

Finally, Minaev's novel, a runaway best-seller, is a first-person narrative from the perspective of a successful new Russian businessman, whose life is spent on an endless round of clubbing, cocaine snorting and sex, and mindless marketing meetings, occasionally interspersed with bouts of "typically Russian" philosophizing about the need for spiritual values and a new national identity. The jaded narrator is outrageously cynical toward contemporary Russia, particularly toward himself and his milieu. Nevertheless, Minaev is unwilling to abandon the role of social doctor, and the goal of diagnosing the ills of Russian society is clearly present in the text. Although the book has been trashed by serious literary critics, it is worth examining in this context, because its popularity with readers indicates that Minaev has struck a chord with readers who still expect literature, albeit badly written literature, to play a significant social role.

Makanin's narrative begins in medias res, with the narrator sitting down to read Heidegger (in Russian translation) but being interrupted by a drunken visitor. The cocktail mixed of high culture and alcohol will turn out to be characteristic for the novel as a whole. By the second page we discover that the narrator is a writer. He is, however, rather a strange sort of writer, as he has never published anything, neither before the fall of the Soviet regime, when his work was apparently not acceptable for official publication, nor after. Still, the fact that he is known to be a writer, that he plays the role of "the writer," is crucial, as he is well aware. Insofar as our narrator will turn out to be representative of a generation, then that generation is Makanin's own, comprised of those who came of age in the Brezhnev era and who lived through late and post Communism.

Although in the new post-Soviet conditions he has had opportunities to "better himself," Petrovich continues to live the life of a demi-monde bohemian, supporting himself through the quintessential Communist-era job for persecuted writers, as a watchman of apartments whose owners are on vacation in an enormous apartment building cum dormitory (a microcosm of Muscovite society). Now, however, he has given up writing, though he continues to take advantage of his reputation: "I don't write. I've given it up. But the typewriter is my old partner (actually a Yugoslav girl), and it gives me a bit of status."[5]

To understand the central point of Makanin's novelistic analysis of his own generation we must carefully analyze Petrovich's seemingly absurd position. Why does a man whose entire life was wrapped up in being a writer have no desire either to publish his old work or to create new work when it becomes possible to reach an audience? Although he never says it in so many words, Petrovich recognizes that in the Communist era the importance of being an underground writer had nothing to do with the literary work one produced. Instead, being a writer (that is being identified and self-identified as one) had everything to do with the social and moral position implied by the activity. In a society that officially valued only the collective, writing (but, emphatically, not reading or publishing) became one of the few available ways to emphasize that a person had retained his individuality. A dissident writer valued himself and was valued by others not so much for what he said (which in any case was pretty much unavailable) but because he represented the possibility of personal freedom within an oppressive world.

When that world disappeared in the wake of Gorbachev's reforms, most members of the underground rejoiced at the possibility of seeing their work in print. They had, apparently, understood the essence of their activity as protest against the Soviet state. With its demise they were free to come to the surface, to take their rightful place in "normal" society. From Petrovich's point of view, however, this was an error. The true meaning of the underground was that it allowed for an assertion of individuality as such (the assertion of "my 'I'" as he puts it many times in the course of his text). An underground writer was, therefore, not fighting the Soviet system but any system that oppresses the ego (and every system does).

Although Petrovich claims to have abandoned writing, the fact that he has produced the long first-person text we are reading implies that he still continues to find the act of producing literature to be valuable and important. In so doing, he clearly indicates his close tie to the traditional litero-centric vision of society that had been typical in Russia for some two hundred years. And although the character is not directly autobiographical, most readers would, we believe, tend to see Petrovich as an alter-ego of his creator Makanin. Whatever his disgust with the particulars of the post-Soviet situation, the reader can clearly see that Petrovich, and by extension

Makanin, still believes in both a personal and a national identity that is created by and through literature. As he puts it at one crucial juncture: As he puts it: "Literature is like a reproof. Like a great virus (literature is always working inside of us)."[6]

In the case of Pelevin's *Generation "P"* the situation is more complex. First of all, whereas Makanin's novel analyzed the final Soviet generation, whose representative Petrovich found the new post-Soviet world almost incomprehensible, Pelevin's hero is of the generation that knew no other reality. Second, although Tatarsky is more or less of Pelevin's generation, the novel is narrated in the third person and it is therefore harder to see the protagonist as the author's alter ego. Thus, when Pelevin's narrator tells us that his hero has turned away from poetry to the production of advertising slogans and TV clips, the reader cannot help but perceive a sharp divide between the author who is writing and the character who has turned his back on literature. Pelevin's choice to make his protagonist a writer who has given up literature betrays an ambivalence towards his own position and, more generally, towards the role of the writer and literature in Russia. This ambivalence is most sharply underscored in those sections in which the novel's main characters begin to discuss the need for a national identity. "We used to have Orthodoxy, Autocracy, and Nationality. Then came this communism. And now that that's all over, there's no idea left except dough . . . We need a short and sweet Russian idea."[7] Tatarsky is given the task of producing a scenario for the new national identity but although he has had no difficulty writing slogans for a variety of Western brands, he finds that the task of defining Russia's essence in the form of an ad campaign is beyond him.

Although he fails to come up with a scenario for Russian identity, Tatarsky is able to enter the inner circle of a certain Azadovsky, whose video production company turns out to be doing something even more shocking than using Madison avenue techniques to produce a national identity. They are, it turns out, exploiting modern media technology to create a simulacrum of Russian reality that has come, through the ubiquity of television, to substitute fully for real social and political life. They learned the tricks for doing this from the Americans (who also supplied the technology), but they have managed, at least in their own minds, to surpass their teachers: They [the Americans] have two candidates for president and only one team of scriptwriters. It's just full of guys who've been dumped by Madison Avenue, because the money's bad in politics. A little while ago I looked at their election campaign material, and it's awful . . . No way, our scriptwriters are ten times better. Just look what rounded characters they write, Yeltsin, Zyuganov, Lebed. It's pure Chekhov. *Three Sisters*. Anyone who says Russia has no brands of its own should have the words shoved down his throat."⁸ Russia's literary abilities and traditions, then, have migrated from the novel and the poem to the fields of PR and advertising, the home of the new Chekhovs who are fully in control of the nation's essence because the nation has no reality beyond what they write.

If Pelevin's novel seems to take a cynical stance vis-à-vis contemporary Russian political, social, and literary life, Minaev's *Soulless* goes much farther down the same road. Like Makanin's *Underground*, this is a first-person narrative, and the author has been at great pains in numerous interviews to tell his readers that they should see the unnamed hero as an autobiographical character. On first reading, this novel seems suffused with an almost boundless cynicism and nastiness. The narrator mocks almost every institution of post-Soviet Russia: the world of money and business, the world of fashion, the world of literature, love and friendship. In his view, sex and money are society's only motivating forces. Nevertheless, amidst all the filth and cynicism, Minaev's man without qualities betrays a desire to escape the dirty world in which he fully participates most of the time. Indeed, looking more closely, we can see that this novel, even more than Makanin's and certainly more than Pelevin's, is an attempt to reclaim a traditional social role for literature. As was the case with Lermontov's Pechorin, the self-flagellation of Minaev's hero is meant to be seen as a diagnosis of the ills of a society which has, in the implied author's view, completely lost its way.

This is not to claim in any way that Minaev's literary talent is equivalent to that of Lermontov. It is merely to note that while the novel seems to be almost purely exploitative on first reading, its attempt to claim the high ground of moral and social criticism places it squarely in the tradition of the classic Russian novel. This aspect of the work is thrown into sharp relief during a discussion between the narrator and his friend Misha, a Petersburg engineer, with whom he meets up a few times a year to smoke marijuana and philosophize. At one point during their conversation Misha opines: "We really need a national idea. Like Autocracy – Orthodoxy – Nationality or, a bit later Stalin – Beria – the Gulag. Basically something that would be comprehensible to everyone. From your Moscow oligarchs to the reindeer herders of far north."⁹ (222). To be sure, their discussion is no more successful than Tatarsky's ad campaign in producing a Russian national program. The point, however, is not in the positive production of a particular idea, but rather in the assertion that a novel is the proper locus for a discussion of the ills and the goals of Russia.

Minaev's novel ends ambiguously and this conclusion is appropriate for our book as well. The narrator, having trashed every aspect of Russian society and having mocked and as a result apparently lost his sometime soul mate, the pure Russian beauty Yulia, takes a train to the outskirts of Moscow. He sits in the train car observing his fellow passengers in a scene reminiscent of Anna Karenina's final journey before her suicide. He heads off along a country road as more or less random and confused thoughts run through his head, again reminiscent of Anna in her final moments. He recalls a BBC program on rats and compares his compatriots to these rodents: "Since we were poisoned long ago by the toxins of cynicism, vulgarity, and hatred of our fellow man, which have built up in our systems during our short life, we will all eventually die, having swallowed each other up. And I hope to God that healthier people will replace us. But this is all total nonsense of course, and I don't know why thoughts like this are coming into my head right now."[10]

This recollection is followed almost immediately by another, which further inclines the reader to expect that the novel will end with the protagonist's suicide. He dredges up his earliest childhood memory of death: a dog that had been hit by a car. He climbs atop a railway bridge, again a perfect spot for a modernized and debased replay of Anna's last moments, lies down by the tracks and ruminates. As he ignites a cigarette lighter, the modern day version of Anna's candle, and the reader awaits the inevitable, thinking "how low the mighty have fallen if this squalid postmodern rerun of arguably Russia's greatest classic has sold more than a million copies." But Minaev fools us, substituting a flaming image that is horribly clichéd, but far more optimistic than Tolstoy's: "Maybe it is my lighter, or perhaps it really is the sun that has begun to rise, far off somewhere beyond the forest. In any case, for some reason I really want to believe that this flame will never be extinguished."[11]

We began our journey through the cultural history of Russian literature with a literary description of a rising sun in the private diary of Andrei Turgenev. That image was set to paper just when literature was coming to be acknowledged as the leading force in Russian society. We end with Minaev's rising sun and with a question. Has Russian literature played itself out as a central social force after an almost unprecedented two-hundred-year run? Or will Russian literature be able to recapture its position as the primary locus for the debate of ideas in Russian society in complex, high quality forms? The ambition of the writers discussed in this conclusion suggests that the desire remains. The willingness of readers to pay attention to their work suggests that even amidst the post-modern cacophony of multi-media entertainment the audience is still receptive to work of this kind. The seemingly inexorable return of strict limits on expression in the political and mass cultural spheres provides the conditions in which Russian literature can reassert its traditional authority. But whether the talent is still there and whether it can be harnessed to produce works sufficiently powerful and expressive to eventually be seen as worthy to stand beside those been considered elsewhere in this book, remains an open question.

Notes

Introduction: Labyrinth of Links: Russian Literature and its Cultural Contexts

  1 Andrei Turgenev, *Diary*, 12–13.

1 The Origins: Russian Medieval Culture

  1 Zenkovsky, *Medieval Russia's Epics*, ed. 82–3. Further quotations from the *Primary Chronicle* are taken from this edition and noted in the main text by page number.
  2 *Ibid.*, 82–3.
  3 This was first published by Tolstoy in 1868. The English translation can be found in the Norton Critical Edition to *War and Peace*, ed. George Gibian (New York, 1966).
  4 Tatishchev, *Istoria rossiiskaia*, vol. 2, 13.
  5 Mazour, *Modern Russian Historiography*, 33. For a summary of the history of the conflict in Russian historiography over the Norman theory, see Pritsak, *The Origins of Rus'*, 3–7.
  6 Mazour, *Modern Russian Historiography*, 34.
  7 Mann, *The Song of Prince Igor*, 22.
  8 Fedotov, *Sviatye drevnei Rusi*, 9.
  9 Avvakum, *The Life Written by Himself*, 58. Further quotations from this work will be from this edition and cited in the main text by page number.

2 The Spirit of Peter: Russian Culture in the Eighteenth Century

  1 Golikov, *Deianiia Petra Velikogo*, 238.
  2 Prokopovich, *Sochineniia*.
  3 Lotman, "O realizme Gogolia," 1996 (1), 142.
  4 i.e. Catherine II's allegorical literary name.
  5 M. P. Pogodin as quoted in Barsukov, *Zhizn' i trudy Mikhaila Pogodina*, 561.
  6 For more on the history of the Russian concept of peasant community see Grant, "Obshchina and Mir."

7 Viazemskii, *Zapisnye knizhki*, 316.
8 Predtechenskii, "Osnovanie Peterburga," 32.
9 Lotman and Uspensky, "Moskva-tretii Rim," 244.
10 *Ibid.*, 239.
11 Gogol, "Peterburgskie zapiski 1836 goda," 178. In Russian the names of the cities follow the concept, with Moscow being a feminine noun and Petersburg a masculine.
12 Lotman and Uspenskii, "Moskva-tretii Rim," 246.
13 Cited from Ovsiannikov, *Tri veka Sankt Peterburga*, 35.
14 Cited from *Ocherki istorii Leningrada*, vol. 1, 170.
15 Pushkin, *Polnoe sobranie sochinenii*, 11, 32.
16 One aspect of Russian life that Peter reformed only partially was the calendar. Until the reform, Russia followed the "old" Julian calendar, but counted years beginning with the purported creation of the world, rather than the birth of Christ (thus, the year 1700 was 7208 according to the old Russian system), and celebrated the new year on September 1, rather than January 1. Peter retained the Julian calendar, which was still employed at that time in protestant England and Sweden. In the eighteenth century, the Julian calendar lagged the Gregorian, used by most of the European nations, by 11 days. Because of the way it calculates dates, the Julian calendar generally falls behind the Gregorian by one day per century. Thus in the nineteenth century the lag was 12 days and in the twentieth, 13. The Julian calendar remained in force in Russia until 1918 when the Bolsheviks replaced it with the Gregorian: January 31, 1918 was followed by February 14. The Julian calendar, however, is still employed by the Orthodox Church.
17 *Lomonosovskii sbornik*, II, 144.
18 Khodasevich, *Sobranie sochinenii*, 1, 219–220.
19 Wortman, *Scenarios of Power*, 1, 113.
20 *Memoirs of Catherine the Great*, 326.

3 The Spirit of Poetry: Russian Culture in the Age of Alexander I (1801–25)

1 See Todd, *Fiction and Society*.
2 Reitblat, "The 'Novel of Literary Failure,'" 19.
3 *Ibid.*, 19.
4 Florovskii, *Puti russkogo bogosloviia*, 131.
5 Cited in Tomsinov, *Svetilo russkoi biurokratii*, 123.
6 Cited in *Portrety istorikov*, 25.
7 See Wachtel, *An Obsession with History*, 1996.
8 Pushkin, *Polnoe sobranie sochinenii*, 12, 305.
9 Gasparov, *Five Operas and a Symphony*, 2005, 37.

4 The Russian Idea: The Quest for National Identity in Nineteenth-Century Russian Culture

1 Chaadaev, "First Letter," 160–73.
2 Cited from Zhikharev, "Dokladnaia zapiska potomstvu o Petre Iakovleviche Chaadaeve," 5.
3 A. S. Pushkin, *Polnoe sobranie sochinenii*, 16, 172 (original in French).
4 Aksakov, *Sochineniia istoricheskie* (Moscow, 1861), 291–2. Cited from Riasanovsky, *Nicholas I*, 1992, 96.
5 Cited Kireevski, *European Culture*, 175–207.
6 Fyodor Dostoyevsky, *The Devils*, 256–9.
7 Belinsky, "Letter to N. V. Gogol."
8 Herzen, *Letters from France and Italy, 1847–1851*, 19–20. Kirsha Danilov is the name of the compiler of a collection of Russian oral folk texts (though there is little evidence that such a person ever existed).
9 Isaiah Berlin, *Russian Thinkers*, 104.
10 Gertsen, *Polnoe sobranie sochinenii*, 7, 326.
11 See Wortman, *Scenarios of Power*, vol. 2, chapters 1–2.
12 Cited in *The Journal of Musicology* (1939), 229.
13 Belinsky, "Letter to Gogol."
14 Hosking, *Russia*, 292, 293–4.
15 Reitblat "The 'Novel of Literary Failure.'"
16 Gasparov, "The Language Situation," 304.
17 Dal', "Naputnoe," 1, xlxviii.
18 I. S. Turgenev, *Polnoe sobranie sochinenii i pisem v 28 tomakh*.
19 Lotman, *Iz istorii russkoi kul'tury* (2), 11.
20 See the Academy Edition of *Zapiski okhotnika*, 558.
21 Riasanovsky, *Nicholas I*, 124.
22 Lomonosov, *Izbrannye proizvedeniia*, 2, 195. Translation ours. The work was written in 1754–5.
23 Quoted in Hokanson, "Literary Imperialism," 340.
24 In his youth, Pushkin was called "the African" by his school chums. Later in life, he mentioned the fact of his African ancestry in his poetry and wrote (but never finished) a prose work entitled "The Blackamoor of Peter the Great" about his maternal great grandmother.
25 Gogol, "Petersburgskie zapiski 1836 goda," 20, 21. It is worth mentioning that the desire expressed by Gogol to identify a national poet whose work would somehow stand for the entire country's spiritual strivings was typical for European Romantic culture. The cults of Shakespeare in England and of Goethe in Germany date from this period, for example. Less developed countries tended, in this as in other areas, to follow suit; thus, the 1840s and 1850s see the apotheosis of Mickiewicz in Poland, of Petöffi in Hungary, and of Njegoš in Serbia. Only in Russia, however, was

the national poet praised for his ability not to epitomize but to transcend his native culture.
26 Dostoevsky, *A Writer's Diary*, 1291.
27 Ibid., 1292.
28 "Utopicheskoe ponimanie istorii," *Diary of a Writer*, June, 1876. F. M. Dostoevsky, *Polnoe sobranie sochinenii v tridtsati tomakh* 23, 47. Translation ours.)
29 "'Anna Karenina' kak fakt osobogo znacheniia," *Diary of a Writer*, July / August, 1877 (25, 199).
30 Quoted in Levitt, *Russian Literary Politics*, 125.
31 Blok, *The Twelve and Other Poems*, 161–2.

5 Russian Psychology: The Quest for Personal Identity in Nineteenth-Century Russian Culture

1 Woolf, "Tolstoy's 'The Cossacks,'" 79.
2 It is, to be sure, reckless to provide psychiatric diagnoses of literary characters, particularly when one is not a psychiatrist and when the characters themselves were created before the discipline of psychiatry existed. Nevertheless, it seems reasonable to say that such characters as Poprishchin in Gogol's "Diary of a Madman," Goliadkin in Dostoevsky's *The Double* and the central character of Vsevolod Garshin's (1855–88) story "The Red Flower" are indeed mentally ill in the medical sense of the term.
3 Ginzburg, *On Psychological Prose*, see especially, 27–101.
4 Lermontov, *A Hero of Our Time*, 2.
5 Goncharov, *Oblomov*, 93.
6 Dobroliubov, "Chto takoe oblomovshchina," 344.
7 "It is difficult . . . and in my opinion simply impossible, to portray a life that has not yet taken form, where its forms have not settled and characters have not been stratified into types." Quoted in Ehre, *Oblomov*, 74.
8 *Essential Turgenev*, 644.
9 Ibid., 646–7.
10 Allen, *Beyond Realism*, 55–6.
11 Joravsky, *Russian Psychology*, 118–19.
12 Dostoevsky, "Notes from Underground," 13.
13 F. M. Dostoevsky, "Zapiski iz podpolia" *Sobranie sochinenii*, vol. 4. Moscow, 1956, 133. Translation ours.
14 Quoted in the notes to F. M. Dostoevsky, *Sobranie sochineni*, 1956, vol. 5, 579. Translation ours.
15 Dostoevsky, *Crime and Punishment*, 471–2.
16 Dostoevsky spent much effort trying to provide a convincing portrait of a perfect man – Myshkin in *The Idiot* and Alesha Karamazov are his two most notable attempts. His inability to produce such a character may well have

been related to the impossibility of providing a convincing psychology for a perfect individual.
17 L. N. Tolstoy, *Polnoe sobranie sochinenii*, v. 46, 67.
18 Belyi, "Formy iskusstva," 20
19 Ginzburg, *On Psychological Prose*, 205.
20 Lermontov, *A Hero of our Time*, 187–8.
21 In the twentieth century, the Russian "martyrology" of poets who died prematurely would include Sergei Esenin (1895–1925), Vladimir Mayakovsky (1893–1930), and Osip Mandelstam (1891–1938).
22 For more on the spiritualist controversy of the 1870s see Vinitsky, "Table Talks," 88–109.
23 Dostoevsky, *A Writer's Diary*, 2, 458–9.

6 Life as Theatre: Russian Modernism

1 Belyi, "Formy iskusstva," 105.
2 Kandinsky, "Content and Form," quoted in Bowlt, *Russian Art*, 21.
3 Quoted in Khardzhiev, "Poèziia i zhivopis'," 52.
4 Quoted in Green, *Russian Symbolist Theatre*, 135. Bely's essay originally appeared in the book *Teatr: Kniga o novom teatre* (*Theater: A Book about the New Theater*), St. Petersburg, 1908.
5 Rudnitsky, *Russian and Soviet Theatre*, 9
6 Lunacharskii, "Sotsializm i iskusstvo," 28.
7 Pushkin, *Eugene Onegin*, 23.
8 Quoted in Leach and Borovsky, *History of Russian Theatre*, 166.
9 *Rech'*, February 25, 1909
10 Baer, *Theatre in Revolution*, 73.
11 Maclean, *Eastern Approaches*, 28.
12 Quoted in Braun, *Meyerhold on Theatre*, 69.
13 Rudnitsky, *Russian and Soviet Theatre*, 42.
14 *Ibid.*, 92
15 *Ibid.*, 17.
16 Letter from July 21, 1911 to V. N. Rimsky-Korsakov. Published in Diachkov, *Stravinsky*, 461.
17 Tugenkhol'd, "Itogi sezona," 74.
18 "7-oi simfonicheskii kontsert S. Kussevitskogo," *Russkaia molva*, no. 45 (January 17, 1913).
19 Garafola, *Diaghilev's Ballets Russes*, 19–25.
20 Benois, *Rech'*. August 17, 1911.
21 Quoted in Reeder, *Anna Akhmatova*, 64.
22 Oginskaia in pro et contra, 95.
23 Runt in pro et contra, 102.
24 Reeder, *Anna Akhmatova*, 2, 95.

7 The Art of the Future: The Russian Avant-Garde

1. Cited in V. Kamenskii, *Put' Entuziasta* (Moscow, 1931), 145.
2. Cited in Schruba, *Literaturnye ob'edineniia Moskvy i Peterburga 1890–1917 godov*, 306.
3. Kruchenykh, *Stikhotvoreniia*, 17.
4. Khlebnikov, *Tvoreniia*, 371–2.
5. To hear Mayakovsky reading this poem go to http://max.mmlc.northwestern.edu/~mdenner/Demo/texts/andcouldyou.html and choose the appropriate audio format.
6. Mayakovsky, *The Bedbug and Selected Poetry*, 302.
7. Cited in Kobrinskii, *Daniil Kharms*.
8. All quotes are from Kobrinskii, *Daniel Kharms* (chapter "Tri levykh chasa").

8 The Future as Present: Soviet Culture

1. Edward J. Brown, *Russian Literature Since the Revolution*, 12.
2. *Na postu* (Moscow, 1923), 10.
3. Maiakovskii, *Polnoe sobranie sochinenii v 13 tomakh*. 12, 89.
4. Lunacharskii, "Sotsializm i iskusstvo," 8, 526.
5. See Gutkin, *Cultural Origins*.
6. See Clark, *The Soviet Novel*.
7. Cited in Varlamov, *Alexei Tolstoi*, 259.
8. Cited in Sverdlov, *Po tu storonu dobra i zla*, 111.
9. The Soviet history of Peter the Great's myth is examined in Platt, "Terror and Greatness."
10. Cited in Sverdlov, *Po tu storonu dobra i zla*, 126.
11. *Ibid.*, 12.
12. Cited in Blium, *Sovetskaia tsenzura*, 280.
13. All citations are from *Pervyi vsesoiuznyi s'ezd sovetskikh pisatelei*.
14. Blium, *Sovetskaia tsenzura*, 77.
15. Mandelstam, "The End of the Novel," 199–201.
16. Podoroga, "The Eunuch of the Soul," 191.
17. Platonov, *Kotlovan*, 1. Translation mine. Further references to *Kotlovan* will be made in the main text by page number from this edition.

9 After the Future: Russian Thaw Culture

1. http://azeri.org/Azeri/az_latin/latin_articles/latin_text/latin_73/eng_73/73_stalin_cult.html
2. http://www.fordham.edu/halsall/mod/krushchev-secret.html
3. http://www.sovlit.com/2ndcongress/ehrenburg.html
4. Translated by George Reavey. In *Twentieth-Century Russian Poetry*, 805.
5. Verdery, *What was Socialism?*, 27, emphasis mine.

300 Notes to pages 240–272

6   Erofeev, *Moscow Circles.*
7   *The Blue Lagoon Anthology,* v. 1, 15. To his credit, it should be noted that Bowlt recognized the pitfalls of such a characterization even as he employed it.
8   Quoted in Skilling, *Samizdat,* 7.
9   Quoted in Klimoff, *Ivan Denisovich,* 4.
10 Solzhenitsyn, *Odin den' Ivana Denisovicha,* 5. Translation mine.
11 Losev, *Iosif Brodskii,* 25–6.
12 Brodsky, "Spoils of War," 8.
13 *Ibid.,* 6.
14 Losev, *Iosif Brodskii,* 39–40.
15 Brodsky, "A Guide to a Renamed City," 91–2.
16 Brodskii, "Evropeiskii vozdukh nad Rossiei," 37.
17 Gordin, "Delo Brodskogo."
18 Cited in Losev, *Iosif Brodskii,* 78.
19 On Soviet "punitive medicine" see Bloch and Reddaway, *Psychiatric Terror.*
20 On this period and its reflection in Brodsky's poetry see Lev Loseff, "On Hostile Ground."
21 "The Trial of Iosif Brodsky" (English transcript of Brodsky's trial), 6–7.
22 Cited in Gordin, *Pereklichka vo mrake,* 187.
23 Bethea, *Joseph Brodsky,* 36–47.
24 Brodsky, "Nobel Lecture in Literature."
25 http://rezanov.krasu.ru/eng/roses/poema.php
26 Blake, "Lenin's Rockers."
27 Rybnikov, *"Juno" and "Avos,"* 51.
28 *Ibid.,* 146.

10 Instead of the Apocalypse: Russian Culture Today

1   Smith, *Contemporary Russian Poetry,* ed. 218.
2   To be sure, there are prizes and prizes. The most prestigious of the new Russian awards, such as the Russian Booker prize, do draw a fair amount of attention and provide significant financial rewards.
3   In the post-thaw period émigré publishers continued to bring out editions of suppressed writers as well as the work of contemporary writers that was smuggled out of the Soviet Union for publication abroad.
4   It was published in the US as *Arrested Voices: Resurrecting the Disappeared Writers of the Soviet Union,* trans. John Crowfoot (New York: The Free Press, 1996). The translator (with the author's permission) significantly edited the book in English. When passages cited appear in the American edition we quote from it. When they have been removed, we quote from the Russian edition. Shentalinsky has published two subsequent collections based on his research in the KGB archives, *Za chto? Proza, poeziia, dokumenty* (Moscow: Novyi kliuch, 1999) and *Donos na Sokrata* (Moscow: Formika-S, 2001).

5 Shentalinsky, *Raby svobody*, 22.
6 This is how the Russian edition begins, at least. The English one has been changed
7 Bloom, *Cult Fiction*, 15.
8 Even in the realm of pop music, litero-centricity reigned in the USSR. Thus, one of the characteristics of home-grown Soviet rock and roll and pop was the comparatively great attention paid to the lyrics, which were often, in the cases of such Russian bardic poets as Vladimir Vysotsky and Alexander Galich, serious and difficult poems in themselves.
9 Flyleaf of *Eto ia, Edichka*.
10 Limonov, *Russkoe*, 181.
11 As quoted in an interview in the newspaper *Trud* (March 23, 1996). Excerpted on the website http://imperium.lenin.ru/~verbit/Limonov/nns-limonov.html
12 Limonov, "Poet-bukhgalter," 132–4.
13 Cardin, "In Search of the Right Milieu," 236–7.
14 http://imperium.lenin.ru/~verbit/Limonov/interv-limonov.html
15 *The Russia Journal*, June 14, 1999 as published on the web at http://www.therussiajournal.com/index.htm?obj=324
16 Limonov, *Moia politicheskaia biografia*, 19. The "five hundred days" project" was touted by the early shock therapy economists as a quick fix for the economic problems of the country.
17 http://nbp.gok.ru/program.htm
18 Limonov, *Moia politicheskaia biografiia*, 240
19 *RFE/RL NEWSLINE*., vol. 7, no. 23, Part I, February 5, 2003.
20 Limonov was released from prison in June 2003 having served almost two years of his four-year sentence.

Conclusion: Whither Russian Literature

1 Lyotard, *The Post-Modern Condition*, xxiv.
2 "The Vital Strength of Realism" in Sholokhov, *At the Bidding of the Heart*, 205.
3 Solzhenitsyn, "Odin den' Ivana Denisovicha," 17.
4 Pelevin, *Generation "P,"* 15–16. Translation Andrew Wachtel. Here and elsewhere we quote from the original because the published English translation omits the last sentences of this section and in general is not very good.
5 Makanin, *Andergaund*, 33.
6 Ibid., 186.
7 Pelevin, *Generation "P,"* 175.
8 Ibid., 216.
9 Minaev, *Dukhless*, 222.
10 Ibid., 339.
11 Ibid., 347

Bibliography

Allen, Elizabeth Cheresh. *Beyond Realism. Turgenev's Poetics of Secular Salvation.* Stanford: Stanford University Press, 1992.
Anna Akhmatova. Pro et Contra: Antologiia. ed. D. K. Burlaka. St. Petersburg, Izdatel'stvo Russkogo khristianskogo gumanitarnogo instituta, 2001. 2 vols.
Archpriest Avvakum, The Life written by Himself: With the study of V. V. Vinogradov. Translated, annotated, and edited by Kenneth N. Brostrom. Ann Arbor: Michigan Slavic Publications, 1979.
Baer, Nancy von Norman. *Theatre in Revolution. Russian Avant-Garde Stage Design. 1913–1935.* New York: Thames and Hudson, 1991.
Barsukov, N. *Zhizn' i trudy Mikhaila Pogodina*, vol 16. St. Petersburg, 1902.
Belinsky, V. G. "Letter to N.V. Gogol." Trans. Daniel Field. http://artsci.shu.edu/reesp/documents/Belinskii.htm
Belyi, Andrei, *Petersburg.* Trans. Robert Maguire and John Malmstad. Bloomington: Indiana University Press, 1978.
___ "Formy iskusstva." *Simvolizm kak miroponimanie.* Moscow, 1994, pp. 90–105.
Berlin, Isaiah. *Russian Thinkers.* London: Penguin, 1978.
Bethea, David. *Joseph Brodsky and the Creation of Exile.* Princeton: Princeton University Press, 1994.
Blake, Patricia ,"Lenin's Rockers," *Time*, July 20, 1981.
Blium, A.V. *Sovetskaia tsenzura v epokhu total'nogo terrora. 1929–1953.* St. Petersburg: Akademicheskii proekt, 2000.
Bloch, S. and P. Reddaway. *Psychiatric Terror. How Soviet Psychiatry Is Used to Suppress Dissent.* New York: Basic Books, 1977.
Blok, Alexander. *The Twelve and Other Poems.* Trans. Jon Stallworthy and Peter France. New York: Oxford University Press, 1970.
Bloom, Clive. *Cult Fiction: Popular Reading and Pulp Theory.* New York: St. Martin's, 1996.
Braun, Edward. *Meyerhold on Theatre.* London: Methuen and Co. Ltd., 1969.
Brodskii Iosif, "Evropeiskii vozdukh nad Rossiei," *Strannik*, no. 1 (1991): 37.
Brodsky, Joseph. "A Guide to a Renamed City." *Less Than One. Selected Essays.* New York: Farrar Straus Giroux, 1986.
___ "Nobel Lecture in Literature, December 8, 1987." Trans. Barry Rubin. *Nobel Lectures, Literature 1981–1990.* Singapore: World Scientific Publishing Co., 1993.

___ "Spoils of War." *On Grief and Reason*. New York: Farrar, Straus and Giroux, 1995.
Brown, Edward J. *Russian Literature Since the Revolution*. Cambridge: Harvard University Press, 1982.
Carden, Patricia. "In Search of the Right Milieu: Eduard Limonov's Kharkov Cycle." *Autobiographical Statements in Twentieth-Century Russian Literature*. ed. Jane Gary Harris. Princeton: Princeton University Press, 1990, 227–37.
Catherine the Great. *Memoirs of Catherine the Great*. Trans. Katharine Anthony. New York: Tudor, 1935.
Chaadaev, P. Ia. "First Letter." *Russian Intellectual History: An Anthology*. Trans. Marc Raeff. New York: Prometheus Books, 1966, 160–73.
Clark, Katerina, *The Soviet Novel: History as Ritual*. Chicago, London: University of Chicago Press, 1981.
Dahl, V. I. "Naputnoe." *Slovar' Zhivogo velikorusskogo iazyka*, Moscow, 1955 vol. 1, p. xlxviii.
Diachkov, L. S., ed. *I. F. Stravinsky: Stat'i i materialy*. Moscow: 1973.
Dobroliubov, N. A., "Chto takoe oblomovshchina." *Literaturnaia kritika*. Leningrad, 1984.
Dostoevsky, Fedor. *A Writer's Diary* 2 vols. Trans. Kenneth Lantz. Evanston: Northwestern University Press, 1994.
___ *Sobranie sochinenii v desiati tomakh*. 10 vols. Moscow, 1956.
___ *Polnoe sobranie sochinenii v 30 tomakh*. Leningrad, 1972–90.
___ "Notes from Underground." Trans. Jessie Coulson. London: Penguin, 1972.
___ *Crime and Punishment*. Trans. Constance Garnett. New York: Bantam, 1981.
___ *The Devils*. Trans David Magarshack. London: Penguin Classics, 1971.
Ehre, Milton. *Oblomov and His Creator; The Life and Art of Ivan Goncharov*. Princeton: Princeton University Press, 1973.
Erofeev, Venedikt. *Moscow Circles*. Trans. J. R. Dorrell. London: Writers and Readers Publishing Cooperative, 1981.
Fedotov, G. P. *Sviatye drevnei Rusi*. New York, 1960.
Florovskii, G. *Puti russkogo bogosloviia*.YMKA Press. Paris 1983.
Garafola, Lynn. *Diaghilev's Ballets Russes*. New York: Oxford University Press, 1989.
Garrard, John and Carol. *Inside the Soviet Writers' Union*. New York: Macmillan, 1990.
Gasparov, Boris. "The Language Situation and the Linguistic Polemic in Mid-Nineteenth-Century Russia." *Aspects of the Slavic Language Question*. Eds. Riccardo Picchio and Harvey Goldblatt. New Haven: Yale Concilium on International and Area Studies, 1984, vol. 2.
___ *Five Operas and a Symphony: Word and Music in Russian Culture*. New Haven: Yale University Press, 2005.
Gertsen (Herzen), A. I. *Polnoe sobranie sochinenii*, vol. 7, 326.
Ginzburg, Lidia. *On Psychological Prose*. Trans. Judson Rosengrant. Princeton: Princeton University Press, 1991.

Gogol, N.V. "Peterburgskie zapiski 1836 goda." *Polnoe sobranie sochinenii*, vol. 8. Moscow, Leningrad 1952.

Golikov, I. I. *Deianiia Petra Velikogo, mudrogo preobrazovatelia Rossii; sobrannye iz dostovernykh istochnikov i raspolozhennye po godam*, IX. Moscow, 1789.

Goncharov, Ivan. *Oblomov*. Trans. David Magarshak. London: Penguin, 1954.

Gordin, Ia. "Delo Brodskogo. Istoriia odnoi raspravy," *Neva* 2 (1989).

___ *Pereklichka vo mrake*. St. Petersburg: Pushkinskii fond, 2000.

Gorky, M. *Nesvoevremennye mysli*. Moscow: Sovremennik, 1995.

Grant, Steven A. "Obshchina and Mir." *Slavic Review*, vol. 35, no. 4 (Dec., 1976), 636–51.

Green, Martin, translator and editor. *The Russian Symbolist Theater*. Ann Arbor: Ardis, 1986.

Gutkin, Irina, *The Cultural Origins of the Socialist Realist Aesthetic, 1890–1934*. Evanston, IL: Northwestern University Press, 1999.

Herzen, Alexander. *Letters from France and Italy, 1847–1851*. Ed. and trans. Judith E. Zimmerman. Pittsburgh: University of Pittsburgh Press, 1995.

Hokanson, Katya. "Literary Imperialism, *Narodnost'* and Pushkin's Invention of the Caucasus." *Russian Review*, vol. 53, no. 3 (July, 1994).

Hosking, Geoffrey. *Russia: People and Empire. 1552–1917*. Cambridge: Harvard University Press, 1997.

Joravsky, David. *Russian Psychology. A Critical History*. Oxford: Basil Blackwell, 1989.

Kamenskii, V. *Put' Entuziasta*. Moscow, 1931.

Kandinsky, Vasily. "Content and Form," quoted in Bowlt, John, trans. and ed. *Russian Art of the Avant Garde*. New York: Thames and Hudson, 1988.

Khardzhiev, N. "Poèziia i zhivopis'." *K istorii russkogo avangarda*. Stockholm: Hylea Prints, 1976.

Khlebnikov, Velimir. *Tvoreniia*. Moscow: Sovetskii pisatel' 1986.

Khodasevich.V. *Sobranie sochinenii*, vol. 1. Ann Arbor: Ardis, 1983.

Kireevski, I. S. "On the Nature of European Culture and its Relation to the Culture of Russia." *Russian Intellectual History: An Anthology*. New York: Prometheus Books, 1966, 175–207.

Klimoff, Alexis, ed. *One Day in the Life of Ivan Denisovich. A Critical Companion*. Evanston: Northwestern University Press, 1997.

Kobrinskii, Aleksandr. *Daniil Kharms*. Moscow: Molodaia gvardiia, 2008.

Konrád, György and Szelényi, Iván, *Intellectuals on the Road to Class Power*. New York: Harcourt Brace Jovanovich, 1979.

Kruchenykh, A. E. *Stikhotvoreniia. Poemy. Romany. Opera*. St. Petersburg, 2001.

Leach, Robert and Borovsky, Victor, eds. *A History of Russian Theatre*. Cambridge: Cambridge University Press, 1999.

Lermontov, Mikhail. *A Hero of Our Time*. Trans. Vladimir and Dmitri Nabokov. Ann Arbor: Ardis, 1988.

Levitt, Marcus. *Russian Literary Politics and the Pushkin Celebration of 1880*. Ithaca: Cornell University Press, 1989.

Limonov, Eduard. *Russkoe.* Ann Arbor: Ardis, 1979.
____ "Poet-bukhgalter (Neskol'ko iadovitykh nabliudenii po povodu fenomena I. A. Brodskogo)." Paris: Muleta, 1984.
____ *Moia politicheskaia biografiia.* St. Petersburg: Amfora, 2002.
Lomonosov, M. *Izbrannye proizvedeniia v dvukh tomakh,* 2 vols. Moscow, 1986.
Lomonosovskii sbornik, II (St. Petersburg, 1911).
Lev Loseff. "On Hostile Ground: Madness and Madhouse in Joseph Brodsky's 'Gorbunov and Gorchakov'." *Madness and the Mad in Russian Culture.* Eds. Angela Brintlinger and Ilya Vinitsky. Toronto: University of Toronto Press, 2007, 90–104.
Losev, Lev. *Iosif Brodskii. Opyt literaturnoi biografii.* Moscow: Molodaia gvardiia, 2006.
Lotman, Iu. M. "Ocherki po istorii russkoi kul'tury." *Iz istorii russkoi kul'tury.* Vol. IV (XVIII – nachalo XIX veka) Moscow, 1996.
____ "O realizme Gogolia." *Trudy po russkoi i slavinaskoi filologii (Literaturovedenie). Novaia seriia.* vol. 2. Tartu, 1996.
Lotman, Iu. M. and Uspensky, B.A.,"Otzvuki kontseptsii 'Moskva – tretii Rim' v ideologii Petra Pervogo. (K probleme srednevekovoi traditsii v kul'ture barokko)." *Khudozhestvennyi iazyk srednevekov'ia.* Moscow, 1982.
Lunacharskii, Anatoly, "Sotsializm i iskusstvo." *Teatr. Kniga o novom teatre.* St. Petersburg, 1908.
____ *Sobranie sochinenii,* 8 vols, Moscow, 1967. vol. 8.
Lyotard, Jean-François. *The Postmodern Condition: A Report on Knowledge.* Trans. Geoff Bennington and Brian Massumi. Minneapolis: University of Minnesota Press, 1984.
Maclean, Fitzroy, *Eastern Approaches,* Penguin, 1991.
Makanin, Vladimir. *Andergaund, ili Geroi nashego vremeni.* Moscow: Vagrius, 1999.
Mandelstam, Osip. "The End of the Novel." *Critical Prose and Letters.* Ed. Jane Gary Harris, trans. Jane Gary Harris and Constance Link. Ann Arbor: Ardis, 1979.
Mann, Robert, trans. *The Song of Prince Igor.* Eugene: Vernyhora Press, 1979.
Mayakovsky, Vladimir, *The Bedbug and Selected Poetry.* Ed. Patricia Blake. New York: Meridian Books, 1960.
Maiakovskii, V. V., *Polnoe sobranie sochinenii v 13 tomakh.* 13 vols. Moscow, 1956.
Mazour, Anatole G. *Modern Russian Historiography.* Westport: Greenwood, 1975.
Minaev, Sergei. *Dukhless. Povest' o nenastoiashchem cheloveke.* Moscow: Khranitel', 2006.
Ovsiannikov, Iu. *Tri veka Sankt Peterburga.* St. Petersburg: Gallart, 1997.
Pelevin, Viktor. *Generation "P."* Moscow: Vagrius, 1999.
Pervyi vsesoiuznyi s'ezd sovetskikh pisatelei. Stenograficheskii otchet. Moscow, 1934.
Pis'ma V.A. Zhukovskogo k Alekstrandru Ivanovichu Turgenevu. Moscow, 1895.

Platonov, Andrei, *Kotlovan, Iuvenil'noe more*. Moscow: Khudozhestvennaia literatura, 1987.
Platt, Kevin M. F. "Terror and Greatness: Ivan IV and Peter I as Russian Myths." Cornell University Press, forthcoming.
Podoroga, Valery. "The Eunuch of the Soul." *Late Soviet Culture. From Perestroika to Novostroika* eds. Thomas Lahusen with Gene Kupermann. Durham: Duke University Press, 1993.
Portrety istorikov: vremia i sud'by, vol. 1. Moscow, 2000.
Predtechenskii, A. V. "Osnovanie Peterburga." *Ocherki istorii Leningrada*, vol. 1. Moscow, Leningrad: Izdatel'stvo akademii nauk SSSR, 1955.
Pritsak, Omeljan. *The Origins of Rus'*. Cambridge: Harvard University Press, 1981.
Prokopovich, Feofan. "Slovo na pogrebenie Vsepresvetleishego Derzhavneishego Petra Velikogo . . ." *Sochineniia*. Moscow, Leningrad, 1961.
Pushkin, A. S. *Polnoe sobranie sochinenii v 16 tomakh*. Moscow, Leningrad: Izdatel'stvo Akademii Nauk SSSR, 1937–59.
____ *Eugene Onegin*. Trans. James E. Falen. Carbondale: Southern Illinois University Press, 1990.
Reeder, Roberta. *Anna Akhmatova*. New York: Picador, 1994.
Reitblat, Abram I. "The 'Novel of Literary Failure'." *Russian Studies in Literature*, vol. 40, no. 1 (Winter 2003–4).
Riasanovsky, Nicholas. *Nicholas I and Official Nationality in Russia, 1825–1855*. Berkeley: University of California Press, 1969.
____ *The Emergence of Romanticism*. Oxford: Oxford University Press, 1992.
Rudnitsky, Konstantin. *Russian and Soviet Theatre. 1905–1932*. Trans. Roxane Permar. New York: Harry Abrams, 1988.
Rybnikov, Aleksei, *"Juno" and "Avos."* Moscow, 1988.
Schefski, Harold Klassel. *Boris M. Eikhenbaum: The Evaluation of His Critical Method and His Contribution to Russian Literary Criticism*. Stanford, 1976.
Schruba, Manfred. *Literaturnye ob'edineniia Moskvy i Peterburga 1890–1917 godov*. Moscow: Novoe Literaturnoe Obozrenie, 2004.
Shentalinsky, Vitaly. *Raby svobody. V literaturnykh arkhivakh KGB*. Moscow: Parus, 1995.
Sholokhov, Mikhail. *At the Bidding of the Heart*. Trans. Olga Shartse. Moscow: Progress Publishers, 1973.
Skilling, H. Gordon. *Samizdat and an Independent Society in Central and Eastern Europe*. London: Macmillan, 1989.
Smith, Gerald S., ed. *Contemporary Russian Poetry. Bilingual Anthology*, Bloomington: Indiana University Press, 1993.
Solzhenitsyn, Aleksandr. "Odin den' Ivana Denisovicha," *Rasskazy*. Frankfurt/Main: Posev, 1976.
Sverdlov, Mikhail. *Po tu storonu dobra i zla. Aleksei Tolstoi: ot Buratino do Petra*. Moscow: Globulus ENAS, 2004.

Tatishchev, V. I. *Istoriia rossiiskaia*. 7 vols. Moscow, 1962–8.
Todd, A. C. and Hayward, M., eds. *Twentieth-Century Russian Poetry. Silver and Steel, An Anthology*. New York, Doubleday, 1993.
Todd, William Mills, III. *Fiction and Society in the Age of Pushkin*. Cambridge: Harvard University Press, 1986.
Tolstoy, L. N. *Polnoe sobranie sochinenii*. 90 vols. Moscow, 1928–53.
Tomsinov, V. Ia. *Svetilo russkoi biurokratii*. Moscow: TEIS, 1997.
"The Trial of Iosif Brodsky." *New Leader* August 31, 1964, pp. 6–17.
Tugenkhol'd, Ia. "Itogi sezona." *Apollon*. no. 6, 1911, 65–74
Turgenev, Andrei, *Diary*, Department of Manuscripts, Institute of Russian Literature, St. Petersburg, Russia, 309/272.
Turgenev, I. S. *The Essential Turgenev*, ed. Lisa Cheresh Allen. Evanston: Northwestern University Press, 1994.
____ *Polnoe sobranie sochinenii i pisem v 28 tomakh*, 28 vols. Moscow,
____ *Zapiski okhotnika*. Moscow: Nauka, 1991.
Ufliand, Vladimir. "Odin iz vitkov istorii piterskoi kul'tury: Nekotorye osobennosti nezavisimoi piterskoi poezii 50–60 godov v sootnesenii s sobstvennym opytom," *Petropol'*, no. 3 (1991), 109–10.
Varlamov, Aleksei, *Aleksei Tolstoi*. Moscow: Molodaia gvardiia 2006.
Verdery, Katherine. *What was Socialism and What comes Next?* Princeton: Princeton University Press, 1996.
Viazemskii, P. A. *Zapisnye knizhki*. Moscow: Russkaia kniga, 1992.
Vinitsky, Ilya. "Table Talks: The Spiritualist Controversy of the 1870s and Dostoevsky." *Russian Review*. January 2008, 88–109.
Wachtel, Andrew Baruch. *An Obsession with History: Russian Writers Confront the Past*. Stanford: Stanford University Press, 1996.
Woolf, Virginia, "Tolstoy's 'The Cossacks.'" *The Esssays of Virginia Woolf*, ed. Andrew McNeillie. 4 vols. London: The Hogarth Press, 1987. vol. 2.
Wortman, Richard. *Scenarios of Power. Myth and Ceremony in Russian Monarchy*. 2 vols. Princeton, Princeton University Press, 1995.
Zenkovsky, Serge, ed. *Medieval Russia's Epics, Chronicles, and Tales*. New York: E. P. Dutton and Co. Inc., 1963.
Zhikharev, M. I. "Dokladnaia zapiska potomstvu o Petre Iakovleviche Chaadaeve." *Russkoe obshchestvo 30-kh godov 19 veka*. Moscow: MGU, 1989.

Index

Abramov, Fedor Alexandrovich: 214, 244
Akhmadulina, Bella Akhatovna: 236
Akhmatova, Anna Andreevna: 69, 144, 157, 178–181, 213, 234, 246, 249, 251, 253, 270, 271
  Evening, 179
  "Song of Final Meeting," 179
  Poem without a Hero, 47, 178, 257
  Requiem, 181, 246
  Rosary, 178–181
  "In the Evening," 180
Aksakov, Alexander Nikolaevich: 153, 154
Aksakov, Ivan Sergeevich: 81, 94, 123
Aksakov, Konstantin Sergeevich: 94, 104, 107, 112, 123
Aksenov, Vasily Pavlovich: 237, 241, 248, 263
  The Burn, 264
  The Island of Crimea, 264
  A Ticket to the Stars, 237
Akunin, Boris (pen name for Grigory Shalvovich Chkhartishvili): 276, 277, 279
  F.M., 277–279
Alexander I (Emperor): 2, 14, 46, 53, 57–58, 60–61, 63, 69, 70, 73, 78, 79, 87, 89, 162
Alexander II (Emperor): 69, 70, 75, 101, 103, 114, 123
Alexander III (Emperor): 164
Alexandrov, Grigory Vasilievich: 216
  The Bright Path, 216
  The Circus, 216
  Happy Guys, 216
  Spring, 216
  Volga-Volga, 216
Alexei Mikhailovich (Tsar): 27, 48, 161
Andreev, Daniil Leonidovich: 146
  "The Rose of the World," 146
Andreev, Leonid Nikolaevich: 209
  The Life of Man, 166
Annenkov, Iuri Pavlovich: 168
Annenkov, Pavel Vasilievich: 101
Arakcheev, Alexei Andreevich: 60
Ariosto, Ludovico: 86
  Orlando Furioso, 83

Arzamas (literary society): 63, 66, 83
Aseev, Nikolai Nikolaevich: 191
Astafev, Viktor Petrovich: 244
Averbach, Leopold Leonidovich: 211, 226
Auden, W.H.: 249, 254
Avvakum Petrov: 27
  The Life of the Archpriest Avvakum Written by Himself, 27–30

Babaevsky, Semen Petrovich: 234
Babel, Isaac Emmanuilovich: 272, 273, 274
  Red Cavalry, 207
Bakunin, Mikhail Alexandrovich: 99, 127, 277, 283
Balakirev, Mily Alexeevich: 101, 146
  "Tamara," 146
Baratynsky, Evgeny Abramovich: 57, 63, 67, 249
Batiushkov, Konstantin Nikolaevich: 57, 63, 66, 67
  "The Dying Tasso," 67
  "My Penates," 67
  "Vision on the Shores of Lethe," 66
Batu Khan: 8
Baudelaire, Charles: 157
Demian Bedny (pen name for Efim Alexandrovich Pridvorov): 227
Belinsky, Vissarion Grigorievich: 72, 81, 98, 99, 102, 103, 112, 113, 115, 127, 142, 144, 145
Bely, Andrei (pen name for Boris Nikolaevich Bugaev): 4, 139, 159, 171, 218, 220
  Petersburg, 47, 139–41
Benois, Alexandre: 69, 160, 166, 175, 176, 177, 178, 210
Berdiaev, Nikolai Alexandrovich: 209, 271
Bethea, David: 254
Blok, Alexander Alexandrovich: 4, 69, 75, 113, 124, 146, 157, 171,175, 179, 208–09
  "The City," 47
  The Fairground Booth, 160, 171
  "On the Field of Kulikovo," 24
  "Scythians," 124
  "The Twelve," 207, 209, 219
Bludov, Dmitry Nikolaevich: 66

Boborykin, Petr Dmitrievich: 153, 154, 155
Bogdanov, Alexander Alexandrovich (pen name for Alyaksandr Malinouski): 184, 210, 211
Bogdanovich, Ippolit Fedorovich: 86
  Dushenka, 86
Boris and Gleb (Saints): 17, 18, 23
Borodin, Alexander Porfirievich: 101
  Prince Igor, 24, 65, 82, 164
Borovikovsky, Vladimir Lukich: 57
Botkin, Vasily Petrovich: 99
Bowlt, John: 240
Brezhnev, Leonid Ilich: 239, 254, 259, 276, 288
Brik, Osip Maximovich: 186
Briullov, Karl Pavlovich: 82, 92
  "Siege of Pskov," 82
Briusov, Valery Iakovlevich: 183, 218, 256
Brodsky, Iosif Alexandrovich (Joseph): 144, 238, 241, 247–255, 263, 271, 280
  "Abraham and Isaac," 250
  "A Christmas Romance," 250
  The End of a Beautiful Era, 254
  The Grand Elegy to John Donne," 250
  Less Than One, 254
  Lyrics and Longer Poems, 253
  Marble, 254
  New Stanzas to Augusta, 254
  A Part of Speech, 254
  "On the Death of Robert Frost," 250
  A Stop in the Desert, 254
  "The Year 1972," 254
  Urania, 254
Bukharin, Nikolai Ivanovich: 208, 226, 227
Bulgakov, Mikhail Afanasievich: 4, 168, 213, 273–74
  The Days of the Turbins, 168
  The Master and Margarita, 4, 168, 271, 273, 274
  The White Guard, 219
  Zoya's Apartment, 168
Bulgakov, Sergei Nikolaevich: 209
Bulgarin, Faddei Venediktovich: 109
Bunimovich, Evgeny Abramovich: 282
Bunin, Ivan Alexeevich: 209
Burliuk, David Davidovich: 185, 186, 187, 191
Butlerov, Alexander Mikhailovich: 152, 153, 192
Byron, George Gordon (Lord): 58, 70, 108, 128, 141, 142, 253

Catherine (the Great): 22, 34, 35–36, 38, 42, 44, 45, 47, 53, 54, 55, 57, 91, 92, 94, 99, 108, 150, 161, 162, 256
  "Instruction," 54
  "Tale of the Tsarevich Khlor," 53
Chaadaev, Petr Iakovlevich: 45, 81, 92–94
  "First Philosophical Letter," 92–94

Chakovsky, Alexander Borisovich: 234
Chekhov, Anton Pavlovich: 4, 125, 138, 160, 163, 165, 166, 291
  The Cherry Orchard, 138, 166
  "Dushechka," 138
  "In the Ravine," 138
  The Seagull, 138, 165
  The Three Sisters, 138, 166
  Uncle Vanya, 138, 166
Chenier, André: 142
Chernyshevsky, Nikolai: 3, 19, 116, 125
  What is to be Done? 20, 103
Chukovsky, Kornei Ivanovich: 219, 253
Constant, Benjamin de: 143
The Contemporary (Sovremennik): 100, 116
Cui, César Antonovich: 101
Cyril of Turov: 17

Dahl, Vladimir Ivanovich: 104–105
  Explanatory Dictionary of the Living Russian Language, 104
Daniel, Iuli Markovich: 23, 239
Danilevsky, Nikolai Iakovlevich: 97, 193
  "Russia and Europe: A Look at the Cultural and Political Relations of the Slavic World to the Romano-German World," 97
Dante Alighieri: 253, 275
Dargomyzhsky, Alexander Sergeevich: 92
Dashkov, Dmitry Vasilievich: 70
Dashkova, Ekaterina Romanovna (Princess): 54, 55
Davydov, Denis Vasilievich: 57, 67
Derzhavin, Gavriil Romanovich: 34, 53, 54, 55, 56, 63, 107, 144, 249, 258
  "Depiction of Felitsa," 55
  "Exegi monumentum," 35, 107
  "Felitsa," 53–56
  "Gratitude to Felitsa," 55
  "The Murza's Vision," 55
Diaghilev, Sergei Pavlovich: 146, 160, 174, 177
Dmitriev, Ivan Ivanovich: 63, 77
Dobroliubov, Nikolai Alexandrovich: 116, 130
  "What is Oblomovitis?" 130
Dom pechati (Press House): 200
Donne, John: 249
Dostoevsky, Fedor Mikhailovich: 4, 5, 15, 19, 46, 47, 63, 76, 92, 96, 97, 103, 107, 112, 113, 115, 116, 119–24, 125, 126, 133–136, 137, 138, 139, 152, 153–56, 186, 256, 287–88
  The Brothers Karamazov, 15, 19, 112, 126, 136, 155, 166, 288
  Crime and Punishment, 47, 134–35, 277–78
  The Devils, 97–98, 135
  Diary of a Writer, 15, 123, 153, 155

Dostoevsky, Fedor Mikhailovich (*cont.*)
  The Double, 46, 47, 133–34
  Epoch, 101
  Notes from the House of the Dead, 20, 246
  The Idiot, 19, 47, 126, 131
  Notes from Underground, 133
  Poor Folk, 47
  "Pushkin Speech," 119–124
  Time, 101
  and psychology, 133–37
  and spiritualism, 153–156
Dovlatov, Sergei Donatovich: 264
Dudintsev, Vladimir Dmitrievich: 235
  Not By Bread Alone, 235
Dunaevsky, Isaac Osipovich: 217

Ehrenburg, Ilya Grigorievich: 235, 271
  People, Years, Life, 271
Eidelman, Natan Iakovlevich: 69
Eisenstein, Sergei Mikhailovich: 18, 157, 167, 212
  Ivan the Terrible, 82
Eliot, T. S.: 249
Elizaveta Petrovna (Empress): 161
Engels, Friedrich: 214
Epiphanius the Wise: 19
Epoch (*Epokha*): 101
Ermolov, Alexei Petrovich: 70
Erofeev, Venedikt Vasilievich: 240
  Moscow Circles, 240
Erofeev, Viktor Vladimirovich: 256
Esenin, Sergei Alexandrovich: 38, 205, 213, 220
Euler, Leonard: 49
Evtushenko, Evgeny Alexandrovich: 236, 250, 260
  "Babii Iar," 236
  Mama and the Neutron Bomb, 260
Exter, Alexandra Alexandrovna: 210

Fadeev, Alexander Alexandrovich:
  The Rout, 207, 211
Fedin, Konstantin Alexandrovich: 220, 223
Feltrinelli, Giangiacomo: 237
Fet, Afanasy Afanasievich: 73, 251
Filonov, Pavel Nikolaevich: 184, 186, 188, 190, 200, 201
Florensky, Pavel Alexandrovich: 271, 273
Florovsky, Georgii Vasilievich: 70
Fokine, Mikhail: 146, 160, 175, 177
Fonvizin, Denis Ivanovich: 32, 34, 38, 163
  The Minor, 161
Foucault, Michel:
  Histoire de la folie à l'âge classique, 251
Frank, Semen Liudvigovich: 209
Freud, Sigmund: 114, 132, 133, 137

Frost, Robert: 249
Furmanov, Dmitry Andreevich: 211

Galich, Alexander Arkadievich (stage name for Alexander Aronovich Ginzburg): 241
Gastev, Alexei Kapitonovich: 210
Ge, Nikolai Nikolaevich: 139
German, Iuri Pavlovich: 253
Ginzburg, Evgeniia Semenovna: 246
  Journey into the Whirlwind, 246
Ginzburg, Lydia: 127, 148
Gippius, Zinaida Nikolaevna: 209
Gladilin, Anatoly Tikhonovich: 237
Gladkov, Fedor Vasilievich:
  Cement, 207, 211
Glinka, Mikhail Ivanovich: 63, 87, 92, 146
  A Life for the Tsar, 162
  Ruslan and Liudmila 87–88, 162, 256
Gnedich, Nikolai Ivanovich: 65, 67
  "The Anglers," 67
Goethe, Johann Wolfgang von: 2, 3, 4, 61, 66, 237
  The Sorrows of Young Werther (Die Leiden des jungen Werthers): 1, 2, 3, 61, 71
Gogol, Nikolai Vasilievich: 4, 5, 14, 42, 63, 70, 76, 92, 98, 102, 104, 105, 107–114, 115, 121, 122, 126–27, 164, 256
  Arabeski, 110
  "Confession," 113
  Dead Souls, 15, 20, 38, 93, 111–12, 114
  Evenings on a Farm near Dikan'ka, 109
  "Hans Kiuchelgarten," 108
  The Inspector General, 110–11, 162, 163, 173–74, 190, 200
  The Marriage," 163
  Mirgorod, 110
    "How Ivan Ivanovich Quarreled with Ivan Nikiforovich," 110
    "Taras Bulba," 110
    "A Terrible Vengeance," 110
    "Vii," 110
  "The Nose," 109
  "Notes of a Madman," 45, 109, 127
  "The Order of Vladimir, Third Class," 110
  "The Overcoat," 63, 109
  "Petersburg Tales," 47
  "The Portrait," 113
  Selected Passages from Correspondence with Friends, 113
Golovin, Fedor Alexeevich (Chancellor): 44
Goncharov, Ivan Alexandrovich: 115, 128, 129, 130, 132, 142
  Oblomov, 128–30
Goncharova, Natalia Sergeevna: 157, 186, 187, 210
Gonzago, Pietro: 61

Gorbachev, Mikhail Sergeevich: 261, 265, 289
Gorky, Maxim (pen name for Alexei Maximovich Peshkov): 166, 209, 220, 223, 225, 226, 239, 273
  The Lower Depths, 166
  Mother, 225
  "Song of the Stormy Petrel," 225
Gorodetsky, Sergei Mitrofanovich: 219
Granovsky, Timofei Nikolaevich: 99
Griboedov, Alexander Sergeevich: 57, 65, 70, 142, 163
  Woe from Wit, 65, 163, 173
Grossman, Vasily Semenovich: 233, 266, 271
  Life and Fate, 266, 271
Gumilev, Nikolai Stepanovich: 179, 209, 218

Heaney, Seamas: 255
Henckel, Johann Friedrich: 49
Herald of Europe (Vestnik Evropy): 64, 68, 71, 77, 101, 152
Herald of Zion (Sionskii vestnik): 64
Herder, Johann Gottfried von: 65
Herzen, Alexander Ivanovich: 81, 99, 100, 127, 142
  My Past and Thoughts, 100
Hilarion (Metropolitan): 17, 19
  "Sermon on Law and Grace," 17
Horace (Quintus Horatius Flaccus): 50, 258
  "Exegi monumentum . . .", 35, 107, 258

Iakovlev, Alexei Semenovich: 64
Iazykov, Nikolai Mikhailovich: 82
Ilf, Ilya (pen name for Ilya Arnoldovich Fainzilberg):
  The Twelve Chairs, 207
  The Little Golden Calf, 207
Ilin, Ivan Alexandrovich: 209
Ivan IV (the Terrible): 14, 76, 82, 160, 216, 222
Ivanov, Alexander Andreevich: 59, 92
  "The Appearance of Christ Before the People," 59
Ivanov, Viacheslav Ivanovich: 113, 159, 194, 218
Ivanov, Vsevolod Viacheslavovich: 213

Jeremiah (prophet): 114
Jakobson, Roman Osipovich: 186
Joravsky, David: 133

Kafka, Franz:
  The Trial, 202
Kalatozov, Mikhail: 236
  The Cranes are Flying, 236
Kamensky, Vasily Vasilievich: 186
Kandinsky, Vasily Vasilievich: 157, 159, 186

Kantemir, Antiokh Dmitrievich: 48
Karamzin, Nikolai Mikhailovich: 22, 23, 34, 56, 57, 63, 65, 66, 76, 78, 82, 85, 102
  History of the Russian State, 65, 68, 76–82, 83
  Ilya Muromets, 83
  Letters of a Russian Traveller, 61, 77
  "A Note on Ancient and Modern Russia," 78
  "Poor Lisa," 61, 77
Karsavina, Tamara Platonovna: 175
Kataev, Valentin Petrovich: 168, 216
  Time Forward!, 216
Katenin, Pavel Alexandrovich: 82
Katkov, Mikhail Nikiforovich: 101, 107
Kavelin, Konstantin Dmitrievich: 82
Kaverin, Veniamin (pen name for Veniamin Alexandrovich Zilber): 213
Kharms, Daniil (pen name for Daniil Ivanovich Iuvachev): 191, 199, 200, 201, 202, 203, 271
  Elizaveta Bam, 200, 201, 202
Khlebnikov, Velimir (pen name for Viktor Vladimirovich Khlebnikov): 159, 160, 184, 185, 186, 188, 189, 190, 191–196
  "Bobeobi sang the lips," 194
  The Cheka Chairman, 195
  The Crane, 194
  "Incantation through Laughter," 194
  Ladomir, 195
  The Marquise Dezes, 194
  Night Search, 195
  "Numbers," 193
  "The Tables of Fate," 196
  "Teacher and Pupil. On Words, Cities and Peoples," 194
  "The Trumpet of Martians," 194
  Zangezi, 195
Khodasevich, Vladislav Felitsianovich: 49, 220
Khomiakov, Alexei Stepanovich: 22, 94, 123
  Yermak, 82
Khrushchev, Nikita Sergeevich: 234, 236, 238, 239, 244, 247, 248, 251
Kiev: 8, 13, 18, 20, 21, 22, 23, 25, 84, 85
Kievan Rus': 8–10, 15, 16, 25
Kiprensky, Orest Adamovich: 57
Kireevsky, Ivan Vasilievich: 94, 96, 104, 123
Kireevsky, Petr Vasilievich: 94
Kirshon, Vladimir Mikhailovich: 168, 216
  Grain, 216
Kiukhelbeker, Vilgelm Karlovich: 67
  Prokopy Liapunov, 82
Kliuev, Nikolai Alexeevich: 273
Kniazhnin, Iakov Borisovich: 22, 34
Kopelev, Lev Zalmanovich: 247
Kostomarov, Nikolai Ivanovich: 82
Kotzebue, August Friedrich Ferdinand von: 64

Kozintsev, Grigory Mikhailovich: 212
Kramskoy, Ivan Nikolaevich: 101, 139
Kruchenych, Alexei Eliseevich: 160, 185, 186, 187, 188, 190, 249
  "Dyr bul shchyl," 188
Krylov, Ivan Andreevich: 65, 67, 68
Kukolnik, Nestor Vasilievich:
  The Hand of the Almighty Saved the Fatherland, 91
Kuleshov, Lev Vladimirovich: 212
Kuprin, Alexander Ivanovich: 209
Kutik, Ilya Vitalievich: 265
  "From Catullus," 265
Kutuzov, Mikhail Ilarionovich: 58, 79
Kuzmin, Mikhail Alexeevich: 160, 171, 271

Larionov, Mikhail Fedorovich: 186, 187, 210
The Lay of Prince Igor: 16, 24, 65
Lebedev-Kumach, Vasily Ivanovich: 217
Leblanc, J.B.: 43
LEF (*Levyi Front Iskusstva*, The Left Front of Art): 189, 197, 211, 212, 213, 214, 222
Leibniz, Gottfried: 49
Lelevich, G. (pen name for Labori Gilelevich Kalmanson): 211
Lenin, Vladimir Ilich (nom de guerre for Vladimir Ilich Ulianov): 20, 56, 169, 189, 192, 207, 208, 209, 213, 214, 215, 225, 227, 234, 270, 283
Leontiev, Konstantin Nikolaevich: 271, 283
Lermontov, Mikhail Iurevich: 121, 126, 127, 128, 129, 132, 141–146, 171, 253, 291
  "Alone I Go Out on the Road," 145
  "The Cliff," 145
  "Death of a Poet," 143
  "A Dream," 145
  The Demon, 143, 164
  "Fairy Tale for Children," 143
  A Hero of Our Time, 126, 143, 287, 291
  Masquerade, 143, 163
  The Novice, 143
  "The Prophet," 146
  "The Sea Princess," 145
  "The Song about Tsar Ivan Vasilievich and the Young Oprichnik and Brave Merchant Kalashnikov," 82
  The Tambov Treasurer's Wife, 144
  "Thought," 143
  and psychology, 126–129
Leskov, Nikolai Semenovich: 4, 29, 37, 103, 153–54, 256
  "The Toupee Artist," 162
Levitsky, Dmitry Grigorievich: 45
Libedinsky, Iuri Nikolaevich: 211
Library for Reading (Biblioteka dlia chteniia): 101

Limonov, Eduard (pen name for Eduard Veniaminovich Savenko: 264, 271, 279–284
  Adolescent Savenko, 281
  It's Me, Eddie, 281
Lissitzky, El (pen name for Lazar Markovich Lisitsky): 212
Livshits, Benedikt Konstantinovich: 186
Lomonosov, Mikhail Vasilievich: 13, 32, 33, 47–51, 53, 56, 107, 120, 122, 144, 193, 258
  "Evening Reflection upon God's Grandeur Prompted by the Great Northern Lights," 51
  "Letter on the Properties of Russian Versification," 49
  "Ode on the Capture of Khotin," 49
Lossky, Nikolai Onufrievich: 209
Lotman, Iuri Mikhailovich: 69, 85
Lunacharsky, Anatoly Vasilievich: 159, 168, 208, 214
Lunts, Lev Natanovich: 213

Magnitsky, Leonty Filippovich: 48
Maikov, Vasily Ivanovich: 86
Makanin, Vladimir Semenovich: 241
  Underground, or A Hero of Our Time, 287–290, 291
Makarenko, Anton Semenovich: 216
  The Pedagogical Epic, 216
Malevich, Kazimir Severinovich: 157, 160, 186, 188, 189, 190, 200, 232
Mandelstam, Osip Emilievich: 69, 157, 179, 205, 213, 228, 229, 232, 249, 253, 273
Marshak, Samuil Iakovlevich: 253
Marx, Karl: 2143, 243
Matiushin, Mikhail Vasilievich: 160, 186, 188, 200
Mayakovsky, Vladimir Vladimirovich: 56, 157, 172, 173, 184, 185, 186, 188, 189, 190, 196–197, 198, 199, 204–05, 207, 208, 214
  The Bathhouse, 173, 199
  The Bedbug, 160, 168, 173, 196–199
  Good, 196, 207
  "I suddenly smeared . . ." 196
  Mystery-Bouffe, 172, 189
  "To You!", 188
  Vladimir Ilich Lenin, 196, 257
  Vladimir Mayakovsky, 188
  150,000,000, 196, 207
  and LEF, 189, 197, 212
Mendeleev, Dmitry Ivanovich: 152, 153, 154
Menshikov, Alexander Danilovich: 40, 46
Merezhkovsky, Dmitry Sergeevich: 209
  M. Iu. Lermontov. Poet of the Superhuman, 146
  Peter and Alexei, 29, 47

Meyerhold, Vsevolod Emilievich: 146, 157, 160, 165, 167, 170–174, 177, 189, 197, 198, 208, 212
Milosz, Czeslaw: 255
Minaev, Sergei Sergeevich: 287, 292
  Soulless: The Story of an Unreal Person, 287, 291, 292
Montferrand, Auguste de: 60, 61, 62, 89, 90
Moscow: 9, 13–14, 19, 28, 29, 39, 40, 44, 48, 54, 58, 61, 63, 65, 68, 70, 72, 78, 93, 105, 106, 115, 142, 147, 162, 163, 164, 167, 170, 182, 195, 196, 215, 216, 223, 225, 238, 239, 244, 245, 256, 272, 274, 275, 277, 278, 279, 282, 292
  vs. Petersburg, 42, 46
  as Third Rome, 9, 14, 46, 91, 120
Moscow News (*Moskovskie vedomosti*): 101
Moscow University: 1, 53, 77, 115, 142, 276
Moshkov, Vladimir Ivanovich: 61
Moskvitianin (The Muscovite): 7, 96, 101
Mozart, Wolfgang Amadeus: 84
  The Magic Flute, 84, 86
Musorgsky, Modest Petrovich: 92, 101, 102, 164
  Boris Godunov, 19, 82, 96, 164
  Khovanshchina, 29
The Muscovite: 7, 96, 101
Musset, Alfred de: 143

Nabokov, Vladimir Vladimirovich: 4, 202, 210, 266
  Invitation to a Beheading, 202
  Lolita, 4
Neizvestny, Ernst Iosivovich: 238
Nekrasov, Nikolai Alexeevich: 101, 116
  Petersburg Sketches, 116
  Russian Women, 257
Nestor: 18
New World (*Novyi mir*): 238, 244, 247, 271
Nicholas I (Emperor): 45, 56, 60, 61, 69, 70, 73, 75, 87, 89, 91, 96, 100, 110, 118, 120, 144, 162
Nicholas II (Emperor): 40
Nikon (Patriarch): 27, 28
Nixon, Richard: 254
Notes of the Fatherland (*Otechestvennye zapiski*): 100, 101, 109, 144
Novgorod: 8, 9, 13, 14, 15, 22, 81

OBERIU (acronym for Association of Real Art): 191, 199–203
Odoevsky, Vladimir Fedorovich (Prince): 70
Ogonek: 271
Okudzhava, Bulat Shalvovich: 241
Old Believers: 27, 29, 36, 46, 48
Olesha, Iuri Karlovich: 205, 226
  Envy, 226
  No Day without a Line, 226

Opekushin, Alexander Mikhailovich: 105, 106
Orlovsky, Boris Ivanovich: 89, 90
Ostrovsky, Alexander Nikolaevich: 29, 37, 92, 163, 164, 171
  Even a Wise Man Slips Up, 167
Ostrovsky, Nikolai Alexeevich:
  How the Steel was Tempered, 216
Ovid (Publius Ovidius Naso): 87, 253
Ozerov, Vladislav Alexandrovich: 45, 57, 64, 67, 85

Panin, Nikita Ivanovich: 38
  "Political Testament," 38
Panti, Mihailo: 286
Parshchikov, Alexei Maximovich: 265
Pasternak, Boris Leonidovich: 4, 157, 207, 213, 227, 237, 249, 270, 271
  Doctor Zhivago, 4, 237, 266
  Lieutenant Schmidt," 207
  "My Sister-Life," 207
Paul I (Emperor), 2, 57, 70, 74
Pelevin, Viktor Olegovich: 287
  Homo Zapiens, 287, 288, 290, 291
Perov, Vasily Grigorievich: 92, 101
Peter I (the Great): 7, 31–32, 35, 36, 38, 39, 46, 47, 48, 50, 51, 82, 92, 93, 94, 96, 98, 114, 117–118, 139, 161, 204, 216, 220, 222
  and the "Table of Ranks": 36
  and the founding of Petersburg: 39–45
Peter II (Emperor): 40
Peter III (Emperor): 36
  Decree of 1762, 36
Petrov, Evgeny (pen name for Evgeny Petrovich Kataev):
  The Little Golden Calf, 207
  The Twelve Chairs, 207
Petrov, Vasily Petrovich: 33
Petrushevskaia, Liudmila Stefanovna: 264
Petrushka, 160, 172, 174–178
Pilniak, Boris (pen name for Boris Andreevich Vogau): 220, 273
  The Naked Year, 207
Pisarev, Dmitry Ivanovich: 101, 116
Plato: 214
Platon (Bishop): 3
Platonov, Andrei (pen name for Andrei Platonovich Klimentev): 4, 184, 228–32, 270, 273, 274
  The Foundation Pit, 228–32
Pogodin, Mikhail Petrovich: 7, 35, 91
Polevoi, Nikolai Alexeevich: 67
Pope, Alexander: 86
Postnikov, Petr Vasilievich: 48
Prigov, Dmitry Alexandrovich: 264, 265
Primary Chronicle: 10, 13, 18, 20–25, 83

Pristavkin, Anatoly Ignatievich: 271
  A Golden Cloud Spent the Night, 271
Prokofiev, Sergei Sergeevich: 18, 157, 210
  The Fiery Angel, 256
Prokopovich, Feofan: 31–32, 38, 40
Pugachev, Emelian: 38
Pushkin, Alexander Sergeevich: 19, 22, 32, 47, 56, 58, 59, 63, 67, 68, 69, 70, 72, 73, 75, 76, 77, 80, 81, 82, 92, 93, 105, 108, 109, 110, 111, 112, 115, 116, 121, 122, 123, 126, 142, 143, 144, 146, 164, 186, 188, 194, 196, 251, 253, 256
  Boris Godunov, 19, 82, 102, 163
  Bronze Horseman, A Petersburg Tale, 46–47, 257
  The Captain's Daughter, 38, 63
  Eugene Onegin, 72, 87, 122, 126, 162, 204
  "Exegi monumentum," 107, 258
  Fountain of Bakchisarai, 67
  "Freedom: An Ode," 67
  Gypsies, 67
  History of Pugachev, 38
  "Poltava," 40, 204, 257
  Prisoner of the Caucasus, 67, 144
  "Queen of Spades," 45, 156
  Ruslan and Liudmila, 66, 82–88, 257
  The Tales of Belkin, 63
Pushkin monument (Moscow): 105, 106, 107, 119
Pushkin, Vasily Lvovich: 66
  "A Dangerous Neighbor," 66
Putin, Vladimir Vladimirovich: 262, 283, 286
Pyrev, Ivan Alexandrovich: 216

Quarenghi, Giacomo: 61

Rachmaninov, Sergei Vasilievich: 210
Radishchev, Alexander Nikolaevich: 38
  Journey from Petersburg to Moscow, 38
Rasputin, Valentin Grigorievich: 241, 244
  Farewell to Matera, 244
Red Virgin Soil (*Krasnaia nov'*): 211, 212, 213, 221
Remizov, Alexei Mikhailovich: 220
Repin, Ilya Efimovich: 82, 101, 102, 139, 140, 187
  "Ivan the Terrible and his Son," 82, 92, 186
  "They Did not Expect Him," 139, 140
Rezanov, Nikolai Petrovich: 256, 257, 258
Rimsky-Korsakov, Nikolai Andreevich: 82, 92, 101, 164, 250
  Christmas Eve, 164
  The Golden Cockerel, 164
  The Legend of the Miraculous City of Kitezh, 249
  The Maid of Pskov, 82
  May Night, 164
  The Tale of Tsar Saltan, 164, 256
  The Tsar's Bride, 82

Rodchenko, Alexander Mikhailovich: 160, 197, 198, 212
Rodov, Semen Abramovich: 211
Rossi, Carlo: 57
Rostopchina, Evdokiia Petrovna: 146
  "To Our Future Poets," 146
Rostropovich, Mistislav Leopoldovich: 263
Rousseau, Jean-Jacques: 28, 61, 71, 148, 150
Rozanov, Vasily Vasilievich: 146
  Pushkin and Lermontov, 146
Rozhdestvensky, Robert Ivanovich: 250
Rubinstein, Anton Grigorievich: 146, 164
  The Demon, 146, 164
Rubinstein, Lev Semenovich: 264
The Russian Colloquy (Russkaia beseda): 101
Russian Herald (Russkii vestnik): 64, 101
The Russian Word (Russkoe slovo): 101
Rybnikov, Alexei Lvovich: 258
Ryleev, Kondraty Fedorovich: 22, 60, 65, 67, 82

Saint-Petersburg, 31
  as European city, 33
  founding of, 39–47
  in the first half of the 19th century, 60–61, 83, 86
Salinger, J.D.: 237
Saltykov-Shchedrin, Mikhail Evgrafovich: 101
Samadoghlu, Azeri Vagif: 234
Samarin, Iuri Fedorovich: 94
Sapunov, Nikolai Nikolaevich: 160, 171
Sartre, Jean-Paul: 253
Schiller Friedrich: 66, 71, 108
Schnitke, Alfred Garrievich: 256
Scriabin, Alexander Nikolaevich: 157
Selvinsky, Ilya Lvovich: 191, 227
  Ulialiaevshina, 207
Semenova, Ekaterina Semenovna: 64
Severianin, Igor (pen name for Igor Vasilievich Lotarev): 220
Shaginian, Marietta Sergeevna: 216
  The Hydroelectric Plant, 216
Shakespeare, William: 71, 104, 112, 165, 167, 237, 275
Shakhovskoi, Alexander Alexandrovich: 57, 63, 66
  The New Sterne: 63, 66
Shalamov, Varlaam Tikhonovich: 246
Shaliapin, Fedor Ivanovich: 210
Shentalinsky, Vitaly Alexandrovich: 271–72, 273
Shestov, Lev Isaakovich (pen name for Yehuda Leib Shvartsman): 219
Shevyrev, Stepan Petrovich: 22, 70
Shirinsky-Shakhmatov, S.A. (Prince):
  Pozharsky, Minin, Hermogen, or the Salvation of Russia, 83

Shishkov, Alexander Semenovich (Admiral): 63, 66, 67, 104, 193
Shklovsky, Viktor Borisovich: 186, 220
Shmelev, Ivan Sergeevich: 209
Sholokhov, Mikhail Alexandrovich: 216, 220, 235, 285, 286
  Quiet Flows the Don, 216
  Virgin Soil Upturned, 216
Shostakovich, Dmitry Dmitrievich: 157, 160, 197, 198, 253, 256
  The Bedbug, 197, 198
  Lady Macbeth of Mtsensk, 256
  The Nose, 198, 256
Shukshin, Vasily Makarovich: 243
Simonov, Konstantin Mikhailovich: 233, 234, 235
  Days and Nights, 235
Siniavsky, Andrei Donatovich (Abram Terts): 238, 239, 263
  Fantastic Tales, 239
  Good Night
  On Socialist Realism, 239
  The Trial Begins, 239
Smotritsky, Melety (Maksim Gerasimovich Smotritsky): 48
Sokolov, Sasha (Alexander Vsevolodovich Sokolov): 264, 271
Solimena, Francesco; 51
Solovev, Vladimir: 3, 15, 69, 75, 82, 113, 124, 146, 184
  Lermontov, 146
Solzhenitsyn, Alexander Isaevich: 4, 241, 243, 244–47, 255, 263, 266, 271, 280, 285–86
  Cancer Ward, 245, 247
  The First Circle, 241, 247
  Gulag Archipelago, 245, 266
  "Nobel Speech," 286
  "One Day in the Life of Ivan Denisovich," 238, 244–47
  "Matrena's House," 243
  The Red Wheel, 25, 245
Somov, Orest Mikhailovich: 67, 121
Stalin, Joseph (nom de guerre for Joseph Djugashvili): 168, 169, 190, 208, 214, 215, 216, 222, 224, 225, 226, 227, 233, 234, 235, 245, 255, 270, 291
  Concise History of The Communist Party of the Soviet Union, 216
Stanislavsky, Konstantin (stage name for Alexeev, Konstantin Sergeevich): 157, 160, 165, 166, 167, 170, 172, 174, 177
Stasiulevich, Mikhail Matveevich: 101
Sterne, Laurence: 61
Stravinsky, Igor Fedorovich: 157, 160, 174, 175, 210, 219
  Petrushka, 175

Sumarokov, Alexander Petrovich: 32, 34, 45
Surikov, Vasily Ivanovich
  "Boyarina Morozova," 29, 30, 139

Tairov, Alexander Iakovlevich (stage name for Alexander Iakovlevich Kornblit): 157, 167, 174
Tale of the White Cowl: 14
Tatishchev, Vasily Nikitich: 22
Tatlin, Vladimir Evgrafovich: 157
  Monument to the Third International, 205, 206, 212
Tchaikovsky, Petr Ilich: 63, 146, 164
  Eugene Onegin, 69, 164
  The Nutcracker, 164
  Queen of Spades, 164
  Sleeping Beauty, 164
  Swan Lake, 164
Terentev, Igor Gerasimovich: 190, 200
Theodosius: 18, 19
Time (Vremia): 101
Tiutchev, Fedor Ivanovich: 96, 97, 142, 251
  "A Russian Geography," 96–97
Tolstaia, Tatiana Nikitichna: 264
Tolstoy, Fedor Petrovich: 57
Tolstoy, Alexei Konstantinovich: 82, 165
  Tsar Fedor Ioannovich, 165
Tolstoy, Alexei Nikolaevich (Count): 213, 217–223
  Aelita, 221
  Black Friday, 222
  Bread, 222
  The Hyperboloid of Engineer Garin, 221–222
  Lyrics, 218
  Nevzorov's Adventures, 222
  Nikita's Childhood, 218
  "Peter's Day," 222
  The Revolt of the Cars, 222
  The Road to Calvary, 219, 222, 223
Tolstoy, Lev Nikolaevich (Count): 1, 4, 18, 19, 20, 45, 92, 115, 116, 125, 131, 139, 186, 192, 193, 222, 245
  "A Landowner's Morning," 245
  Anna Karenina, 97, 126, 136–38, 147, 218, 292
  Childhood, 116, 136, 147–151, 245
  Confession, 113
  The Cossacks, 125, 136
  "Father Sergii," 19
  "The Kreutzer Sonata," 279
  War and Peace, 42, 69, 82, 96, 103, 245, 256
  "What is Art?" 96
  and psychology, 136–138, 179, 245
Tomon, Toma de: 57, 61
Trauberg, Leonid Zakharovich: 212
Trediakovsky, Vasily Kirillovich: 48, 49, 50

Trezzini, Domenico: 40
Trifonov, Iuri Alexandrovich: 241
Trotsky, Lev Davidovich (nom de guerre for Lev Davidovich Bronstein): 189, 190, 208, 210, 212, 213, 222, 250, 270
Trubetskoy, Nikolai Sergeevich (Prince): 124
Tsvetaeva, Marina Ivanovna: 69, 157, 181, 210, 249
Turgenev, Andrei: 1–4, 63, 66, 71, 292
Turgenev, Ivan Sergeevich: 4, 38, 63, 99, 107, 125, 138, 139, 163, 220
  A Month in the Country, 163
  Fathers and Children, 103, 131–32
  Notes of a Hunter, 38, 114–120
    "Khor and Kalinych," 117–18, 243
    "Singers," 118–120
  On the Eve, 220
  "The Russian Language," 105
  and psychology, 131–33, 136
Tvardovsky, Alexander Trifonovich: 233, 244, 247, 253
Tynianov, Iuri Nikolaevich: 69, 186, 220

Uvarov, Sergei Semenovich: 91
Ustrialov, Nikolai Gerasimovich: 91

Vadim of Novgorod: 22
Vagner, Nikolai Petrovich: 152, 153, 192
Venetsianov, Alexei Gavrilovich: 57
Venevitinov, Dmitry Vladimirovich: 70
Vesnin, Alexander Alexandrovich: 212
Vesnin Leonid Alexandrovich: 212
Vesnin, Viktor Alexandrovich: 212
Vertov, Dziga (pseudonym for David Abelevich Kaufman): 157, 212
Viazemsky, Petr Andreevich: 39, 57, 66, 67, 78
  "Indignation," 67
Victory over the Sun, 160, 188
Vigdorova, Frida Abramovna: 252
Virgil (Publius Vergilius Maro):
  The Aeneid, 83
Vitberg, Alexander Lavrentievich: 59
Vladimir (Prince): 10, 11, 15, 17, 23, 83, 84, 88
Vladimov, Georgy Nikolaevich: 240, 242
Voiekov, Alexander Fedorovich: 66
  "Insane Asylum," 66
Voinovich, Vladimir Nikolaevich: 237, 241, 264
  Ivankiada, 264
Volkov, Fedor Grigorievich: 32
Volkov, Roman Maximovich: 61
Voloshin, Maximilian Alexandrovich: 218
Voltaire (pen name for François-Marie Arouet): 86
  Henriade, 83

Voronikhin, Andrei Nikiforovich: 57, 60
Voronsky, Alexander Konstantinovich: 211, 212, 213
Voznesensky, Andrei Andreevich: 236, 241, 255–60
  "Avos'," 256
  Iunona i Avos', 255–260
Vrubel, Mikhail Alexandrovich: 146
Vysotsky, Vladimir Semenovich: 88, 241
  "The magic shore has disappeared," 88

Wanderers (Peredvizhniki): 101, 138
Wachtel, Andrew Baruch: 81
Walcott, Derek: 255
Wells, H.G.: 221
Wieland, Christoph Martin: 83
  Oberon, 83
Wolff, Christian: 49

Yeltsin, Boris Nikolaevich: 261

Zabolotsky, Nikolai Alexeevich: 184, 191, 199, 201, 203
  "Movement," 201
Zaitsev, Boris Konstantinovich: 209
Zakharov, Adrian Dmitrievich.: 61
Zakharov, Mark Anatolievich: 259
Zelinsky, Kornely Liutsianovich: 222
Zhdanov, Andrei Alexandrovich: 225, 227, 234, 249
Zhdanov, Ivan Fedorovich: 265
Zhirinovsky, Vladimir Volfovich: 282
Zhukovsky, Vasily Andreevich: 1, 3, 22, 57, 63, 65, 67, 69–76, 81, 83, 85, 87, 89, 108, 109, 121, 142
  Ahasueros, 76
  "The Appearance of Poetry in the Image of Lalla Rookh," 73
  "Elegy Written in a Country Churchyard," 71
  "Kamoens," 76
  "Lalla Rookh," 73
  "Lenore," 72
  "Liudmila," 67
  The Odyssey (translation), 76
  The Prisoner or Chillon, 67
  "Singer in the Kremlin," 59, 73
  "Singer in the Russian Military Camp," 65, 72
  "Svetlana," 67, 72
  "The Twelve Sleeping Maidens, A Story in Two Ballads," 83, 86–87
  "Vadim," 5, 59
Zoshchenko, Mikhail Mikhailovich: 213, 234
  The Stories of Nazar Il'ich, Mr. Sinebriukhov, 207